Practical Software Requirements

Practical Software Requirements

A MANUAL OF CONTENT AND STYLE

BENJAMIN L. KOVITZ

MANNING

Greenwich
(74° w. long.)

For electronic browsing of this book, see http://www.manning.com

The publisher offers discounts on this book when ordered in quantity. For more information, please contact:

Special Sales Department
Manning Publications Co.
32 Lafayette Place
Greenwich, CT 06830

Fax: (203) 661-9018
email: orders@manning.com

Library of Congress Cataloging-in-Publication Data
Kovitz, Benjamin L., 1965
        Practical software requirements / Benjamin L. Kovitz.
            p.   cm.
        Includes bibliographical references and index.
        ISBN 1-884777-59-7 (alk. paper)
        1. Computer software development.   I. Title.
QA76.76.D47K684   1998
005.1—dc21   98-29162
                                                                 CIP

  Manning Publications Co.
        32 Lafayette Place
        Greenwich, CT 06830

        Copyeditor: Leslie Aicken
        Typesetter: Nicholas A. Kosar
        Cover designer: Leslie Haimes

Printed in the United States of America
    3 4 5 6 7 8 9 10 – CR – 00 99

For Rufus and Skeezix.

contents

introduction

This book is about how to write two kinds of documents needed in the early stages of many software development projects: a *requirements document,* which describes desired effects to be produced by the software, and a *program specification,* or *interface design,* which describes the outward behavior of the computer that produces those effects—the behavior of input/output devices.

Together, these documents provide the information that programmers need to create a program that causes the behavior described in the specification and ultimately fulfills the requirements. The same information provides the baseline against which a tester can design test plans, as well as the operating procedures and background information that a technical writer can put into a user's manual or on-line help.

Many people have a need to write these documents:

- System analysts—the people who serve as the liaison between the customer and the rest of the development team. In larger organizations, writing requirements is traditionally the responsibility of a system analyst. This book provides system analysts with many writing techniques to make their documents clearer and more useful to the people who read them, as well as a clearer delimitation of requirements from other aspects of the software than that found in most books.

- User-interface designers—the people who draw the screens and invent the conceptual world in terms of which an end user is to think when operating the software. For user-interface designers, this book explains the information that programmers, testers, and technical writers need from a user-interface design document to do their jobs, and how to present it tersely and crisply.

- Programmers—particularly those in small companies that are in the process of adding more rigor to their development processes. Many of these companies don't have system analysts and are now recruiting their programmers to write requirements documents for the first time. Indeed, many programmers already do a great deal of requirements engineering and interface design without calling them by those names. For many programmers, defining the problem and choosing the interface behavior to solve that problem is the part of their job that they find most fascinating; many consider these jobs the most essential part of programming. This book construes the word *programming* more narrowly, to allow careful focus on requirements and interface design as distinct tasks.

- Project managers called upon to write requirements. Especially in small shops, people work in many roles. Often a project manager has the most contact with a customer and is, therefore, the most logical choice to write the requirements document. This can be a daunting task, especially the first time, and especially if no one else in the company has experience writing requirements. This book provides many concrete examples and both high-level and detailed guidance to help a newcomer get started.

Part I, *Groundwork,* presents the underlying principles that distinguish requirements, interface design, and program design. These principles draw heavily on the landmark work of Michael Jackson, presented in more theoretical form in his book, *Software Requirements & Specifications: A Lexicon of Practice, Principles and Prejudices.*

Chapters 1 and 2 cover background about how programmers really write programs and how requirements must be tailored to be useful to them. Chapter 2 defines the concept of a *software problem.* Chapter 3 relates software problems to the principal elements of their solutions, creating the foundation upon which the rest of the book is built.

Chapters 4 through 6 present Jackson's concept of a *problem frame:* a way of casting the principal elements of a software problem into a form suitable for detailed documentation and for solution by known (or unknown) techniques. Chapter 4 introduces the fundamental elements of domains, shared phenomena, and requirements. Chapter 5 describes five commonly recurring types of software problems and how to frame them. Chapter 6 gives examples of how to apply problem frames to the task of breaking down large, complex problems into simple ones. The technique, unlike most, does not work by hierarchical decomposition. Instead, it works more flexibly, allowing any kind of overlap between the elements of one subproblem and the elements of another.

Part II, *Content,* gives detailed information about the content to include in each type of document, along with tips on how to describe that content simply and clearly.

Chapter 7 describes the jobs of each person on the development team who reads requirements or specifications, and the information they need. Chapter 8 is a set of two content checklists, one for each type of document. The checklists are flexible guidelines to help you spot needed information that you might overlook, and are not generic tables of contents to force onto any document. Software problems and their solutions are far too varied for that.

Chapter 9 explains how to document two kinds of sets that appear in the vast majority of software problems: classes and relations between classes. The principal technique shown is the standard entity-relation diagram, or class diagram, supplemented by guidance on how to describe, in text, all of the information sketched in the diagram. Chapter 9 also shows how to describe queries that a piece of software is to answer.

Chapter 10 is about techniques for describing sequences and, in particular, sequences of events. This includes description techniques for events themselves, which are needed in a requirements document, and for the computer's and users' responses to these events, which are needed in the program specification.

Chapter 11 attacks the particularly tough problem of how to describe causal relations and rules. These causal relations can exist among the phenomena in the world that the software interacts with, in which case they are described in a requirements document, or they can be the causal rules according to which the computer behaves, in which case they are described in a program specification. As in chapter 10, a variety of techniques are presented for the reader to adapt to the peculiarities of a particular problem.

Chapter 12 addresses a number of miscellaneous topics related to content, including elicitation, the temptation to force the concepts of object-oriented design onto problem-domain description, and the hazards of use cases.

Part III, *Style,* is about how to choose among the many forms with which to present the same content. Much of this information is standard elements of good technical writing, though focused exclusively on requirements and specifications.

Chapter 13 presents a number of broad principles of technical writing, followed by a list of common mistakes in requirements documents with advice on how to correct them. Most of these mistakes grow out of a too-rigid set of concepts or procedures for writing requirements—forcing the content to fit the descriptions rather than the other way around.

Chapter 14 presents techniques of organization: how to group information together and how to choose the sequence in which to present that information. The strategy is always to build a table of contents from the content identified in Part II, and not to start with a table of contents and fill it in without regard to the specifics of the project.

Chapter 15 is a haphazard collection of guidance on small details: guidance on laying out the page to be most readable, how to reword vague sentences, information to put on the title page, how to word a definition, and so on.

Part IV, *Examples,* contains two example documents from a real project.

Chapter 16 is the requirements document for a small piece of software to track bugs discovered during software development at Information + Graphics Systems, Inc., in Boulder, Colorado.

Chapter 17 is a set of excerpts from the user-interface design document for the same project. These excerpts contain many examples of information that is very tricky to document simply.

acknowledgements

I am particularly grateful to Michael Jackson for much patient help in the writing of this book. In addition to carefully reviewing the manuscript, he many times answered my rambling, somewhat inarticulate questions about requirements and software engineering with just the insight I needed to unravel my confusions. It's been a great privilege to learn from one of the world's foremost teachers of software engineering.

I owe many thanks to Ray Agostinelli, Paul Agostinelli, Heidi Anderson, Harold Cheney, and Asim Jalis for much stimulating late-night conversation—or rather, for tolerating my combination of ranting and thinking out loud, even during Monday Night Football. The manuscript is especially improved as a result of Ray's careful reading of multiple drafts, exposing subtle errors in content and many unclear passages.

Sonia Kovitz, my mother, gave me some of the sternest criticism of the most difficult chapters. She often found the exact point where the logical thread got lost, helping me to improve the text immeasurably. It helps quite a lot to have a professor in the family.

Many others kindly gave their time to review different drafts of the manuscript: William Bail, Steve Colwell, Bruce Ediger, Anne Frank, Richard Gabriel, Earl Glynn, Lon Gowen, Haim Kilov, Peter Luise, and Charlie Whiting. Their feedback, drawn from experience far surpassing my own, has filtered out many mistakes and added much valuable content to the book.

Thanks also to the many people who gave me detailed information about software problem domains that they were familiar with as programmers, requirements writers, or users: Michael Burton, Joanne Curme, Ben Eng, Lisa Higgins, Brent Jones, James Jones, Charles Libicki, Craig Lloyd, Scott Meyers, Scott Peter, Darrin Smith, Kim Swaney, Rachel Tillman, Gina Vick, Don Whiteside, and Bob "Zimbob" Zimering. Some allowed me to grill them for hours about the minutiae of their areas of expertise. This book is filled with examples taken from a very broad range of software applications. I couldn't have included such a variety of examples without the help of these people. James Jones practically gave me an introductory course in bonds—over the phone. Rachel Tillman also reviewed the manuscript; her insights and wide experience are reflected throughout the book.

A special thanks goes to Craig Bachmann and Steven Bruny of Information + Graphics Systems, Inc. They've graciously allowed me to publish some of the requirements documents that I've written at IGS. This is an all-too-rare phenomenon within our industry: most books about requirements contain only contrived examples from imaginary projects because documentation from real projects is proprietary. But only real-world documentation has the irregular, unpredictable complexity of a real project. People need to see real examples of how other people have struggled with the way real problems never quite fit simple schemes for writing requirements.

Thanks also to the Bug Log team at IGS: Judy Bennett, Rae Bernhardson, Stacey Glazer, Jennifer Key, Bjorn Laukli, Randy Law, Tim Phillips, and Ivan Storck. A good set of requirements embodies much more knowledge than the system analyst brings to it. The example documents embody their ideas as much as mine.

None of the many people who've helped me agrees with every idea presented in this book, of course. I've worked hard to remove mistaken ideas and poor techniques, but I am all too aware of the book's flaws. Any of the people listed above could probably point out plenty more.

Finally, thanks to the outstanding staff at Manning Publications. I couldn't ask for a more devoted and professional team, nor one more pleasurable to work with. I am especially grateful to Marjan Bace. He has somehow known exactly when to allow the creative process to run free and when to push, ever so subtly yet firmly, to meet a deadline or radically revise a chapter organization that took months to evolve. Marjan's calm, almost invisible presence has improved this book in many profound and subtle ways, probably in more ways than either of us can know.

author online

Purchase of *Practical Software Requirements* includes free access to a private Internet forum where you can make comments about the book, ask technical questions, and receive help from the author and from other readers. To access the forum, point your Web browser to:

http://www.manning.com/Kovitz

where you will be able to subscribe to the forum. This site also provides information on how to access the forum once you are registered, what kind of help is available, and the rules of conduct on the forum.

I have tried to be complete and accurate within the limits of this book; however, errors and omissions are inevitable. If you find mistakes in this book, or if you think I have left something out, please let me know. There may be another edition of the book, and, if so, I would like to make as many corrections and implement as many suggestions as possible. Please direct them to me using the Author Online forum.

PART **1**

Groundwork

C H A P T E R   1

Problem solving

This book is not about programming. It is about how to *define a problem* for people to solve by programming a computer. Defining such a problem means providing all of the information that programmers and interface designers need in order to make a computer bring about effects outside of the computer. The complete statement of this problem is called the *requirements* for the software.

Whereas programming is the act of configuring a machine to behave in a certain way, writing software requirements is a form of communication between people. The people who desire effects from the software—the people who want to print reports, control manufacturing processes, generate 3D images, or whatever may be the intended use of the software—need to communicate those desires to the people who design the machine behavior that brings about those effects: the interface designers. The people who design the machine behavior need to communicate their ideas to the people who actually configure the machines: the programmers. Other people who work on the software—the testers and the people who write the user manuals—need the same information in order to do their jobs. This book is about how to give all of these people the information they need.

Thus, this book is about a certain kind of technical writing: how to write software requirements documents. Sometimes technical writing is narrowly construed as covering

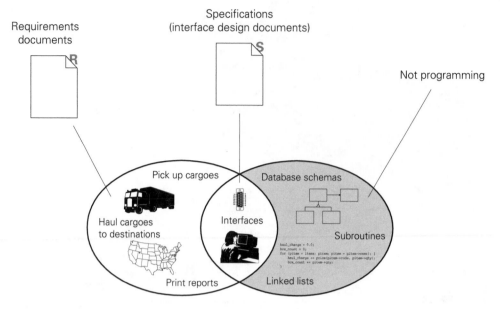

Requirements documents

Specifications (interface design documents)

Not programming

Pick up cargoes

Database schemas

Haul cargoes to destinations

Interfaces

Subroutines

Print reports

Linked lists

Figure 1.1 What this book is about

only the mechanics of grammar and formatting. This book takes a much broader view: both the choice of the content to include in the document and all aspects of the choices about how to present it, from small details of wording to the largest decisions about overall organization.*

The niceties of grammar and punctuation are covered in hundreds of other books about writing, so we won't cover them here. We also won't cover the principles of what makes a good choice for a problem to solve, or how to think up good problems to solve, or what makes a good user interface, and so forth. This book is only about how to write documents in order to make them useful to a software development team, including all of the information they need, and techniques for presenting that information so real people can understand and use it.

In chapter 1, we'll explore the fundamental principles of requirements, interfaces, and programs—what they are and how they're different from each other. But first, before we can define software problems well, we'll need to understand how programmers go about solving them in real life. We'll start by learning a few lessons from the software industry's experiences of the last few decades—a period of still-unfinished transition from software as pure research field to software as engineering discipline.

---

* [Schriver 1997] is an excellent, wide-ranging introduction to this broad conception of technical writing.

1.1 The myth of functional decomposition

The goal of any kind of engineering, not just software engineering, is to give people the ability to do something that they currently can't do—for example, travel from Los Angeles to Sydney in less than 24 hours, get information no more than five seconds out of date about any stock trading at the New York Stock Exchange, wash clothes with very little muscular effort. The task of the engineer is to design a device that gives people the desired ability—an airplane, an information system, or a washing machine.

Loosely defined, *requirements* are any criteria that an artifact to be designed must meet in order to be considered successful—roughly, what the customer can't do until the artifact is created, and the reason for creating it. We'll provide a more precise definition of requirements in chapter 3, but this will serve for now. To write a useful requirements document, we will need to understand what engineers do in order to produce a design that meets the requirements.

Engineering is essentially bridging the gap between requirements and available materials. Different engineering fields consist of techniques for bridging different kinds of gaps between different kinds of requirements and different kinds of materials. An aeronautical engineer is a person who knows how metal and other materials can be shaped and combined to make an airplane, meeting requirements pertaining to flight; a chemical engineer is someone who knows how to design apparatus to drive chemical reactions, meeting requirements pertaining to substances to be produced; and so forth.

A software engineer is someone who knows how to configure computers to perform various tasks related to information, such as providing information to people, transmitting information, and causing objects to behave in accordance with specified rules. The materials of a software engineer are unusual because they are intangible. They are the instructions that the computer is capable of executing, or the subroutines and instruction blocks made available by operating systems, subroutine libraries, and high-level programming languages.

Bridging the requirements/materials gap is seldom an easy business, particularly when the gap is large. Given a sponge, it's easy to see a way to get dishes clean, but there's an enormous gap between having only natural materials on hand and building a dishwasher. It took centuries for engineers to find a way to make airplanes, involving exploration of countless dead ends. Once someone figures out how to bridge the gap, as the Wright brothers did in the case of flight, the design can be repeated and slightly varied to solve new problems, but how do you bridge the gap when it's very large? How, for example, do you approach writing a program to manage the operations of a nationwide business when your materials are tiny statements in computer languages that merely add or substract numbers, write and read blocks of data to and from a disk, execute either one block of instructions or another depending on the value of a certain memory location, and so on?

1.1.1 Functional decomposition

Many theories about how to bridge large engineering gaps have been proposed. In the 1970s, one theory about how engineers can reliably bridge a large gap between materials and requirements became popular. Known as *functional decomposition*, or sometimes *top-down design* or *stepwise refinement*, it dominated the software industry for about twenty years and had particular influence on system analysts—the people who write software requirements.

According to the theory of functional decomposition, by following the steps shown below, an engineer can produce a design that meets any requirements that can be met:

1   The engineer identifies the function of the system to be built. The function is *what* the system is to do, as opposed to *how* the system will do it or what the system will *be*. So, for example, we don't say that the customer wants a washing machine; we say only that the customer wants to be able to wash a load of clothes of a specified size within a specified time, using no more than a specified amount of muscular effort.

2   If the function maps directly onto available parts—nuts, bolts, computer instructions—the engineer allocates the function to those parts and the design is done.

3   Otherwise, the engineer divides the function into subfunctions and repeats steps 2 and 3 until every subfunction is small enough to map onto the smallest parts of the design. The engineer is careful to exclude any design decisions from the specification of these subfunctions. Again, each subfunction says what the subsystem must do, not how it will do it.

For example, the subfunctions of the *wash clothes* function might include: accept clothes from user, return clothes to user, and remove dirt particles from clothes. The first two would be allocated to the door of the washing machine; the last function would be further subdivided. Notice that the last function is specified without mentioning soap or a rinse cycle or a motor. Those would be describing how the dirt particles are to be removed and would, therefore, be a design decision.

At first glance, this appears to be a perfectly rational, systematic approach to engineering. If a function is too big for the human mind to figure out how to implement it all at once, then break it down into smaller functions and repeat until you reach functions small enough to handle. Every main function required by the user gets allocated to exactly one element of the design, ensuring that every function is implemented. Every design element traces back to the required functions, ensuring that the design includes no superfluous elements.

An added bonus is that different subfunctions can be allocated to different engineers. On a large project, such as an airplane or an operating system, such a division of labor is a necessity. On a large project, a major task of the analyst or system engineer is to identify the major subfunctions of the system so that they can be allocated to distinct design units. People can then implement and test the design units independently before integrating them.

It sounds good—until you try it.

1.1.2 *Let's put it to the test*

While this book isn't about how to write programs, we need to understand what programmers do when writing a program in order to write useful requirements documents for them. To see how functional decomposition works in practice—or rather, doesn't work—let's follow the plight of a student taking a beginning programming course. Here is a typical, simple assignment given to a student in such a course:

Assignment—functional requirements:

(1) Convert numbers expressed in binary digits to decimal.
(2) Convert numbers expressed in decimal digits to binary.

For both types of numbers, allow fractions, indicated by digits to the right of a decimal point, and a plus or minus sign at the beginning of the number to indicate whether the number is positive or negative.

The student knows only the statements available in one programming language, such as C or BASIC, and has been taught that the rational approach to program design is functional decomposition. Those are the only weapons the student has to attack this assignment: knowledge of the programming language plus the theory of functional decomposition.

Notice that for the student, despite the fact that the assignment is fairly elementary, the engineering gap is quite large. He or she knows of no C or BASIC statements to perform the desired functions, has access to no subroutine libraries to do the job, and has never solved a problem like this before. So the student will have to break the functions down, perhaps to many levels, in order to implement them.

So, what are the subfunctions? Nearly any beginning programmer will draw a total blank. If they do come up with something, it might go like this:

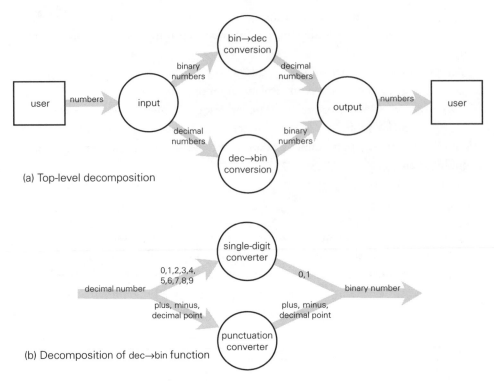

Figure 1.2 Beginning programmer's attempt at functional decomposition of base conversion program

"Let's see, I suppose there's an input function and an output function, and I guess there will be two conversion functions. Now, how should I decompose the conversion functions? Umm...maybe one subfunction handles the digits and the other subfunction handles the punctuation marks. Each time a conversion function receives a character, it calls the appropriate subfunction to convert it and sends the converted character to the output function." Figure 1.2 diagrams this functional breakdown.

An experienced programmer would know that such a program structure is a disaster. It's bug-prone because nearly all the subroutines "know" too much about what the others do; their responsibilities overlap in ways that can easily become unsynchronized. The program is unnecessarily long (and therefore bug-prone) because four functions are doing very similar work which could be done more cleanly by a single function. Finally, the requirement that each conversion function output a digit each time it receives a digit is impossible to fulfill. When the single-digit binary-to-decimal conversion function receives a 1, what can it output? There's no way to know until it receives more digits: 101 should produce 5, 10110 should produce 22, and so forth.

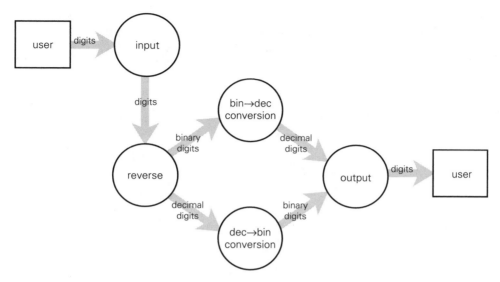

Figure 1.3 Second attempt at functional decomposition

After writing some code, the student would likely discover most of these problems. Okay, back to the drawing board. Brooks says, "Plan to throw one away; you will, anyhow."*

After struggling a while with the conversion functions—the hard part of the assignment—the student now decides that maybe there should be a digit-reversing function. One difficulty the student encountered in writing the conversion functions was the need to access digits that appear later in the stream in order to determine the numerical value of earlier digits. For example, the function can't tell that the 4 in 426 stands for 400, not 40 or 40,000, until it's read the remaining two digits. So the input function collects the entire string of digits, and, when the entire number is done, the input function sends the string to the reversing function. The reversing function then sends the string to the appropriate conversion functions, but in reverse order. Now the conversion functions know that the first digit received—at least in a number with no fractional part—is in the ones position, the second digit is in the tens position, and so on.

The new design (shown in figure 1.3) is a little better—maybe—but an experienced programmer would do it very differently. He knows some tricks such as internal representations that are independent of input or output formats, and something called a parser. The programmer sees that these tricks apply very nicely to this problem, and adds a parameter to the parser indicating what base to convert from, thereby collapsing two functions into one. The parser is concerned with creating the base-

* [Brooks 1975], p. 116.

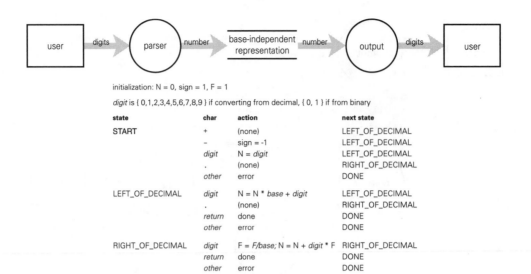

initialization: N = 0, sign = 1, F = 1

digit is { 0,1,2,3,4,5,6,7,8,9 } if converting from decimal, { 0, 1 } if from binary

state	char	action	next state
START	+	(none)	LEFT_OF_DECIMAL
	−	sign = -1	LEFT_OF_DECIMAL
	digit	N = *digit*	LEFT_OF_DECIMAL
	.	(none)	RIGHT_OF_DECIMAL
	other	error	DONE
LEFT_OF_DECIMAL	*digit*	N = N * *base* + *digit*	LEFT_OF_DECIMAL
	.	(none)	RIGHT_OF_DECIMAL
	return	done	DONE
	other	error	DONE
RIGHT_OF_DECIMAL	*digit*	F = *F/base*; N = N + *digit* * F	RIGHT_OF_DECIMAL
	return	done	DONE
	other	error	DONE

Figure 1.4 Experienced programmer's design

independent representation, but not with generating the output. The programmer gives to the output function the job of converting the base-independent representation to a specific base, effecting a very different separation of concerns than that found in the student's program. Coding the parser requires a trick called a state-transition table, but the programmer has written those before and tosses it off in five minutes without a mistake. This approach is shown in figure 1.4.

Why, armed with the theory of functional decomposition, was the beginning student unable to invent a design even remotely like the design produced almost instantaneously by the experienced programmer? The beginning student could have decomposed functions into subfunctions into subsubfunctions for the next six months and still not found the idea of a state-transition table—the key to a simple, bug-free design.

1.2 Problem solving and design patterns

Functional decomposition is just one of many generalized techniques of problem solving—that is, techniques that aim to help people solve a wide variety of problems across a wide variety of fields. The following is an exhaustive list of *all* problem solving techniques, arranged in order of decreasing effectiveness:

1 Already knowing the solution

2 Already knowing the solution to a similar problem

3 All other techniques

The third—enormous—category lumps functional decomposition together with whacks on the side of the head, thinking outside the box, and all the others because, compared to the first two techniques, they are nearly worthless. All of them, including functional decomposition, have considerable value, but none can compare with either already having the solution or already having the solution to a problem similar enough that it requires no great leaps of creativity to make the necessary adjustments.

This might seem like cheating. Already knowing the solution hardly seems like a technique for solving problems. Maybe so. But as engineers, we are not interested in giving problems a sporting chance. We want dependable ways to create designs that meet requirements and please customers, and the fact is that none of the techniques, other than the first two, reliably generate results.

There's a simple reason for this: only the first two techniques have features that are specific to the problem to be solved. Engineering problems are so different from each other that very few of the ideas or knowledge that enable you to solve one problem will help you solve a problem from a different field. Knowing how to design a sailboat doesn't tell you much about how to design a low-power light source. Completely generalized ideas that are so unfocused that they apply equally to all problems can give you some help, but not much. What help does "break the problem down into subproblems" give you when your problem is to build an accounting system out of computer instructions? However, knowing how to design a small sailboat gives you an enormous head start on designing a slightly larger one.

1.2.1 How engineering really works

Now we can see both why functional decomposition doesn't work and how engineering really works.

> Functional decomposition doesn't work because there are many different ways to divide a high-level function into subfunctions, and there is no way to tell which of those possible divisions are good or bad until you've gotten to the lowest level of design.

That's one reason why the student was at a loss to come up with a good functional breakdown, and why the first two that he tried worked out so poorly. The student couldn't tell that he or she had made the conversion functions impossible to write until they had started trying to write them. It's only at the bottom level, once you've started writing code, that you're in a position to evaluate a particular functional breakdown. By then, it's often too late to correct errors at the top level, especially if you've allocated the subfunctions to different programmers and you're three months into the project.

The way engineering really works is as follows:

1 Engineers apply and slightly vary already existing, time-tested designs.

2 Engineers engage in unstructured exploration of new designs and new ways to put old designs together.

Both types of problem solving can occur in the same project, of course.

The reason the experienced programmer was able to invent a wonderful design on the spot is because an experienced programmer knows several excellent designs that have been used thousands of times before. They know about parsers and display-independent representations, as well as a few other tricks, and see how they can solve the base conversion problem. That's all there is to it.

The reason the student failed to invent a good program structure is because the student didn't know about such clever tricks as state-transition tables and display-independent representations. There's nothing in the idea of functional decomposition that says "make a state-transition table and a display-independent representation," so functional decomposition didn't help him.

You might object that the student should have known better than to specify the conversion functions in their first design in a way that was impossible to implement—that he or she should have known more number theory, or should have known some programming techniques that would have made the job easier. However, that amounts to demanding that the student already know some of the major elements of the solution. Of course, students will learn these things from later courses and as they find good designs to imitate. Those will help the student—not general problem solving techniques.

1.2.2 Design patterns

Strangely, despite the importance of standard designs in all engineering fields, the concept has never been given a common name, and its role in engineering has mostly been left implicit in engineering practice and curricula. People learn standard designs for bridges, D.C. generators, brakes, smelters, microphones, and so forth, but they don't learn that use of standard designs is what separates professional engineering from tinkering.

In software, the term *design pattern* has recently come to denote such a standard design.* The word *pattern* emphasizes that the design can be applied "a million times

---

* Brought to widespread use mainly by [Gamma 1995].

over, without ever doing it the same way twice."* While some patterns (like the brick) vary little from one application to another, most (like the suspension bridge) are flexible ideas that require intelligence and imagination to apply. Thus, no two suspension bridges are alike.

This use of the word *pattern* comes from the work of architect Christopher Alexander, who found the same principle at work in town planning and architecture. In *A Pattern Language*, Alexander set about cataloging numerous patterns commonly found in towns and buildings that people like. Many of these patterns are simple things that we all know: *street cafe* is a pattern, *corner grocery* is a pattern, *dormer window* is a pattern, *waist-high shelf* is a pattern. Just as possessing a rich vocabulary of words enables you to write well, possessing a rich vocabulary of design patterns enables you to design well.

A pattern is not the same thing as a reusable component. A component is a specific physical object (or, in the case of software, a specific configuration). Two different instances of the same component are identical; both are instances of the same design. A pattern is a reusable *idea*. No two instances of a pattern are quite the same. The application of patterns is called design or engineering; the creation of new instances of the same design is called manufacturing.

1.3 Why software is hard

Early in the history of an engineering field, its practices tend more toward unstructured exploration than toward application of time-tested designs. This is natural because, in the early days, there are fewer time-tested designs.

Also in the early days, because of the emphasis on innovation, the field does not produce reliable results. Every new design involves numerous untested ideas, and untested ideas often fail.

When an engineering field is mature, engineers spend most of their time combining and making tiny variations to time-tested designs. They solve problems from a well-defined set of problems. For example, one well-defined set of problems is how to build transformers that convert between different voltages. For different voltages and power ratings, there are precise, step-by-step methods to build the transformer: how to choose the materials for the windings and the cores, how many windings to make, and so forth. Since transformers are part of the standard designs in electrical engineering, you can go to an electrical engineer, tell him the electrical characteristics that you desire, and be

---

* [Alexander 1977], page x.

confident that he can build exactly what you have asked for. If you ask him for something that he can't design, he can probably tell you on the spot. Whenever a solution technique is well defined, so is the type of problem that it applies to.

Naturally, the vast majority of projects still require ingenuity to solve unexpected problems. Combining existing designs always requires imagination. Also, the invention of entirely new kinds of designs continues, such as the tiles on the Space Shuttle and composites for airplane wings and bodies. Every large project still involves trying out and rejecting a number of designs until a good one is found. But an extensive vocabulary of time-tested designs makes possible a remarkably systematic and reliable engineering discipline. Few bridges or homes collapse of their own weight today; few transformer designs fail to meet their electrical requirements.

We'll distinguish, then, between two types of engineering project, corresponding to two types of activity, keeping in mind that these are a continuum rather than a sharp dichotomy:

> *Orderly engineering* is characterized more by the application and slight variation of time-tested design patterns.

> *Exploratory engineering* is characterized more by the unstructured exploration of new kinds of designs.

These are simply names for the two kinds of engineering activities described earlier. Both types of activities occur in any project, of course. Every problem contains something new, and no problem is without some similarity to problems solved before. But overall, the more mature the field, the more it is characterized by orderly engineering.

Software engineering is still in an immature state, although this is rapidly changing. The reason for the high failure rate of software projects is not primarily because of bad business processes or because programmers don't derive their code from calculations. The major reason is that often there is a large gap between the system that the customer wants delivered and the available time-tested designs.

For example, suppose that you're writing the software for a phone switch. A phone switch is a device that attaches to many (hundreds, thousands, even more) pairs of wires, each pair capable of connecting to a telephone. Hardware inside the switch has the ability to electrically connect any pair to any other pair. The job of the software is to control the creation and dissolution of connections between pairs in order to connect calls. The switch also needs to forward calls according to user requests, generate busy and ring signals, parse touch tones, as well as many other support functions.

What algorithms are available to draw upon in order to solve this quite complex problem? What standard data structures apply to it with little or no modification?

Not many. Therefore, the programmers will have to exercise great ingenuity in order to write the software. And, therefore, they will likely finish behind schedule and the code will likely contain bugs.

If you haven't programmed, the following task (see figure 1.5) should illustrate why software projects so often fail or come in late:

 Solve this—but first, schedule each phase of your solution, and figure out how long it will take you to solve it.

Figure 1.5 Exploratory engineering is difficult to plan

Solving a Rubik's cube is mostly a matter of stumbling onto a few key insights such as the following:

> There's a sequence of four moves that rotates three pieces without disturbing any others: [cube image] .

> If you have a useful sequence A that moves only a few pieces, such as the one shown above, you can easily change which pieces it moves by preceding it with a sequence B and following it with B in reverse. B moves pieces into position to be moved by A. The key is that B is very easy to invent because you needn't worry about causing side effects elsewhere on the cube. Running B in reverse after A cancels the side effects, leaving only the desired changes. $BAB^{-1} =$ [cube image] .

No one can possibly anticipate such insights. You can't even vaguely anticipate what they'll be like. Nor is there any systematic way to search for such insights. You can't base plans around the totally unknown. All you can do is keep your mind alert for the unexpected and struggle a while until you do find them.

Programming is often the same way. However, once you have solved a Rubik's cube, it's fairly easy to solve similar puzzles, such as those shown in figure 1.6:

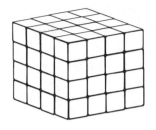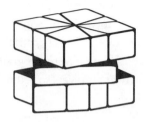

Figure 1.6 Solve one, and the rest become easier

The same insights apply. It's still difficult to know in advance how long it will take to solve these, but you now have a fairly well-defined class of problems along with a set of solution techniques, or *heuristics,* for solving them. Such solution techniques are, of course, analogous to design patterns.*

1.4 *Pattern composition and decomposition*

Fortunately, a great number of patterns have arisen in the world of software. There are sorting algorithms, searching algorithms, numerous types of data structures, algorithms for performing all manner of floating-point calculations, parsing techniques, algorithms for rendering three-dimensional images, and many more—far more than can fit into even a four-year college curriculum. Thus, the situation is not quite as bad as the Rubik's cube analogy suggests.

These patterns are what enabled the experienced programmer to make design decisions with confidence at a higher level than program code. Whereas the beginning programmer could only tentatively explore different ways to divide the program into modules, trying out different functional decompositions and hoping to find some key insight, the experienced programmer knew that dividing the program into a state-transition table for parsing input, a display-independent representation, and an output function would produce a program that both worked and was simple. So there is such a thing as orderly software engineering, at least for many types of software.

The experienced programmer is able to perform a task superficially similar to functional decomposition but, in reality, quite different. The experienced programmer

---

* See [Polya 1957] for the classic work on heuristics, the art of finding hypotheses worth investigating, or *provisional reasoning.*

engages in what we can call *pattern decomposition* or *artifact decomposition*—recognizing a pattern that is built from smaller patterns, and either implementing the smaller patterns or specifying them in enough detail that someone else can implement them. The programmer recognizes that the problem to be solved requires a parser, and he also knows that a parser is composed of a few elementary patterns: the state-transition table and the little trick of accumulating an ever-growing number in a variable. So he can decompose the pattern into subpatterns.

But there is a big difference between this and functional decomposition. The programmer was able to decompose the high-level pattern into subpatterns only because those subpatterns have been put together before. That's how the high-level pattern was created. In functional decomposition, you avoid any consideration of the underlying design. Rather, you try to deduce the design by breaking down the top-level function into subfunctions that you don't necessarily know in advance how to design. In pattern decomposition, you only break down a known design into known parts.

In functional decomposition, an engineer divides a complex task into smaller tasks. He divides "I need a way to do *a*" into "I need ways to do *b*, *c*, and *d*, such that if all those were done, *a* would be done." The *things* that perform these tasks are intentionally omitted from functional decomposition. Functions—tasks to be done, conditions to be achieved, or mappings between inputs and outputs—are mapped onto smaller functions at each stage of decomposition, with allocation to specific things deferred until the very end.

The real myth of functional decomposition is that we're capable of deferring concrete decisions to such an extent, deriving a working, concrete design from such a long train of purely abstract deductions and divisions. In fact, when people divide large functions into simpler functions, they always draw heavily upon their knowledge of the types of artifacts that they know can be built. However, this knowledge is left implicit. It guides the functional breakdown—as, indeed, it should—but the myth that design considerations are left out of their thinking goes unexamined. Thus, functional decomposition gets the credit for breaking down large, complex problems when, in fact, the problems were already broken down by existing knowledge of design patterns.

It's been said that functional decomposition is what enabled the Wright brothers to succeed where their predecessors failed. Whereas other people who attempted to enable people to fly created designs that borrowed heavily from the structure of birds, the Wright brothers decomposed flight into its subfunctions, enabling them to implement each subfunction by further decomposition, as shown in figure 1.7.

However, understanding that there are an unimaginably large number of ways to break down a function, you can see how unlikely it is that they designed their airplane by functional decomposition. Without assuming *any* design decisions about

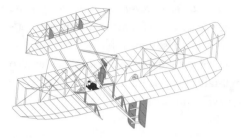

Subfunction	Implementation
Forward propulsion	Four-cylinder engine, propeller
Lift	Wings
Steering	Rudder, bendable wingtips

Figure 1.7 Functional decomposition of Wright brothers' airplane

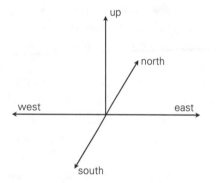

Subfunction	Implementation
Up/down propulsion	?
North/south propulsion	?
East/west propulsion	?

Figure 1.8 Another functional decomposition of flight

what objects the airplane will be made from, how can you criticize the functional decomposition in figure 1.8? If each subfunction were implemented, then the complete flight function would be implemented. Why not allocate one team of engineers to up/down propulsion, another to north/south propulsion, and a third team to east/west propulsion?

The reason the Wright brothers used wings, an engine, a propeller, and a rudder was because they had those things. Currently, no one has components that implement the up/down, north/south, and east/west functions, so no one breaks airplane design down that way, despite its mathematical elegance.

If we had components that implemented those functions, then we could indeed allocate each function to one component and the design would work. The fact that we do not have any such components nor do we see any way to make them is not supposed to deter us when decomposing functions. We're supposed to apply the procedure to the smaller functions and repeat until we find functions small enough to implement. But the great difficulty of functional decomposition is finding a way of dividing the top-level functions in such a way that we won't be further subdividing them until the end of time, like the beginning student trying to write the base conversion program. All that can enable us to do that is knowledge of specific things that can implement the functions—thoroughly tainting our functional decomposition with early design decisions.

If the internal combustion engine were not available, it's unlikely that the Wright brothers would have specified a forward propulsion function and then, through continuing stepwise refinement, deduced cylinders, pistons, spark plugs, and crankshafts. The only reason they used an engine was because it was an available component that they knew how to use. Indeed, the majority of the Wright brothers' airplane was designed by imitation. The idea of wings, with their peculiar shape, came from birds. One of the steering mechanisms came from observing the way that birds bend their wings to change direction. And, of course, the Wright brothers did not invent the internal combustion engine, though they did design their own—a variation on existing designs, tailored to the needs of the airplane.*

In pattern decomposition, people think, "I want an artifact of type *x* that meets such-and-such requirements." For example, a town planner can request of a civil engineer, "Build me a bridge that goes across this bay, has two lanes going in each direction, can support 30-ton semi-trailers, and meets the land at these two points." The civil engineer then opens up the *bridge* pattern into its subpatterns—the girders, supports, rivets, and so on—which have been put together many times before, though always in slightly different ways. Each level of pattern decomposition consists of smaller *things*, not smaller abstract functions. At every level, we know what we're talking about and we know how to build it.

Exploratory engineering usually works the other way around—*composing* patterns into larger designs in new ways. People have existing patterns and think, "I wonder what we could build out of these?" When people first built computers in the 1940s, they had no idea that computers could be used for digital manipulation of photographs, page layout in newspapers and magazines, paint mixing at hardware stores, or nearly any other modern application of computers. They simply explored ways in which you could build highly configurable machines, different ways that you could configure them, and what kinds of results you could achieve.

As is often the case in exploratory engineering, they built a solution in search of a problem. They did not start with the problem, "enable people to lay out pages in magazines on a screen." Their problem was to find out what is possible to do with these new machines. We're still a long way from finding out all of it; hence, the continued large amount of exploratory engineering in software.

In orderly engineering, where pattern decomposition is the rule, we start with problems for which there are known solutions, like "print a list of employees in alphabetical order." We exploit our existing knowledge of what is possible to build, rather than expanding it. Earlier exploratory engineering has found the techniques; now we

* Before we leave functional decomposition behind, there were two key elements to the Wright brothers' success that are well worth noting.

The first was [Cayley 1809]'s famous observation that (a) machines could generate much more force in proportion to their weight than could animals, and (b) birds are capable of generating lift without flapping their wings, that is, forward motion of the wing through the air produces enough lift to keep the bird from falling. This article is sometimes taken as a demonstration that lift and propulsion are distinct functions, though it's better understood as a demonstration that a certain kind of design is feasible. In other words, Cayley did not discover the true subfunctions of flight because, as we have seen, other divisions are possible. He argued that a certain breakdown of functions could be implemented by technology that seemed right around the corner. The article concludes with a design for a toy that lifts itself off the ground by spinning little propellers made from feathers, proving that it is possible to generate substantial lift merely by pushing a wing shape through the air instead of flapping the wing—just the sort of design that seemed feasible given current understanding of machines capable of continuously exerting force far in excess of their weight.

The second element, which truly distinguished the Wright brothers from their competitors, was genuinely successful functional decomposition. Other people at the time built whole airplanes, flew them, and then tried to guess why they crashed. Because they measured only global characteristics of the airplane, like "how far did it fly?", they could seldom trace problems to their source. Indeed, the source was seldom one wrong variable, but many: a combination of wing placement, wing shape, rudder placement, skill in rudder control, and so on. The Wright brothers, on the other hand, created and tested designs for one function at a time. They built their own wind tunnel to measure the lift that different wing shapes produced. They flew gliders to test different methods of steering. At each stage, the Wright brothers had a much smaller design space to search than aviators who wandered through the much vaster space of complete airplane designs. Once they had a successful design for lift, another for steering, and another for propulsion, they were able to combine them into a successful whole-airplane design. Read [Bradshaw 1992] for a short but very insightful discussion about the role of functional decomposition in the Wright brothers' success.

The success of the Wright brothers (and many exploratory engineering projects that followed similar methods) shows that functional decomposition is a useful general-purpose problem-solving technique, well worth its space in any engineer's bag of tricks. However, it does not show that functional decomposition is a reliable, systematic engineering method unto itself. Imitation of birds and Cayley's observation that machines could produce lift by pushing a wing shape through the air were equally important parts of designing the first airplane. Even armed with these preliminary and ultimately successful design ideas, as well as the technique of refining one subsystem at a time, the Wright brothers could not have scheduled their first flight when they first began designing.

Notice also that for many problems, functional decomposition does not even provide a hint of a solution. How, for example, do you break speech recognition into subfunctions? In general, for functional decomposition to be helpful, the number of creative steps between function and design must be very small, and it must be possible to create a fairly independent design for each function. If the Wright brothers had also to invent the internal combustion engine for propulsion, they probably would not have succeeded in building an airplane; and if the available methods of generating propulsion interfered with the methods of generating lift, the decomposition into lift and propulsion would not have significantly reduced the size of the design space they had to search.

The fact remains that, when trying to build something for which there are no existing, time-tested design patterns, or when the gap between the patterns and the problem is large, there is no guarantee of *ever* finding a solution that meets requirements, much less a systematic method for doing so, and still less a way to know in advance how long it will take.

apply them.

While the principles of requirements documentation taught in this book can apply to exploratory engineering, we will concentrate on orderly engineering—projects where the goal is to apply existing knowledge of software techniques to problems that we know we can solve. In exploratory engineering, requirements can even be a hindrance. The idea is to find out what's possible, to grow the new techniques organically from the existing techniques, and to discover what program code can do—especially, what it can do easily.* You can't predict in advance what you're going to discover, whereas requirements define exactly what problem the program code is to solve.

Pattern decomposition enables an important division of labor in engineering. You don't need to know how to design all the patterns that, together, form an artifact. You only need to know that the patterns exist and that people can build the artifacts. The town planner does not need to know all about bridge building in order to ask the civil engineer to build the bridge. The civil engineer specializes in understanding different types of bridges and how to build them. From the town planner's point of view, the bridge is just one of many elements of his own design. Furthermore, the civil engineer, while able to decompose the bridge pattern into subpatterns, need not know how to design instances of those subpatterns. If the bridge needs to raise up to allow ships to pass through, the civil engineer doesn't need to know how to design the motor to lift the bridge. He just needs to know that such motors can be built and who can build them.

---

* [Booch 1996] calls this an "architecture-driven project" as opposed to a "requirements-driven project." These are apt terms. An architecture-driven project starts with an implementation idea and looks for ways to extend it that provide new and unanticipated benefits to the customer. A requirements-driven project starts with well-defined benefits and draws upon existing, proven implementation ideas.

C H A P T E R   2

Problem defining

2.1 Requirements and design patterns

When a town planner decides that the ferry that transports people across a bay in his city no longer has sufficient capacity to carry all the traffic, he is likely to ask a civil engineer to design a bridge. The town planner does not ask the civil engineer, "Say, I've got people on opposite sides of this bay, and I need some way to transport them across. Got any ideas?" Before the town planner contacts an engineer, he has already decided what he wants built. He knows a standard type of artifact—a bridge—and he knows who is capable of designing one specifically for the traffic across the bay.

The fact that orderly engineering starts with some type of design pattern has an important implication for requirements:

> Rigorous research and definition of requirements is possible only in relation to a specific design pattern.

Only because the civil engineer knows that he's going to build a bridge can he ask pertinent questions of the town planner. "What traffic do you want the bridge to carry? Cars, or just pedestrians? Trucks? If so, what maximum weight? How many lanes do you want? Where on the land do you want the points of access to the bridge?" These questions enable the civil engineer to calculate parameters such as the width of the bridge and the load that it needs to support. He can also inspect underwater to learn how deep the bay is where the bridge is needed, and how solid its floor is in those places.

With a ferry, there is a whole different set of questions to ask. "How many lanes?" would be silly. Instead, one would ask, "How many cars and trucks do you want to be able to carry on each trip? How much total tonnage? How fast do you want the ferry to go? Are there any bridges in the way that the ferry must pass under? How high is their clearance? How wide is the entrance to the harbor?"

If we were to write requirements on the premise that engineers design by functional decomposition, every requirement purely a matter of what the device must do without assuming any design decision as to how it will do it, then the questions for the town planner would float into starry-eyed abstraction. Why try to find out the width of the bridge when you might, instead, build a ferry? Or a fleet of cargo planes? Or a teleportation device? We don't want our questions to rule out any possible design, after all. Perhaps the civil engineer should get the town planner to specify the speed at which the bay-transit device is to move the cars and trucks and then write this into the contract in order to specify every parameter that any design would have to meet. Oops—such a parameter makes no sense in regard to bridges.

Now we can explain one of the common complaints about requirements documents, heard from customers, programmers, testers, and everyone else involved in software development—they're so abstract that no one can understand them. This is the result of the analyst's diligence in avoiding assuming any imaginable design decision. (More common problems in requirements documents are described in sections 13.3 through 13.5.)

Implicit in the *bridge* pattern is the set of questions asked by the civil engineer about how the bridge is to be used. The answers to these questions define the problem to be solved by the bridge in enough detail to enable the engineer to apply and adjust the pattern to the town planner's needs. These answers constitute the requirements of the bridge.

Thus:

> Corresponding to every design pattern is a set of questions to ask about the type of problem that the pattern solves. A requirements document answers these questions.

Writing requirements, then, is answering a set of questions. The particular set of questions is determined by the type of artifact—the design pattern—for which you are writing requirements. The answers define a problem in enough detail—and the right kinds of details—to enable an engineer to apply that design pattern to create a new design.

2.2 Software problems

We know what sort of problem a bridge solves: provide a path for certain objects to move by ground travel (that is, with weight fully supported) from one place to another without falling into the space below. The generic problem definition makes clear what kind of questions you need to ask to write the requirements for a bridge. Most fundamentally, they are: what are the size and weight of the objects that are to move across, and what are the points where the bridge is to meet with the land on either side? Additional information pertains to the environment of the bridge: other types of loads on the bridge, such as wind, and where the bridge can get its own support, such as the floor of a river.

What sort of problems, then, does software solve? All software problems are of this form:

Configure machine M to produce effects R in domain D.

The machine M is the computer to be programmed, including its input/output devices. The effects R are the requirements. The domain D is a necessary part of the problem definition because it is the part of the world in terms of which the requirements are defined, and because the machine can rarely produce the desired effects all by itself. The design of the software exploits properties of its environment by making use of redundancy to detect errors, making use of people or other software to gather information, making use of motors to control other machinery, and so forth.

The reason that computers are so powerful and so useful throughout so many industries is the fact that they are extraordinarily configurable machines. Every program is just one of the astronomical number of useful configurations of the bits in the computer. On most computers, you can load one program—that is, one configuration—and operate it for a while and then replace it with a completely different program later; for example, swapping a word processor for a spreadsheet. (The reason for saying "most computers" instead of "all" is that in embedded applications, where the program is stored in read-only memory, reconfiguring is difficult or impossible.) The same program can even reside in different places in memory at different times, or it can be swapped in and out from disk in segments, if the computer lacks sufficient memory to hold the entire program at once.

This is also the reason that software is so easily misunderstood and that software engineering is so different from other engineering fields. Software is not a tangible artifact, like a bridge, a motor, or a computer. Software is a particular configuration of a computer—not the hardware, but the way the hardware is set up, a possible state of the hardware. Being a mere potentiality for configuration, software does not weigh anything or occupy any space. The software can exist, in the form of source code or object code stored on tape, even if no computer currently bears that configuration. To put it another way, the materials of software are not physical objects, as in other engineering fields; they are the instructions that a computer is capable of executing, or, more broadly, the bits in a computer.

Adding to the potential for confusion, the machine M of which a piece of software is a potential configuration might well be a combination of hardware and other software. We don't usually write software simply for PCs. Writing software for a PC running Windows is very different from writing software for a PC running Linux. From the standpoint of a programmer, the operating system is itself part of the machine to be configured.

Software engineering, then, is the art of exploiting the extraordinary configurability of computers—the art of inventing useful ways to configure them. The general form of all software problems suggests three fundamental questions to answer in order to write software requirements: what type of machine do you want configured, what effects do you want the configuration to produce, and what are the properties of the outside world that the machine can exploit to produce those effects?

In orderly engineering, we must limit ourselves to the types of software problems that people already know how to solve—effects that we know how to achieve. Chapter 5, *Five problem frames,* describes five standard types of software problem in detail, including all the questions to ask to fully define each problem. The following is just a taste.

One of these standard problems is the *information problem*. In an information problem, the task of the software developer is to configure a computer into an information system—that is, a combination of hardware and software that supplies information to users, on demand, about the current state of some part of the world. The principal questions to answer in a requirements document for an information system are therefore: (1) What machine is to be configured to act as an information system?, (2) What questions can the users ask of the information system?, (3) What part of the world do these questions concern, and what events happen there?, and (4) How can the machine get access to these events? For example, must people relay the information to the machine by typing it in manually, or are there automatic sensors, or are there other computers or databases that can supply the information? Information problems have many variations, and different variations need different questions answered, but these illustrate the fundamental pattern. Question (2) provides the requirements: answer these questions on demand. Questions (3) and (4) provide the relevant information about the domain of the requirements.

In practice, question (1), about the type of machine, or platform, to be configured into the desired information system tends to fade into the background, especially in large-scale information systems where we have a great number of machine-independent programming techniques. Programs written in high-level languages, for example, can be compiled to run on a variety of different machines with very little modification to the source code. However, high-level languages mainly make possible a high degree of CPU (central processing unit) independence, not independence from the input/output devices.

In most requirements documents, the principal information that we need to know about the machine is its input/output devices. The interface design is essentially a design for how the input/output devices should behave; the program is what makes them behave according to the interface design. Without knowing the input/output devices, we would not be able to create the interface design.

For example, it makes a great difference to the design of both interfaces and programs whether there are bar-code readers attached to the computer or whether users must enter data manually. If a computer that controls a laboratory apparatus has a pH sensor, the programmers need to know how the pH sensor works in order to write code to control it and read data from it. A user-interface design for a Macintosh or Windows program can call upon different hardware and operating-system services than a user-interface design for software that communicates only through 25 × 80 text-only terminals.

And in some projects, facts about the machine's CPU, memory, and non-volatile storage are no less important to include in the requirements document. In an embedded system, where the software runs on, say, a custom microprocessor in a very limited amount of memory, describing the internals of the machine takes on a level of importance that cannot be masked through such tools as high-level programming languages.

2.3 Requirements engineering

Requirements are sometimes contrasted with *design*, where design is understood as a choice of means to bring about a desired effect. The requirements are the desired effect, and the interfaces, program code, and so forth are the means to bring it about. This is unfortunate because requirements themselves are design—no less than program code.

To take a simple example, suppose that a company's marketing department has made a Web site and wants to evaluate the site's effectiveness for purposes of improving it. Someone might propose writing a tiny information system with the following requirement: "report how many hits each page received and from what Internet domains." This requirement is an effect to be produced by the software, but it's also a means to bring about another effect: improving the Web site by helping the marketing department tune the pages to the people who are actually reading them.

The decision to write software that meets that requirement is a creative act—an invention, a choice, a design, a perceived way of bringing about improvement—no less than the design of a subroutine or data structure. If this is an effect that no one desires, then people will likely reject the software or leave it unused. If people want this effect, then the software will likely be successful.

Requirements engineering—the design of requirements—is very often the most critical phase of a software project. The requirements are the desired effects to be achieved by the software. Someone has to think up those effects. Someone must decide that those effects would be good to achieve. If the effects do not bring about any real improvement—that is, further effects, such as improvements to the Web site and increases in sales—then the software will fail even if it implements the requirements perfectly.

Software quality is, therefore, much more than meeting requirements. The requirements themselves must be a good design. Many times, software has failed not because it contained bugs or ran too slowly or contained any other fault within the purview of program code. It failed because people refused to buy or use the software because the problem that it solved was of no concern to them, or even because they preferred to leave that problem unsolved. A typical example is software for doctors' offices that facilitated communication among doctors about diagnoses of a patient. It turns out that while the software worked perfectly, most doctors preferred to form their diagnoses from scratch. The culture of doctors' offices made software to perform this task unwanted. Thus, the software, for all practical purposes, was of low quality because the requirements were of low quality, not because of the quality of the user interface or program code.

Furthermore, there are always many, many ways of meeting requirements. No one, for example, can write down all the criteria for judging one user interface superior to another. No one can measure how readable or modifiable program source code is. Requirements engineering certainly has the greatest influence on software quality, but all aspects of software design affect quality in a variety of different ways. There is no formula for measuring the quality of requirements, no formula for measuring the quality of a user interface, and no formula for measuring the quality of program code. We simply design each as well as we can, drawing upon the accumulated knowledge of the field as embodied in both theory and the software design patterns that have evolved so far.

Even though requirements are design no less than user interfaces and program code, there is a key difference. A set of requirements defines a problem such that we can say that the interfaces and program code either solve it or fail to solve it. The software either meets the requirements or it doesn't. As just mentioned, there is much more to software quality than meeting requirements, but requirements do provide the baseline for the remainder of a software design.

Inventing requirements is a matter of inventing a well-defined problem to solve:

> A *well-defined problem* is a set of criteria according to which proposed
> solutions either definitely solve the problem or definitely fail to solve it,

along with any ancillary information, such as which materials are available to solve the problem.

The requirements themselves, however, do not necessarily measure up against strict criteria of success and failure. During requirements engineering, you design against an open-ended problem:

> An *open-ended problem* is a situation in which we believe that some improvement is possible, but we have no definite criteria for measuring improvement. Discovering good criteria is, itself, part of the problem.

A typical example of an open-ended problem is that faced by the town planner before asking the civil engineer to design a bridge. The town planner's problem was to do something about the traffic along the roads connecting two sides of a bay. But did the town planner have any definite requirements to meet? Was the requirement to reduce the number of cars traveling along the existing roads by at least 10%? Well, no, that could easily be achieved by blocking off the roads. Was it to increase the speed of trips during rush hour by at least 10%? Well, no, that might not even be possible.

In fact, the town planner simply faces an enormous set of alternative actions. A major part of his effort will be discovering and exploring those options, as well as trying to discover good criteria for determining which options are better and which are worse. The town planner could widen the existing roads, build a bridge, dig a tunnel, order a new freeway, or he could do some surprising things. He could *narrow* the existing roads in order to cause people more frustration as they drive to work, encouraging them to either ride the bus or move to within walking distance of their jobs. If he changes the zoning laws to allow offices to be interspersed among residences, and apartments to be built above shops at street level, people just might move their place of residence and stop driving so much.

How is he to measure such an option? Traffic along the existing roads might flow much more slowly than before, but people would get to work faster. If he had tried to start with a well-defined problem where the requirement was to speed up traffic, this option would have been ruled out prematurely. Furthermore, as he examines each of his many options, he continually discovers new criteria for evaluating them. By causing less traffic to flow instead of more, he would help out the city's smog problem—a problem that he wasn't even trying to solve. By encouraging people to walk, the streets become more alive with pedestrians, changing the culture and character of the city—an aspect of town planning that he might not even have thought about before. Now he has new criteria for measuring the options of widening the roads, building a bridge, and all of the rest. Perhaps, when he re-examines those options, he will discover new criteria by which to evaluate the option to frustrate people into moving closer to their destinations.

All engineering begins with open-ended problems: no requirements, just the belief that some sort of improvement is possible. Noticing that rush-hour traffic was becoming a nuisance, the town planner thought he could do something to "improve the situation."

By understanding that requirements are design, we know to avoid two common mistakes: settling on strict evaluation criteria too early, and trying to write requirements so vaguely—so untainted by design decisions—that they don't define any definite problem at all. For example, "design a data model that meets the needs of the business" or "design a system to ensure that baggage is processed correctly" are useless criteria without a precise description of the business's needs or an extensive definition of "correctly."

In requirements engineering, you start with an open-ended problem, and finish with a well-defined problem—so well defined that you can entrust it to someone else to work out a solution. The decision about what type of artifact to build—in our case, the decision to write a piece of software—is the most fundamental decision in requirements engineering. If you haven't yet made the decision to write software, you are not yet ready to hand off the problem to software engineers. You're still engaged in requirements design, not interface design or program design.

A software requirements document presents software engineers with a well-defined software problem. There is no sense in giving software engineers a problem in town planning, business management, manufacturing, typesetting, or anything other than software.

The full subject of requirements engineering—the art of inventing and choosing requirements—is far beyond the scope of this book, or indeed any book. Here, we cover only what information needs to be put into written form for the rest of the development staff to implement software requirements. We won't explore techniques for coming up with ideas for requirements or criteria for judging whether those requirements would serve customers well or poorly.

2.4 Lessons learned

Before we move on to a precise definition of requirements and their relation to interfaces and programs, let's pause to look over what we've learned in the first two chapters about how engineering really works. What we've learned boils down to just this:

> Generalized problem-solving methods don't work, at least not well
> enough to base a method of requirements-writing on them.

So, we won't premise that programmers and interface designers will implement requirements by decomposing high-level functions into low-level functions. Real-life programming just doesn't work that way. Therefore, we won't write a set of high-level software functions connected by data flows; we'll let the programmers write their own subroutines.

We won't try to document an entire open-ended problem in a requirements document. So, in the case of the software to count Web hits, we won't make the requirement anything so broad as "help the marketing department improve the Web pages" or "increase sales."

Instead, we will always premise that programmers and interface designers will implement requirements by making *software*. The only type of problem we'll describe in a software requirements document is a software problem, as defined in section 2.2.

We'll go even further and tailor the information in requirements documents to specific kinds of software and specific known design patterns and programming techniques. "Provide information about specific events in domain *D*" is a type of requirement that we know how to fulfill, so that's the type of requirement that we write for the software to monitor the marketing department's Web page: "Provide reports showing the number of hits to the Web page."

While the specificity of our documentation techniques has the great advantage that it allows us to write very concretely and in a way instantly and obviously useful to interface designers and programmers, we need to be aware of an important implication: the documentation techniques taught in this book do not apply to every conceivable type of software. Neural nets and expert systems, to take two examples, are types of software whose design techniques work in different ways than most ordinary software; each has an unusual set of questions to ask in order to apply the design patterns.

Another type of software excluded by this book's focus on natural-language documentation is software that performs tasks so complex that it is difficult to be sure that the design of the interface or program is correct. If you're writing software where you can't prove the validity of a design by fairly straightforward, simple techniques, then you need to investigate *formal methods*. Formal methods are ways of making and validating descriptions—of the requirements, interfaces, and program—that derive from mathematical notations. Mathematical notations make it possible to express mathematical ideas of much higher complexity than we can achieve with natural language and simple graphics. Formal methods also make possible, to some extent, automated validation of interfaces and programs. For example, sometimes you can run software to check whether the software will really meet the requirements or whether the requirements contain gaps or internal contradictions.

Nevertheless, the basic principles taught in the next chapter do apply to virtually all kinds of software, and you can probably vary many of the techniques to come in later chapters to work with other kinds of software. That's how patterns are—not inflexible rules, but helpful ideas that always need a little bit of creativity and variation to apply in each case.

CHAPTER 3

Two worlds and three designs

3.1 The problem domain

Imagine that you are working on a project to develop software for a trucking company. The company has trucks, drivers, cargoes, and customers scattered all over the country. The job of the software is to track all of these things so that employees can know where any truck, driver, or cargo is at any time. Your task is to write the requirements document. What information do you include?

You might start by describing the behavior of the software desired by the customer in as much detail as possible: the appearance of the screens, what information goes in each field, and how the program responds to keystrokes and mouse clicks.

If you start by documenting those things, then you have skipped requirements.

This might come as a surprise. Didn't we just say that we know what kind of thing we're going to build, and that this knowledge should guide the way we write requirements? Yes, but that doesn't mean that we confuse description of the software with requirements. Requirements define the problem to be solved by the software; they do not describe the software that solves it.

A customer rarely desires software behavior. What the customer wants was described above: "employees can know where any truck, driver, or cargo is at any time." Trucks, drivers, and cargoes are not part of the software, nor is knowledge held by the company staff. These make up the part of the world that is of interest to the customer.

This part of the world is called the *problem domain*. It gets its name from the fact that the problem to be solved by the software is defined in terms of it. What the customer wants is for certain conditions to be realized in the problem domain—in this case, for employees to be able to know the locations of the company's trucks, drivers, and cargoes.

More precisely:

> The *problem domain* is the part of the world where the computer is to produce desired effects, together with the means available to produce them, directly or indirectly.

The problem domain includes everything relevant to describing the desired effects: objects that queries pertain to, people to be informed, objects to be controlled, parameters (such as voltage) to be kept within a certain range, even desired output formats for queries.

The means available to the software designers to produce these effects are also part of the problem domain. Indirect means include users whom the computer can ask to perform tasks, motors that the machine can turn on and off, people or other machines that can supply information—anything that is not part of the software to be written. For example, a requirement of the trucking company's software might be to send cargoes from one location to another, on command. The means available include trucks and drivers. The software fulfills the requirement by scheduling trucks and calling upon drivers to drive them.

Where there are indirect means, there must be direct means. The only type of effect that a computer can cause directly is the behavior of its input/output devices. The most obvious examples are keyboards, screens, and printers—the means by which the computer receives commands for where to pick up and deliver cargoes, and the means by which the computer communicates instructions to the drivers. In embedded applications, input/output devices are a more obvious part of the problem domain. In order to write, for example, machine code to control a microwave oven, the programmers need to know what inputs the microprocessor receives from the control panel and how the microprocessor is connected electrically to the other parts of the oven.

It might be convenient to define the problem domain as "the world outside of the computer," but this is not quite true, for three reasons. First, without knowledge of the input/output devices, we would have an abstract problem, not a concrete engineering problem. To design the software, we must be able to follow the causal chain from objects in the external part of the problem domain all the way to the computer. Otherwise, for example, we wouldn't know how to cause the microwave oven to behave in the specified way. The program would be in one world, and the problem domain would be in another, neither able to affect the other.

Second, sometimes the problem domain does not exist outside the computer. The classic example is the problem domain of a word processor or computer-aided design (CAD) program. The documents that people create with a word processor exist only inside the computer. The principal effect that the software is to achieve is to *create* the problem domain. Simulation programs have the same type of problem domain.

We'll call such a domain a *realized domain* when we discuss domain description further in chapter 4. A software problem involving a realized domain is somewhat different from other problem types. It's a *workpiece problem.* The problem is not to report on or control existing objects, but to create entirely new, intangible, software objects inside the computer for people to work on.

Some of the most widely used software in the world solves workpiece problems— word processors, spreadsheets, even operating systems. However, most software development solves problems in which the problem domain already exists—custom inventory software, embedded applications, software to perform scientific calculations, and so forth. So, while we will cover workpiece software, most of our emphasis will be on the other types of problems.

The third reason why the problem domain is more than just the world outside the computer is that, in some applications, the requirements are specifically for the input/output devices to behave a certain way. A customer might want forms to appear a certain way on the screen. Entertainment software provides the most extreme examples. In a video game, the on-screen appearance makes up the majority of the requirements.

3.2 Requirements

We are now ready for a precise definition of requirements:

> *Requirements* are the effects that the computer is to exert in the problem domain, by virtue of the computer's programming.

These are the "effects *R*" discussed in section 2.2. We've made the definition more precise and more useful by limiting requirements to conditions in the problem domain. We are interested, not in software behavior, but in the effects produced *by* software behavior.

Another way to think of the relation between requirements and the problem domain is as follows. Requirements are statements identifying what the customer wants to achieve: to be able to perform some type of action in the problem domain, to have access to information about some part of the problem domain, to keep parameters in the problem domain (such as temperature) within a certain range, and so forth. Each term in a requirement statement refers to something in the problem domain.

So, for example, the requirements for the trucking company's software use terms like *truck, cargo, client, driver, road,* and so on. Those all refer to objects in that software's problem domain. For example, "an employee can find out, for any given truck, what cargo, if any, it is currently holding."

The requirements do not include terms like *database, keystroke, doubly-linked list, file,* or *field.* These terms all refer to the software. The software developer will probably create all those things in order to fulfill the requirements, but let's not confuse the solution with the problem.

3.3 Interface design

The solution to the problem defined by the requirements and description of the problem domain is to write a program, of course—to configure a computer to execute instructions that bring about the requirements. However, no current-day computer's instruction set includes such operations as "Find out where Burnside's truck is right now and make this known to Smithers."

Software solves problems by interacting with the outside world. While there are no computer instructions that put information in people's minds, there are instructions that write to memory that corresponds to pixels on a monitor. There are instructions that read input registers that are activated by keystrokes, instructions that control read/write heads on disks, and so on. What each of these examples has in common is that each action takes place simultaneously within the machine world and the outside world—that is, each instruction either affects or is affected by the machine's input/output devices.

The program *specification*, or *interface design*, is a set of rules relating behavior of the computer's output devices to all possible behavior of the input devices. We design the specification to cause the requirements—that is, to cause desired effects in the problem domain, directly or indirectly. The specification thus pertains to the tiny part of the world that instructions inside the program can affect or be affected by directly—the tiny part of the world that the computer shares with the problem domain.

The program, in turn, is the configuration of the computer's memory that results in its behaving as described in the specification. The program, not being a tangible input/output device, is no part of the problem domain at all. Intangible things, such as a possible way for an object to be configured, cannot cause effects by themselves. Strictly speaking, the object is what interacts with the rest of the world; the configuration determines which of the object's many possible ways of behaving actually occurs. For convenience, we will speak of the program causing the computer to behave a certain way, but never of the program directly exerting effects outside the computer.

For example, software to control a printing press is responsible for moving paper through the press and applying ink at the correct locations on the page. The computer lacks instructions to cause these effects directly, so it causes them indirectly, through its connection with the motors that attach to rollers in the printing press. While the requirements describe paper and ink movements, the specification describes the activation and deactivation (changing of voltage to 5 volts or 0 volts) of the wires connecting the computer to the motors. These activations and deactivations initiate the chain of events that result in paper moving through the press and receiving the desired images. Finally, the program is what makes the computer cause the activations and deactivations of the wires to occur, as described in the specification.

Thus, software design as a whole involves three principal designs: the design of the requirements, the design of the interfaces that bring about the requirements, and the design of the program that makes the computer behave as specified by the interface design. These three designs span two worlds: the requirements are contained completely within the problem domain and exclude the machine; the interfaces pertain to the tiny overlap between the problem domain and the machine; and the program design describes only the configuration of the machine. All of these relationships are shown together in figure 3.1.*

Most specifications contain two further pieces of information beyond a strict description of the behavior of input/output devices. First, in order to relate past events at the input devices to future events at output devices, a specification usually must postulate *states* of the machine. The specification can say that a certain input event, such as typing in some data at one time, changes the state of the machine such that *if* another event occurs later, such as requesting a query, the data displayed in the query is the data typed in earlier. If someone types in new data, that can change the state of the machine again, so that now the same query would produce different results.

The one rule for describing machine states in a specification is that these states must make some distinguishable difference in the problem domain. So we can say that the machine stores data, such as names and phone numbers, and even say how many characters are allowed in the names and how long the phone numbers can be, but we don't say anything about the internal representation of this data inside the computer.

---

* Figure 3.1 is adapted from the diagram on p. 170 of [Jackson 1995].

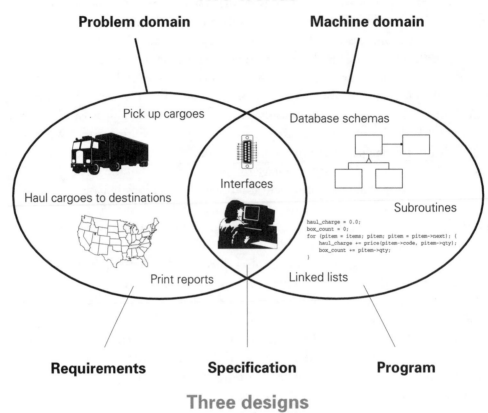

Figure 3.1 Relationship between requirements, specifications, and programs

We must say how many characters a user can type in when entering a name, but we have no reason to say whether the name is stored in an object-oriented, relational, network, flat-file, or other type of database. We don't even need to say whether the characters in the name are represented according to the American Standard Code for Information Interchange (ASCII) code. For purposes of this book, the design of database tables is considered a part of programming; it's "behind the scenes."

The second main type of additional information to include in a specification is any rules that parts of the problem domain must follow in order for the software to work properly. For example, when a program interfaces with human users, you do more than design screens and invent data for the computer to store. You also impose responsibilities on the users. If the users are the computer's source of information about maintenance being performed on trucks, then you make it the users' responsibility to enter this information as it happens.

The behavior that the software requires of users is called the software's *operating procedures*. The users must follow the operating procedures correctly, or you can't guarantee that the computer will call for maintenance checks at appropriate times, print correct data in reports, and so forth. A specification must document all operating procedures, or the testers, programmers, technical writers, and especially the users will be at quite a disadvantage.

Naturally, the option to make demands on parts of the problem domain is not available to all specifications. Software to control a crane must take the behavioral properties of the crane as they are. Normally, when users are involved, an interface designer can impose responsibilities on them. There is little or no leeway when designing an interface to hardware or other software.

Creating a specification often involves a great deal of imagination and ingenuity. There are often many possible specifications that could solve the problem defined in the requirements, some better and some worse. Especially in designing a user interface, the job of specifying software is often exploratory engineering rather than orderly engineering. Despite the fairly refined vocabulary of user-interface patterns already in use, the open-endedness of user-interface design is not likely to end soon, or ever. Thus user-interface design is a stage of software development especially in need of prototyping and early testing. Interfaces to software and hardware, on the other hand, tend not to admit of such flexibility.

Very often, the customer needs to be involved in both requirements design and interface design. Though two user interfaces might both meet requirements, the customer might greatly prefer one to the other. The customer might consider one of them completely unacceptable. When presenting an interface design, you need to explain how it addresses each requirement. In addition to letting the customer judge the interface, this gives the customer an opportunity to notice requirements that were missing or improperly defined and to judge for himself whether or not the interface really satisfies the requirement.

3.4 Validation of interfaces and programs

Figure 3.2 shows how the principal elements of a complete software design are related to each other logically. It should always be possible to prove the validity of the interface design on the basis of the description of the problem domain plus the requirements. The reasoning runs as follows. Premises: (1) The behavior described in the interface design occurs; (2) The computer's environment matches the description of the problem

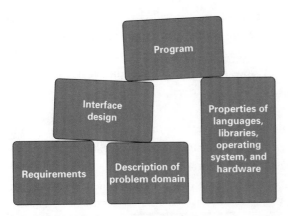

Figure 3.2 Logical structure of requirements, specifications, and programs

domain. Conclusion: the requirements are fulfilled. If the conclusion does not follow from the premises, then the interface design is invalid.*

The reason for including premise (2) is that the computer fulfills requirements by interacting with objects in its environment. If the interface designer has misunderstood the environment, it is unlikely that the interface will be correct. For example, part of the problem domain of the software that controls a printing press is the motors that attach to the rollers. One of the premises of the interface design, then, is that when the motor runs, the roller turns. Another premise is that the motor is attached to a certain output port on the computer—when the output port is at 5 volts, the motor runs. Only by adding premises about the computer's environment to premises about the behavior of the input/output devices can we deduce that the requirements will be fulfilled.

The relation of programming to interface design follows the same pattern. You prove the validity of a program as follows. Premises: (1) The program consists of the specified instructions. (2) The platform on which the program runs possesses the specified library, operating-system, and hardware properties. Conclusion: the behavior described in the interface design occurs.

Or, more simply, a program design is validated against a specification; a specification is validated against requirements and the problem domain. Therefore:

> Without requirements, there is no way to validate a program design—that is, no way to logically connect the program to the customer's desires.

This is true even if the requirements are not documented. Writing down requirements is primarily a device to help many people work together on the same project, as

---

* [Jackson 1995], p. 171.

we will discuss in chapter 13. Requirements, domain descriptions, and interface designs are propositions and concepts, not sentences or diagrams on paper. This book has much to say about sentences and diagrams on paper, but this is always for the purpose of communication between people. Sometimes you might want to trust less formal techniques of communication; for some factors to consider, see section 12.6.

The fundamental reason for carefully distinguishing interface design from requirements is that requirements are designed in response to an open-ended problem, but interfaces are defined in response to a well defined problem. That is, there are no rigid criteria for evaluating requirements; we simply make a decision to build software to bring about certain effects. An interface, on the other hand, derives from a well-defined problem—the one provided by the requirements. You can prove deductively that an interface meets requirements. But you can't validate requirements by such a deductive method; you, or the customer, simply judge them as good or bad effects to achieve.

A further reason for distinguishing interface design from requirements is to consciously focus on the problem domain. Especially for a programmer just moving into system analysis, this shift in perspective is difficult. It's tempting to push the unfamiliar world of the problem domain aside, directing your attention instead to the familiar world of software. But the interfaces and program code will be much more useful to the customer if you've carefully framed the problem entirely in terms other than program structure.

3.5 Description

It follows from the principles of validating an interface design that you need to *describe* the problem domain in addition to writing requirement statements. That is, in addition to statements about how the problem domain is to be affected, you need to say how the problem domain *is*.

Table 3.1 includes some common problem-domain information that needs to be in a requirements document.

Table 3.1 Types of information needed in a problem-domain description

Information	Examples
Entities in the domain and their attributes	Trucks: manufacturer, maximum cargo weight, maintenance record, whether includes refrigeration, and so forth. Hurricanes: name, location, shape, direction of rotation, and so forth.
Cardinalities of relations between entities	For every customer, there can be zero or more invoices; for every invoice, there is exactly one customer.
Events that the entities are capable of	Trucks move along roads, from city to city. A new truck can be bought; the company can sell or otherwise retire a truck from service. A hurricane can move, possibly overlapping a city.

Table 3.1 Types of information needed in a problem-domain description (continued)

Information	Examples
Causal rules	A cargo never moves unless it is in a moving truck. A truck never moves unless moved by a driver. When a truck moves, its driver moves to the same place. The fuel injector releases 1 ml of fuel into the cylinder when address line A17 goes high.
Interfaces that provide the software indirect access to entities of interest	A time clock that connects to the computer that the software will run on, providing electronic records of when employees punched in and out
Data formats	The format of the data sent by the time clock

Notice that it's not the responsibility of the software to enforce any of the above statements. Rather, knowledge of the above statements is needed by the software designers in order to design software to bring about the requirements. If the software is to print reports on how many hours each employee works each week, the programmers need to know that there is a time clock, that the employees are supposed to punch it, and the format of the data sent by the time clock.

Without purely descriptive information about the problem domain, designing software to meet the needs of the customer would be impossible. Requirements, or prescriptive statements, are not enough.*

In fact, on most software projects, a well-written requirements document needs much more problem-domain description than requirement statements. The number of pages of pure description might easily be five times as many as the number of pages of requirement statements.

This might not be as much of a surprise as the principle that requirements say little or nothing about the software to be built. The principle is really the same in both cases, though. The problem that the customer wants to solve is always to make certain things happen in the problem domain. The job of a requirements document is to define that problem in enough detail that people can design software to make those things happen. In real-world problems, the problem domain tends to be complex, while requirements are often not much more than, "Let me query about anything in our inventory" or "Play back the recorded messages into the phone line when the caller dials the passcode."

---

* [Jackson 1995], pp. 125–128, and [Zave 1997] propose a more elegant terminology, distinguishing between statements in the *indicative* and *optative* moods. Indicative statements are those that merely point out facts; optative statements say what we consider good, what we would opt for. We'll say *descriptive* and *prescriptive* in this book only because they're more familiar.

The complexity of the problem domain might make it seem hopeless to even attempt to describe it in detail. How can you know, while still writing the requirements document, which facts about the problem domain will turn out to be relevant and which won't? And aren't there millions of such facts?

The key to keeping domain description from becoming open-ended is the principle that the information in a requirements document always derives from the type of artifact to be built or, more specifically, from the type of well defined problem solved by that artifact. When writing the requirements document for an information system, there are specific questions to answer about the problem domain: what objects reside there about which the user can initiate queries, what events do those objects undergo that change the proper results of those queries, and what sources of information share phenomena with the machine, enabling it to track those events? Chapter 5 provides detailed checklists of all the problem-domain information needed to define five of the most common problem types.

Further restricting the type of information needed in a requirements document is the principle that you need only include the very specific information needed by a well-defined software problem, not the potentially limitless information needed to choose the requirements themselves. When building an information system, the requirements reflect (but do not justify) your decision to build such a system, what queries to allow users to initiate, and so forth. You do not need to attempt to document such aspects of the outside world as the culture of the users, upon which you based your judgement that they would accept and make use of such a system.

3.6 Invention versus validation

Validation works one way only: you validate an interface design on the basis of requirements and problem-domain description, and you validate a program on the basis of the interface design. The process of *inventing* requirements and interfaces, however, follows no such simple pattern. Requirements stimulate ideas for interfaces, but designing an interface can also lead to new ideas for requirements. Similarly, even though a program is an implementation of an interface design, writing the program often leads to new ideas for the interface, and often, the act of designing an internal data structure can lead people to discover clearer ways of understanding the problem domain or omissions in the requirements.

A typical example is that you show some users a mockup of a screen to perform a type of query, and the users say, "You mean you can do that?" By the time you answer affirmatively, they've noticed what a small leap it would be to provide many more queries that would be even more useful to them. Any kind of designing, including requirements engineering, is a creative process, and creative processes seldom follow a predictable path. Every new idea leads people to notice new, previously unanticipated possibilities. A beneficial side effect of exploring and documenting requirements is that everyone on the project can contribute ideas for requirements and specifications—users, programmers, testers, and technical writers, too, not just the analysts and interface designers.

While we always evaluate interface designs for *correctness* according to whether they produce the requirements (and programs for correctness according to whether they produce the specified interface behavior), there is nothing wrong with *choosing* requirements on the basis of what we know about interface designs and programming. Indeed, this is the idea of basing the questions answered in a requirements document on known design patterns. There's nothing unseemly about changing requirements because of the difficulties with making an easy-to-use or elegant interface, or changing an interface design because it's difficult to program. We invent requirements and interface designs on the basis of what we believe we can feasibly implement. To put it another way, knowledge of programming guides our choice of requirements (similarly for interface designs) no less than knowledge of the open-ended problem that the software solves. In the same way, knowledge of building materials guides an architect's choice of how to shape a house, no less than knowledge of how people live and work.

So, while we try to make our techniques for documenting requirements such that there are existing programming techniques for implementing them, we should not think that writing requirements necessitates a rigid, clockwork progression of software development. While the art of project management is far beyond the scope of this book, a few words are in order.

It's virtually impossible to write excellent requirements at the very beginning of a complex project. Only when we see the interfaces and allow programming to start can we begin to truly refine our ideas for the requirements. This is a brute fact that a project manager must contend with, not a problem that can be solved by a "perfect" method of requirements design. To enable the requirements to profit from what we learn from interface design and programming, we can develop the software incrementally, improving the requirements at each stage.

There are two principal strategies for managing incremental improvement of design (remembering that requirements are designed, no less than interface designs and program designs). One is to start with sketchy requirements, adding detail at each stage, or to postpone rigorous requirements definition until the very end, at which time the requirements are somewhat superfluous. In this case, we do not start with a well-defined problem; we start by tentatively building solutions and hope that a well-defined problem eventually comes into focus.

The other strategy is to take a spiral approach: start with a modest, well-defined problem, solve it, and then expand the problem in the next phase, repeating the process as many times as necessary. With the spiral approach, you have rigor, not sketchiness, at each stage of development. Each stage produces a provably correct solution to a well-defined problem, resulting in software that runs and contains few, if any, holes. From each solution, we learn how to expand the problem—that is, improve the requirements—in the next stage.

Perhaps the most famous example of the strategy of rigorously solving a series of progressively more complex problems was the United States space program of the 1960s. The goal was to land a man on the Moon and return him safely to Earth, but that was far too ambitious to attempt all at once. Over a decade, NASA designed, built, and launched numerous complete spacecraft solely for the purpose of learning about each of the many problems involved in a Moon mission. Project Mercury solved problems of orbital dynamics and human life support in space; Project Gemini solved the problems of extravehicular activity and space docking, among many others; Project Apollo, in many stages, solved the final problems of actually landing on the Moon and returning. Each of the many spacecraft designs was driven rigorously by requirements, and each experience improved the requirements for the next design.

The advantage of the strategy of growing the solution in whichever direction it wants to grow is that it can solve problems we had never before thought to identify. When successful, it can generate spectacular results, such as new programming tools and entirely new kinds of software. Its danger, as in any exploratory engineering, is that it can stray considerably from what a customer wants, veering instead toward areas that the programmers find most interesting and within their area of expertise. This danger is especially clear in contract programming, in which a customer simply wants software to perform a specific task, for example, to control a certain piece of machinery or to keep track of accounts and inventory. With no well-defined problem against which to validate the interfaces and program, holes and problem misfits turn up well after the software has been installed, when they're most expensive to correct.

The spiral approach, with well-defined requirements supporting validation of each version of the interface design (and well-defined interfaces supporting validation of each version of the program), is much more conducive to rigor. Since you consciously design the desired effects of the software in the problem domain at each stage, you have more opportunity to catch mistakes early in the process—while they're still requirements on paper rather than thousands of lines of inappropriate code. Also, you have something well defined to test against at each stage. The disadvantage—a small price in most everyday software projects—is that the more clearly defined the goal, the less likely it is that you'll make totally unexpected kinds of innovations.

Rapid prototyping is a strategy for inventing requirements that blends the benefits of both approaches: free-form exploration of interfaces and program designs that do not fully solve a well-defined problem, as well as rigorous problem definition and solution. When you write the real software, you throw away the prototype—the sloppy part that you made only to stimulate ideas. Pencil-and-paper mockups of screens, sometimes called *paper prototypes,* are one example of this technique. They are very tentative user-interface designs that are inexpensive to produce and whose sole purpose is to stimulate ideas for both requirements and the final, detailed user-interface specification.

So, while writing requirements does not preclude a flexible, incremental style of development, neither must flexibility conflict with rigor. Modern project management techniques, such as the spiral method and rapid prototyping, enable programs to rigorously map to requirements even as we improve requirements by observing the software in action.

3.7 What software requirements are not

Terminology in the software industry is far from standardized, especially in regard to the term *requirements.* This book rigorously adheres to one definition, but many others are also in common use. The following serves both to distinguish this book's concept of requirements from some older ones, as well as to clarify it by describing other concepts with which it is easily confused. Section 12.5 briefly describes a few more.

3.7.1 Not top-down

Structured analysis is an approach to requirements based on the idea of extending certain techniques of program design outward to requirements. The program design techniques are:

- Form each subroutine by combining blocks of code without gotos, iterations of such blocks, and execution of one block or another based on a condition.

- Functional decomposition: when a given function is too complex to implement in a single subroutine, break it into smaller functions. When one function is decomposed into several, the functions exchange data with each other, as shown in a data-flow diagram like that of figure 1.2.

These are the principles of structured programming. In structured analysis, the idea is to bring the same hierarchical, structured method to requirements.

The analyst, then, describes a set of top-level functions, perhaps leveling (decomposing) them a few times to make functions small enough to begin implementing. The intent is that the programmers will translate each of these functions into a high-level subroutine in the program. The requirements document is, thus, a high-level description of the program structure, making software development flow smoothly from beginning to end.

A requirements document made according to the principles of structured analysis consists of a collection of functions to be performed by the software, together with the data input and output by these functions. Each function is described in terms of the rule relating each possible input to the corresponding desired output. Different functions can be allocated to different programmers, enabling them to work in parallel. Different functions can also be allocated to different testers.

We've already seen that programming does not consist of breaking down high-level functions hierarchically into low-level functions.* Structured analysis, however, has an additional flaw. It is concerned with the wrong subject matter—the program rather than the problem domain.

If software development starts by describing the top level of the program structure and working down to individual instructions, the only thing that ever gets described is the configuration of the machine—the program. Regardless of the fact that this kind of functional decomposition doesn't work, no logical connection from the problem domain to the program is ever established. In many projects that try to follow structured analysis and design, the important job of interface design (especially user-interface design) is neglected—perhaps sketched out by the analyst and later completed by a programmer, regarded as part of coding a subroutine rather than a separate task in its own right.

The rules for drawing the context diagram of structured analysis—the highest-level functional diagram, of which all the others are decompositions—expressly forbids showing any connections between domains outside the system.† The context diagram shows only the inputs and outputs that directly supply or receive data to or from the system.‡ Effects to be achieved indirectly by the software, as well as indirect sources of data, are

---

* There are many more practical difficulties with functional decomposition in software than this book covers, such as the difficulty of modifying the program to adapt to (very common) changes that cut across functions. The practical difficulty of modifying programs designed top-down is described further in [Jackson 1983], pp. 9–11, as well as in most texts on object-oriented design, such as [Jacobson 1992], pp. 73–76 and pp. 135–141. Further difficulties, discussed in [Jackson 1995] , pp. 196–199, are the fact that functional decomposition leads you to make the most momentous decisions when you understand the problem the least, and, perhaps most fundamentally, the real world does not have the kind of neat, hierarchical structure found in a hierarchy of functions, making it difficult to devise a simple, robust mapping between a real-world problem and the elements of a program designed top-down. See also [Jackson 1983], pp. 370–371.

† See [Yourdon 1989a] or nearly any other book on structured analysis.

explicitly excluded from the context diagram, and consequently excluded from consideration. We will see in chapter 4 that these indirect connections between the machine to be configured and the domain of interest are the source of much of the complexity in software problems. It's tempting enough to sweep them under the rug, without a method of writing requirements that explicitly demands it.

A better metaphor for the progression of the principal design stages in software development (or each trip around a spiral) than "top-down" is the "left-to-right" progression shown in figure 3.1. Each stage of design is concerned with a different *subject matter* than the previous stage. This is very different from starting with a description of high-level subroutines and fleshing them out with program code and low-level subroutines. Our concern is to relate the program to desired effects in the outside world, logically or causally. And indeed, in both requirements and specifications, we do not describe the program *at all*. Programming is the programmers' job.*

3.7.2 *Not sketches*

In practice, trying to approach software development top-down often leads people to view requirements as a *sketch* of the program. In this approach, the requirements phase of the project is the creation of an outline of the major features of the program, leaving the details for later, similar to the way an architect's first drawing of a house is a sketch that omits many details. The key distinction between requirements and later stages of design, following the sketch approach, is the level of abstraction. Requirements are supposed to abstract out details, allowing them to be filled in as development progresses. The requirements are high-level; the final design is low-level or detailed.

So, for example, development might start with a requirement like: "The program must enable paralegals to research statutes pertaining to workmen's compensation claims." Program design consists of progressively adding more detail to this fundamental idea: fleshing out data structures, algorithms, screen designs, and so forth.

How, though, can programmers make good decisions about these data structures without knowledge of small details of the problem domain, such as the formats of legal citations? To write the program well, someone needs to inform the programmers that one type of statutory law citation has the following format:

---

‡ In the terminology of chapter 5 of this book, structured analysis demands that all software problems be framed as transformation problems.

* However, don't get the idea that structured analysis is worthless. Its strength has been its techniques for describing data—actually, a borrowing from relational database theory. These techniques for describing models are so good that they can also be applied to describing the problem domain itself. This book freely draws upon them in chapter 9. Data-flow diagrams are good for describing things that are already well understood; we'll see them again in chapter 11. And our graphics for describing software problems, presented in chapter 4, are a variation on data-flow diagrams.

A.R.S. 23-613(A)(2)(a)   ⟶   Arizona Revised Statutes Annotated, Title 23, section 613, section A, subsection 2, sub-subsection a

while citations from case law have a different format:

San Francisco Arts & Athletics, Inc. v. U.S. Olympic Committee, 107 S.Ct. 2971, 483 U.S. 522, 97 L.Ed.2d 427 (1987)   ⟶   Case: San Francisco Arts & Athletics, Inc. v. U.S. Olympic Committee.

Published in: Supreme Court Reports, volume 107, page 2971.

Also published in: United States Reports, volume 483, page 522.

Also published in: Supreme Court Reports, Lawyers Edition, second series, volume 97, page 427.

Date of decision: 1987. Because the main citation implies the court of record, it is not indicated next to the date; otherwise, the last part would read: (U.S.; S.Ct. 1987).

The rules for legal citations are among the tiniest of details, yet the program must parse and print legal citations in a wide variety of formats or it won't be of much use in legal research. Unless the programmers just happen to have basic legal training, they would never guess these details correctly.

This, once again, illustrates that the difference between requirements and program design is not level of detail or level of abstraction, but subject matter. The formats of legal citations, whether described sketchily or down to the last detail, are facts from the problem domain, discovered by research and by talking with the customer. Facts about data structures are facts entirely within the machine domain, invented by the programmers to solve a problem expressed entirely in terms of the problem domain.

A further difficulty with writing a sketch of a single domain, rather than a detailed description of one domain and how it is to be affected by another, is that there is no well defined problem to solve—no baseline against which to test or evaluate the final design. If a tester finds that the program allows a citation to list only a single publication, should he mark this as a bug, or should he infer that this was one of the detailed decisions made by the programmers?

The principle of exhaustive detail is worth formulating explicitly:

> When a requirements document is done, the development staff should

need to undertake no further research of the problem domain in order to design the software.

In other words, a completed requirements document must contain every last relevant detail about the problem domain. A completed interface design contains every last detail about an interface. Programmers don't flesh out missing details; they create an entirely new domain, which indirectly brings about the indicated effects in the problem domain.

There is one main exception to the above principle. Much of the project-specific knowledge needed by a user-interface designer is an intuitive understanding of the users: what they understand, how they speak, what they like and don't like, and so forth. Since this kind of information cannot be written down precisely, no attempt should be made to do so.

Sometimes you simply can't get access to all of the necessary problem-domain information early in the project. As noted at the beginning of section 3.6, there is nothing wrong with revising the requirements and the description of the problem domain after having done some prototyping or building some interfaces. Like the other principles, the "no further research" principle describes the logical relation between the program and the requirements to be achieved by the time the software is completed and accepted by the customer, but getting to that acceptance is not necessarily a neat, clockwork sequence of development stages. The principle says that, at *some* point, all the domain information must be available to the programmers and interface designers, even if it isn't all available on day one of the project.* To put it another way, people can begin tentative interface design and program design even if the requirements document is not completely finished.

Furthermore, by no means does the above discussion mean that rough sketches have no role to play in orderly software development. On the contrary, they play an indispensible role in nearly every project. In the early stages of designing the requirements, you will likely create a sketch of the requirements in order to help you refine your ideas and to help you communicate them with others on the project. You might throw out all, some, or none of the ideas in this sketch when you write the completed requirements document. Similarly, you might sketch out a specification before writing the detailed version, and similarly again for the program.

The two important things to understand are that a sketch of the requirements is not sufficient to make a detailed interface design or program, and that a sketch of requirements is not an outline of a program. Also, because a sketch is made without full

---

* [Parnas 1986] discusses many aspects of bringing together all the parts of software documentation logically even when the process cannot occur in the ideal chronological sequence.

knowledge of details, you cannot bank on a smooth flow from high-level to detailed description. If you had enough information to guarantee that, you wouldn't need to write a sketch; you would be ready to write the final, detailed document. A sketch is an exploration of ideas, an essay into the unknown. When you explore, you do not know in advance what you will find.

3.7.3 Not what versus how

Requirements are sometimes defined as "what" software must do, while design is "how" the software does it. These definitions are far too vague to be of use in a real project, as a simple example will demonstrate. Suppose that you're creating a program to map data between certain relational databases and object-oriented databases. You plan to run this program to enable some new insurance software to work with existing databases in the insurance industry, permitting incremental change instead of large, instantaneous change. You've decided that to effect the mapping, you'll have a human being manually create a map file for every pair of databases that need to exchange data. The software will then translate data according to the mappings in the map file specified when the software starts up.

Now, which is "what the software does" and which is "how it does it"? Should the requirements describe the insurance business? What the software does there is reduce costs and increase profits. The requirements would be, "The mapping software shall reduce total operating costs by at least 0.8%." Or does the software map data between databases? If so, should we exclude discussion of the map file from the requirements, as part of "how" the software performs the mapping? Or does the software read the map file and map data between databases in accordance with a set of map-file interpretation rules?

In fact, everything in engineering is what and everything is how. Everything that a piece of software does is what it does, and everything that a piece of software does is how it does something.* This is true equally of databases, user interfaces, subroutine calls, local variables, and arithmetic instructions.

The program is a design for performing mappings according to the map-file interpretation rules. The map file is also designed by software engineers to serve the purpose of mapping. The map file overlaps between the world of users and databases and the world of the program, so it's part of the specification, as are the user interfaces for any programs for editing map files, along with the procedures for operating those programs. The problem domain is the database files. The requirements of the program are to perform the mappings. The requirements are *also* how. They are a set of conditions to be

---

* See also [Davis 1993], p. 17, for an amusing refutation of the what/how distinction.

achieved in the problem domain, which people carefully designed in order to bring about still other effects: helping shepherd the insurance industry toward acceptance of new standards, and reducing operating costs.

3.8 Summary

Figure 3.3 summarizes all the fundamental components of software problems and their solutions.

A software problem

Configure machine *M* to bring about effects *R* in domain *D*.

The *machine domain* is the computer, including its input/output devices.

We solve a software problem by designing behavior of the machine's input/output devices that causes the effects *R*, and by programming the machine to behave as specified. The specification is correct if the behavior produces the desired effects in the problem domain. The program is correct if it produces the specified behavior.

machine *M*

Database schemas

Subroutines

```
haul_charge = 0.0;
box_count = 0;
for (pitem = items; pitem; pitem->next); {
    haul_charge += price(pitem->code, pitem->qty);
    box_count += pitem->qty;
```

Linked lists

Interfaces

A *program* is a configuration of a machine, which determines the machine's behavior.

A software *specification* is a design for how the machine's input/output devices are to behave: an interface design.

A specification states rules relating desired behavior of the output devices to all possible behavior of the input devices, as well as any rules that other parts of the problem domain must obey, such as operating procedures for users to carry out. To help state those rules, a specification can also postulate machine states, such as data stored in the computer, that relate past input events to future output events.

Pick up cargoes

Haul cargoes to destinations

Print reports

domain *D*

effects *R*

The *problem domain* is the part of the world where the computer is to produce effects, together with the means available to produce them, directly or indirectly.

Indirect means include users whom the machine can ask to perform tasks, motors that the machine can turn on and off, people or other machines that can supply information—anything that is not part of the machine. Direct means are the machine's input/output devices: keyboards, serial connections, screens, and so forth.

Software *requirements* are the effects that the machine is to exert in the problem domain by virtue of its programming.

R A software requirements document includes both a list of requirements and a description of the problem domain. The exact problem-domain information needed in a requirements document is determined by the type of software problem (details in chapters 4 through 6).

Figure 3.3 Software problems and their solutions

C H A P T E R   4

Problem framing

4.1 The knight's tour

Consider the following problem, known as the *knight's tour*. The knight starts at the center of the board, as shown in figure 4.1. The problem is to find a sequence of moves that lands the knight on every square, without landing on any square more than once.*

Even on the miniature chessboard, this is a difficult problem. You try out a sequence of moves and soon can't remember which squares you've already covered. Lacking a systematic approach, you resort to trial and error, never able to know if you've painted yourself into a corner until it's too late. Should you try to cover the quadrants of the board one at a time? Or spiral outward from the middle? The difficulty of the task and lack of a systematic approach remind one a little of solving a

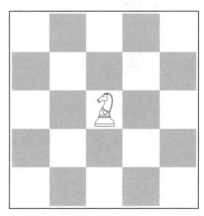

Figure 4.1 The knight's tour

Rubik's cube, as in section 1.3.

Now, in figure 4.2, look at a new version of the same problem.

In the new diagram, the squares of the chessboard have been moved. Each square is connected by a line to all the squares that are a single knight's move away. Miraculously, the "difficult problem" is now trivial. You can find a path that touches each square only once in only a second or two. Just start on square 13 and follow the lines.

What makes the second version of the knight's tour so much easier is that the problem has been *reframed* to expose its essentials. The real problem is to find a chain of squares such that a knight can jump, in a single move, between the two squares connected by any one link of the chain. The arrangement of the squares on the chessboard is of secondary importance, so we can freely modify it in order to make the "chain" aspect of the problem more conspicuous.*

The first and perhaps most important step in documenting software requirements is to *frame* the problem—to put it into a definite form, with definite parts, and definite relations between the parts.† The way the problem is framed should make the details of the problem, no matter how complex, fit into a simple, coherent framework so that a person can systematically analyze them without becoming overwhelmed. In the knight's tour, the numbers on the squares—that is, the locations of the squares on the original board—are the potentially overwhelming details. The chain diagram still includes all the details, but puts them into a framework that allows you to see each in proper relation to the others, referring to the numbers only as necessary.

4.2 Domains

Software problems seldom fit into frames like the knight's tour, of course. How, then, do you frame a software problem? You've already seen the most fundamental technique, *separation into domains,* in the general diagram of a software problem from chapter 3, reproduced here in figure 4.3.

---

* For non-chessplayers, a knight's move goes either two squares vertically and one square horizontally, or two squares horizontally and one square vertically.

* Figure 4.2 is adapted from [Sawyer 1955], a book overflowing with similar examples and insights from all throughout mathematics.

† Framing the problem is also one of the most important steps in researching it, as there's no way to do systematic research without specific questions to ask.

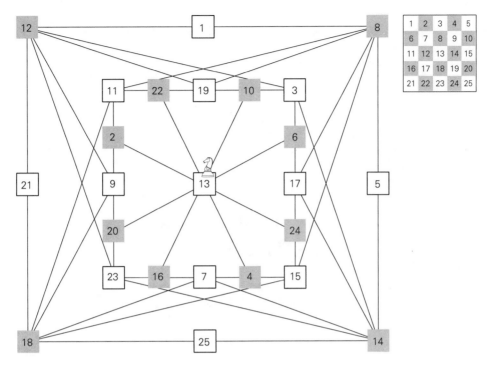

Figure 4.2 The knight's tour, reframed

What, exactly, is the difference between the two domains indicated by the ovals? Each domain contains a set of *individuals*—that is, distinguishable things about which we want to make statements. The individuals in the problem domain are the trucks, cities, cargoes, drivers, customers, users, and so forth—the physical part of the world in terms of which the requirements are defined. The individuals in the machine domain are all the subroutines and data structures that make up the machine's programming, as well as the input/output devices of the machine. The only rule about individuals is that you can always distinguish one individual from another—no individual is also another individual.

Also included in each domain is everything that we want to say *about* those individuals. So, for example, we can say about a certain truck and a certain cargo that the former *is now carrying* the latter, or that a certain driver *drove* a certain truck at a certain time, that a certain customer *owns* a certain cargo, and so forth. Everything that we want to be able to assert or deny of one or more individuals, we will call a *predicate*. The machine domain contains a different set of predicates: a subroutine *occupies* a certain range of memory locations, one subroutine *calls* another, and so forth.

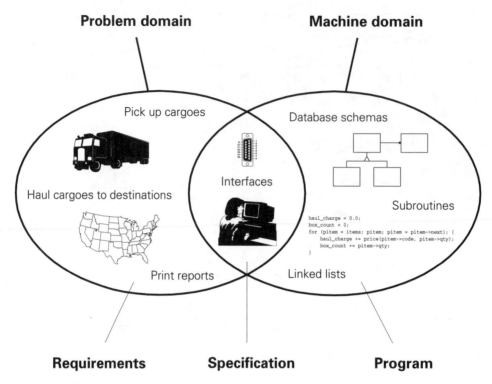

Problem domain

Machine domain

Pick up cargoes

Database schemas

Interfaces

Haul cargoes to destinations

Subroutines

```
haul_charge = 0.0;
box_count = 0;
for (pitem = items; pitem; pitem = pitem->next) {
    haul_charge += price(pitem->code, pitem->qty);
    box_count += pitem->qty;
}
```

Print reports

Linked lists

Requirements

Specification

Program

Figure 4.3 Separation into domains

A *domain,* then, is a set of individuals with accompanying predicates. The individuals need not be individuals that exist now or ever; they can be merely potential individuals that the software must be capable of dealing with. So, for example, all potential customers are part of the problem domain in the trucking example. When defining a domain, we do not necessarily know all of the actual individuals that it now contains or will contain; however, we do specify all the predicates that we intend to apply to them.

When we make statements within the problem domain, the individuals and predicates that exist only in the machine domain are not available to talk about. Occupying a certain range of memory is not the kind of predicate that one asserts of a truck driver. Since requirements are expressed in terms of the problem domain, they can only refer to individuals in the problem domain, and all they can assert about those individuals is predicates from the problem domain. So the requirements document says nothing about linked lists and subroutines.

Domain description generally occupies the majority of a requirements document—even more than the list of requirements. For readers to understand a domain well enough to design software to function with it, you must provide one or more of the following types of information, depending on the type of problem:

Table 4.1 Domain information

Type of information	Details in
What kinds of entities are or can be in the domain—for example, people, cars, musical compositions, fuel injectors, road names.	Chapter 9
What kinds of attributes those entities can possess—for example, color, completion status, due date, how much money is in an account.	Chapter 9
Relationships that can exist between the entities—for example, a driver *owns* a vehicle, two parties are *plaintiff* and *defendant* in a court case.	Chapter 9
The types of events that can occur within the domain—for example, that cars can be sold, that rollers can turn, that the Supreme Court can decide to hear a case or throw it out.	Chapter 10
The causal laws according to which the entities behave—for example, that servomotor A is on if and only if bit 7 of I/O port 0xF00 is high, and when servomotor A is on, roller R1 rotates clockwise.	Chapter 11

Events are often best treated as individuals, just like entities. When you frame the problem, you don't necessarily know which events will happen, but you know all of the possible attributes they can possess and all of the relations of interest between them. The attributes of an event are the entities that participated in the event, and possibly the time and duration of the event; relations between events are such things as *before* and *after*.

Understanding the information described in table 4.1, you can incorporate it into *propositions:* assertions or denials that certain individuals possess certain attributes or bear certain relations to each other. Attributes and relations can either identify an individual for the purpose of making a proposition about it, or they can server as the predicate asserted about the individual. A question, such as a query that a user asks of a piece of software, is also a proposition—a proposition whose truth or falsity is unknown, or a proposition with the type of predicate stated but the specific predicate missing. (For example, you know that a quantity of tires was sold, but not exactly how many.) A user runs a query to find out whether the proposition is true or to find out the missing predicate.

Everything that you can say with individuals and predicates, along with various types of relations between propositions, is the subject of two branches of mathematics known as the *predicate calculus* and the *propositional calculus*. In this book, we'll limit ourselves to the relatively simple types of propositions that you can express in natural languages. The predicate and propositional calculi play a more explicit role in formal methods.

For purposes of most everyday software projects, all you need to know is that in describing each domain, you must explain the entire vocabulary in terms of which you describe it—all the types of individuals that you want to talk about and all the predicates that you want to use to describe them—and frame all of your descriptions in terms of that vocabulary. Usually, this means providing each of the five types of information listed in table 4.1.

The choice of what to call an individual and what to call a predicate depends only on what propositions you are interested in asserting or asking. It is not a rule that physical objects have to be individuals, nor is it a rule that intangible things, like names and numbers, have to be predicates. If you make an assertion about a name or a number, then you are treating that name or number as an individual. The only rules are that no part of the domain can be two individuals at once, and you must know in advance all of the predicates that you want to assert of the individuals. Sometimes, the choice of how to go about describing a domain—what individuals to talk about what what predicates to use in describing them—is one of the trickiest and most critical parts of framing the problem, as the following simple example demonstrates.

Suppose that you are writing the requirements for software to figure out routes for bus riders to take to get from one place to another. Many of the propositions of interest to you will involve roads, such as: "Route 102 stops at the northwest corner of 28th street and Pearl street." It might be very tempting to make roads your individuals, and road names your predicates. But there is a problem with this scheme. Roads sometimes overlap. For example, 28th Street might also be Highway 36 for a stretch of a few miles and then the two roads go their separate ways. Are they one individual or two? The solution is to define two kinds of individuals: road segments and road names. Highway 36 then becomes a collection of individuals: all road segments with name *Highway 36*. Some of these segments also have the name *28th Street.** A single road segment can have more than one road name. Your main predicate is now: has such-and-such name.

---

* Adapted from [Jackson 1995], pp. 100–103.

4.3 Shared phenomena

Separation into domains is the most fundamental technique of framing software problems. We separate domains for two main reasons.

First, if we choose our individuals and predicates wisely, we can limit the scope of our concerns. We can talk about one set of phenomena without having to include another. It's hard enough to describe the problem domain for the trucking software without having to describe the program at the same time.

Second, we can talk about causation across domains, or other relations between domains, such as representation, in a carefully delimited and disciplined way. In order for one domain to exert effects in or communicate information to another, it must partially overlap with that other domain. In the case of figure 4.3, this overlap is the input/output devices of the computer. There are actions, such as the user typing in data about a new driver, that are simultaneously acts in the problem domain and in the machine domain. Following Jackson, we will call these overlaps between domains *shared phenomena.**

Shared phenomena are all states, events, and objects that are shared between two domains. The input/output devices whose behavior is described in a software specification are only one type of shared phenomena. They can occur between any two domains. If you choose to treat the trucks as one domain and the drivers as another, then there are truck driving events that occur in both domains—that is, events in which a driver drives a truck, causing them both to move from one location to another—as well as events that occur in only one domain, such as engine maintenance and hiring.

Here are some typical examples of shared phenomena:

- Keystrokes typed by a user are keystrokes received by software.
- Every pixel displayed on a monitor by software is also a pixel seen by the user.
- A block of memory shared by two running processes in a computer, holding semaphores by which one process tells the other whether or not it's safe to perform a certain operation. Record-locking is a typical example of this.
- The signals sent by an oxygen sensor to a microprocessor inside a car
- The signals sent by the same microprocessor to the car's fuel injectors
- A directory in which one program places files for later retrieval by another program, or a mail folder in which a mail receiver places new mail for later retrieval by a mail reader

---

* [Jackson 1995], pp. 178–181.

- All of the data sent over coaxial cables in a local area network is shared by the network software running on all the computers connected to the network.

- Ink being sprayed onto paper by an inkjet printer is also the paper receiving ink at the location where the ink lands.

- An employee punching a time clock is the time clock recording the event.

In this book, our main interest in shared phenomena is to identify which individuals in one domain can directly affect or be affected by individuals in another, and in precisely what ways. There are, however, more advanced uses of the concept of shared phenomena, for example, the types of overlap studied in process algebras, such as that described in [Hoare 1985].

Sometimes, for purposes of requirements, we treat slightly disconnected phenomena as if they were truly shared. For example, you would treat 'motion of subject in front of video camera' as shared with 'change of state of image on camera' even though these two events are mediated by light traveling from the subject to the camera. This is no serious distortion of reality, because all that matters from the standpoint of shared phenomena is that the same event can occur within and be described in terms of two (or more) domains. If, however, the in-between domain can introduce serious distortion or delay—such as the data-entry staff who type information into the computer—then you cannot ignore it. It is a *connection domain,* described in the next section.

4.4 Connection domains

Consider an information system to report on current temperatures all over the world. The computer sits in a room at a meteorological research center and, consequently, has no direct access to these temperatures. Instead, there are weather stations placed all over the world, containing both temperature sensors and communication equipment. The computer must communicate with the weather stations to learn the temperatures and report these temperatures to researchers on demand. We thus have four domains, as shown in figure 4.4. The problem domain as a whole consists of three of them: the temperatures, weather stations, and researchers.

The weather stations share phenomena with the actual temperatures that the computer is supposed to report on because events that affect temperature also affect the temperature sensors on the weather stations. Inside the weather stations there is equipment to convert the analog readings at the temperature sensors into digital signals suitable for sending to the computer. The computer shares phenomena with the weather stations because data sent or received by a weather station is data received or sent by

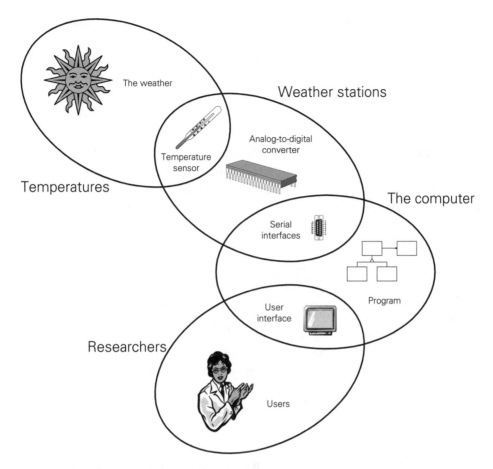

Figure 4.4 A software problem with four domains

the computer. Finally, the computer shares phenomena with the researchers so it can communicate directly with them via the screens and keyboard.

The requirement of the software is to create a relation between the researchers and the temperatures all over the world: the researchers must be able to query the temperatures on demand. The weather stations thus form a special type of domain: a *connection domain,* that is, a domain that shares phenomena with two domains that we wish had a direct connection, but don't—in this case, the computer and the temperatures.

Connection domains play an important role in most real-life software problems because they put upper limits on how well you can fulfill requirements. A connection domain nearly always introduces some form of distortion and delay which may impact the users of the software. The weather stations do not always function properly. Sometimes their power goes out, sometimes their serial connection to the computer is broken, and sometimes their temperature sensors go out of calibration. During these times, the software is unable to fulfill its requirement of delivering current, accurate information about the temperatures in each location where a weather station is placed. You'll need to inform the customer, while still discussing the requirements, about these limitations that are imposed by the connection domain.

You will also need to invent desired results when any of these conditions holds, and you'll need to learn enough about the temperature and weather-station domains to enable the software to detect those conditions. If you know that air temperature never changes by more than ten degrees in one second, and a weather station reports just that, you can exploit this knowledge in the design of the software. The software can reject the weather station's report and output "unknown" in queries about the temperature at that station's location.

4.5 Realized domains

A pharmacy and a health insurance company have computers that talk to each other. When a patient fills a prescription at the pharmacy, the pharmacy's computer asks for approval from the insurance company's computer. If the transaction meets the insurance company's approval rules, the insurance company's computer sends back the amount of the co-payment to be paid by the patient. The pharmacist then collects the co-payment, and the insurance company owes the pharmacy the price of the drug minus the co-payment.

Where is the domain that contains the amount owed by the insurance company? It's not part of the insurance company's approval rules. It's not part of the pharmacy's drugs or prices. Is it shared phenomena connecting the two? Of course not. If it's neither in one nor the other, it can't be common to both. But we have to know where the debts are in order to design the system containing both computers because we have to know how the system can get access to them in order to control them or report on them.

The answer is that the debts have no tangible existence outside the system. Therefore, the system can enact no cause to control them, and no activity in the debts domain can ever exert an effect detectable by the system. Debts exist only within the conceptual world of human agreement.

What the system can do, however, is create a proxy for the debts inside itself. The pharmacy and the insurance company agree that when certain bit patterns exist within the computer, the insurance company will owe a corresponding amount of money to the pharmacy, as long as these bit patterns were created in accordance with various rules, such as, "Only an authorized employee can create a debt." We will say, then, that the system *realizes* the debts within itself; the debts are a *realized domain*.

By creating a realized domain as a proxy for the real debts, the system is able to control the debts. Without the agreement between the insurance company and the pharmacy, there would be no point in fiddling with the bits in the computer. Neither party would really owe anything to the other.

Another computer system, perhaps run by the government, that reports on the amount spent on prescriptions all throughout the country also needs to access the debts, but its job is not to realize the debts within itself. No one is bound by the debt records stored in the government computer. The debts exist entirely outside the government computer. It accesses debts only for information-gathering purposes, perhaps by communicating with the insurance company's computer.

This distinction between a realized domain and a real domain is both simple and subtle. It is something people rarely need to articulate, but it is critically important. Nearly any type of commitment between people, if a computer is to manage it, must appear as a realized domain in a requirements document. This includes most debts, accounts, responsibilities to perform tasks, scheduled times at which to meet, the right to use a conference room at a certain time, and so on. If the debts, accounts, and so on are not to be realized, but merely reported on, then the requirements document must treat them very differently. The document must indicate how the computer can access them (perhaps through a connection domain—a realized domain in another computer).

A much more familiar type of realized domain are documents created in a word processor or graphics in a graphics editor. Here, too, the domains do not exist prior to the operation of the software. A word processor doesn't access a document by interacting with something in the outside world either directly or through a connection domain. The word processor's job—one of its requirements—is to realize documents within itself in response to user commands, just as the insurance company's computer realizes debts within itself in response to commands initiated by a pharmacist.

4.6 Frame diagrams

The notation of overlapping ovals, as in figure 4.4, does a nice job of illustrating domains, shared phenomena, and direct versus indirect connections, but it's somewhat unwieldy. In this section, we introduce a simple graphical notation for depicting all the principal parts of a software problem. We'll call a diagram made in this notation a *frame diagram.**

In a frame diagram, each domain is represented by a rectangle, and shared phenomena between two domains are represented by a line connecting two rectangles. The

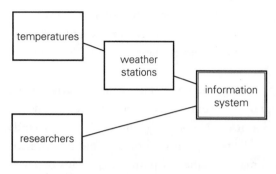

Figure 4.5 Part of the frame diagram for the temperature information system: domains only

machine to be programmed is indicated by a rectangle with a double border. The words written inside the double border are the type of machine that the computer becomes as a result of programming, for example, the name of the software, or (in generic examples as in this book) a phrase like "information system" or "controller." The domains in the temperature information system are drawn in this notation in figure 4.5.

If one domain is contained entirely within another, such as the set of documents that is contained entirely within a computer, a frame diagram represents this with a big dot, as in figure 4.6. The big dot also provides a way to draw the rare case of shared phenomena between three or more domains, as would occur if you chose to distinguish trucks, drivers, locations, and cargoes as distinct domains. Shared phenomena are, by definition, wholly contained in two or more domains at once.

We now have symbols for two of the principal parts of a software problem: the machine M and the domain D.* All that's left is the effects R that the machine is to bring about by virtue of its programming—the requirements. We symbolize the requirements by an oval, with one or more lines connecting it to the domains that the requirements pertain to. Requirements always assert either relations within a domain or between domains. Inside the oval, we write either a short assertion summarizing the requirements, or a noun indicating a type of thing to be provided by the software, such as queries about a domain or a mapping between domains. The complete frame diagram for the weather information system is shown in figure 4.7.

The frame diagram for a program, or part of a program, that manipulates digital images of photographs is shown in figure 4.8. The problem domain consists of two

---

* Frame diagrams are from [Jackson 1995], pp. 158–162 and 84–87; the underlying concepts are presented in the same book. The sample problem frames described in the following chapters are derived from, but are not identical to, the problem frames also described in that book.

* See section 2.2.

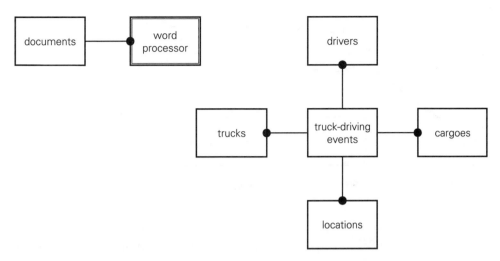

Figure 4.6 The big dot indicates that one domain is wholly contained in another

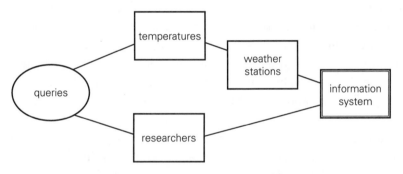

Figure 4.7 Complete frame diagram for temperature information system

collections of data: input images and corresponding output images. The requirement is to produce an output image from an input image according to a specified image-processing algorithm. We'll see many more frame diagrams in chapters 5 and 6.

The way to read a frame diagram is to follow two steps. First, read the oval and notice which domains it relates. These are the primary domains of interest. The problem, in its most fundamental form, is to create this relation between these domains in order to enable users to make queries about temperatures (as in figure 4.7) or to create output images with a certain correspondence to input images (as in figure 4.8).

The second step is to find the machine domain and see how it directly or indirectly connects to the domains of interest. That is, you trace a path from the machine to the primary domains of interest. In figure 4.7, the machine does not have direct access to the temperatures. It can communicate with them only indirectly through the weather

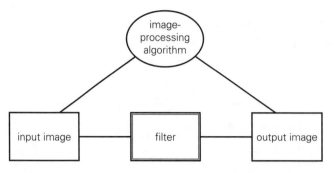

Figure 4.8 Frame diagram for image-processing software

stations. The weather stations, thus, add an important element of complexity to the problem. In figure 4.8, however, both primary domains of interest connect directly to the machine because the machine can read and write image files directly. Therefore, no connection domains complicate this problem.

Notice that a frame diagram does not attempt to depict all aspects of a problem. Users initiate queries, and the queries are about temperatures; temperatures do not initiate queries about users. This asymmetry is not shown in figure 4.7. The diagram provides you with a quick way to sketch out all of the major elements of the problem in order to help you plan out a systematic way to document them. The detailed, rigorous description is what you'll create when you write the document. No simple diagram can do all that.

Therefore, you can only understand a frame diagram with some accompanying commentary. The requirement is not simply queries, as shown in the oval in figure 4.7, but to answer queries on demand. Frame diagrams are perhaps best understood as napkin art—not necessarily something to include in a requirements document, but an aid for sketching out a software problem as a first step toward writing a requirements document.

Of course, you might want to include a frame diagram in the overview section of a requirements document. It does indicate all the principal elements of most software problems, but most people are not familiar with the notation. Or you might add arrows to it to indicate one-way flows of information, thus converting it into a sort of data-flow diagram, or add notational devices that are specific to the one problem you're trying to describe. The examples in the following chapters will add a few nuances as the need arises.

4.7 From diagram to documentation

Having framed the problem to be solved by the temperature information system (see figure 4.7), you can now document it systematically by writing the details corresponding to each element of the frame diagram. Include all of the following information, and your requirements document will contain enough information to enable the rest of the development staff to devise and implement a solution:

- A list of all the queries that users can initiate, that is, all the questions that they can ask about temperatures and that we want the system to be able to answer. If the customer desires, the format of these queries—both format of the input and the format of the results—can be included in the problem.

- A description of temperatures (very easy)

- A description of how the weather stations interact with temperature. Usually, the instruments at the weather station accurately record the temperature, but not always, such as during malfunctions, power outages, and instruments falling out of calibration. The requirements document needs to cover everything that can go wrong in the connection between the computer and the temperatures.

- A description of how the weather stations interact with the computer, that is, the communication protocols that the system will need to adhere to in order to extract information about temperature from the weather stations.

- A description of the connection between the researchers and the computers, that is, the input/output devices available to the user-interface designer. If the software is to run on a standard type of machine and operating system, such as a Windows machine or Macintosh, then you need say only that, along with any more specific information, such as the lowest screen resolution that the user interface must support.

- Possibly, a description of the researchers, if there's anything unusual about them that would affect the design of the user interface

Notice that frame diagrams depict only the information to include in a requirements document. The diagram breaks the problem domain into its principal elements, and shows how the machine to be programmed connects with them. A frame diagram is not an outline of program structure, nor is it a description of the behavior rules that make up the specification. It's strictly a graphical overview of a software problem, not its solution.

Once the problem is framed, people can approach documenting and solving it systematically, but there is no systematic way to frame a problem. There is no rigorous method for finding a rigorous method. There are, however, common patterns to recognize and draw upon when framing new problems. Presenting these patterns is the purpose of chapters 5 and 6.

When you frame a problem well, you are readying it for the development staff to apply the design patterns that they know. Ideally, when you write up the descriptions of the queries, a programmer is able to think, "Ah, I know just the search algorithm for this—Algorithm T from [Knuth 1973], p. 481." The problem description doesn't describe the algorithm, of course; it describes the problem solved by the algorithm in such a way that it's easy to recognize.

4.8 Notation summary

For reference, the meaning of each symbol in a frame diagram is summarized in figure 4.9.

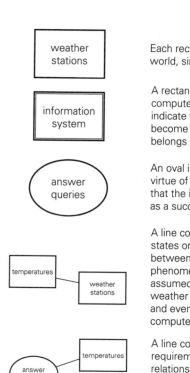

Each rectangle is a *domain:* a collection of objects or portion of the world, singled out for the purpose of making statements about it.

A rectangle with a double border is the *machine domain:* the computer to be programmed. The words inside the rectangle indicate what kind of special-purpose machine the computer will become when it runs the program; usually the name of the program belongs here.

An oval is a set of *requirements:* propositions to be made true by virtue of the computer's programming. Ovals collect together criteria that the interface designs and program must meet in order to count as a success. In this case, the system's job is to answer queries.

A line connecting two domains represents *shared phenomena:* states or events that overlap between two domains. Causation between domains and flow of data always involve shared phenomena. In this case, the state of the outdoor temperature is assumed to overlap with the state of measuring instruments on the weather stations—they reach the same temperature. The states and events by which the weather stations communicate with the computer are different, of course.

A line connecting an oval to one or more domains indicates that the requirements apply to those domains. Requirements always specify relationships to be realized within or between domains. In this case, the job of the system is to maintain a relationship between the users and the temperatures: the users are able to get information about temperatures by making queries.

A big dot indicates that one domain is completely contained in another: the entire domain is phenomena shared with the domain marked by the dot. The dot is needed to describe any problem where part of the software's job is to create or embody a domain within the machine. A domain created by the software is called a realized domain.

Figure 4.9 Symbols used in frame diagrams

C H A P T E R 5

Five problem frames

5.1 Overview

This chapter presents five different problem frames, corresponding to the five types of requirements shown in table 5.1:

Table 5.1 Five different problem frames

Requirement type	Description	Problem frame
Queries	Requests for information about some part of the problem domain	Information
Behavioral rules	Rules according to which the problem domain is to behave	Control
Mappings	Mappings between data input to and output by the software	Transformation
Operations on realized domains	Operations that users can perform on objects that exist only inside the software	Workpiece
Correspondences between domains	Keeping domains that have no shared phenomena in corresponding states	Connection

For each type of requirement, there is a corresponding set of problem-domain information needed to devise a specification that implements the requirement. Queries, for example, need a description of the part of the world that the queries are about. The five problem frames of this chapter include both the requirements and associated problem-domain information.

These five problem frames are not an exhaustive list. They describe very common large scale software patterns. Like any pattern, each describes a specific kind of problem, never claiming to be a general method of describing all problems solvable by software. They help you in the same way that knowledge of hashing techniques helps a programmer. When a programmer sees a situation where a hashing algorithm is appropriate, he applies hashing, perhaps varying the implementation slightly if the problem is a little different from what the books describe. No one claims that a programmer should try to solve all programming problems only with hashing algorithms.

When you see a problem to document that fits one of these problem frames, you'll know how to systematically document the problem in a manner useful to programmers, though perhaps varying the frame slightly if the problem is a little different. If none of the problem frames fit, then you'll have to invent a new one, but hopefully they'll still help you by providing successful models to start from.

Furthermore, most software problems involve several of the above types of requirements at the same time. In this case, you have a *multi-frame problem.** Chapter 6 provides some guidelines for combining problem frames.

To summarize, then:

> The purpose of framing problems is not to force-fit them into existing categories; rather, it is to recognize familiar problems when you see them and gain a head start on unfamiliar problems by varying the familiar.

The following is a brief introduction to each of the problem frames discussed in the rest of this chapter.

Software that solves an *information problem* answers queries about a certain part of the real world. Documenting an information problem involves describing the types of information requests to be satisfied, the part of the real world to which the requests apply, and how the software can get access to that part of the real world. See section 5.2.

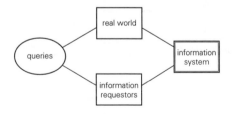

Information problem

---

* [Jackson 1995], pp. 128–134.

In a *control problem*, the software is responsible for ensuring that some part of the world behaves in accordance with specified rules. Documenting a control problem involves describing the objects that inhabit that part of the world and the causal rules they obey,

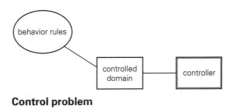

Control problem

the rules according to which they are supposed to behave, and the phenomena shared with the software through which the software can monitor the state of the world and initiate causal chains that result in the rules being followed. See section 5.3.

To solve a *transformation problem*, the software generates output data that maps to input data in accordance with specified rules. Documenting a transformation problem involves describing the entire set of all possible inputs and the mapping rules that indicate, for each possible input, the correct output. See section 5.4.

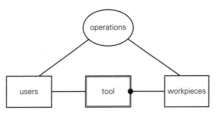

Transformation problem

In a *workpiece problem*, the software serves as a tool for creating objects that exist only within the software, the same way a lathe is a tool for creating wooden workpieces. Documenting a workpiece problem consists of describing the objects to exist within the computer and the operations that users can perform on them. See section 5.5.

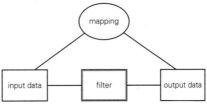

Workpiece problem

Finally, in a *connection problem* the software must simulate or make do with a connection between domains that do not really share phenomena. This diagram shows one form of connection problem in which the principal information to document is the delay and distortion characteristics of the connection domain, and the behavioral

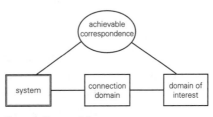

Connection problem

characteristics of the domain of interest, so that the system can detect invalid data received from the connection domain. See section 5.6.

5.2 Information problems

In an information problem, you are charged with building software that satisfies queries for information about some part of the world, usually outside the software. Hence, to document the requirements for an information problem, you must describe the relevant part of the world, the queries, and the people or things that initiate the queries.

All of this is shown in the information problem's frame diagram in figure 5.1:

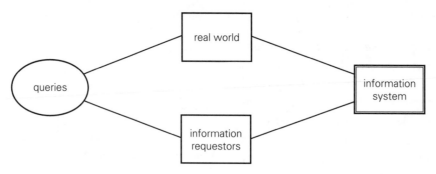

Figure 5.1 Information problem

The requirement is to satisfy queries initiated by the information requestors—users, hardware, or software that needs information. The query oval is connected to the real world and the information requestors to indicate that the job of the system is to maintain a relationship between the two in order to enable the information requestors to get information about the real world on demand.

Queries are always defined in terms of content—a question about the real world that the system is required to answer. Sometimes, but not always, customers have particular ideas about the form in which they want to ask the questions or the form in which they want the answers to be presented. An example of the latter is a preprinted form, such as bills that contain the company logo along with spaces to fill in customer name, address, amount, and so on. In this case, describing the format of the bills—that is, the output of the queries—is also part of defining the problem.

In most information problems, describing the queries is fairly easy. You simply write, "User can receive a list of all purchases made by any specified customer," and so on for each type of question that you want to make the computer answer, perhaps including the output format if the customer specified one. The larger job is describing the real world—that is, the part of the world, usually outside the software, that the queries pertain to. You must describe all of the types of objects that the queries can ask about, as well as all the events that happen to them that affect the results of the queries.

Often the information requestors require little or no description. They may be end users, or perhaps any line of code that calls a function that returns information. If, however, the information requestors are special hardware, such as electronic devices that change voltages on wires connected to the computer on which the software is to run, the hardware needs to be described, or at least what the changing voltages on each wire mean.

Notice that since the only requirement is to satisfy queries, causation is no part of an information problem. The system reports on the state of the world, but it is not responsible for affecting the state of the world. Affecting the world is a different kind of requirement, described in section 5.3. Both types of requirements can be different parts of a single, complex problem, of course.

Example software that solves information problems:

- Part of an inventory control system: displays amount in stock of any item, prints reports of items low on stock, prints reports of sales at end of each day, week, month, and year

- A program to search texts of Cretan Linear A documents for user-specified sequences of characters

- A web search engine: finds pages on the world-wide web relevant to user-specified topics

- A subroutine or operating-system function that returns information about the graphics adapter attached to the computer: current resolution, current color palette, amount of video RAM, list of supported graphics modes

- An electronic thesaurus

- A library catalog system: informs users of what books are in the library, their call letters and other attributes, and whether or not the books have been checked out

- A small part of a library catalog system: logs library searches by content, which terminal the search was initiated from, and number of matches, to help people look for ways to improve the searching system described just above. In this case, the real world component of the problem is another part of the software—a part that solves a different information problem.

5.2.1 Connection domains

Because computers are not psychic, nearly all information problems include a connection domain—something that relays information from the real world to the software to be built. Typically, this connection domain is people performing manual data entry.

Thus, many real life information problems have frame diagrams that look like figure 5.2.

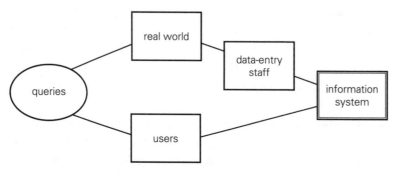

Figure 5.2 Information problem including a typical connection domain

Data gathering equipment is another likely connection domain, as illustrated by the weather stations in figure 4.7.

An example of an information system with no connection domain is a program that lists the files contained in a directory on the same computer that the program runs on. Such information systems are definitely the exception rather than the rule.

5.2.2 Static and dynamic

Most information systems report on the state or history of a real world that is constantly changing—changes to account balances, current stock prices, current contents of a warehouse. These we can call *dynamic information systems.*

A *static information system,* by contrast, reports on a real world that changes little or not at all—the interaction properties of drugs, strengths of materials, decisions and opinions of the United States Supreme Court, the collected dialogues of Plato. The distinction is not precise, of course. While Plato's dialogues will never change, new information is continually discovered about drug interactions, and the Supreme Court announces new decisions and opinions each year. Nevertheless, there are somewhat different approaches to implementing information systems that report on a static or a dynamic world.

In a dynamic information system, the collection of information available to report on builds up while the system is in operation. Typically, a static information system comes with all of its available information built in. The texts of the Supreme Court decisions, for example, might be stored on the same compact disc that includes the program. If the information changes very slowly, the software manufacturer might provide quarterly or yearly updates.

To document a dynamic information problem, you must indicate how the software can get access to each event that changes the results of possible queries. For example, is the information available only from users performing manual data entry?

If so, how will they get access to the information—from newspapers, from customers, by direct observation? Is there equipment that registers when these events happen? Are there existing databases or computers that already supply this information? If more than one data source is available for the same information, which is more trustworthy or up-to-date?

To document a static information problem, you must indicate, not how the software can access the relevant part of the real world, but how the software developers can. They may have to get it from people who type it in manually, as in the case of software that enables users to search and display Plato's dialogues in the original, ancient Greek. If there are existing sources for the data, the requirements document should indicate these, along with any shortcomings, such as missing sections or a manner of representation that omits diacritical marks. Often in a static information problem, the great majority of the work is not programming or even writing requirements, but entering and editing the data.

Many real life dynamic information problems require that the system start off able to answer queries about events that occurred before the system is put into operation. This is most often the case when the customer already has an information system in place, and the new system is merely a replacement for it. The customer does not want to lose access to the years' worth of data stored in the old system. Just as in a static information problem, the requirements document must indicate how the software developers can access the legacy data. Often this involves documenting the file formats, or at least documenting your guesses about the format because documentation on the details of the old system is often poor, if it exists at all. You need to document the meaning of the data, not just the files and record types and fields. The programmers need to know how to map the data to the real world if they are to build a system that answers questions about that real world. If the legacy data is not sufficient to answer all the queries that the customer wants to make, the customer should know this as early as possible.

Finally, a *snapshot* problem is a very simple case of dynamic information problem. In a snapshot problem, the system reports on the current state of some part of the real world, such as the current temperature, or perhaps displays a snapshot, via the World Wide Web, of Times Square in New York. Such problems are usually best framed as connection problems, described in section 5.6.

5.2.3 Passive and active

So far, we've mentioned only queries initiated by users: user types in query about *x*, system displays requested information about *x*. In these cases, an information system responds only passively to user input.

Some information systems also deliver information to their users without their having requested it. For example, a burglar alarm notifies police or security personnel that an intruder has entered a building without the people at the police station continually querying to see if anything has happened. Similarly, an inventory control system might notify employees in the purchasing department whenever an item is running low on stock and needs to be reordered. Other software, rather than a person, might be the recipient of a notification, as in UNIX, where the operating system notifies a process when one of that process's child-processes dies. In these cases, the information system plays an active role, effectively initiating queries and showing users their results.

Active queries, or *notifications*, sometimes require a little more documentation in requirements than do passive queries. What event triggers the notification? What kind of lag between the occurrence of the event and the notification of the user is permissible? If the user does not receive the notification, must the system take some other action? If so, how can the system know that the notification has succeeded?

Very often, the real reason for requiring that the system perform notifications is to ensure that a business operate according to certain rules. In this case, the notifications are the means by which the system exerts control over a domain, and the problem is better framed as a control problem, described in section 5.3.

5.2.4 Solving an information problem

The normal solution to an information problem is to build a model of the real world inside the computer. The model consists of bits in the computer that change state following rules that map them to activity in the real world. The model, then, behaves in a manner analogous to the real world, enabling the software to answer queries directly, on the basis of the model, instead of contacting the real world in response to each new query.*

For example, when a clothing store receives a new shipment of sweaters, the model maintained by its inventory software changes: the qty_in_stock field in the item record

---

* The software industry is somewhat notorious for its nearly all-encompassing use of the word *model*. In this book, *model* means only the most mundane sense of the word: an object whose properties bear a useful analogy to something else, as a model of a building is useful to examine when planning to construct a real building, or you can examine a model of a molecule to learn about the actual molecule. The analogy between a model and what it is a model of can be useful to varying degrees, but the model itself is neither true nor false; it's just another object. A *description*, or statement, by contrast, is true or false. Requirements and specifications, then, are descriptions, not models. They describe the problem domain, the effects that the software is to achieve there, and the interface between the software and the problem domain. The problem domain description is simply true or false, and the requirements and specifications become true when and if the software is implemented without bugs and operated correctly. The bits in a computer that bear a useful analogy to the real world are a genuine model. As these two concepts are among the most fundamental to keep distinct, we will not use the words that stand for them interchangeably.

corresponding to that style of sweater increases by the number of sweaters in the shipment. When a user queries on the number of sweaters of that style in the store, the software simply reports the current contents of the same qty_in_stock field.

Therefore, the specification that describes the solution to an information problem needs to describe the model maintained by the software as well as, for each event in the real world that changes the answer to any possible query, the corresponding interface event that changes the model.

For example, when the store receives the new shipment, it becomes the responsibility of a user to type in the item type and the quantity of the shipment. The software updates the model in response to the user-interface event, not the actual receipt of the shipment, since the software has no direct access to the latter. We will call each such action an *event response.*

An event response involving human users has two parts: the action that the user is responsible for performing (getting to a certain screen in the program and typing in some data) and the update of the model. The user's action is one of the operating procedures for the software. If the users do not operate the software as described in the specification, the software cannot be relied upon to answer queries correctly.

The description of the model describes the data only insofar as it affects the outcome of queries—that is, only states of the model that are distinguishable at the interface to the problem domain. Whether the model is implemented as a relational, hierarchical, network, object-oriented, or other type of database is no part of the specification.

When hardware or software, rather than users, supplies information at the interface, the principle is the same. The specification must state, for each event initiated by the hardware or software, how the system responds to it—that is, how the system updates the model. In most cases, these event responses do not include anything analogous to operating procedures because only rarely is it possible for the interface designer to specify how the hardware or software that it communicates with must behave. Rather, the design must conform to known and unalterable behavior of the hardware and software.

The specification of a static information system does not include any event responses, of course, because no events happen in the problem domain. The specification does include a description of how the information gets into the system in the first place. This might involve writing requirements for another program to create and edit the model. Such a tool would most likely fit the workpiece frame, described in section 5.5.

If the problem domain changes occasionally, or if knowledge of it changes—such as pharmacologists' knowledge of drug interactions—then the specification must describe how these events lead to an update of the model. For example, if there is to be a monthly update of pharmacies' databases, the specification must describe how the new drug interaction information enters the main system, how the main system generates updates for distribution to end users, and how users enter the updates into their own systems.

To try to counteract the distortions introduced by a connection domain, a specification usually includes a set of validation rules. Each rule must state criteria for rejecting data and what the system does if a user (or hardware or software) attempts to enter data that fails the criteria. For other types of connection problem and their solution, see section 5.6.

Lastly, the specification contains all of the screens in the application, including a description of every action that a user can take. The user-interface description tells how the users enter queries and how the results appear on the screen. In most projects, before designing the screens, it's wise to write up each event response only in terms of data entered by the user and the effect on the model. The user-interface designer then adds the screens, indicating exactly what fields the user enters and buttons the user presses in each event response. The programmers can implement the operations on the model while the user-interface designer designs and tests the screens.

5.2.5 Checklists

Tables 5.2 and 5.3 list the information needed to fully document both the requirements and the specification for an information problem. See also chapter 8 for generic information that applies to nearly all software, such as installation and backup procedures.

Table 5.2 Information problem: requirements document

Topic	See
Objects in the real world and their attributes and relations	Chapter 9
Data to be stored about the objects[a]	Chapter 9
All real world events that change the results of queries, and all possible sequences in which those events can occur	Chapter 10
Queries	Section 9.9
How can the system access the objects and events? (Or, in a static information problem, how can the software developers access them?)	(Not covered in this book)
File formats for any existing files that the system needs to access (or refer to existing documentation)	Chapter 10
Distortions and delays introduced by any connection domains	(Not covered in this book)

a. As mentioned in section 8.1, while a description of data to be stored is technically part of the specification, it's usually most convenient to include it in the requirements document.

Table 5.3 Information problem: specification

Topic	See
Event responses	Section 10.3
Validation rules[a]	(Not covered in this book)
User interface, and any additions to the data model necessitated by the user interface, such as preferences	Section 8.2
Operating procedures	Section 11.5

a. Validation rules can also be appropriate to include in the requirements document instead of in the specification. The specification says, in addition, what the system does in response to entry of any data that violates the validation rules.

5.3 Control problems

A control problem focuses exclusively on causation—that is, in making part of the world behave in accordance with specified rules.

To document a control problem, you need to describe three things: (a) the causal properties of the relevant part of the world and the rules that the objects in that world follow by virtue of their nature, regardless of the software; (b) the rules that we would like them to follow; and (c) the phenomena shared between the computer and the problem domain, through which the software monitors the problem domain and initiates actions that result in the rules in (b) being followed.

Part (b) is the requirement, shown in the figure 5.3 as *behavior rules*. The rest is problem-domain description.

The software in a microprocessor-controlled video camera solves a simple control problem. The behavior rules link button presses with motor activity, as in, "Motor runs at normal speed while record button is depressed, unless tape cartridge is at end of tape or no cartridge is loaded." The description of the controlled domain consists of

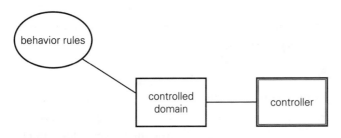

Figure 5.3 Control problem

statements such as, "The motor is always in one of the following three states: off, running at normal speed, running at high speed" and "The motor can only run at high speed when the battery charge is at least 0.2." Finally, the shared phenomena are described by statements connecting the I/O ports on the microprocessor to other parts of the problem domain, such as, "When output port 0x0A00 is 0x01, the motor runs at normal speed" and "Input port 0x0A01, bit 0, registers the current status of the record button: 1 if depressed, 0 if raised."

More examples of software that solve control problems:

- Heating control system in a large office building: turns fans, furnaces, and air-conditioning units on and off to make the best compromise among the varying settings of numerous thermostats located throughout the building

- Traffic-light controller: switches lights between red, green, and yellow according to timing rules, activity registered at sensors, and timing relationships with activity at neighboring traffic lights

- Telephone switch software: directs switches to connect incoming calls to wires that lead directly to telephones, parses pulses and touch tones from telephones to find out what number they're calling, and connects the two telephones or connects the call to another service, such as a long-distance carrier, to complete the next segment of the connection

- Inventory control system: fills or rejects orders, logs the acquisition of new inventory, directs stock pickers to the correct shelves, reorders new inventory at economically most efficient times

- Mail transfer agent: software that runs on an electronic mail server that receives notifications from delivery programs that new email has arrived, calls upon appropriate delivery programs to forward email to its destination address according to rules about how bandwidth is to be used and knowledge about which communication protocols are supported by each destination computer. (A delivery program is one that exchanges email via a specific communication protocol.)

As diverse as these examples are, stating their requirements involves essentially the same principles: state the causal rules that describe how the relevant objects in the world behave, and state the desired behavior that the system should cause.

5.3.1 Connection domains

A very common type of control problem, especially in business applications, involves directing people to perform various activities. This is perhaps better named a *direction problem*, because the computer can only direct people, it can't control them. They might

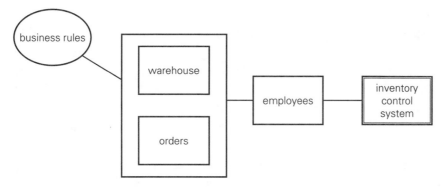

Figure 5.4 Connection domain in a control problem

or might not do as the computer directs them. Thus, the users in such a problem are a connection domain, as shown in figure 5.4.

The behavior rules say only to move inventory into the warehouse when it's received and to ship it to customers in response to orders. The inventory control system must rely on employees to tell it when inventory and new orders are received. The only way the inventory control system can cause inventory to move is by directing employees to move it.

The inventory control system also keeps track of accounts and responds to queries. These, however, form an information problem, and we should not let them distract us when considering the control aspects of the problem. More information about the inventory control system's multiple problem frames is in section 6.2.

In addition to sometimes moving the wrong items, or entering order data incorrectly, the employees introduce another difficulty. There is a delay between the time the system gives a direction and an employee moves the inventory, and a delay between the time inventory or an order is received and an employee enters this into the system. Furthermore, the software cannot tell when or whether inventory was actually shipped.

The software designers cannot entirely remove distortion and delay, but they can reduce them to some extent. If there is redundancy in the problem domain—for example, products that have unique numbers as well as unique names—the software can require that users enter both the number and a name, and reject the data if they don't match.

What's that big rectangle enclosing the warehouse and the orders? It wasn't on the list of symbols in figure 4.9. It's just a way to group domains together so that one line can connect to all of them without making a messy diagram. Frame diagrams are not a formal language. They are diagrams that you can draw on a napkin in two minutes or less. Modify them to suit whatever you want to depict.

5.3.2 Solving a control problem

The specification of a program that solves a control problem is a description of yet more behavior rules: rules that describe the behavior of the shared phenomena, this time including the behavior of the computer. Continuing the example of the video camera, part of the specification might state, "When input port 0x0A01, bit 0, changes from 0 to 1, program changes output port 0x0A00 to 0x01."

Often, timing plays a role in the specification, just as in the requirements. If the requirements state that the VCR's motor must not run in pause mode on the same segment of tape for more than 180 seconds, then the specification includes rules for changing the settings of output ports in accordance with similar timing rules.

In many cases, the behavior rules in the specification are more complex than can be expressed by statements in the form of, "When x happens, y happens." Often, the program must respond differently to the same event, depending on which events preceded it. In this case, the solution is to postulate a set of states that the software takes on. Each state specifies, for each possible input, the visible response in the problem domain and the next state for the software to change to. For example, if a single press of a clear button on a photocopier is supposed to cancel the current job, and a second press is supposed to clear all the copier settings to their defaults, the specification would need to describe two states. More information about states and state-transitions is in chapter 11.

When you solve a direction problem, you create a specification describing two things: notifications to tell users when to perform tasks, and event responses to tell the system when relevant events happen. Both notifications and event responses are the same as described under information problems. Both typically need a special user interface designed.

5.3.3 Checklists

Tables 5.4 and 5.5 list the information needed to fully document both the requirements and the specification for a control problem. See also chapter 8 for generic information that applies to nearly all software, such as installation and backup procedures.

Table 5.4 Control problem: requirements document

Topic	See
Objects in the controlled domain; data model, if any	Chapter 9
Causal laws of the controlled domain, including events that the objects are capable of	Chapter 11
Behavior rules	Section 11.5
Actions in the problem domain that the computer is capable of initiating	Section 11.2

Table 5.4 Control problem: requirements document (continued)

Topic	See
Shared phenomena through which the computer can monitor the controlled domain	(Not covered in this book)
Any connection domains	(Not covered in this book)

Table 5.5 Control problem: specification

Topic	See
Trigger rules or state tables, relating actions initiated by the computer to detectable actions in the problem domain	Section 11.1
Event responses, if the system maintains a data model	Section 10.3
User interface and operating procedures, if any	Section 10.3

5.4 Transformation problems

Software that solves a transformation problem generates output data that maps to input data according to specified rules. Its problem frame is shown in figure 5.5.

The input data and output data are elements from two sets. Documenting a transformation problem consists of describing the following: the set of all possible inputs, the set of all possible outputs, and the rule relating each possible input to its corresponding output. The rule, shown in the frame diagram as mapping, is the only requirement.

A transformation problem could just as easily be called a calculation or mapping problem. Calculation is simply mapping input numbers to output numbers according to a rule. A four-function hand calculator solves four straightforward transformation

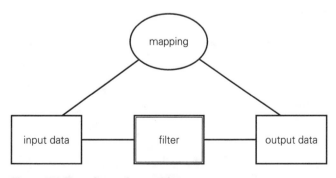

Figure 5.5 Transformation problem

problems: given a pair numbers, output their sum; given a pair of numbers, output their difference; given a pair of numbers, output their product; and given a pair of numbers, output their quotient.

More examples of software that solves transformation problems:

- A program to convert between the file formats of two different word processors, or two different graphics file formats
- A subroutine that translates bar codes into numbers
- A program to assign students, professors, and classes to rooms for a semester at a university
- Image-processing software to perform such operations as removing dust and scratches from digitized photographs
- A program that tells a bus rider which buses to take to get from one location to another, arriving by a specified time
- A program to generate weather maps from meteorological data
- A printer driver: converts printer-control commands from the operating system into equivalent commands to control a specific printer
- Software that helps archaeologists find buried villages based on satellite data. Such software applies complex rules to transform information about how the surface of the Earth reflects light both within and beyond the visible spectrum, into guesses about what lies beneath the surface.

It is the job of requirements to specify the entire mapping completely. Software that tries to place elements of complex diagrams into aesthetically pleasing and readable arrangements should not have the requirement "arrangements must be aesthetically pleasing and readable." Converting "aesthetically pleasing and readable" into mathematical rules would be the main work of writing the requirements in this case. Similarly, for software that calculates a most efficient route, the requirements must define "most efficient" in the form of a rule specifying, for any two possible routes, which is most efficient.

5.4.1 Solving a transformation problem

The great majority of the work of solving a transformation problem is programming, not interface design. All that a specification needs to add to the requirements is the user interface, if needed, or an API if the software is to be accessed by other programs.

5.4.2 Checklists

Tables 5.6 and 5.7 list the information needed to fully document both the requirements and the specification for a control problem. See also chapter 8 for generic information that applies to nearly all software, such as installation and backup procedures.

Table 5.6 Transformation problem: requirements document

Topic	See
Input and output sets	Chapters 9 and 10
Source and destination of the data	(Not covered in this book)
Mapping between input and output sets	Subsection 11.5

Table 5.7 Transformation problem: specification

Topic	See
User interface and operating procedures, if any	Subsection 10.3
API, if any	(Not covered in this book)

5.5 *Workpiece problems*

In a workpiece problem, the job of the software is to enable users to create objects, such as documents or designs, similar to the way a lathe helps a carpenter create wooden workpieces. The workpieces are intangible, software objects that exist only in a realized domain, though the software may also generate tangible versions of them, such as printed documents.

There are two requirements: to enable the users to perform the given operations on the workpieces, and to realize the workpieces within the software. The vast majority of documenting a workpiece problem is describing the workpieces.

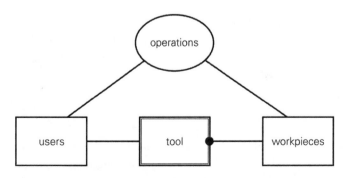

Figure 5.6 Workpiece problem

Example software that solves workpiece problems:

- A word processor: creates documents inside the computer. The documents contain sections, pages, paragraphs, characters, graphics, and so on. All of these are to have properties and behavior invented by the software designer.
- A program to create business graphics
- A program for designing cable TV networks. A user places each type of cable and equipment on a map of a neighborhood to receive service.
- A program to build and display models of organic molecules
- A music editor
- A program to generate composite sketches of police suspects. A witness selects from a library of chins, mouths, hairlines, cheekbones, and so on, to create an accurate drawing of a person they saw.
- A recipe file

Not all programs that solve workpiece problems involve letting users *create* workpieces. In typical educational software, students can manipulate objects within the computer—for example, taking tests—but they can't create their own tests. A companion program would likely enable a test designer to create them.

The workpiece problem, perhaps better than any other type of software problem, illustrates that requirements themselves are creative design, usually a solution to some other problem not solvable directly by software techniques. The requirements for a workpiece problem are not "Create an outline processor tailored to the needs of lawyers," but a detailed description of all of the text elements and outlining operations that the software is to realize. Only a person who knew a lot about the needs of lawyers could invent these text elements and outlining operations. Therefore it's part of requirements, not specification or programming.

5.5.1 Solving a workpiece problem

The majority of the work in solving a workpiece problem is usually user-interface design. The rest is programming: representing the workpieces and performing the operations, which don't concern us in this book.

5.5.2 Checklists

Tables 5.8 and 5.9 list the information needed to fully document both the requirements and the specification for a control problem. See also chapter 8 for generic information that applies to nearly all software, such as installation and backup procedures.

Table 5.8 Workpiece problem: requirements document

Topic	See
Workpieces	Chapter 9
Operations	Same as event responses, in section 10.3

Table 5.9 Workpiece problem: specification

Topic	See
User interface and operating procedures	Section 10.3

5.6 Connection problems

In a connection problem, there are domains that do not share phenomena directly but are, instead, connected by another domain between them—a connection domain. The problem is to make the two indirectly connected domains behave as if they were directly connected, to the extent that this is possible.

Figure 5.7 shows the two principal types of connection problem. In type (a), the system needs to interact with the domain of interest, but must make do with a connection domain to relay information from the domain of interest to the system, or carry out commands sent by the system. In type (b), the system to be built *is* the connection domain, responsible for bringing system *B* into states corresponding to the current state of system *A*, as system *A* changes (or vice versa). The requirement, in both cases, is merely an achievable correspondence of states, not a perfect correspondence, because a perfect correspondence is usually impossible to achieve.

Connection problems seldom occur in isolation. Rather, they usually occur as part of a larger problem. We've already seen them in information problems and control problems. Inside another problem, a connection problem usually does not need requirements spelled out explicitly, such as "Achieve such-and-such level of correspondence." But the requirements document should spell out such matters as the timeliness of the data to be elicited by queries (so the interface designers can design a way to achieve it), as well as the limitations imposed by the connection domain (so the customer knows what is possible and what is not).

Example connection problems:

- The data-entry staff that supports an information system (discussed in section 5.2). Human data entry introduces distortion, in the form of typographical

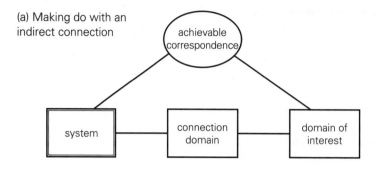

(a) Making do with an indirect connection

achievable correspondence

system — connection domain — domain of interest

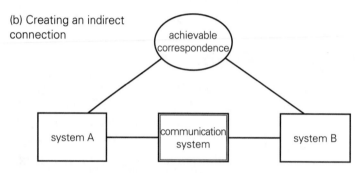

(b) Creating an indirect connection

achievable correspondence

system A — communication system — system B

Figure 5.7 Connection problems

errors, and delay, in that events often happen well before people have time to enter data about them.

- A data warehouse answers queries based on the data in a number of *operational data stores*—databases, such as order-entry systems, inventory systems, and so on, that are each tailored to a specific task that they support on a daily basis. The data warehouse allows exploration of all that data in unanticipated ways. The real problem, however, is to get information about the real world. Often, different operational data stores overlap in the parts of the world they cover, and they differ in the accuracy and timeliness with which they cover it. The designer of the data warehouse, therefore, faces a problem: how to supply the most accurate and up-to-date information in response to queries, given a variety of different sources of data.

- Error-free data transfer across a noisy phone line. Of course, it can't be completely error-free because random line noise can foil any error-correction scheme. All error-correcting protocols sacrifice speed for accuracy. The more careful the error-detection, the more overhead the protocol introduces and the slower the transmission.

- Video conferencing: as people move and speak in one location, they can be seen and heard in another.

Documenting a connection problem like that in figure 5.7(a) consists of describing the mapping between the shared phenomena linking the connection domain to the domain of interest, and the shared phenomena between the system and the connection domain. This mapping should include the types of distortion and delay introduced by the connection domain: which type of information is the least reliable? how long is the lag between an event at one end of the connection domain and the corresponding event at the other?

It is especially valuable to document ways by which the system can detect that the connection domain is not functioning properly. Continuing the weather station example, if there are shared phenomena by means of which the system can detect that the weather stations are off or in need of calibration, these should be described in the requirements document. Information about what types of activity in the domain of interest are possible and what types are impossible also enables the system to detect errors.

When the connection domain is human users, of course the requirements document need not explain the numerous patterns of human error. The branch of cognitive psychology known as *mistake theory* is part of the background knowledge of a user-interface designer, and, as noted in chapter 7.1, does not belong in a requirements document. However, the requirements document should still contain as much information as possible about the domain of interest in order to detect invalid data entered by users.

If, as in figure 5.8, there are multiple connection domains that connect to the same domain of interest, then the reliability of each can be rated relative to the others. For

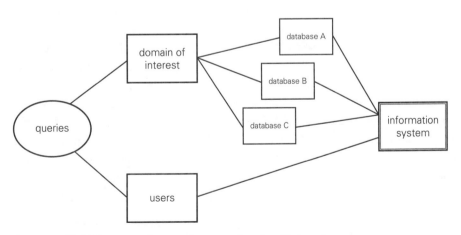

Figure 5.8 Multiple connections to the same domain of interest

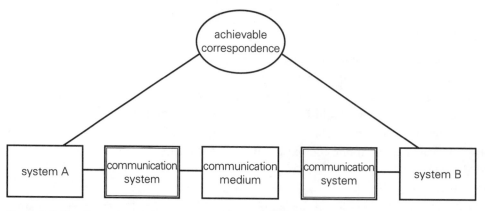

Figure 5.9 Creating a connection across a communication medium

example, if three different databases contain information about people's names, addresses, and phone numbers, the requirements document can state that for names, database *A* is more reliable than database *B*, and *B* is more reliable than *C*, but for addresses, *B* and *C* are of equal reliability, and both are better than *A*. If the databases contain information about the reliability of a particular record, such as a date_entered field, the requirements document should indicate that too, so a specification can take advantage of it. The requirements document can also describe "voting rules" to resolve disagreements when two databases give results disagreeing with one another.

Documenting a connection problem like that in figure 5.7(b) involves describing the same type of mapping between states and/or events, except that now it is a *desired* mapping, with desired distortion and delay characteristics—requirements rather than problem-domain description.

Often in a type (b) connection problem, the problem domain includes yet another connection domain, as shown in figure 5.9. An error-correcting protocol runs simultaneously at two different systems separated by a communication medium. The distortion characteristics of the medium need to be described in the requirements document, just as in a type (a) connection problem.

Communication media, such as copper wires, often have very different distortion characteristics at different data rates, different radio frequencies, and so on. Also, the medium may have different distortion characteristics at different times. Some telephone connections, for example, are much clearer than others. The requirements document should describe distortion as a function of these other variables, to enable the specification to take fullest advantage of the capabilities of the communication medium.

5.6.1 Solving a connection problem

Solving a connection problem is primarily a matter of exploiting redundancy in the problem domain and, in the case of a type (b) connection problem, creating redundancy to exploit.

In a type (a) connection problem, the specification states rules according to which the system rejects data, and what the system does in response to bad data. If there is no redundancy whatsoever in the domain of interest—that is, if every theoretically possible state or event of interest is equally likely, and every possible state or event in the connection domain maps to a legitimate state or event in the domain of interest—then no solution to the connection problem is possible. The system can't reject any data from the connection domain because any data might be valid.

Fortunately, nearly all problem domains contain large amounts of redundancy. People's names don't contain control characters; atmospheric temperatures do not change faster than one degree per second; ISBN numbers map to book titles, and so forth. Even if there is no simple rule for detecting invalid data received from a connection domain, the development staff can define operating procedures, such as double entry, on the assumption that two different people are unlikely to make the same error typing in the same data.

Another trick, applicable to a few types of connection problem, is to have the system make guesses in response to queries when data from a connection domain is delayed. For example, if the news last heard from an airplane was that it would arrive at a certain time, the system can report this arrival time in response to queries even if no news has been heard from the airplane or the originating airport for the last five hours. Guessing that the arrival time is unchanged might be right 95% of the time, and this accuracy might be good enough for displaying on public monitors in airports. On the other hand, if a loss of communication correlates with a long delay in arrival time, then the specification can indicate that the system makes a different guess, taking this correlation into account.

If the connection problem appears in a control problem, as in the inventory control system mentioned in section 5.3, a common difficulty is to ensure that the requested actions actually got performed in the domain of interest. The specification may state that users must click a certain button in the software to indicate that the action is complete, or the software might be able to recognize that the action was not completed or not done correctly if it later fails to detect expected activity, such as boxes being barcoded for shipment.

In a type (b) connection problem, the usual solution is to add various checks to the data. These, in turn, become redundancy to exploit in the same manner as in a type (a) problem. Checksums, sent along with the data, are related to the data by a precise mathematical rule. The receiver can then reject data blocks whose checksums do not match the data. This doesn't guarantee that the receiver never accepts bad data, of course, but sophisticated mathematical techniques can reduce the probability to any desired level.

Redundancy in the data to be transmitted also figures into the design of a communication protocol. The protocol can exploit redundancy by the way it encodes data for transmission over the communication medium by encoding the most probable pieces of data with the shortest sequences of bits. This enables the protocol to achieve the same high reliability of accurate transmission without sacrificing as much speed. Modems that perform data compression exploit redundancy in the English language; they send text at a faster bit rate than they send executable programs.

5.6.2 Checklists

It's difficult to make a checklist for connection problems because they vary so much from case to case. Tables 5.10 and 5.11 list information to consider for inclusion in both requirements documents and specifications that involve connection problems. Very few real problems would involve everything listed here, and many problems would probably need additional information.

Table 5.10 Connection problem: requirements document

Topic	See
States and events in domain of interest	Section 11.1
Redundancy in domain of interest	(Not covered in this book)
Mapping, actual or desired, between states and events in different domains	Section 11.5
Distortion and delay introduced by connection domain, actual or desired	(Not covered in this book)
Rules for telling which of several connection domains has the most reliable data	Section 11.5

Table 5.11 Connection problem: specification

Topic	See
Validation rules; actions that the system takes when validation rules are violated	Chapter 7
Operating procedures that increase redundancy	Chapter 8
Communication protocols	(Not covered in this book)
Guessing rules	Chapter 7

CHAPTER 6

Multi-frame problems

6.1 Combining problem frames

The clock is a well known design pattern. The AM/FM radio is another. They have nothing to do with each other. One continuously displays the current time, and one translates electromagnetic signals into sound. Yet they are often combined—into the clock radio.

For the most part, each part of the clock-radio problem can be described independently of the other. The clock needs to rotate hands or display numbers at a certain rate and sound a buzzer at an hour specified by the user. The radio needs to translate signals in certain parts of the electro-magnetic spectrum into sound with a certain degree of fidelity. But there is a small area where they interact. The radio must turn on and off according to times set *on the clock* by the user.

Ideally, whenever you encounter a complex problem in software, you can break it into distinct problem frames that interact through a similarly narrow logical channel in which the description of the part of the problem that fits one frame refers very little to the part of the problem that fits the other frame. Some problems just won't yield to any simple breakdown, but fortunately, in practice, the vast majority do.

Framing the total problem as a set of smaller problems that overlap slightly—sharing only one or a few domains—is your most important weapon against overwhelming complexity in a requirements document. By framing the problem in this way, you can talk about one thing at a time—the only way to write comprehensibly—but still systematically cover everything and everything's relation to everything else.

An opposite approach would be to describe a great number of different scenarios, each involving many aspects of the system. Each scenario is difficult to understand without first understanding all the others. The scenarios involve effects that overlap in ways that can be understood only by carefully looking over each one, holding them all in your mind in their entirety, and comparing them against each other. And, without a systematic approach, it's difficult to be sure that the scenarios have not left any holes in the description—categories of domain activity left unaddressed in the requirements. This entanglement is the result of failing to divide a problem at its seams.

While you need a systematic approach to fully document requirements, it need not be the same systematic approach that you follow on a different project. There's no need to subscribe to one "methodology" for all software; all you need is a method suited to the one piece of software that you're working on right now. Framing the problem is the step wherein you create a systematic method specially tailored to just that one problem. More than anything else, experience with other software (enough to have noticed the patterns of software) is what enables you to frame a new problem well.

The seams of a large problem usually follow groups of requirements of the same kind, that is, requirements that correspond to one type of problem frame and pertain to the same set of domains. For example, a piece of software might need to both report on an activity and control it. Reporting calls for the information frame; control calls for the control frame. Having split up the problem this way, you can describe each set of requirements without mingling it with the other. You can describe the domains that are common to each part of the problem one at a time, without mingling them with the requirements. The table at the beginning of section 5.1 shows the correspondence between requirement types and frame types.

The rest of this chapter provides a few examples to show how problem frames combine in practice.

6.2 Inventory control system

The primary job of an inventory control system is to guide the transport of goods in and out of a warehouse: directing employees to store goods as they come in, and directing the employees to retrieve the goods when orders are received and ship them to customers. However, filling orders follows certain rules: customers who are too far behind in

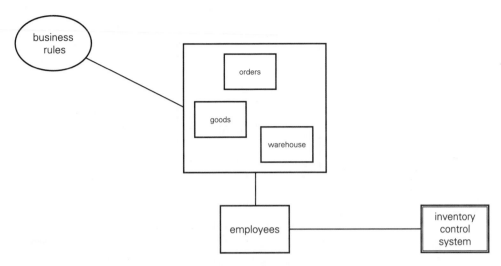

Figure 6.1 "Move goods through warehouse" part of inventory problem

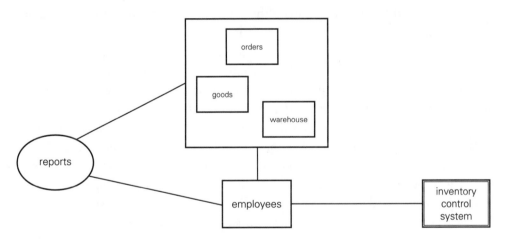

Figure 6.2 "Print reports" part of inventory problem

their payments are not to have their orders filled, different orders get different priority, and so on.

Another job of an inventory control system is to report on the activity of the warehouse: its current state and the past flow of money and goods. Talking about reports means describing information to be supplied to a user (the contents of the report) and possibly how the report is to be formatted. This is very different than describing the rules for how the business would like to see goods flow in and out of the warehouse.

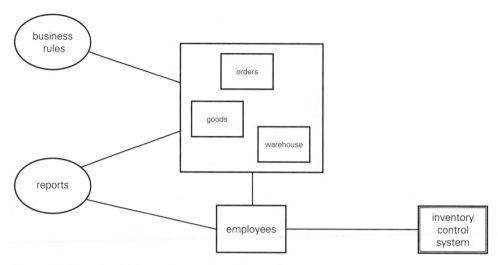

Figure 6.3 Control and information aspects of inventory problem on one diagram

So, you need two problem frames: the control frame and the information frame. These are shown in the frame diagrams in figures 6.1 and 6.2.

The employees are the only direct connection to the system. The business rules, defining the flow of goods through the warehouse in response to orders, pertain only to the goods, warehouse, and orders, but not to employees. The employees are simply means called upon by the control system to implement the business rules. Because this is a control frame, it calls upon you to document the causal powers of the employees: what they can do and how the inventory control system can get them to do it. The employees can affect the goods, warehouse, and orders; therefore, a line connects them.

The diagram in figure 6.2 shows the information problem: generating reports about the goods, warehouse, and orders in response to employee requests. The employees once again are a connection domain. In addition to requesting information, they supply the system with all of its information about the goods, warehouse, and orders.

You can also put both types of requirement on the same diagram, as in figure 6.3.

A very common requirement is for users to be able to change the rules by which the system operates. For example, managers might need to modify the business rules from time to time. This means that we also have a workpiece problem: the managers must be able to define the business rules. A frame diagram that simultaneously shows all three types of requirement is in figure 6.4.

It may seem a little strange to treat the business rules as a domain, but, in fact, all sets of requirements are domains. Anything that you could ever talk about with the same set of concepts is a domain. For example, a set of like requirements is a domain.

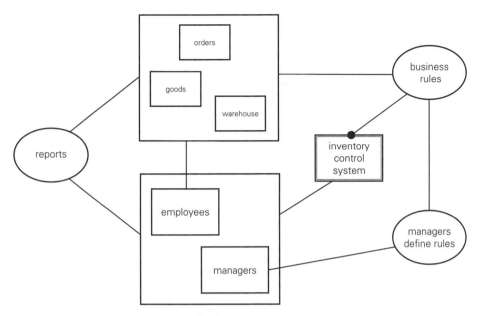

Figure 6.4 Composite frame diagram for inventory control system

Even the reports could be a realized domain, in the very likely possibility that users would be able to define their own reports.

So, from the standpoint of the "managers define rules" problem—a workpiece problem—the business rules are workpieces realized within the system. From the standpoint of the "move goods through warehouse" problem—a control problem—the (variable) business rules are the requirements. This is fairly typical overlap between problem frames. You can see how important it is that the text cover each domain in each of its roles one at a time (a domain typically having one role per problem frame). In still more complex problems, this kind of overlap could become mind-boggling without a careful breakdown into small problem frames.

Notice that even though these frame diagrams describe something very complex— the requirements and problem domain of an inventory control system—each diagram, with the possible exception of figure 6.4, is very simple. The business rules might be very complex, but now you can see how to document them. One section says what they are and their relation to the motion of goods in and out of the warehouse. Another section describes the operations that managers can perform on them. The different employees' roles in moving goods around might be somewhat complex, but you can talk about those elsewhere in the document without simultaneously talking about the business rules. No matter how complex the problem, you can—you must—break it down into humanly comprehensible subproblems, or else no human will be able to comprehend the problem as a whole.

6.3 Statistics package

A program to perform complex, user-definable statistical calculations combines a transformation frame and a workpiece frame. The transformation frame covers the calculations, of course. The workpiece frame covers the user's ability to define the formulas used in those calculations. Both subproblems are presented in a single diagram in figure 6.5.

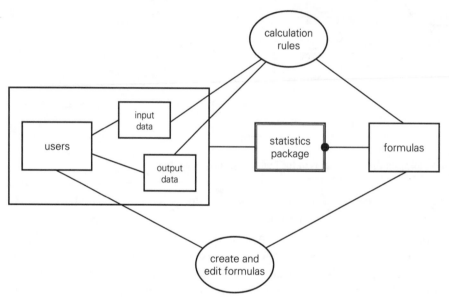

Figure 6.5 Frame diagram for a statistics package, combining transformation frame and workpiece frame

6.4 Digital answering machine

The software inside an answering machine that stores messages digitally rather than on an audio cassette combines a control frame and a transformation frame. The control frame addresses the recording and playing of messages in response to activity at the controls and on the phone line. The transformation frame addresses the mapping between sound and its representation in memory.

Ordinarily, statements about representation in memory would not belong in a requirements document. However, the answering machine is specifically a digital answering machine. The rules for digitizing speech are part of the problem domain, not

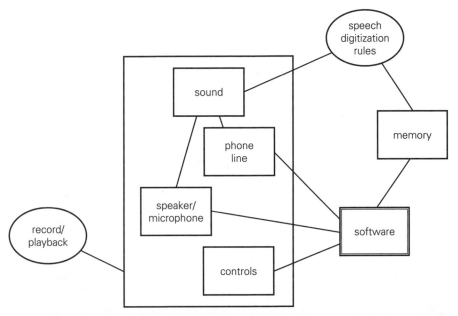

Figure 6.6 Frame diagram for digital answering machine, combining control frame and transformation frame

part of ordinary programming knowledge. Also, the intent is that the software implement certain digitizing techniques because these will be one of the main selling points of the answering machine. The digitization rules are, thus, one of the givens of the problem, something that the programmers must implement, not something the programmers must invent. Figure 6.6 diagrams these relationships.

Notice that the software has no shared phenomena with the sound, but the sound is supposed to be represented in memory. The phone line and the speaker/microphone and telephone line are actually connection domains to sound, whether generated or received. If the requirements document describes known, common patterns of distortion, the programmers can design ways to recognize and compensate for them, improving sound quality.

As is nearly always the case in embedded applications, the user is not mentioned in the requirements. The user is mentioned in the system requirements, but not the software requirements. From the standpoint of the software, the only problem is to respond to activity at the controls. The controls are assumed simple enough to reflect the user's intentions without distortion.

6.5 Compiler

A compiler is often thought of as purely a transformation problem, shown in figure 6.7. There is a mapping between source code and the object file, and the job of the compiler is to produce the object file in accordance with that mapping.

The truth is that inventing the mapping is actually the main work of compiler design. The rule is that the mapping must be such that when the compiled program runs, the target machine behaves according to the semantics of the source file. So here we have a variation on the usual way that problem frames combine. Part of the solution is to define a transformation problem such that solving it will also solve a control problem. The transformation problem is the mapping from source statements to machine instructions. The control problem is to make the target machine behave as specified in the source file.

The correct problem frame, shown in figure 6.8, shows a critical element missing from figure 6.7: the target machine. The programmers need to know the instruction set of the target machine in order to design the translation rules. The requirement is to make the target machine behave as specified in a source file written in a given language, by generating an object file that, when run on the target machine, brings about the specified behavior.

Compilers are a well understood type of program, so it's unlikely that anyone would make a mistake like that shown in figure 6.7. When writing a C compiler for a new microprocessor, no one would demand that the manufacturer supply the translation rules to go from a source file to machine instructions, and no one would forget to get documentation on the instruction set from the manufacturer.

But in a less well understood type of program—say, one being written for the first time—this type of mistake is very easy to make. Many requirements documents omit the domains that the requirements pertain to, leaving the programmers to infer them.

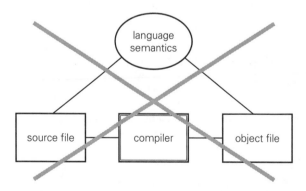

Figure 6.7 Compiler misframed as a transformation problem

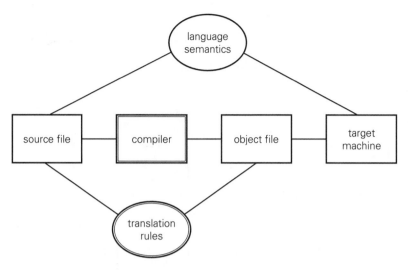

Figure 6.8 Correct problem frame for compiler

6.6 *Electronic mail*

An electronic mail system combines the workpiece and connection frames. Both frames are combined in figure 6.9.

The main domain information needed to solve the connection problem "send and receive mail" is the protocols followed by both the Internet and the other mail systems. The requirement is to get mail to the other users, not merely to the Internet or the other mail systems. As in most connection problems, the requirement is impossible to meet perfectly. The Internet is not always reliable; other mail systems do not always follow the protocols correctly; and other users do not always log in regularly.

The workpiece problem "create and edit email" is straightforward, and can even be offloaded onto an existing editor.

The mail itself bears extensive description in the document. Is the mail just text or can it contain binary attachments? The more sophisticated the type of mail to be sent, the more complications enter the connection problem as well as the workpiece problem. The other mail systems need to be described, too. Which ones can support which types of attachments? Which ones can support rich (formatted) text? The other mail systems include the readers operated by the other users. Is there any way for the system to find out what encodings an addressee's mail reader supports? (Yes, and when our user finds out, he or she can type it into our system. The choice to do that, however, is part of interface design and belongs in the specification.)

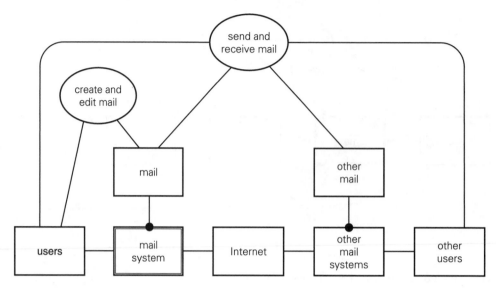

Figure 6.9 Frame diagram for an electronic mail system

An information problem frame would likely be added to any real electronic mail system, for reports given to a system administrator about Internet traffic and usage. Notice that the other problems can be described independently of this one. Once the other problems are documented, including the domains, the real world part of the information problem is already documented. All that remains is to write the requirements: the queries or automatically generated reports available to the system administrator.

This information problem would likely be added as part of the specification, not the requirements, because system administrators are not part of the problem domain and because the details of mail traffic can't be known until much of the specification has been designed.

6.7 Satellite reconnaissance

The following description of the requirements for a program to control a satellite that gets images of the Earth's surface, simplified though it is, involves five simultaneous problem frames. An interesting exercise is to see how much more complicated you could make it, without adding any more information, by dividing it differently.

Most fundamentally, the job of retrieving images is shown in figure 6.10 in an information frame. Here we have an instance of a snapshot problem because the object of the queries is changing, but the problem is not to keep track of the object, only to report its current state on demand.

CHAPTER 6 MULTI-FRAME PROBLEMS

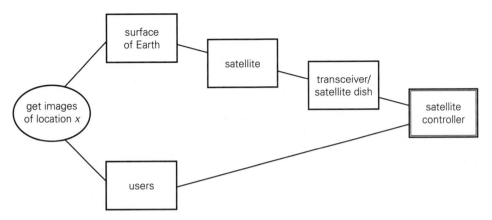

Figure 6.10 Most fundamental frame diagram for satellite controller: get images of surface of Earth on demand

There are two connection domains: first, the satellite creates images that must be relayed to the controller, and second, the satellite dish (antenna) must receive the images from the satellite. Establishing communication with the satellite involves a control problem. The dish must be pointed at the satellite, requiring that the commands for controlling the dish be documented, as well as the rules for determining exactly where to point it. This control problem is shown in figure 6.11.

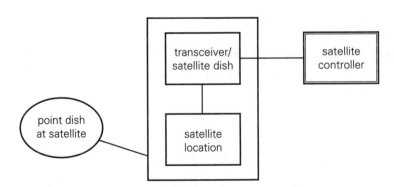

Figure 6.11 Control problem: point dish at satellite to make communication possible

Where does the satellite location come from? This is a transformation problem shown in figure 6.12. The controller must calculate the current location of the satellite based on its last known location. There is no other source for this information.

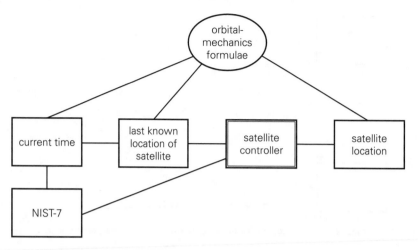

Figure 6.12 Transformation problem: calculate the satellite's current location

Figure 6.12 includes a connection domain: NIST-7, the atomic clock operated by the National Institute of Science and Technology in Boulder, Colorado, is the controller's source for the current time.

Once the satellite controller has established communication with the satellite, there is another control problem: to point the satellite at the desired location on the surface of the Earth, shown in figure 6.13. The *x* in the requirement comes from the request made by the user in figure 6.10.

This second control problem omits the connection domain of the satellite dish. For purposes of this problem, we assume that the commands sent by the satellite controller are phenomena shared with the satellite, so we can concentrate on documenting the commands that control the satellite and how they affect the satellite in relation to the surface of the Earth.

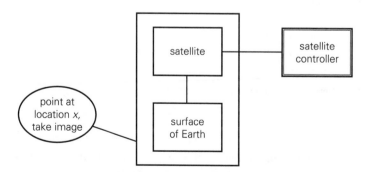

Figure 6.13 Another control problem: pointing the satellite at the desired location on the surface of the Earth and taking the image

CHAPTER 6 MULTI-FRAME PROBLEMS

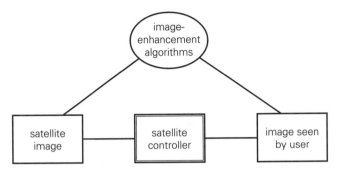

Figure 6.14 Another transformation problem: enhancing the image for human viewing

Finally, once the image is retrieved from the satellite, the controller must enhance it for human viewing. This is another transformation problem, shown in figure 6.14.

PART 2

Content

C H A P T E R   7

Software development

To write any kind of technical document, you first need to know who will read the document and what jobs they will perform with the information that it contains. This chapter tells who are the members of the software development team who read (and write) requirements and specifications, and how they apply them to their jobs. We do not cover each job in detail, nor undertake a comprehensive coverage of software development, such as can already be found in such texts as [Metzger 1981], [Sommerville 1989], and [Pressman 1996]. We are concerned here only with the people who read and write requirements and specifications, and how they use the information in them.

7.1 A division of cognitive labor

If you regularly switch between two mail programs, you might write a program to convert mail messages between each program's folder format. When you write a program all by yourself like this, to use all by yourself, you understand everything. You understand the purpose of the program; you've researched the file formats; you've carefully thought through what information needs to be displayed on the screen and how it should look; you know exactly how to invent tests that exercise the most critical junctures in the program; you know what changes you're most likely to want in the future. Consequently, when you write the program code, you can make the hundreds of small trade-offs and design decisions that tailor the program code perfectly to your needs.

When a group of people work together on a software project, all of this thinking, analysis, and background knowledge needs to be at least partly shared among all the participants. Ideally, if the information is shared perfectly, the final product is made as if by a single, multi-talented person who possesses the knowledge of all the participants—far more knowledge than any one person could possess, resulting in a higher-quality product than any one person could create.

The purpose of internal documentation is to share the knowledge of the participants, to come as close to that ideal as possible.

Except for the documentation of the problem domain, internal documentation does not describe generalities. It describes only specific information needed by each participant for each job. For example, it is not the task of internal documentation to explain to everyone on the project how to design good user interfaces. That kind of knowledge is nearly impossible to put into words. Rather, internal documentation captures the result of the user-interface designer's thinking about this one project so that the programmers can implement it without knowing how to invent such a design themselves. The resulting program is made as if by a single person who is both an expert user-interface designer and an expert programmer, even though neither the user-interface designer nor the programmers has the other's expertise.

As the project progresses, each new document or artifact embodies more and more knowledge, as depicted by the gradually widening arrow in figure 7.1.

Even more types of knowledge figure into a complete software project. A manager applies management knowledge; the deployment team applies its own brand of knowledge, and so forth. These groups are not the principal audience of requirements and specifications, but we will mention them when relevant.

Figure 7.1 should not be construed as a depiction of a waterfall process—a step-by-step procedure for designing software in which once a step is complete, its results are never revisited or revised. Iterative or spiral processes also result in the same kind of

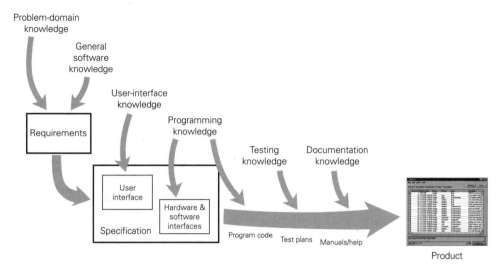

Figure 7.1 Division of cognitive labor in software engineering

division of cognitive labor, each participant contributing the type of knowledge shown in the figure.

Notice that the difference between each type of knowledge that feeds into the final product is about a different subject matter: the problem domain, user-interface design, programming, and so on. This is very different than a division of labor in which each party contributes knowledge of the same subject matter but in progressively more detail. Such a division of labor is possible, but it has more the character of a brainstorming session. In a brainstorming session, each person hears a vague idea from another participant and attempts to refine it or allow themselves to be led in an entirely new direction of thought. The participants are not given well-defined problems to solve on their own; they're given vague problems to flesh out or modify however they see fit.

Due to the size and complexity of software projects, as well as the diversity of specialized knowledge applied in them, the brainstorming approach is not feasible as an overall strategy of software development. In section 1.1 we've already examined the dangers of functional decomposition—another conception of software engineering based on progressing from less detail to more.

7.1.1 Five tasks and five audiences

Five tasks related to requirements and specifications, and five audiences for them, are shown in figure 7.2:

The rest of this chapter gives an overview of each task.

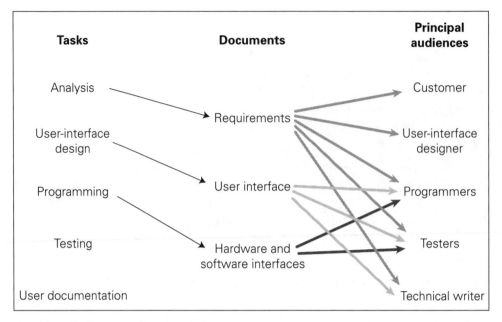

Figure 7.2 Tasks, documents, and audiences

7.2 *Analysis*

Notice that the first kind of knowledge shown in figure 7.1 is problem-domain knowledge normally provided by the customer. Thus, the customer is the first participant in the division of cognitive labor that results in the completed software. The *system analyst* is the liaison between the customer ("subject-matter expert") and the rest of the development team.

Analysis has two main parts:

- Learning the problem and the problem domain from the customer, known as *elicitation*.

- Communicating this information to the rest of the development staff by writing a requirements document.

The analyst, however, is more than just a funnel of information. Overlapping both of these two main parts is the job of *framing the problem*, as described in chapters 4 through 6.

Framing the problem is casting it in a form suitable for solution with software. The customer, not being an expert in software, is not likely to know how to do this particularly well; customers really don't know all the ways in which business problems can map to software problems. Thus, in the process of framing the problem, the analyst can suggest changing the problem from what the customer had originally intended so that the resulting software delivers a greater benefit. At the same time, by expressing the problem in terms appropriate to software solution, the analyst has taken the first step toward writing the requirements. The way in which the analyst chooses to frame the problem dictates both the types of results the customer will expect and the organization of the requirements document.

Of all the work the analyst does, nothing better fits the word *analysis* than answering such questions as, "Is the customer interested in using the computer simply to retrieve information, or is the software better understood as a controller for the operations of his business? Does this software respond to a long list of requests for data sent by other applications, or does it most fundamentally map data from one database to another?" Framing the problem in these ways is the act of finding the essential simplicity that underlies any system, no matter how complex.

Though there might be hundreds of pages of details in the final document, there must be a simple, one-sentence answer to the question, "What is this for?" If the analyst can find the answer and communicate it, the project makes sense and everyone can see how every part fits neatly into the whole. If not, the details of the project disperse like ink into cotton, never making sense. Later in the project, it seems that every bug fixed leads to two new bugs cropping up, because no one had the global perspective to see how every part interacts with every other part.

Thus the analyst, perhaps more than any other participant, has the greatest influence over the success or failure of the project, through the quality of the thinking that he or she puts into the requirements document.

As noted in the preface, writing the requirements document is technical writing. Conceivably, an analyst could hand off this job to a technical writer—the same type of person who writes the user documentation and on-line help—but many prefer to do it themselves.

Some analysts double in other roles. "Programmer/analyst" was once a popular job title. Indeed, many programmers do analysis as part of their jobs, but they don't call it analysis and don't include it in their job title. An analyst is just anyone who defines a software problem, whether called by that name or not. Many programmers find this part of their job the most fascinating.

Analysts with an artistic bent sometimes double in user-interface design, an apt combination because both analysis and user-interface design require close understanding of the problem domain. A role particularly enjoyed by many analysts is data modeling—especially, designing a relational database to model a problem domain. Many analysts started off working in a problem domain—say, chemical engineering—and only later in their careers moved to system analysis. In such esoteric fields, few other people could do a good job of analysis because the amount of time it takes to become familiar with the problem domain is so great.

Ideally, the analyst oversees and reviews all other work in the project, finding unanticipated places to apply his or her up-close knowledge of the problem domain.

7.3 User-interface design

The job of the user-interface designer is to (a) draw each screen in the software under development and describe the behavior of each control—each button, each text field, and so on—in enough detail for programmers to implement it; and (b) design the operating procedures for the software. One user-interface designer is enough on most software projects, but larger projects may require more than one.

Not all programs have user interfaces, or at least not user interfaces that a special member of the development team must design. In many embedded systems, such as a controller for a microwave oven, the user interface is just another part of the hardware that the software communicates with. Others, such as controllers for fuel injectors in automotive engines, have no direct user interface at all. Naturally, in regard to programs such as these, you should simply disregard statements in this book about how to write requirements to best serve the needs of the user-interface designer.

A user-interface designer needs the following information to make a good user interface:

- The vocabulary of the problem domain—specifically, the vocabulary of the users
- The data types to be stored by the software—that is, the data model. These usually correspond closely to the problem-domain vocabulary. (The user-interface designer often adds more data types, such as user preferences.)
- All the tasks to be performed by the user. These tasks should be easy to derive from the requirement statements.
- Supplementary information, such as sample data, patterns of common errors learned from previous versions of the software, and the most common sequences in which users are expected to perform tasks
- An understanding of how the users think, what their tastes and preferences are, and what they find easy or difficult to understand

All but the last item belong in a requirements document and/or data model. As mentioned at the beginning of section 2.4, the last item is too difficult to express precisely in written form. Therefore, this book will provide no tips for documenting it. The user-interface designer can learn it only through direct interaction with real users.

As a means to creating the screens and operating procedures, a user-interface designer also invents a set of concepts for the user to learn and apply while operating the software—in effect, an abstract world for the user to imagine existing behind the screens. The user-interface designer might want to document this conceptual framework for his own benefit, for future designers who will work on later versions of the software. Documentation of this conceptual framework can also help the technical writer write a useful manual.

Not even the most skillful user-interface designer can come up with a good design the first time. A high-quality user-interface design almost always grows out of several iterations of prototyping and testing on real users. A fortunate side effect of the proto-type is that the user-interface designer can capture the screens and put them into the user-interface design document.

The customer is not listed in figure 7.2 as one of the audiences of the user-interface design document. This may come as a surprise because feedback from the customer is so important in making a good user interface. However, a user-interface design document, like any specification, is somewhat terse, difficult reading. It's simply a list a screens, but-tons, fields, and so on, along with the effect of every possible user action on the database or the hardware/software interfaces. The best way for a customer to understand the user interface is to experiment with a prototype, perhaps guided by the user-interface designer who can describe the effects of functionality that won't be implemented until the first release.

The user-interface designer needs to consult with the programmers before commit-ting to a design. User-interface designers can easily come up with wonderful ideas that are not feasible to implement with the tools available to the programmers. The pro-grammers then need to point out which parts are difficult, possibly suggesting changes. This is as it should be. Programmers are likely to invent only user-interface ideas that are easy and obvious in their favored tool. "Anything is possible to the man who does not have to do it himself." The user-interface designer can often suggest more innovative and difficult designs, stretching the programmers to search for implementation strate-gies they would otherwise have bypassed. Often, the crazy design requires only a few more lines of code than designs that are squarely on the beaten path.

7.4 Programming

In this book, the word *programmers* refers to all the people who create the configuration of the machine—the program domain, not the problem domain and not the user interface. This includes the people who write the program code, the people who design the program architecture, and the people who design the physical database. Some members of this group might not want to be lumped in with the rest, but from the point of view of requirements and specifications, their concerns are the same: the program domain rather than the problem domain.

Once upon a time, programmers did everything: analysis, user-interface design, testing, and, if there were a few hours left before the deadline, documentation. Even today, many companies adhere to no rigorous distinction between requirements design, interface design, and program design, and many programmers see all of these as programming. This is particularly true if the company takes the sketch approach to requirements.* In this book, however, we take a very restricted view of programming: devising a configuration of the machine to produce defined interface behavior, where the interface, in turn, was designed to produce defined effects in the problem domain. That is, by programming we mean writing the source code, configuring the database tables, and so on—inventing the parts of the machine configuration that remain stable even as the machine stores different data.

Naturally, many programmers are good at requirements design and user-interface design as well as programming, because all three tasks require the combination of rigor and creativity that makes for a good program. However, we want to carefully distinguish between problem domain, interface, and program. We want to judge the program ultimately by how well it produces certain effects in the problem domain, and we can't do that if we don't carefully distinguish between designing effects in the problem domain (requirements design), designing physical machine behavior to produce those effects (interface design), and designing the intangible configuration of the machine that produces that behavior (programming).

In some companies, designing the user interface and programming it are regarded as the same task. This is unfortunate because when program design is put into conflict with user-interface design, program design usually wins. Programmers, usually the furthest removed from the problem domain of anyone on the project, have a natural tendency to design screens and error messages that reflect the internal structure of the program rather than concepts familiar to the user.†

This is explained by the nature of programming. Programming is an intricate task with an intricate set of concepts that are far removed from anything outside software. To write a program is to build a little world of loops, functions, objects, local variables, jump tables, and so forth. Being immersed in this world, it's difficult to retain the ability

---

* See section 3.7.2.

† See figure 7.4 for an example.

to see the program in any way except from this behind-the-scenes perspective. For this reason, and because of the tendency to let user interfaces be governed by what is easiest to implement, it's best that a user-interface designer not double as a programmer on the same project, even if the same person possesses both skills.

A non-programming task that *is* best left to programmers is the design of non-human interfaces: interfaces to hardware and other software. These require software expertise and, unlike user interfaces, are best designed with an eye toward the resulting program code. Of course the analyst or anyone else can design them, but designing them is much more like solving a programming problem than designing a human interface.

In order to start programming, programmers need to know the following:

- The requirements and problem-domain description and/or data model (the data as seen in the outside world, not the internal representation of the data)

- The program specification: the user interface, and all interfaces to hardware or software

- The hardware and operating system on which the software is to run

- Supplementary information, such as test data, information about the frequencies of different kinds of data and sequences of operations, to help the programmers design the program to run efficiently

- A list of changes anticipated in later releases, to help the programmers design the program for easy modification in the future

The description of the problem domain is usually of secondary interest to programmers, although, if they read about it, they can often point out subtle holes that others overlook because of their focus on the details of how to model it.

7.5 Testing

Requirements and specifications are necessarily abstract, as they cover an infinity of possible cases. The first job of a tester is *test planning*: converting requirements and specifications into a set of concrete actions to take, that prove that the software as actually built really brings about the requirements—or to prove this with as much completeness as is practical. Each of these actions to take, together with its expected response, is called a *test case*.

Of course, there is no way to test software completely. If one were to make a test case for every possible pathway through the software—not just every possible input, but

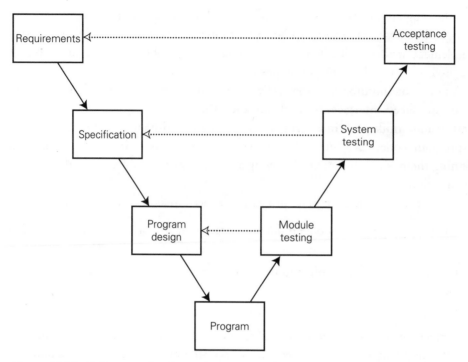

Figure 7.3 The V diagram, showing each main type of test in relation to the documents that supply the propositions to be tested

every possible sequence of inputs—one could never finish the test plan. A tester must be judicious, strategically choosing test cases that exercise the most important sections of the software in ways carefully designed to expose the parts that are most prone to bugs. To find those potential weak points and to aid in choosing the most effective test strategies, testers often make use not only of requirements and specification documents, but program design documents and the program source code as well.

Testing is often broken down into *acceptance testing, system testing*, and *module testing*, shown in the traditional V diagram in figure 7.3.

In *module testing*, large chunks of the program are tested to verify that they perform as the program design specifies that they should. Not shown on the diagram is *unit testing*, the testing of the smallest pieces of the program. Unit testing is normally performed by programmers.

In *system testing*, testers supply inputs at the interfaces of the system to verify that the program generates the outputs described in the specification.

In *acceptance testing*, the system is given a trial run in its real environment, or possibly in a realistic substitute, to verify that the requirements are really achieved. Whereas system testing verifies only that the microprocessor activates bits in its I/O ports at the specified time, acceptance testing verifies that, for example, the fuel injectors really squirt gasoline into the cylinders in the correct sequence, correctly synchronized with the spark plugs and throttle. In an inventory system, acceptance testing verifies that the system really does tell receivers the names of real shelves on which to place new inventory, that stock pickers really do find inventory on the shelves indicated by the software, that the orders delivered to the packers really do match the orders placed, and so on. Acceptance testing gets its name because the contract to develop the software usually specifies that if all the test cases in the acceptance test plan happen as indicated, the customer will then accept the software and pay up.

If something goes wrong during acceptance testing, there can be two reasons: either the program is not operating according to specification, or the specification itself is wrong. A specification is derived from both the requirements and the description of the problem domain: what makes the fuel injectors squirt, how the software can determine the state of the throttle, or how many shelves are in the warehouse. If these premises about the problem domain are wrong, the specification can be perfectly faithful to the requirements document but still fail to generate the required phenomena. A third problem that can be exposed during acceptance testing is simply that requirements of interest to the customer were omitted.

Correcting mistakes in the description of the problem domain can have the most far-reaching effects on a program because the logical foundation upon which the program was constructed has been undermined. Unfortunately, acceptance testing necessarily comes last in the sequence. You need a program before you can give it a trial run, and you need the modules to be working before you can test the program in the lab.

Approaches to software development, such as the spiral method, attempt to alleviate this difficulty by going through many small acceptance tests, the earliest ones testing the barest minimum of functionality that can usefully be tried out. The choice of the sequence in which to develop and test parts of the program is not part of the requirements and specification, of course, and is not covered in this book.

Naturally, the testing terminology is far from standardized. *Integration testing* sometimes means the same as *system testing*, and sometimes means only testing a group of modules that do not, together, compose the whole system.

Acceptance testing is not to be confused with the *usability testing* often performed by a user-interface designer with real users, usually done early in the development process. The intent of usability testing is to find out what screen layouts and terminology the users find easiest to understand and most efficient to work with. Usability testing is not usually the responsibility of the testing staff.

To write system and acceptance test plans, testers need to know:

• The requirements and problem-domain description and/or data model

- The program specification: the user interface and all interfaces to hardware or software

- As much about the problem domain as possible to design realistic tests such as realistic data and information about the frequencies of different kinds of data and sequences of operations

- The hardware and operating system on which the software is to run. If the customer has a variety of different machines, such as a network of PCs of varying speeds, the testers need to know the most typical machines and slowest machines that will run the software in order to catch performance problems as early as possible. Information about such troublemakers as TSRs (terminate-and-stay-resident utilities) and operating-system extensions on users' machines also enables testers to reproduce problems before they have a chance to happen on users' machines.

Testers test requirements and behavioral statements in specifications. They do not test preferences. There is no way to test whether the designers gave higher priority to speed than to storage space. However, preferences listed in a requirements document do provide information to testers about what aspects of the system should be given highest priority when testing.*

A good idea when writing requirements is always to bear in mind that when a tester is reading them, one question is on the tester's mind: "How could this be tested?" The answer should be fairly obvious, at least in principle. For example, it is no puzzle to think of how to test a requirement that a user can query to find out all flights to a specified destination with arrival times on Saturday or Sunday.

On the other hand, a requirement that says, "The general design philosophy of the user interface should be to arrange screens so that work proceeds as efficiently as possible," is no requirement at all. Neither is "The DEX system shall communicate with VERBIS" a genuine requirement, as you can see by trying to invent a test case for it. A real requirement says something that you can try out to see if it's true—something like "System prints day-end report at time of day specified by administrator," along with a precise description of all the information included in the day-end report. You can run the system, specify a time of day, see if the day-end report really gets printed at that time, and if it contains all the information stated in the description.

By framing problems as described in chapters 4 through 6, you'll seldom find yourself writing requirement statements that say nothing specific. Lack of specificity in many requirements documents is often the result of stopping at sketch of the system, where the details are left to be filled in by programmers.† Even without writing sketch requirements,

---

* For an explanation of preferences, see section 8.1.

† Described in the last part of section 2.3.

it pays to imagine yourself in the tester's position as you are writing. Often you can catch and correct vagueness very early that way.

7.6 User documentation

Usually delayed until the last possible moment, a technical writer creates the user's manuals and online help (more than one technical writer in a large project). If coding or debugging takes longer than expected, as it always does, the time will just have to come out of documentation's share of the schedule. The technical writer can't write much before the program is done because the only way to find out what the program does is to try it out and see.

It doesn't have to be this way. If the requirements and user interface are documented, the technical writer can begin organizing the manual, writing the procedures for using the software, and writing the glossary well before the program is done. Ideally, the technical writer can even cut and paste from the requirements document. Screens do change a lot during development, but recapturing a screen and putting it into the manual with a few changes to the text is a short task. The hard part of writing the manual is understanding what the users do with the software and choosing the content and organization.

When requirements are not well documented, the technical writer must research the problem domain in order to write the manual, either by spending a long time interviewing the analyst, or by doing the analyst's work. The latter requires calling people at the customer site and asking them about their jargon and what they expect to do with the software.

The technical writer is also often called upon to patch up mistakes in the user interface. A common reason why screens aren't done until the very end is because programmers sometimes design them as an afterthought to the underlying code. The programmers, knowing only the world inside the computer, often design screens like figure 7.4.

In figure 7.4 you see a somewhat simplistic screen to control a (very fictitious) mass spectrometer. A mass spectrometer is a machine used by scientists to find out what things are made of by knocking molecules off them, attaching a charge to the molecules (ionizing them) so they'll fly through a detector in a magnetic field, and then sorting the molecules by mass. If you don't understand, you're not alone.

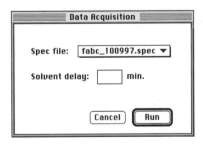

Figure 7.4 Screen that exposes program design

Just imagine trying to write a user's manual for a program to control a mass spectrometer without understanding what one is.

The spec file list in figure 7.4 has the following options:

```
esic_081597.spec
esid_011898.spec
fabc_100997.spec
fabd_090997.spec
malc_091297.spec
mald_093097.spec
```

Here is the story behind this list. The mass spectrometer can work with three different ionization sources, which the programmers abbreviated esi, fab, and mal. For each ionization source, there are two possible acquisition modes: continuous and discrete, which the programmers abbreviated to c and d. Controlling the mass spectrometer properly involves setting many, many parameters exactly right, and the parameters vary for each combination of ionization source and acquisition mode.

The programmers decided to invent a special text-file format to describe all of these parameters. Each such file they called a *spec file*. Finding just the right settings was difficult and took a lot of experimentation. During development, the programmers had to make many different versions of the spec files, so they included the date of the revision in the filename in order to distinguish them and to keep track of which worked best.

From the programmers' point of view, the job of the program code that runs the screen in figure 7.4 is to send the name of the spec file for the next run of the mass spectrometer to a subroutine that reads the file and sets up the mass spectrometer according to the settings in the file. The job of the user, then, is to choose a spec file. What, then, could be more logical than showing the user a list of all the most up-to-date spec files?

However, spec files are not part of the problem domain. From the user's point of view, the screen should look like the one in figure 7.5. You might not know what all those words mean, but the type of person who would use this mass spectrometer does. Notice that the ionization sources are not in alphabetical order. The top option, which is also the default, is the

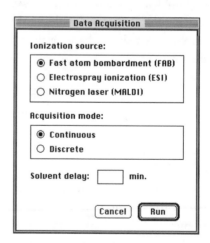

Figure 7.5 Screen redrawn with terms from problem domain

one that the users at this particular site will select most frequently. Alas, the technical writer is not in a position to improve the user interface.

What the technical writer is called upon to do in this situation is explain the mapping between the problem-domain concepts and the spec files, without letting the dates in the filenames sound too foolish. To figure out how to write this section of the manual, the technical writer needs to know what the spec file names mean, as well as the types of measurements that call for each combination of ionization source and acquisition mode. That would be the most pertinent possible information to put into the manual. Even if the user interface is designed well, the manual should still contain this information.

If no one has researched and documented these things early in the project, they'll be difficult to find out with only a week until the deadline—which is often when a technical writer is introduced to the project for the first time. Also, if no one understands these things, it's unlikely that the program will work correctly.

In summary, to write the user's manual or on-line help, a technical writer needs to know the exact same information as a user-interface designer, plus one more:

- The user-interface design

There are a number of reasons why software documentation has a reputation for being incomprehensible. One of most common reasons is not that the technical writer couldn't write well, but that information about the problem domain just wasn't available to him. Good requirements and specifications documents can fix that.

C H A P T E R   8

Two documents

Chapter 5 provided checklists of problem-specific information for each of five standard problem frames. This chapter presents complete lists of contents for both requirements and specifications: the additional details that flesh out each document as well as the main building blocks.

Note that figure 8.1 shows *lists* of contents, not *tables* of contents. Choosing a table of contents is a matter of document organization, the topic of chapter 14. Some organizations try to follow industry standard tables of contents, but it's hard to think of a worse error in technical writing than to fit one document's information into the table of contents from a document that described the requirements for some other project. That's what following a prefabricated table of contents amounts to. For that matter, you may well decide to break either document into many—the requirements document perhaps being split into several domain-description documents, a system overview document, several documents that give only brief lists of requirements, and a project glossary.

Furthermore, while the lists of contents are very extensive, there is no way that they can be exhaustive. Software is simply too varied a subject. The lists cover all the information needed in the vast majority of software projects, but don't hesitate to add more if you believe that your project needs them. However, in most projects, you

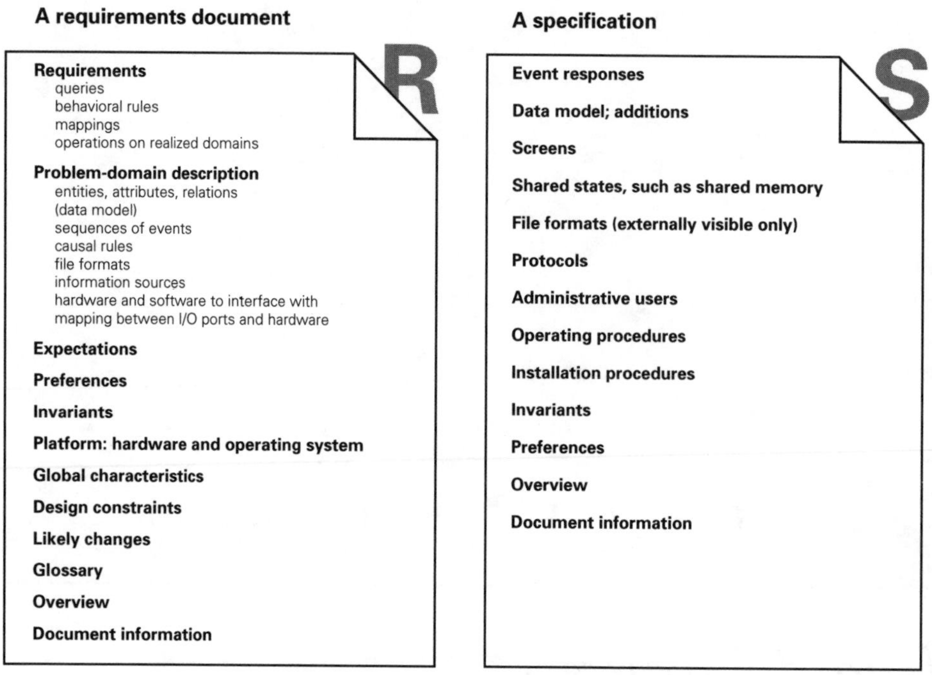

A requirements document

Requirements
  queries
  behavioral rules
  mappings
  operations on realized domains
	R

Problem-domain description
  entities, attributes, relations
  (data model)
  sequences of events
  causal rules
  file formats
  information sources
  hardware and software to interface with
  mapping between I/O ports and hardware

Expectations

Preferences

Invariants

Platform: hardware and operating system

Global characteristics

Design constraints

Likely changes

Glossary

Overview

Document information

A specification

Event responses

Data model; additions

Screens

Shared states, such as shared memory

File formats (externally visible only)

Protocols

Administrative users

Operating procedures

Installation procedures

Invariants

Preferences

Overview

Document information

S

Figure 8.1 Contents of the two types of document that this book is about

should describe fewer. Only a very large project would require everything shown in figure 8.1.

8.1 Contents of a requirements document

Requirements are the effects that the computer is to exert in the problem domain by virtue of the computer's programming. Different types of requirements and the problem-domain information that each needs have already been described in chapter 5.

Also, you may want to include some measure of each requirement's relative importance or priority, for purposes of deciding what to cut if the schedule starts to slip. However, it's difficult to be precise about importance. You can define a little set of importance ratings, each with a somewhat vague definition, like "3: critical to success of project," "2: strongly desired but possible to do without," "1: nice but not necessary." Unfortunately, these rating systems often leave much to be desired. Why not rate importance like this: "3: Must be implemented perfectly," "2: Needs to work, but not spectacularly well," "1: May have bugs"?

A simpler approach, however, is perfectly precise—just indicate the release numbers in which every requirement is to be implemented. The only reason you care about priority is to decide the sequence in which to implement features. Trying to numerically encode all the information that the customer would use to choose a sequence in which to implement features, such that you can make that choice without consulting the customer, is similar to the mistake of trying to document an entire open-ended problem in a requirements document. Since you need agreement from the customer to determine the sequence in which to implement features anyway, you actually gain nothing by trying to precisely document the customer's decision-making criteria.

You can, however, communicate the importance of implementing a feature correctly, at least to some extent, by explaining why the customer wants it—that is, the use to which the customer plans to apply the feature. "The ability to enter diacritical marks into messages is a convenience now that extended character sets are becoming standard," suggests one level of importance. "Most of the messages will be in Vietnamese, where diacritical marks carry a great deal of the meaning: for example, *ba* means father, *bá* means aunt, and *bà* means grandmother," clearly indicates a very different level of importance.

Remarks like these will help the development team make a good compromise between time spent designing and verifying all the different features. They also enable the team to make a type of judgement that the simple, numerical ratings don't help with: judgements about whether one feature would be useless without another feature. Knowing that most of the messages will be in Vietnamese probably affects many different features, not just one.

Problem-domain description, as noted earlier, normally takes up the majority of the document. Techniques of domain description are presented throughout chapters 9 through 11.

This book recommends, in most cases, including the data model with the domain description, even though the data model is part of the specification. The data model is simply the sets of data elements that are stored in the computer and is not to be confused with the part of the world it represents. Also, the description of the data model that belongs in either a requirements or specification document describes only states of the software that can be distinguished from the outside. It doesn't specify a relational database, an object-oriented database, an array of bytes in memory, or any other aspect of how the data is represented by the software.

The reason for merging specification into requirements in this one instance is that a good domain description maps very simply to a good data model. It's often simplest to just write both descriptions at once. We might as well say things like, "Customer name has a maximum of 40 characters," right along with the description of customer name.

File formats are also listed under domain description for programs whose requirements necessitate their reading files generated by other software. File formats *should* already be documented. But they often aren't, and understanding them precisely is often critical to a successful project. If the file formats are already documented, however, then you needn't duplicate the documentation. Just refer the reader to the correct place in another document.

In fact, you should try to refer as much as possible to existing documentation. Problem-domain description is a time-consuming and difficult task. If it's already been done, you can save yourself a great deal of effort by simply referring to it. If you refer to other documentation, though, you must provide a map between your own terminology and that found in the other document. A reader should not have to guess that loader in your document is filler in the document you referred to.

If your organization plans to make a number of different programs for roughly the same problem domain, then a useful strategy is to create a single, master problem-domain document. Each program's requirements document can then be very short because it merely refers to the master problem-domain document rather than duplicates it.

Expectations are the results of the software that are the customer's motive for paying for it—the expected effect of fulfilling the requirements. This does not have to be a detailed section, nor does it need to be included at all in many documents (for example, in the requirements for a controller for an anti-skid braking system). However, it's a great advantage to the development staff to know that the reason new software is being ordered is because the previous software was too difficult to use, or because employees were spending too much time going to the shelves to verify that inventory records were correct. Expectations tells the staff what the customer is really interested in.

Preferences are criteria for choosing among different designs that meet requirements: principles by which to make trade-offs. You may have thought, with all the emphasis on precision in requirements, that surely something is missing because not everything that a customer wants is so precise. Indeed, there are two common mistakes regarding vague desires about the software: to omit them, or to force them into precise language. Preferences are the place to describe vague desires.

For example, it may be most important to the customer that the user interface be as fast as possible. The customer may consider ease of learning, and ease of use for people without long experience with the software, fairly unimportant. This is valuable information, so mention it as a preference. It can't be a requirement because you cannot test a statement like, "The designers chose speed over ease of learning whenever faced with a trade-off."

It would be a mistake, however, to describe this preference in precise, quantative terms. Should you specify a precise, numerical formula to balance operation time against ease of use as reported by first-time users on a scale of 1 to 10, like this?

Maximize: $3 \times (10 \text{ sec.} - \text{median operation time}) + 2 \times (\text{median ease-of-use learning rating})$

By trying to be so precise, it's easy to lose sight of the actual preference. So, just write down, "Speed of use by experienced users is more important than ease of learning," and explain the reasons for this preference. Knowing that the customer plans to hire only four daily users for this program, the development staff understands much more about how to make trade-offs to serve the customer than any numerical rating could possibly communicate.

Note that preferences are not necessarily vague. They're just the one place where vagueness is acceptable. A more precise preference might be, "The faster the block-transmission speeds, the better, but only up to 1 block per 0.7 milliseconds. Speeds faster than that provide no benefit, since the microwave transmitter won't be able to keep up." Notice again how explaining the rationale makes the preference much clearer.

Invariants are conditions that are never to change, or at least never to be violated between events even though they may be temporarily violated during an event. There are two main types of invariants: (a) requirements that state conditions that the system is supposed to maintain even as other operations take place, such as "Room temperature stays between high-setting and low-setting of thermostat"; and (b) redundancy added to requirements to help ensure their correctness.

There's no need to treat type (a) invariants any differently from other requirements. The interface designer tries to design machine behavior that keeps them true, the same as any other type of requirement. Type (b) invariants are different. They state conditions that the requirements themselves are intended to maintain so that if some combination of the behavior described by the requirements would violate the invariant, then there is an error in the requirements. Because readers must interpret these statements differently from requirements, you must distinguish them by explicitly calling them invariants.

For example, the requirements may describe accounts to be stored in the computer, along with a set of transaction types that can affect them.* Each transaction in the document has been carefully defined so that the books always balance; that is, the result of any transaction is to add as much to account *A* as it removes from account *B*. Defining the more complex transactions is tricky and error-prone. A way to help catch errors in the requirements is to explicitly state the condition that each transaction was trying to achieve: "Invariant: For any transaction, the sum of all additions and subtractions to all affected accounts is zero," and/or "Invariant: assets plus liabilities equals equity."

---

* Such accounts would form a realized domain, described in section 4.5.

Explicitly stating these invariants becomes especially helpful when people modify the requirements in future versions of the software. Often the people who make the changes are not as familiar with the problem as the people who wrote the original document, yet they must define more-complex features. If they add a transaction that shuffles money between three different accounts, they may well inadvertently violate one of the invariants. A person reviewing the document, even without knowledge of accounting, might well spot the error if the invariants are stated explicitly.

Invariants are supported by *assertions*, a programming technique that also works by redundantly stating what the rest of the program is intended to bring about. (Assertions are explained more in depth in the glossary.) Thus, the program itself can serve as a check on the correctness of requirements. Furthermore, if the requirements are correct, assertions based on invariants help find programming errors. In formal methods, special software can check requirements and specifications directly against the invariant statements. See *Invariants* in chapter 15 for specific writing tips.

The *platform* is the machine to be configured. As software is a configuration of a very configurable machine, the most fundamental piece of information needed to create any piece of software is what kind of machine is to be configured. Here *machine* means both hardware and operating system and/or other software that runs on the same hardware. A PC running Windows and a PC running Linux are the same hardware, but from the standpoint of a programmer, they are two different machines. For a Java program that is interpreted by a Web browser, the Web browser is the platform. The hardware and operating system are, implicitly, anything that can run the Web browser. Be sure to include version numbers: "XYZ/OS version 4.6 or later." See also the information needed by testers in section 7.5.

Global characteristics (a non-standard term) are properties that the system as a whole is to possess, as opposed to the separate requirement statements that usually have a nearly one-to-one mapping to segments of program code. Four of the most common global characteristics that people want to see included in a requirements document are system availability, reliability, safety, and security. Another that is worth mentioning is scale.

System availability is the time each day that the system is to be available for use and able to fulfill the requirements. For example, if users must be able to operate the system 24 hours a day, 7 days a week, this needs to be stated explicitly.

Reliability is a tricky matter in software. Most other engineering fields build artifacts out of components that break down at known rates. For example, a beam made of a certain material supporting a certain load might have a mean time to failure (MTTF) of ten years. You can specify that the assembly that the beam is part of has an MTTF of as long as you like—say, a hundred years or a thousand years. The engineers can choose different materials, different manufacturing techniques, or different testing techniques to achieve the desired MTTF, or they can add redundancy to the assembly: more beams that support the same load, other subsystems that perform the same tasks, and so on. The more redundant subsystems in an assembly, the longer the assembly's MTTF—longer than the MTTF of any individual component.

Software doesn't work that way. Software never wears out. The storage medium containing the software has an MTTF, but the software itself always works exactly the same way. A fuel pump might work fine today and fail tomorrow, but software is a pattern of bits—a configuration of a machine, not the machine itself—and therefore follows the same rules every day.

Software failures are due to those rules being wrong. There is currently no way to design software to a specified MTTF—to design the rules so that they generate inappropriate behavior only once every ten or hundred years. Adding redundant code—say, two or three subroutines to perform the same function—may well cause new bugs rather than mask them.

This makes reliability requirements for software somewhat useless. What's the point of telling the programmers to design the system to have an MTTF of a hundred years if they know of no design techniques to achieve this? Some people are doing research on statistical checks for faulty lines of code, but it's a long way from something that programmers or testers can apply to yield a specified MTTF. What if the problem is not that an individual line is wrong, but that the logic of the whole subroutine is wrong? What about the likelihood—much more important in most software—that programmers will introduce new bugs when making modifications because the comments were incorrect or too hard to understand? How do you design the comments to achieve a specified MTTF over ten years of maintenance?

Instead of making a quantitative statement of how reliable the software is supposed to be, you can try to give some measure of the *cost* of bugs and downtime. For example, if the customer's salesmen bring in $120,000 per hour while the system is up, from 1:00 p.m. to 4:00 p.m. on business days, this should indicate how important it is that the system not crash during those times. This is not a genuine reliability requirement, but it's much better than nothing.

If safety is a factor in the design of the software, it is best treated as either an ordinary requirement or an invariant, such as, "Invariant: The paper-cutting blade never moves while any part of a human operator is within the blade path." Statistical measures of safety apply to software no better than statistical measures of reliability.

In many cases, security is best treated as a requirement or attribute of requirements. If there are queries that only managers are allowed to run, then those queries should say, "Can be run only by managers." Security as a global characteristic should pertain to who is to be allowed to operate the software, who is to be allowed to access its data, or who is to be prevented from doing so. Again, a brief description of the costs of allowing data out, or allowing it to be corrupted, gives people a better idea of how they should figure security into their specifications and program designs. The cost need not be in dollars: "Allowing Splenetix Corporation's chemical-bond database to leave the company would completely destroy its competitive advantage. Sacrifice performance, functionality, and the schedule rather than allow any breach of security on this database."

For many projects, the above global characteristics are not very important. When they're not important, trying to state them precisely makes the document sound silly and undermines its credibility. "Required security level on cat-lover's mailing list: 0.0. Safety requirements: the cat-lover's mailing list shall not cause injury to persons or property." In these cases, it's best to omit them entirely.

A global characteristic that is worth stating for virtually all software, however, is scale. Scale is the number of instances of the various objects and activities described in the requirements and problem-domain description. An accounting system for ten or twenty people to run in a small business might have identical requirements and problem-domain concepts as an accounting system for a small business with offices in three cities. The software, however, needs to be designed very differently. The larger system needs much more parallelism, which is more complex and difficult to design.

So, how many users will there be? How many queries will they likely run per day? How many flights take off per day? How many planes are there? The answers to these questions do not have to be precise, but they should at least give an order-of-magnitude estimate, providing enough precision to enable the programmers to design a system that can handle a real workload.

Peak levels are also important to document, especially in large systems, such as how many flights are booked on an average day, and how many the day before Thanksgiving. If the system works beautifully for 364 days and crashes on the airline's most profitable day of the year, you can imagine how the customer will react.

Sometimes included among global characteristics is *performance:* how fast the system runs. However, performance is usually best understood as an attribute of specific requirements, not as a global characteristic. If the system needs to generate a certain report in no more than fifteen minutes, this is best documented as part of the description of that report. If the software must generate an acknowledgement signal within 0.2 μs upon receipt of a cerain input signal, this is best documented as part of the rules for how the software is to respond to the input signal.

Documenting performance characteristics can be tricky, again because software is different from physical artifacts. The average response time for a type of query depends heavily on exactly which queries the users make most often and what data is currently stored in the system. Again, a good strategy is to provide the programmers with some background so they can make intelligent trade offs. For example, knowing that the users nearly always run queries about transactions within the past month, but during a yearly audit, they run queries stretching back the past year, allows the programmers to optimize performance accordingly.

However, programmers can often design for specific worst-case response times. If you know that the system would be useless if it took more than a certain amount of time to answer a query, this is critical information to include in the document. Don't, however, pull numbers out of the air just for the sake of being numerical and precise; this undermines the credibility of the document.

Because the phrase *global characteristics* is neither self-explanatory nor standard, it's best not to title a section by that name. Just find places for each topic that you need to cover. They can all be subsections of an introductory section, or you can have a Safety and Reliability section—whatever provides the simplest organization within that one document.

Design constraints are statements that deliberately violate the separation of subject matters shown in figure 3.1. If the customer insists that every variable in the source code be in upper case, you know that that's part of program design and not a requirement, but what are you going to say? In the document, call this a design constraint rather than a requirement. This shows that you aren't confused about the difference between requirements and program design.

More realistic design constraints include matters pertaining to the source code's usefulness to the customer once development is done. For example, the customer may have a staff of COBOL programmers who will take over maintenance of the program once development is done. In this case, it may be of the highest importance to the customer that the program be written in COBOL, and even that it follow their coding conventions—say, putting every variable in the source code in upper case.

As this example illustrates, you should explain the reason for each design constraint—the descriptive statements that are the basis for the prescriptive constraint. If a design constraint sounds arbitrary, programmers are likely to disregard it, thinking that you put it in only because you either didn't know what you were doing or because you were following a standard that demands that the programming language and coding conventions be mentioned in every requirements document.

Likely changes are changes that you expect in future versions of the software, such as future requirements or changes to the problem domain. You don't have to describe the changes in enough detail to implement them. The purpose of writing them down now is to help the programmers design in order to make the future modifications easier. It is impossible to design a program to make any kind of modification easy. You can design to allow modifications in one direction or modifications in another direction, but seldom—even with object-oriented programming—can you design for all possible directions of modification, and it's unlikely that a program will be easy to modify in ways that are totally unexpected. You can't possibly anticipate all future changes, but you can usually anticipate some. Documenting them now, however briefly, can be a very effective way to cut future development costs.

A *glossary* is a great help in all but the smallest documents. Include not only the major terms from the problem domain, but any term that you use that some readers might not understand. For example, if you mention TSRs in an example somewhere, you should define TSR in the glossary, even if TSRs are only tangentially related to the subject of the document.

On a large project with many requirements documents, you can save yourself a lot of duplication by creating a single glossary for all of them and just refer to it in each document. Or, people can cut and paste from the master glossary when they write new requirements documents. See *glossary* in chapter 15 for specific writing tips.

An *overview* is almost always necessary to show readers how each of the document's many parts—all the different requirements as well as the many parts of the problem domain—fit together. An overview says the very same thing as the rest of the document; it is a helpful redundancy. The difference is that the overview omits details in order to make the overall structure clear. It is similar to a rough sketch.

Document information is the following information about the document:

- Table of contents
- List of related documents
- Typographical conventions
- Software version that the document applies to
- Date when the document was last modified
- Change log
- Document preparer(s)
- An index, for large documents

Naturally, information about the document should take up a tiny proportion of both the document and your time. The document is about requirements, not itself.

The list of related documents is especially important if there are file formats or protocols that the programmers need to read.

If the document is especially huge, or you've split it into a group of documents, then you may need to write a document overview to explain how all the parts fit together. Normally, though, the table of contents alone should provide an adequate overview of the document.

A requirements document should briefly state its typographical conventions for indicating which statements are requirements and which statements are not, that is, which statements are prescriptive and which are descriptive. For example:

Typographical Conventions

Requirements and preferences are shown in bold sans-serif type, like this:

R-2.4 Approve no prescription refill if the number of days since the last fill is less than 90% (rounding up) of the number of daily doses in the last fill.

All other text is purely descriptive, unless otherwise indicated.

The example to illustrate the convention should be a real example, copied from later in the document. In many documents, the convention is so obvious that it doesn't even need to be stated explicitly. See *table of contents* and *title page* in chapter 15 for more tips.

8.2 Contents of a specification

A program specification is the description of interfaces. A specification document contains little else but descriptions of events that involve both a user or a piece of hardware or software that interacts with the system, and the system's response to that event. If the system interfaces with two or more other systems, perhaps in addition to human users, it's often wisest to create a separate document for each interface.

Most of the concepts and techniques for describing interfaces are the same as those for describing requirements and the problem domain: there are externally visible objects in the system (instead of outside the system) to describe, state transitions made by the system in response to events (instead of state transitions that happen outside the system), decision rules about how the system behaves (instead of rules describing how objects outside the system behave), and so forth.

Event responses are how the system responds to events in the problem domain: what data stored by the system changes, and any activity initiated by the system in response. Very often, the events of interest are not phenomena shared with the system. So, the specification addresses the question of how the event of interest gets to the system—for example, by manual data entry, or by other means. See section 10.3 for more information.

Additions to the data model are data to be stored in the system that was not described in the requirements document, usually to serve a purpose pertaining to the maintenance of the software rather than a purpose found in the problem domain. For example, the system needs to store user preferences and passwords, even if these do not correspond directly to any requirements or problem-domain phenomena.

The specification of a user interface must contain *screens*. Screen layout is a subtle, skilled job, best performed by a user-interface designer with a prototyping tool, and not left for a programmer to do casually while coding. Ideally, the screens in the document are bitmaps captured from the prototyping tool. If you don't have a prototyping tool, drawing the screens with pencil and paper and scanning them in also works.

Shared states are objects or states of objects that the system shares with the outside world, as opposed to events. The most common type of shared state is a shared segment of memory, as in a program that communicates by semaphore with other programs running concurrently. The specification needs to document all the information needed to implement this shared memory: its location, size, and contents.

The specification also needs to document the *file formats* of any files that are designed to fulfill the requirements and are of importance outside the software. A typical example is a configuration file, such as a .INI file in Microsoft Windows. Documenting file formats is similar to documenting shared memory. You need to indicate the name of the file, the directory where it resides, and its contents. Files that users can conceivably access but which they have no reason to access don't need to be described in the specification.

Protocols are any communication protocols that the development staff designs in order to fulfill requirements, as opposed to protocols already defined in the problem domain. Most software doesn't include them, but software that provides services to other, software not yet written, often does. Similarly, if the software has an application program interface (API), the specification must include that, too; in fact, that may be the vast majority of the specification.

Administrative users are special users whose roles are invented in order to fulfill requirements, rather than users found in the problem domain. Typical roles for administrative users are editing configuration files, setting up user privileges, and backing up and restoring data.

Descriptions of administrative users should not be allowed to pollute the requirements document. They are strictly part of the solution, not of the problem. Describing them in a requirements document makes it appear that the purpose of the software is to serve them, whereas the truth is that their purpose is to serve the software. Inventing them is only one of many possible design decisions.

Operating procedures are activities that users are responsible for performing—that is, the correct way to operate the software. When you design screens and buttons and fields, you have in mind particular sequences in which users are supposed to open the screens, click the buttons, and fill the fields. If you keep this information only in your head, it is unlikely that users will be able to divine it. The operating procedures are series of action-response pairs. Each pair says what the user is supposed to do, and what the system does in response.

The testers and technical writer are especially interested in the operating procedures. You might simply tell them to the technical writer, who can immediately put them into the user's manual.

An important type of operating procedure is backing up and restoring data. This does not correspond to any particular requirement or element of the problem domain because it corresponds simultaneously to all the requirements. It's an action taken to keep the software functioning. Backup and restore procedures are strictly specification, not requirements. Like administrative users, they serve the software, rather than the software being designed to serve them.

Installation procedures are a special type of operating procedures to install the software onto its platform. It's often difficult to know what the installation procedures will be until most of the programming is done. There's no harm in deferring the writing of this part of the specification until near the end of the project. However, every time the programmers produce an interim release for the testers and technical writer to look at, they should document the installation procedures. Especially in those chaotic times, it can be difficult for the staff to figure out how to install the program correctly without written documentation.

The installation procedures should also state how the program recognizes previous versions of the software and what the program does to them. In effect, the platform and existing versions of the software form a secondary problem domain that the specification must address, just as it addresses the problem domain described in the requirements. This means that the installation procedures also have to describe every possible kind of thing that can go wrong, such as running out of disk space and how the software behaves in response.

Finally, *invariants* and *preferences* are the same as in requirements, except they're a direction to the programmers who implement the interfaces, as opposed to a direction to the interface-designers who devise ways to fulfill requirements. The *overview* and *document information* are, again, the same as in requirements.

C H A P T E R   9

Classes and relations

What's in the problem domain? This chapter shows how to answer that question and how to describe the individuals in the problem domain, the attributes they possess, and the types of relations that can exist between individuals.

The techniques for describing individuals, attributes, and relations apply equally well to describing the problem domain as to describing sets of data to be stored in the computer, so you might apply these techniques in both a requirements document and a specification. Data items are individuals in the machine domain, just as the real world objects they represent are individuals in the problem domain. As noted in chapter 8, in many projects, particularly simpler ones, it's most convenient to describe both the problem domain and data in the requirements document by including this one part of the specification in the requirements.

The next two chapters tell how to answer the questions, "What happens in the problem domain?" and "What causes it to happen?"

9.1 Two kinds of sets

Figure 9.1 depicts two kinds of sets that appear in many different domains, especially in information problems:

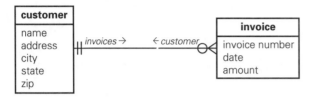

Figure 9.1 A class diagram

One kind of set is shown by the two boxes marked customer and invoice. Sometimes called an *entity set* or *class*, this is a set whose members all possess the same attributes. Every customer has a name, address, city, state, and zip code. Every invoice has an invoice number, date, and amount.

Sometimes it's convenient to draw a class diagram without attributes, as shown in figure 9.2. This can be a helpful choice if a diagram becomes especially complex.

Figure 9.2 Class diagram without attributes

The word entity literally means "thing," but these sets do not need to contain physical objects. They can contain anything from elements of a database to scenes in seventeenth-century British plays. The only rule is that all the members of an entity set have attributes that make sense to compare: any two names are comparable, any two addresses are comparable, and so on.

The other kind of set is shown by the line connecting the two boxes. Called a *relation*, each element of this kind of set is a pair of members of entity sets (or, less commonly, groups of three or four or more). In this case, the relation matches each customer with that customer's invoices. The set of pairs (*customer, invoice*) includes one pair for each invoice, showing which customer the invoice belongs to. For example, these two pairs:

    (George Gibbons, invoice #1019)
    (George Gibbons, invoice #1184)

Figure 9.3 Chen ERD

link the customer George Gibbons with both of his invoices.

Relations are described further in section 9.5. For now, it will suffice to say that the funny symbols on the line connecting customer and invoice indicate that for every customer, there correspond zero or more invoices, but for every invoice there is only one customer.

The term class is becoming more popular than entity set, so this book will stay with class and *class diagram*. However, a term still in common use for the type of diagram shown in figure 9.1 is *entity-relation diagram*, or *ERD*, invented by Peter Chen. Chen's original entity-relation diagrams depicted relations with triangles, as shown in figure 9.3; this notation is also still in use.

Much of the terminology in the world of software is in a state of flux, including the terminology for concepts pertaining to sets. Whereas entity-relation diagrams were originally conceived as a way to describe the world outside the computer, the term *class* originated in object-oriented programming. There, it referred not to a set but rather to the combination of a data structure with program code that operated on it. The subroutines associated with the data structure are listed in a third segment of the class's box in a class diagram. Consequently, sometimes *class* is defined in ways like "an abstraction of behavior."* As people have attempted to apply concepts from object-oriented programming to requirements, the word *class* has started to lose some of its connection to programming.

In this book, by *class* we mean nothing more or less than a set of comparable elements. The elements can be things in the real world, like trucks, tractors, and cornfields, or they can be data stored in a database, such as the records stored on disk of a corporation's trucks, tractors, and cornfields. They can be anything whatsoever. However, since the focus of this book is requirements, here we most often define classes of things that exist outside the computer.

Naturally, in your own documentation, substitute *entity-set, type, category, set* or whatever you, the customer, and the development staff are most comfortable with.

Be aware that there is a danger in using the word *class*. Many programmers and other people who've read about object-oriented programming stop hearing the word

---

* A little more information about object-oriented programming techniques versus requirements is in section 12.2.

class in its everyday sense of a set of like elements, and understand it to mean only a type of representation created in object-oriented programming—a data structure with a set of associated subroutines. It's not unusual for them to keep interpreting it that way even if you tell them otherwise, and even if you add text to the requirements document telling them that that's not what you mean. This is a common effect of a programmer's natural concern with the world of programming: the problem domain disappears over the horizon, along with the vocabulary for talking about it.

"This is all design," someone complains, "because you're talking about objects." In fact, the word *object* never appears in the document. Only the word class does, but sometimes that's enough to trigger the the mental association with object-oriented programming.

"But the world is filled with objects," you reply, "and I need to talk about them. What do you suggest?"

The complainer suggests, "You're supposed to describe the software in a design-independent way: a logical model of the system, without specifying whether the design will be object-oriented or not."

You reply, "But I'm not trying to describe the software at all. I'm trying to describe bicycle parts and the stages in which people assemble them into bicycles."

If this happens to you, try calling them *sets*. This book would call them sets, were there not a host of other kinds of sets to describe, too.

9.2 Classes

The purpose of documenting classes and relations is to provide the vocabulary in terms of which to make statements later on, such as requirement statements, statements about actions that occur in the problem domain, and statements about causal rules. To serve this purpose, a requirements document must provide the following information about each class:

Table 9.1 Information to document about each class

Class information	Where described
The name of the class	(Not covered in this book)
A definition of what kind of thing the class can contain. In other words, an answer to the question, "What are you talking about?"	*Definitions* in chapter 15
A list of each of the class's attributes, including a definition of each attribute, the set of all possible values of the attribute, and the meaning of each possible value	Sections 9.2–9.4

Table 9.1 Information to document about each class

Class information	Where described
Which attributes uniquely identify members of the class, if any	Section 9.8
Each class to which the class bears a relation	Sections 9.5–9.7
Each event, if any, that affects members of the class, and which attributes and relations it affects	Section 10.2

Here is an example from requirements for restaurant software:

2.4 Orders

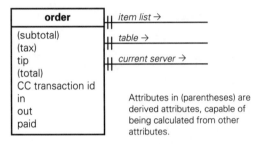

Attributes in (parentheses) are derived attributes, capable of being calculated from other attributes.

An *order* is a set of menu items ordered by one or more people at a table. A party at a single table might have more than one order, such as if they ask for "separate checks." Also called a "check," "bill," or "tab."

Attribute	Description	Affected by
item list	One-to-many: The list of items on this order (see section 2.9). For any order, there are zero or more items in the item list; for any item, there is exactly one order. An order has zero items when the party has sat down at the table but not yet ordered anything.	open, change
table	Many-to-one: The table where the party who placed the order is currently sitting. For any order, there is exactly one table; for any table, there are zero or more orders.	open, order-moves

Attribute	Description	Affected by
current server	Many-to-one: The server currently responsible for this order. For any order, there is exactly one current server; at any time, a server is responsible for zero or more orders.	open, server-takes-over
subtotal	Dollars and cents: the sum of the amounts of each item in the order. (Derived attribute.)	open, change
tax	Dollars and cents: the amount of sales tax on the order.	open, change
tip	Dollars and cents: the amount of the tip.	close
total	Dollars and cents: the sum of subtotal + tax + tip. (Derived attribute.)	open, change, close
CC transaction id	20-character alphanumeric ID code returned by credit card bank, uniquely identifying the transaction in which a customer paid the order. Applicable only if the customer paid by credit card.	close
in	Date/time: when the order was opened.	open
out	Date/time: when the order was closed.	close
paid	True/false: whether the bill was paid.	close

The preceding documentation is called a *class description*. A class description describes, in text, the following:

- The definition of the kind of thing included in the class, as shown by the first sentence above: "An order is a set of menu items ordered by one or more people at a table."

- A definition of each of the class's attributes, including the set of all the possible values of each attribute

- Optionally, a list of each of the events that affect the attribute, or a complete description of each of the events along with the set of all possible sequences in which they occur. This information needs to be somewhere in the document, not necessarily in a class description. Deciding where to place the description of events is a matter of organization, discussed in chapter 14. Techniques for describing events are in section 10.2.

- Any other information about the class that you think would be helpful to a reader

A nice technique is to cut the class's rectangle out of a larger class diagram, including the connecting lines, and paste it above the class description, as shown at the top of the example. (The larger class diagram is shown in figure 9.11.) This serves a number of purposes. It helps the reader see the class in relation to all the other classes without being overwhelmed by a complex diagram. It encourages the reader to go look at the more complex diagram that includes all the classes, because now the reader has something specific to look for—this class, and the other classes that it connects to. Finally, the graphic breaks up a section of the document that could easily consist of many pages of uninterrupted text, making the document easier to skim through when looking for highlights or an overall feel for the content.

Describing the attributes in a table is another good technique. This makes the attributes much easier to find than if they were buried within a stream of paragraphs. The first three attributes in the example, item list, table, and current server, are relations, described in section 9.5.

There are several noteworthy points about this particular class description. First of all, even though it's from a familiar, everyday domain, it makes some distinctions that we normally pass by. For example, one might have simply associated an order with a table: one order, one table. The definition above carefully notes that a single table can have multiple orders.

Second, note that the Affected by column is strictly descriptive. It makes statements about events that take place in the real world, regardless of how the software behaves. It does not state that the software must affect anything. That will come when we write requirement statements.

Third, notice that after current-server, there is not a single complete sentence. Instead of writing:

in	The in attribute is the exact date and time when the order was opened. The in attribute's type is date/time.	The in attribute is affected by the open event.

we simply write:

in	Date/time: when the order was opened.	open

The shorter version is easier to read and understand, and omits no information. It's also easier to write.

Finally, there is nothing sacred about the layout of the table. Even the Affected by column is just a convenience for the reader, not a necessity. You should feel free to adjust or completely rework the format of the table to suit whatever you are describing, perhaps omitting the Affected by column if you see no need to cross-reference attributes to events or if a lot of the attributes are affected by many events. Add lines to the table if it becomes difficult to read without them. (See *tables* in chapter 15.)

If an attribute requires a long description, then it's best to describe it only briefly in the table and reserve the long description for the text that follows the table. The need for this is most common in attributes that are states that the members of a class can take on. We'll see some of these in the next section.

9.2.1 Esoteric problem domains

A common mistake in writing requirements for fields that everyone knows about is to omit critical details, either because the analyst assumed that the programmers would know them or because the analyst didn't research the problem domain carefully—"I already know all that stuff." So typical mistakes in restaurant software include failing to track commonplace aspects of the restaurant business that most of us seldom think about: that a server's shift ended before a customer finished eating, leaving the server who replaces him to take the entire tip, or failing to track the percentage of tips that is owed to the busboys.

When the problem domain is esoteric, a more common problem is that the analyst is very familiar with the problem domain, perhaps because they worked in it for many years, and while the analyst researches and understands the problem domain perfectly, the analyst writes documentation that only a fellow expert can understand.

Here is an example of a poorly written class description from the somewhat esoteric field of telephone networks:

A *node* is the top-level division of the network. Nodes are the most important breakdown for purposes of design.

Attribute	Description
name	This is the node's six-letter code.
state	The status of the node with respect to its point in the design cycle.
polygon	This is the precise location of the node.

Attribute	Description
house count	Identifies the node's house count.

The problem with this description is that if you don't already know what a node is, or you don't already know how nodes are named, or you don't already know what states nodes go through, and so on, this description doesn't tell you. The analyst is writing in his own internal mental shorthand, and not the language of readers who are ignorant of nodes. Saying that nodes are "important" communicates nothing to someone who doesn't already know why they're important.

Here is a much better description:

A *node* is the geographical area served by a single launch amp. It includes up to 440 subscriber services—the maximum that a single launch amp can supply.

Attribute	Description
name	A six-letter code uniquely identifying the node. Format is described below.
state	The current phase of the node's design cycle. See below for complete description.
polygon	A series of *x, y* coordinates (NAD86), each of which is a vertex of a polygon bounding the node. Typical node polygons have no more than 10 vertices, though conceivably one could have as many as several hundred.
house count	The number of buildings in the node.

The format of a node name is as follows:

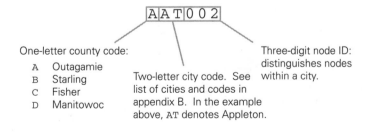

One-letter county code:
- A   Outagamie
- B   Starling
- C   Fisher
- D   Manitowoc

Two-letter city code. See list of cities and codes in appendix B. In the example above, AT denotes Appleton.

Three-digit node ID: distinguishes nodes within a city.

No two nodes have the same node name.

The possible states of a node are as follows:

proposed   The phone company has proposed to the public utilities commission to build the node and is awaiting approval.

design   The node is currently being designed.

construction   The design is currently being constructed.

operational   The node is delivering service to subscribers.

The terms *launch amp, subscriber service,* and *NAD86* would likely be explained elsewhere, following the principle of not trying to say everything at once. Here is how those definitions might read:

A *launch amp* is a piece of equipment that converts the digital signals from a fiber-optic cable into equivalent analog signals to be sent over coaxial cable. A single launch amp can source up to 440 subscriber services connected via coaxial cable.

A *subscriber service* is a single phone line and/or cable TV hookup. That is, a subscriber service can be a phone line, a cable TV subscription, or both at once. This is because our equipment sends both types of signals over the same cable; we need only connect a single coaxial cable to deliver both services. Sometimes called "service" for short.*

NAD86 (North American Datum 1986) is a coordinate system describing the entire surface of the Earth, based on satellite measurements made in 1986, and superseding the NAD27 coordinate system made by land measurements in 1927. To give the accuracy required to locate telephone equipment, NAD86 coordinates require at least six digits both to the right and left of the decimal point.

This isn't easy reading, but it's readable, and when you've read it, you know what nodes are. The information is now on paper, not just in the analyst's head.

Now you, too, know something of the language of the problem domain. You can think of new questions to ask, like, "Once a node is operational, does all design stop, or does the phone company continue to design and construct changes even while people are receiving service?" or "Does the public utilities commission approve *designing* the node or *constructing* the node? If the latter, does the phone company ever start designing

---

* If you're interested in learning about telephony, be aware that these definitions vary a bit from reality in order to illustrate techniques of documentation.

while the node is still proposed but not approved?" These are possible errors in the analysis. Perhaps the reality is that there are three somewhat independent status attributes. A programmer, thinking about how to model these states, could come up with these questions despite having no prior knowledge of what is done at telephone companies. That probably wouldn't happen if all the document provided was the names of the four node states, or, worse, a single-letter code for each state.

The brief description of polygons provides important information often left out of requirements documents: what are the most likely values, and what are the most extreme values? Without the mention of "typically no more than 10" and "conceivably as many as several hundred," a programmer may have assumed that no more than eight vertices would ever be needed and hard-coded the data structure for nodes to contain exactly eight slots for polygon vertices. Now the programmer knows to apply a more flexible design pattern when designing the data structure. The numbers provided are not precise, but they are good enough.

There's nothing like a simple graphic to describe each segment of an alphanumeric code. Note that both the graphic and the discussion of node states go after the table of attributes, not inside it. Even this is not a rule; but it's a option to keep in mind if a table you're making becomes unwieldy.

9.3 All possible values

Table 9.1 suggests that you need to indicate all the possible values that each attribute can have. That may seem like an outlandish demand—"All of them? But there could be trillions!" Actually, in most cases it is very easy.

There are two main strategies. One is to refer to a well-known set of possible values, such as the sets of integers or real numbers. Often this is called a data type, but of course you aren't necessarily describing data when you talk about attributes. Figure 9.2 some common attribute types and information that you need to specify whenever you describe an attribute.

If people had always indicated what future dates they were interested in, or the programmers had told customers what range of dates their software supported, there would have been no Year 2000 problem. (In the latter case, the customers would have protested long before the year 2000.)

Also of interest to the programmers are the most common values, as well as the extreme ones. Sometimes, by knowing that a narrow range of values is most common, a programmer can make great improvements to the speed of the program.

Table 9.2 Common attribute types

Type	Extra information
Integer	Is zero allowed, or just positive numbers? Are negative numbers possible? What is the highest integer value possible? The lowest?
Real number	How many digits to the right of the decimal point? How many to the left? What are the highest and lowest values possible?
Dollars and cents	Keep track of pennies? What is the greatest possible amount? Are negative amounts allowed?
Date	What is the earliest date of interest? The furthest in the future?
Time of day	With what precision—hours, hours and minutes, hours and minutes and seconds, or even more precise than that?
Date/time	Same as for date and time of day.
True/false	(None.)
Text	Maximum number of characters. Do any characters not occur, such as lower-case characters? Are any special characters possible, such as characters with diacritical marks, like å?

If all or most of the dates and times that will be of interest to the program will be between 1990 and 2050, you can save yourself the trouble of repeating this in every attribute definition by stating it once near the beginning of the document in a little section called Attribute Types. Similarly, for integers or other types of numeric ranges, you might want to define—"Angle (real number in range 0..360, or 0..2π)," "Capacity (0..100,000 gallons)," and so on.

If you define such a set of attribute types, you can also define one- or two-letter codes for them. You can then put these codes into a middle column in a table of attributes:

Attribute	Type	Description
item list	1→M	The list of items on this order (see section 2.9). For any order, there are zero or more items in the item list; for any item, there is exactly one order. An order has zero items when the party has sat down at the table but not yet ordered anything.
table	M→1	The table where the party who placed the order is currently sitting. For any order, there is exactly one table; for any table, there are zero or more orders.
current server	M→1	The server currently responsible for this order. For any order, there is exactly one current server; at any time, a server is responsible for zero or more orders.

Attribute	Type	Description
subtotal	$	The sum of the amounts of each item in the order. (Derived attribute.)
tax	$	The amount of sales tax on the order.
tip	$	The amount that the customer tipped the server.
total	$	The sum of subtotal + tax + tip. (Derived attribute.)
CC transaction id	S20	20-character alphanumeric ID code returned by credit card bank, uniquely identifying the transaction in which a customer paid the order. Applicable only if the customer paid by credit card.
in	DT	Date/time when the order was opened.
out	DT	Date/time when the order was closed.
paid	T/F	Whether the bill was paid.

In this case, you would define each type code early in the document, in a table like this:

Type code	Description
I	Integer: a whole number in the range −32768 to +32767. Range may be restricted in attribute description.
I+	A positive integer—a "count."
0+	A natural number: an integer zero or greater.
$	Dollars and cents.
F$m.n$	A floating-point number with up to m digits to the left of the decimal point and up to n digits to the right.
Sn	A string: text containing up to n characters. Characters may come only from the 7-bit ASCII character set
text	Free-form text, with no limit on the number of characters. Implementation must support at least 4096 characters, preferably more.

Type code	Description
D	A date from January 1, 1900 to December 31, 2099. (Implementation may support a wider date range.)
T	A time of day: includes hours and minutes, but not seconds.
DT	Combination of D and T.
T/F	True or false.
*	Special type; list of possible values is provided in attribute description.
M→1	Many-to-one relation: a member of another class that can correspond to many members of this class.
1→M	One-to-many relation: a set of members in another class that correspond to a single member of this class.
M→M	Many-to-many relation: a set of members in another class that correspond to a set of members of this class.

Of course, there is no standard set of type codes; this list is only an example.

Notice that the true/false type is called T/F, not B or boolean. Everyone knows what true and false are, but few aside from programmers and mathematicians know what Boolean algebra is.

The second main strategy for indicating all the possible values of an attribute is simply to list them all, one by one. This strategy works best on two types of attributes: state attributes and attributes whose values must be described with words rather than numbers. We've seen an example of state attributes in the node states previously described. States are further described in section 11.1.

Here are some typical examples of attributes whose values need words. Such attributes are often said to have *enumerated types*.

inkjet	cyan, magenta, yellow, black
phosphor type	green, amber, color
outlet type	grounded, ungrounded
outlet voltage	110 volts AC, 220 volts AC

The last example uses numbers, but we still consider it an enumerated type, because it has such a small set of possible values.

Notice that outlet type is "grounded or ungrounded," not "outlet is grounded: true or false." The true/false pair of attribute values is best reserved for attributes whose names you want to use in sentences to describe a condition, as in "If approved, initiate transaction," or "List all invoices that are not paid." The adjectives *true* and *false* apply to any proposition whatsoever, and therefore aren't very descriptive. By choosing words or phrases that apply only to this one attribute, you can often give the reader a clearer idea of what you're describing.

In light of this, we can revise the description of the paid attribute. Instead of:

paid	True/false: whether the bill was paid.

we can omit true/false by writing:

closing status	Either of these values:	
	paid	Customer paid.
	walked out	Customer walked out without paying.

The latter version tells the reader much more about what this attribute is and why it's an important part of the problem domain. To keep true/false but provide more information, write:

paid	True if the customer paid, false if the customer walked out without paying.

When naming true/false attributes, choose the name so that in the sentences in which that name will appear, you'll need the word *not* as little as possible. Since the attribute above would most likely appear in sentences like "Total all paid orders," naming it paid is better than naming it walked out. The latter would result in sentences like "Total all not-walked out orders." Especially try to avoid names that require negating a negative: "Total all not-unpaid orders." There's nothing ungrammatical about such sentences, but they're confusing.

If you find yourself listing an enormous number of possible values or, especially, if the attribute's set of possible values is capable of change during the lifecycle of the program, then you do not have an attribute, you have a whole different class. For example, flower type is not merely an attribute of flower. As there are hundreds of thousands of flower types, all of which must be entered into the program, flower type is a class that bears a one-to-many relation with flower. (See section 9.5 for more information about relations.)

A less common strategy for indicating all the possible values of an attribute is illustrated by the polygon attribute. It's described as a "series of vertices." A series or list or collection of anything is a perfectly acceptable attribute in a domain description. When the programmers create a representation of polygon, they will probably create a distinct vertex class, or perhaps a distinct table in a relational database, for purposes of storage and retrieval. But that does not mean that we should define a separate class for a concept that is well known to the customer, well known to the programmers, and contains no variations specific to this problem.

9.4 Impossible values

Listing all the possible values of attributes is mandatory. It is helpful, but not mandatory, to indicate the *impossible* values, too. This kind of information helps a user-interface designer invent ways to prevent invalid data from being inadvertently entered into the computer, and helps a programmer to add checks and redundancy to the program to catch bugs, including all the kinds of tricks described in section 4.4.

If you know, for example, that a table cannot possibly have two legs, then you can indicate in the description of the table class that its legs attribute must be three or more. By stating the range of possible values, you automatically exclude all the impossible values.

Be aware, however, that this strategy can backfire. Reality is filled with oddball cases that violate the rules we thought they would always obey. For example, in a program for a company that insures cars, you might write:

appraised value	Dollars and cents: value of the car; amount that we pay if the car is totaled. Range: $100 to $200,000.

Now the user-interface designer knows to design the system to display an error message if a user enters a number greater than 200,000 for appraised value. This prevents data-entry mistakes, such as those caused by unwittingly holding down a number key long enough to make it auto-repeat.

One day, however, a customer walks in to insure a 1961 Volkswagen Beetle that he's spent a decade customizing—a huge, computerized array of light bulbs on the outside that display a spectacular light show, larger engine, expensive metallic trim, and numerous other work. He estimates that it would cost $500,000 to replace; it's a one-of-a-kind car, probably destined for a museum.

If the system rejects the appraised value, it will reject what is probably the largest and most exciting order in the insurance agent's career!

Fortunately, there's an easy solution. Just say that violations of these kinds of rules are *unlikely*, not impossible:

appraised value	Dollars and cents: value of the car; amount that we pay if the car is totaled. Range: above $0. Very rarely below $200 or above $100,000.

Now, the user-interface designer can design the system to not reject the large values, but to display, perhaps, a confirmation screen if the user enters a large appraised value:

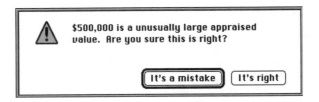

Notice also that we narrowed the range somewhat, down to $200 to $100,000. We can do this because we don't have to worry about excluding the occasional strange case.

Most frequently, the impossibilities that a system can exploit to detect invalid data involve relations between attribute values, not just individual attribute values. For example, software for the Department of Motor Vehicles tracks powered vehicles of all kinds. One of the parameters for a vehicle is wheels: some trucks have as many as eighteen, while boats have none. Another is vehicle type: car, truck, motorcycle, and so on. A motorcycle can have only two wheels, but a car can't. Therefore we know that if the user enters both "car" and "2 wheels", one of those must be in error.

A few attributes contain redundancy already designed in the problem domain. For example, credit card numbers are calculated from a formula that allows only about one in 20,000 sixteen-digit numbers to be valid, making credit card fraud more difficult. ISBN numbers (International Standard Book Numbers), used by libraries to identify book titles, include a check digit. In cases like these, all you have to do to exclude the impossible values is describe the validation formula or explain how the check digit is calculated.

9.5 Relations

In Hawaii, there's a business that offers boat rides among several of the islands. Any given boat can travel from any island to any other on any given day. The business rotates the boats through the islands according to weather conditions that day and which boats are in working order. Abigail Stevenson, a customer, suspects that she dropped her address book in one of the boats within the last few days. She would like us to search the boat for her, but she doesn't remember the ID number of the boat, of course, and she doesn't remember exactly which day it was. All she remembers is the starting island and destination island of the journey.

What kind of set does the computer need to keep track of in order to tell us which boat Abigail Stevenson rode? Looking at the set of all customers wouldn't suffice. A single customer can go on many different rides on many different boats, so the customer class couldn't have a boat ridden attribute that would answer our question. Searching the set of all islands or the set of all boats wouldn't give us the information we need, either. Each boat can visit all the islands, so boat docked couldn't be an attribute of island, nor could island visited be an attribute of boat.

What we need is a type of set called a *relation*: a set of tuples, each of which contains elements from other sets.* A *tuple* is an ordered set, such as:

(Abigail Stevenson, Moloka'i, Lana'i, 76R805)

"Ordered set" means only that the order of the elements in the set is significant. We couldn't, say, reverse their order and have the same tuple. Ordinary sets, such as classes, have no particular order.

The tuple above has elements from three different classes:

Tuple element(s)	Class
Abigail Stevenson	customer
Moloka'i, Lana'i	island
76R805	boat

---

* In some terminology, including that of UML (Unified Modeling Language), a relation is called an *association*. The term *relation* is standard in mathematics in the sense used here—as a set that maps elements from one set to elements in one or more other sets. Since we mean the mathematical concept, and not a concept pertaining to the peculiarities of object-oriented implementations, adhering to the terminology of mathematics is more appropriate.

This relation contains one tuple for each passenger-trip: each time a boat carried a passenger from one island to another, counting all the passengers on each trip separately. Described schematically, each tuple looks like this:

(*customer, from-island, to-island, boat*)

The complete set would contain many, many tuples:

(Mark Spencer, Maui, Hawai'i, 76R802)
(Jane Spencer, Maui, Hawai'i, 76R802)
(Ikuro Ishigure, Moloka'i, Lana'i, 76R805)
(Abigail Stevenson, Moloka'i, Lana'i, 76R805)
(Maynard Williams, O'ahu, Moloka'i, 76R802)

· · ·

Now we can rephrase the query to find the boat as:

Find the *boat* element of the tuple in this relation having Abigail Stevenson as *customer*, Moloka'i as *from-island*, and Lana'i as *to-island*.

If more than one tuple satisfies those conditions, then there may be more than one boat to search.

Happily, the vast majority of relations contain tuples with only two elements, known as *pairs*. For the curious, table 9.3 shows the terminology for all different tuple sizes.* Nonstandardly, we'll call each of the positions within a tuple a *slot*. Each tuple in the boat example, therefore, has four slots: *boat, customer, from-island,* and *to-island*.

Table 9.3 What tuples and relations of various sizes are called

Number of elements in each tuple	Type of relation	Name of tuple
2	binary	pair
3	ternary	triple
4	quaternary	quadruple
any	*n*-ary	*n*-uple, tuple

On class diagrams, binary relations are indicated by lines between the classes represented in each slot of the pairs, as shown in figure 9.4.

---

* More rigorous circles would demand that we call these *ordered pair, ordered triple,* and so on, but this is more than enough terminology for our purposes.

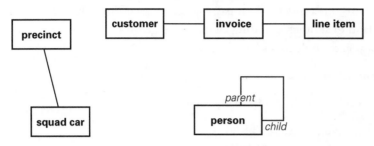

Figure 9.4 Some binary relations

The (*precinct, squad car*) relation indicates, for each precinct, all of the squad cars based there. Customers are connected with invoice line items by a chain of two relations, one mapping each customer to all of his invoices and another mapping each invoices to all of the line items that it contains. The (*parent, child*) relation is an example of a relation in which both elements of each pair are from the same class: person.

How to diagram ternary and higher-order relations will be shown on page 169.

If tuples seem a bit strange, you might note that if you understand classes, you are already familiar with tuples. A class is nothing more than a set of tuples, having one slot for each attribute. The only difference between a class and a relation is that a class's tuples contain members of attribute sets, whereas a relation's tuples contain members of classes.

9.6 Cardinality

There are two fundamental rules to state about the correspondence between customers and invoices:

(1) For every customer, there correspond zero or more invoices.

(2) For every invoice, there corresponds exactly one customer.

Together, these two rules define the *cardinality* of the relation—the range of possible numbers of tuples having the same element in any one slot, corresponding to a single element found in the other slot.* To put it another way, a relation's cardinality is the answer to the question, "Given specific elements for all but one slot, how many different tuples can the relation contain having different elements in the remaining slot?" The concept is more intuitive than its definition sounds; it's easiest to learn through examples.

---

* In some terminology, including that of UML, cardinality is called *multiplicity*.

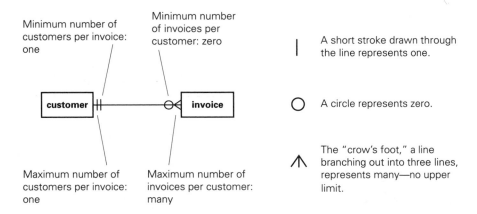

Figure 9.5 Cardinality symbols

In a class diagram, a relation is symbolized by a line connecting two classes. The relation's cardinality is symbolized by the symbols at each end of the line, as shown in figure 9.5.

The maximum number of tuples that contain elements from class *A* corresponding to a single element from class *B* is shown by the symbol closest to class *A*. Thus, in the example, the crow's foot next to invoice indicates that a single customer may have an unlimited number of invoices. The short perpendicular line next to customer indicates that an invoice can correspond to no more than one customer.

The minimum number of tuples that contain elements from class *A* corresponding to a single element from class *B* is shown by the symbol second-nearest to *A*. Thus the circle near invoice indicates that a customer need not have an invoice. The short perpendicular line second-nearest to customer indicates that for any invoice, there must correspond at least one customer.

There are numerous other conventions for indicating cardinality. Two are shown in figure 9.6. UML simply writes numbers, an asterisk serving as shorthand for "any number." OMT (Object Modeling Technique) had a notation that resulted in some pretty and very readable diagrams: a hollow ball meant "zero or one," a solid ball meant "zero or more," an unadorned line meant "exactly one," and other ranges were indicated explicitly with numbers.

What is important is not the graphical notation, but describing cardinalities precisely. Regardless of your graphical notation, you should always describe cardinalities in the text, as in item list in section 9.2. A reader can easily skim over some symbols in a graphic. A sentence prompts a reviewer to stop and judge whether the sentence is true or false.

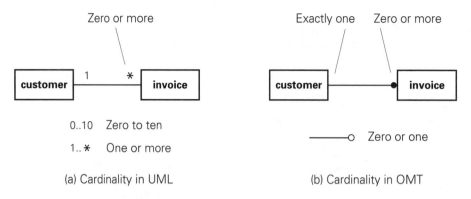

Figure 9.6 Other cardinality symbols

Yourdon* recommends simply drawing a line to indicate a relation and not attempting to show its cardinality at all on the graphic, leaving that information for the accompanying text. That is always a good option to consider when drawing a class diagram because the purpose of a class diagram is only to provide an overview of the details described in the text, not to make statements that appear nowhere in the text. If the diagram becomes too cluttered to serve as an overview, it's not serving its purpose.

Relations and their cardinalities can be very tricky to get right. Yet they contain a great deal of the structure of the problem domain. Understand why a relation is one-or-more-to-zero-or-more rather than one-or-more-to-zero-or-one, and you often uncover subtle but critical distinctions in the problem domain.

To aid in recognizing some of the different cardinalities, figure 9.7 shows a set of concrete examples. For many people, it's easier to remember the "ranch/horse" relation than the "zero-or-one-to-zero-to-many" relation. Included with each relation is the text description of the cardinality. There is no substitute for the text description in documentation, especially if it explains why the cardinality is as it is.

These examples are meant to be easy to remember and understand because they deal with commonplace classes. It's easy to remember that "a horse can roam free." They are not necessarily the best ways to describe the above classes and relations in a real requirements document. For example, making a class diagram for the square/piece relation is overkill. It's better to just draw a chessboard with pieces on it, and explain the relation in text. Classes and relations, remember, are types of sets, not graphics.

The professor/class relation brings up an important point about the difference between writing a requirements document and designing a database. Relational databases do not allow many-to-many relations. The database designer must break them up

---

* [Yourdon 1989a], p. 240.

For every customer, there are zero
or more invoices. Every invoice
belongs to exactly one customer.

For every city, there are one or
more postal codes. Every postal
code belongs to a single city; no
postal code straddles two cities.

At every ranch there reside zero or
more horses. A horse either resides
at a ranch or roams free.

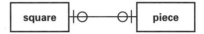

A square on a chessboard is either
empty or occupied by one piece. A
piece either occupies a square or
has been captured, in which case it
occupies no square.

During any one semester, a
professor teaches zero or more
classes. Every class in that
semester is taught by one or more
professors.

Every vehicle owner owns one or
more vehicles. Every vehicle is
owned by a set of one or more
vehicle owners (possibly the state).

Figure 9.7 Some cardinalities to remember

into two relations, many-to-one and one-to-many. So, our professor/class relation
would be invalid according to relational-database theory.

However, we are not describing a relational database. In a requirements document,
we are first of all describing the real world of professors and classes. There, a professor
can teach many classes in one semester, and the same class can be taught by more than
one professor in the same semester. That is the way it is. If a type of database software
needs to have the description modified, the programmers can make the modification in
their design documents. In object-oriented databases, many-to-many relations are
allowed. This type of distinction is invisible to the problem domain. Users don't know
or care about it, so it has no role to play in requirements. In requirements, we provide all
the information about the problem domain necessary to design software using available
tools and techniques. We don't distort descriptions of the real world in order to conform
to the quirks of one particular database management system.

The "one semester" qualifier in the professor/class relation raises one final point
about cardinalities:

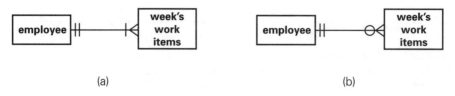

Figure 9.8 Two versions of a relation in a timesheet system

> To state the cardinality of a relation is to make assertions about the problem domain *over a certain range of time.*

This range of time is normally the time between events of interest to the system, that is, any two consecutive events that require a change to the data stored in the system. There is no reason to limit the scope of the assertion to such a small range, however. In the case of the professor/class relation, this range of time is one semester. Over a professor's entire career, the professor would have to teach at least one class. The "zero" in the cardinality is for sabbaticals and summer vacations. Whatever the range of time over which the cardinality is to apply, it is important that the reader know what it is.

The assertion, in the case of a minimum and maximum of one tuple, is a *guarantee* that a member of class *A* has exactly one corresponding member of class *B*. Thus, you guarantee to the programmers and user-interface designer that for every invoice, there is a corresponding customer. If, in fact, a single invoice can have multiple customers, contrary to all the diagrams so far, then the description is wrong and the programmers and user-interface designer will design the system on false premises. Such mistakes, unfortunately, are commonplace and quite frustrating to end users.

A typical example is in a system for employees to track their hours. The only hours tracked are those for which an employee is paid: hours billable to clients, hours in training classes, hours working on internal projects, vacation hours, and so on. Following the relation in figure 9.8(a), a programmer would set up the database to disallow any completed weeks with zero work items, and a user-interface designer would specify that the program refuse to accept a timesheet with zero items, displaying an error message instead.

However, if an employee takes off for a two-week unpaid sabbatical to write some difficult chapters in a book, the system won't accept the employee's timesheets. It then becomes necessary for the employee and the accounting staff to sort through spurious error messages every day as the system displays reminders that the timesheets are late. Or, in a common type of workaround, they can adopt a convention for entering spurious items into timesheets to make the system accept these weeks, and then manually subtract them from the totals output on reports. The correct cardinality is that shown in figure 9.8(b). Identifying this in the requirements would save a lot of people a lot of time.

CHAPTER 9   CLASSES AND RELATIONS

9.7 Relations as attributes

What do you call the relation between customers and invoices? One method is to name it as in figure 9.9, with a verb or preposition that you would use in making a statement about the relation, such as, "Every customer has zero or more invoices."

Figure 9.9 Awkward method of naming relations

For many relations, this results in some surprisingly undescriptive names . Has is as bland and generalized as can be. Even when the name is descriptive, as in "officer arrests suspect," where do you describe the arrests relation—in the description of officer, in the description of suspect, or separately from both? It seems that all three are unsatisfactory.

Fortunately, in most cases there is a better way: treat the relation as an attribute of both classes. The value of the attribute in class *A* is the subset of class *B* corresponding to a given member of class *A*. We'll call such an attribute a *reference attribute* because it refers to members of another class.*

In figure 9.10, the relation between customers and invoices is shown as two attributes, one attaching to customer and one attaching to invoice. The other, non-reference attributes are omitted from this diagram. The attribute attaching to customer is invoices: the set of invoices that are payable by one customer. Attaching to invoice is an attribute called customer: the customer responsible for paying a given invoice.

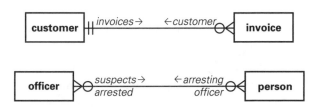

Figure 9.10 Relations as attributes

---

* Programmers will notice the similarity between reference attributes and pointer variables. However, reference attributes are just a way of describing sets of tuples. Whether they're implemented as pointer variables or as table joins in a relational database is a matter of program design.

The officer/suspect relation has changed in figure 9.10. A person who was not a suspect can become one; from the point of view of his attorney, he is a client; from the point of view of his prison, he is an inmate. Thus, a person is a suspect only in relation to another class. So we call a person a "suspect arrested" in relation to the arresting officer, a "client" in relation to his attorney, and so forth. The accompanying text must indicate that if a person is an arrested suspect, he has an arresting officer. A graphic can only show so much.*

Relations are sets of tuples, but talking about sets of tuples is often confusing. The above method of treating relations as attributes takes a lot of the confusion out of describing relations. By always talking only about the subsets of class B that correspond to a single member of class A, we can talk about a simpler kind of set—just a set of members of class B.

Reference attributes also enable you to naturally describe relations without a separate "Relations" section following all the classes. Such a section tends to be awkward reading, containing many small snippets of text, each describing one set of tuples, and difficult to understand without repeatedly cross-indexing back to the classes. The class descriptions, too, are difficult to understand because, in many cases, a relation that a class participates in is the most important aspect of the class. Defer describing the relation until forty pages later in the document, and the class can easily seem like an arbitrary collection of attributes.

Even when a relation is described as a pair of reference attributes, the reader must still cross-index between two classes. However, in general, a reader can read a single class description and understand it without having to jump ahead in the document. All the information that is directly pertinent to the class is collected in one place. The fact that other, related information—the relation as seen from the other class—is described elsewhere is not a fault.

The description of the order class in section 9.2 is an example of how to document relations as attributes. The item list from which the subtotal is calculated is described right in the class description, as part of the class, which is how the customer and end users think about it most naturally. The complete set of classes that order connects to is shown in figure 9.11.

Notice that order item lacks a reference attribute for its relation with order. Similarly for menu item's relation with order item. No attribute is named because there is no occasion in the requirements to speak of the order corresponding to a given order item. An

---

* Readers familiar with UML or OMT should take care not to confuse the *roles* from those notations with reference attributes. In fact, they are exactly opposite. The  person's role in relation to the officer is "arrested suspect"; the officer's role is "arresting officer."

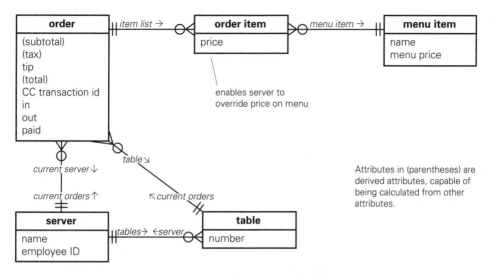

Figure 9.11 Some classes and relations in a restaurant application

order has an item list, and that's all. What we never need to talk about, we don't bother to name.

The text accompanying the relation between order item and menu item should note explicitly that a single order can contain multiple instances of a single menu item. The cardinality symbols are ambiguous as to what range they apply to. The diagram above does not indicate whether a single menu item can correspond to many order items within a single order or only across the set of all orders—that is, whether a single menu item could correspond to different order items only if the order items came from different orders.

This ambiguity is a further argument in favor of Yourdon's recommendation to omit cardinality symbols from graphics. You should decide on a project-by-project basis whether to include them; there is no general rule. This book shows cardinality symbols in nearly all class diagrams, mainly for the purpose of teaching concepts of cardinality. In real documentation, you should omit them far more often. Sometimes they illuminate, sometimes they obfuscate—or, worse, convey an impression of more rigor than they really deliver.

9.7.1 Ternary relations

A hospital wants to collect data to evaluate the effectiveness of different treatments for different conditions. Linking in the patients on whom treatments are applied yields a ternary relation, shown in figure 9.12.

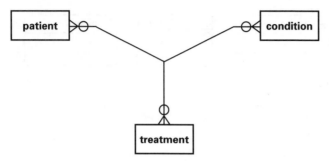

Figure 9.12 A ternary relation

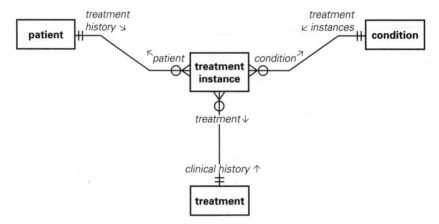

Figure 9.13 Ternary relation shown as a class

In a ternary relation, our trick of avoiding talk of tuples by treating relations as reference attributes won't work, at least not as well. The problem is that there are two other classes, not just one. Every patient corresponds to a set of (*condition, treatment*) pairs. Each condition and treatment similarly corresponds to pairs of elements from the other two classes. We could define a "set of pairs" attribute, with a name like condition/treatment, but there's another strategy: treat the relation as a class.

Creating a treatment instance class consisting of nothing but reference attributes, as in figure 9.13, we can refer to the relation from every class via meaningful attribute names. A patient has a patient history, a treatment has a clinical history, and so forth.

The new diagram conveys much more information about the medical activity about which data is to be collected, and it leads the reader very naturally to think in terms of a set of triples connecting patient, condition, and treatment. The four sets depicted are exactly the same as those in figure 9.12, but now, because the description is entirely in terms of binary relations, they're much easier to understand.

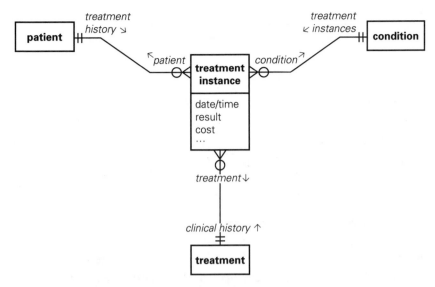

Figure 9.14 Attributes added to the ternary relation

In a real application, the relation would be even more complicated because the doctor administering the treatment would have to be included, making treatment instance a quaternary relation. By following the strategy of figure 9.13, adding a doctor class would not unduly complicate the diagram.

Converting ternary relations into classes is especially natural because, in nearly all real-world cases, there is further information to describe about each triple in the relation. This means that the ternary relation needs to be a class anyway. Figure 9.14 shows some of the non-reference attributes that belong to treatment instance.*

9.7.2 Directed attributes

In some cases, it's inconvenient to treat a relation as a class just because it has one or two attributes. For example, a business might buy the same product from several different vendors. The price is not simply an attribute of the product because the same product

---

* UML and OMT would call treatment instance a *link class*: an association with accompanying attributes. In requirements and specifications, however, there is no need to distinguish between a link class and any other class that participates in relations with other classes. It is important, however, to state in the accompanying text what all the cardinalities are: that a single patient can be treated for many conditions, that many treatments can be applied to the same patient for the same condition, and that many patients can have the same conditions and receive the same treatments. The fact that a class diagram does not show these cardinalities is true not only for link classes, but for any classes related as *A–B–C*: the cardinality of the implicit relation between *A* and *C,* if it is of any importance, must always be described explicitly in text accompanying the diagram.

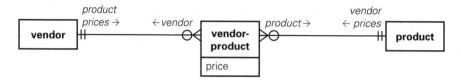

(a) Relating price to vendor and product via a class

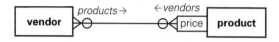

(b) Diagramming price as a directed attribute

Figure 9.15 Two ways to diagram a directed attribute

can have a different price for each vendor. Nor is the price an attribute of the vendor because each vendor can offer many products. Mathematically, prices are related to vendors and products by a set of triples: (*vendor, product, price*).

Figure 9.15 shows two ways to describe the price. In diagram (a), the price has been put into a class with three attributes: price, the vendor associated with the price and product, and the product associated with that price and vendor. The vendor-product class, then, is simply the set of triples described above.

Diagram (b) shows another way to link prices to vendors and products: by making the price what we shall call, non-standardly, a *directed attribute*. A directed attribute is an attribute of class *B* that has a different value for different elements of class *A*. People naturally think of price as an attribute of a product, regardless of the fact that it all boils down to the set of triples (*vendor, product, price*). To make the document easier for them to understand, you can treat price as a special kind of attribute of product. Draw price outside product, connected to the relation to vendor, as shown. Now, in the class description, you can simply treat both price and vendor as attributes, as illustrated below.*

---

* A directed attribute is different from the *qualifier* found in UML's and OMT's notations. A qualifier is an attribute attaching to class *A* that distin-

guishes elements in class *B*. For example, no two patrons of the same library may have the same card number at that library, but a single patron may have the same card number at different libraries. In the author's experience, many people, even programmers, find qualifiers confusing because it's more natural to think of card number as an attribute of patron, not of library. They tend to draw qualifier attributes as described above—that is, attaching to class *B*—not as the UML standards stipulate. Also, note that price could not be a qualifier attaching to vendor because products are not distinguished by price: two products sold by the same vendor could have the same price.

2.11 Product

A *product* is anything that XYZ Corporation purchases from any vendor.

Attribute	Description
vendors	One-to-many: The set of vendors that sell this product.
price	Dollars and cents: The price at which a specific vendor sells this product. There is one price for each vendor in the vendors set.

Note that diagram 9.15(a) provides the general solution. In a real application, it is likely that a set of mere triples would not be enough. Vendors also have, for each product, a product code, a minimum quantity, a lot size or even a set of several lot sizes, a delivery time, a rush-order delivery time, a rush-order premium, and so on. The directed attribute approach becomes cumbersome with more than two or three attributes. On the other hand, you can simply draw price, lot size, and so on. the same as any other attributes, and just describe their relation to vendor in the text, as above. The text is king; the graphic merely aids the reader in seeing how the different statements in the text fit together.

9.8 Uniqueness and functional dependence

A car-parts warehouse stores many different types of parts, each with type, weight, and unit price. The software they've ordered needs to track how many of each are in stock, for purposes of reordering. Which diagram in figure 9.16 is the better division into classes?

The part type set contains one element for each type of part that the warehouse carries. The part set contains one element for each part currently in stock. So part type would contain one element for gasket type A64G. The part set would contain zero or more corresponding elements, one for each gasket of type A64G in stock.

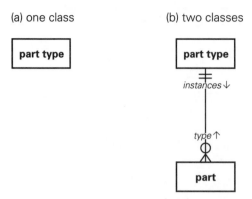

(a) one class

(b) two classes

part type

part type

instances ↓

type ↑

part

Figure 9.16 Two class diagrams for car parts

Diagram (a) is better, because the warehouse does not distinguish individual parts of the same type. This brings up an important principle of class diagrams:

> The only classes and relations worth describing are those in which *individual elements* are distinguished by propositions or questions about the problem domain.

The part type class would have a quantity attribute: the number of parts of that type currently in stock. That would suffice for defining rules that tell when to reorder new stock, and it would suffice for queries about how many of any type of part are in stock.

Diagram (b) would be appropriate only if the warehouse needed to find out the answers to questions like, "Which customer bought the type A64G gasket with ID 780-D1-09?" In that case, you would add an attribute named ID to part.

Another important piece of information to include in each class's description, therefore, is what attribute or combination of attributes the development staff can depend on to uniquely identify each member of the class.

The simplest way to indicate which attributes uniquely distinguish members of a class is a sentence in the class description that speaks of "no two" members of the class, like this:

> No two employees can have the same employee ID.

If there are two or more rules guaranteeing methods of uniquely identifying class members, express them as a list, so you don't have to repeat the same sentence structure over and over:

No two patients can have the same:

- Social security number.

- Combination of insurer and insurance ID.

Diagrams used for relational database software often include a special segment in the class box (there called an *entity*), to indicate which attributes can distinguish individual members of classes. Sometimes there are two such boxes: one for attributes contained within in the class ("keys"), and one for attributes in related classes ("foreign keys"). This technique is helpful for designing a relational database, but it's more complexity than a diagram needs for describing the problem domain when no particular method of representation has been chosen.

Sometimes the problem domain does not provide any information that can be relied upon with certainty to distinguish individual members of a class, but they must be distinguished anyway. For example, orders in a restaurant* have a time at which they were created, a table number, a server, and so on, but none of these or any combination can be guaranteed to be unique for any order. In these cases, you might want to mention in the class description that the available attributes can't uniquely identify any one order. The user-interface designer can then either add an ID-number attribute, or not, if there are other ways to distinguish orders on the screen, such as by displaying them in separate windows.

9.8.1 *Functional dependence*

If there is a rule in the problem domain such that for any value of one attribute (or a set of attributes), another attribute (or set of attributes) can only have a certain, corresponding value, the second attribute is said to be *functionally dependent* on the first. For example, every product might have both a number and a corresponding name. In this case, product name would be functionally dependent on product number (and vice versa, if no two products can have the same name).

A database designer must understand all the functional dependencies in the problem domain in order to take full advantage of the capabilities of relational database software. One of the stages of creating the tables of a relational database is to *normalize* them—convert a single table into multiple tables, redefine keys, and so on, such that no operation on the database can put it into an invalid state.† An invalid state is one in which the information stored in the database is not merely false, but internally

---

* See section 9.2.

† See, among many other sources on database normalization, [Date 1977], chapter 9.

inconsistent. Internally inconsistent means only that it violates functional dependencies—for example, a line item on an invoice having a product number and product name that did not correspond.

The correspondence rule referred to in the definition of functional dependence is a rule in effect at a certain time, not necessarily permanently. That is, the rule may change, though there is always *some* rule in effect. For example, a user may change the name of product #1547 from Southwestern Couch to Southwestern Sofa. What is important for functional dependence is that the problem domain follow a rule that can be stated independently of a list of all the product numbers and corresponding product names. A different kind of correspondence is that between customer numbers and invoice numbers. We wouldn't say, if a certain customer somehow got associated with an invoice from some other customer, that the association was logically *inconsistent*; it would just be wrong.

By explicitly stating uniqueness rules, you have already described the vast majority of information about functional dependence that a database designer needs to know. However, it's valuable to understand the concept explicitly in order to recognize and document any unusual kinds of functional dependence that you might come across.

9.9 Queries

All the previous sections of this chapter have presented only techniques for describing the problem domain—specifically, sets. At last, we are ready to make a requirement statement.

A *query* is a request for information—a question. Some typical types of questions to ask about sets are:

- What are all the elements in the set?

- How many elements are in the set?

- Are there any elements in the set having values x, y, and z for attributes a, b, and c?

- What are the values of attributes a and b for all elements having attribute c = x?

- What are all the elements in set B, corresponding via relation R to the elements in set A having attribute a = x?

As the above query types illustrate, a query always contains information: a specific set of elements to receive information about, and the type of information to receive. To describe a query, then, all that's necessary is to describe two things: the information that the user enters and the information that the user receives in response. In most cases, the set to search is implied by the choice of query, so this can be left out of the list of information entered by the user. Most queries do, however, need the user to supply some attribute values.

A variety of typical example queries is shown in the table below. The queries described are unrealistically drawn from a wide mix of applications so that the table can realistically show what a list of queries looks like.

R-1 The system answers the following queries on demand:

Query	User Specifies	Result
Q1 Find flights between specified cities	city *start*, city *dest*	List of all flights *f* such that *f*.start = *start* and *f*.dest = *dest*; total number of such flights. Attributes displayed for each *f*: number, service_type, airplane_type. Sort by: *f*.number.
Q2 One customer's prescriptions	*text*, up to 40 characters, where *len* is the number of characters actually entered	List of all prescriptions *p* such that the leftmost *len* characters of *p*.customer.name = *text*. Display all attributes of *p*. Sort by: *p*.refill_date, earliest date first.
Q3 Department expenditure detail	Month *mon* (including year; for example, 05/98)	For each department *d*: *d*.name; list of all expenditures *e* where *e*.department = d and *e*.date is within *mon*; sum of all *e*.amount. For each expenditure *e*: *e*.employee.name, *e*.date. *e*.amount. Sort departments by *d*.name, expenditures by *e*.date.

The promised requirement statement appeared at the beginning of the list of queries, numbered R-1. If the requirements document describes only a simple information problem, you can leave off the R number, and refer only to the Q numbers in other documentation. Another workable strategy is to assign a different requirement number (R number) to each query, in place of the Q number.

The query descriptions follow two typographical conventions in addition to putting query and requirement numbers in a bold sans serif font. The first is that, as anywhere else in the document, names of classes and attributes are in a special font: here, a normal-weight sans serif font. The second is that attribute values and references to specific elements of classes—anything that can vary from one query or from element to element within the same query—are in italics in the serif font. This enables the attribute value or class element to be referred to more than once without the use of ungainly phrases like "the prescription that matched the first condition above" or "the second telephone number that the user entered." Everyone who has ever seen a mathematics text for even a moment is already familiar with this convention, at least subconsciously, so it needs no explanation.

The period between words indicates an attribute of an element of a class:

$$element.\text{attribute\_name}$$

So p.refill_date means the refill_date of element p, which was defined earlier as an element of the prescription class. When an attribute is a set of elements from another class, two (or more) periods in a row can denote the resulting chain of relations:

$$p.\text{customer.name}$$

denotes the name attribute of the customer related to p.

Notice that in Q1, the user specifies two cities, not the names of two cities. This way of describing the query lets the user-interface designer decide how the user specifies the cities: by typing in their names, by selecting the cities from a list, and so forth.

The algebraic style of describing queries provides precision and flexibility for very complex queries. Sometimes, however, you can describe queries more simply, depending a little more on the reader's understanding of the problem domain to interpret the description, as shown below:

Query	User specifies	Result
Q1 Find flights between specified cities	Start and destination cities.	The number, service_type, and airplane_type of all flights from the start city to the destination city, sorted by flight.number.
Q2 Customer's prescriptions	*text*, up to 40 characters, where *len* is the number of characters actually entered	List of all attributes of all prescriptions with leftmost *len* characters matching customer.name. Sort by: refill_date, earliest date first.

Query	User specifies	Result
Q3 Department expenditure detail	Month *mon* (including year; for example, 05/98)	For each department: name, list of all expenditures with date within *mon*, sum of amounts of all expenditures. For each expenditure: the name of the employee who made the expenditure, the date of the expenditure, and the amount. Sort departments by name, expenditures by date.

As always, you should look for the simplest way to describe a query. The simplest way is seldom a completely general method for describing any imaginable query. What is important in a requirements document is only to describe what data the user enters and what data the system displays in response, and to do so clearly enough for any likely reader of the document to understand.

Notice that the second version of Q3 contains an ambiguity: does the "sum of amounts of all expenditures" refer to all expenditures within one department/month, all expenditures displayed in the query, or all expenditures in the entire history of the system? A reader who understands the purpose of the query is likely to be able to tell which interpretation is correct. But in more esoteric domains, the customer will often make the correct interpretation when reviewing the document, failing to notice that there are others, while the programmers are likely to make a different interpretation, again not noticing that there are others.

The example queries above were all defined purely in terms of content. Often a customer has specific ideas about the format of the output of a query—or even the input. This is especially common in the cases of queries that are printed reports. In this case, include the customer's specifications along with the query. With the availability of today's sophisticated report generators, an option to consider is creating the definition of the format of a report in the report generator and only referring to it in the requirements document. There, it's easy to modify, usually easy to understand, and, best of all, implemented exactly as specified.

For reports that print onto preprinted forms, such as bills or invoices bearing the customer's logo, attach a copy of the preprinted form to the requirements document, or include a scanned image, and simply provide a table mapping the names of fields on the form to names of attributes in the query.

9.10 Naming classes, attributes, and relations

The following are a few guidelines for naming classes, attributes, and relations—collectively called *sets*.

- Wherever possible, name sets whatever they're called in the problem domain—that is, whatever the customer calls them. A requirements document should invent as little new terminology as possible.

- Often, unfortunately, the customer uses the same name for several different sets that you must distinguish. The word *shipper*, for example, might apply equivocally to both the people who put packages onto trucks for delivery to customers, and the companies that actually perform the delivery. Sometimes, in a case like this, you can find synonyms already in use: *shipping clerk* and *shipping company*. Do not call either set by the ambiguous word; avoid it entirely. In other cases, you must invent genuinely new terms. See also the section on *Type* in chapter 15.*

- If at all possible, when inventing terminology, do not invent new acronyms. (See *Acronyms* in chapter 15.) Acronyms already in common use by the customer are fine, however. The development staff needs to learn the language of the customer, including its acronyms.

- Make a set's name singular or plural according to what best applies to an *individual element* of the set. A class whose elements are trucks, then, should be named truck, not trucks. If a single truck can have more than one license plate, then the attribute linking to the license plate class should be license plates, because each instance of the attribute is a set of one or more license plates. The license plate class, on the other hand, has a singular name, because each of its elements is just a single license plate.

- Don't name a binary relation if you don't have to, or at least don't define it separately from the classes that it connects. As described in section 9.7, define reference attributes in the classes at both ends of the relation, whose values are subsets of the other class—for example, an invoices attribute of customer, whose value is

---

* An excellent example of how to meet the need to replace the customer's terminology is in [Zave 1998]. The word *call* does not single out telephone-equipment activity with enough precision to write requirements for software to control that equipment. Zave shows how she solved this problem and many others. An especially good example of coining a new term is *voice path*, her name for the series of connections that carries a signal through the telephone network from one place to one or more others. Many people's lives are made much easier by such an intuitive term; but finding such a term is often quite difficult.

the set of a given customer's invoices, rather than a has relation, which is awkward to talk about.

- Consider converting ternary relations into named classes, as described in section 9.7.

- If you must name a binary relation, consider making its name a noun, especially if the relation is symmetrical (that is, neither class is "first" or "second"). A binary relation is a set of pairs, so its name should suggest that, for example, sister-cities, not is sister city of. Another technique is to create a class consisting of nothing but two relation attributes; for example, twin-pair or twins, whose attributes are the two members of the person class who are twins.

- Naming a relation a verb or prepositional phrase, like arrests or lives at, is most suitable when you want to speak of the relation as a predicate, that is, as an expression that is either true or false. For example, in a query you might want to say "for specified officer, list all persons such that arrests(officer, person)." Note, however, that in such a case, as in many relations named with a verb, the name of the arrests relation is better converted to the past participle: arrested(officer, person). Also in this case, the query is more simply described if the relation is named following the class attribute strategy recommended above: "for specified officer, list all suspects_arrested."

- If your programmers are using a tool, such as a commercial database or a CASE (computer-aided software engineering) tool, you might want to follow the tool's naming conventions. This might make life a little easier for the programmers. For example, if the tool does not allow spaces in names, then substitute hyphens or underscores for spaces in your own names. This is convenient for other reasons, as well, such as describing queries as in section 9.9. Don't, however, pollute your description of the problem domain with any programming concepts—a strong temptation if one is thinking in terms of a programming tool—and don't follow the tool's naming conventions if they're too restrictive, such as a maximum of eight characters per name.

- Never give a name to any set that you don't refer to elsewhere in the document.

- Whenever you refer either to a set or to data to be stored in the computer, put the name of a set in a special, sans serif font, to distinguish it from different usages of the same word. For example, road is the name of the set of all roads. Actual instances of roads, you should just call "roads."

C H A P T E R   1 0

Sequences and events

Now that you know how to describe the inhabitants of the problem domain, the next question is: What events happen to them? In this chapter, we'll see how to describe the events themselves, how to describe all the possible sequences of those events, and how to describe the machine's response to those events. The events and their possible sequences are information that belongs in a requirements document; the responses to events are part of the program specification. The techniques for describing sequences of events also apply to any other kind of sequence, including the sequence of data in a file, as we'll see in the first example.

10.1 Structure

Here is a simple log file for a mail server—a program that exchanges electronic mail with other mail servers. It contains data recording each message sent and received by the server. Your task is to document the format of the file so that programmers can write programs to read it and answer queries about the mail server's activity.

```
ALIASES
forbin=apteryx@splenetix.com,gibbons@splenetix.com,zimmer@marquette.edu
support=f.hall@splenetix.com
MESSAGES
receive,887923440,chalmers@cogswell.com,forbin
send,887923448,gibbons@splenetix.com,fairbourne@dat.com
send,887923480,clark@splenetix.com,info@camshaft.org
receive,887923489,morisawa@mail1.torque.com,support
receive,887923501,services@camshaft.org,clark@splenetix.com
```

A text file is a sequence of characters. To describe its format, you collect characters together into groups, enabling you to see the file as a sequence of groups. Those groups, in turn, you collect together into larger groups, and so on, forming a hierarchical structure.

The characters in the log file are organized into lines. The lines, in turn, compose two main sections in the file: an ALIASES section defining aliases that stand for one or more email addresses, followed by a MESSAGES section listing each message's time sent, 'from' address, and 'to' address. This structure is depicted in a *Jackson diagram*, shown in figure 10.1.

A Jackson diagram breaks down a structure in four ways:

- By *sequence*: one element always follows another, illustrated by the left-to-right sequence of four boxes in the second row.

- By *selection*: exactly one of a set of elements occurs, illustrated by the send and receive boxes in the third row. The circles in the upper right corners indicate that send and receive are alternatives rather than elements in a sequence.

- By *iteration*: a single element occurs zero or more times, illustrated by the alias and message boxes. The asterisks in the upper right corners indicate that alias and message can occur any number of times.

- By *hierarchy*: one element is composed of one or more subelements, illustrated by the lines branching out from log file and message.

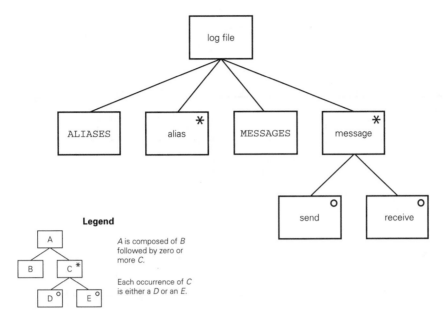

Figure 10.1 A Jackson diagram

What the Jackson diagram describes is a set: the set of all possible sequences in which lines in the log file can appear, that is, all possible log files in this format. Readers with programming experience will notice that the four types of breakdown correspond to the elements of structured programming: a sequence of instructions containing no branches, an if-then or switch statement, a while loop, and block structure.*

When describing a file format, you must describe the set of *all* possible valid files, whether you're describing a file that the program reads or a file that the program generates. The same applies to any sequence of relevance to the program: a sequence of events in the problem domain, a sequence of keystrokes, a sequence of mouse clicks, a sequence of hardware interrupts, a sequence of statements in a programming language, and so forth. To write the program, the programmers must know the set of all possible valid sequences.

Even though such sets are almost always infinite, describing them is often very straightforward when you break the format down in the four ways listed above. What makes the set infinite is the presence of iterated elements which occur zero or more times.

---

* Jackson diagrams, also called *structure diagrams*, were introduced in [Jackson 1975], a book on how to translate such sets of all possible sequences into program code. Though many of the examples involve decks of punch cards, the principles are timeless, and the book is still a classic work on program design.

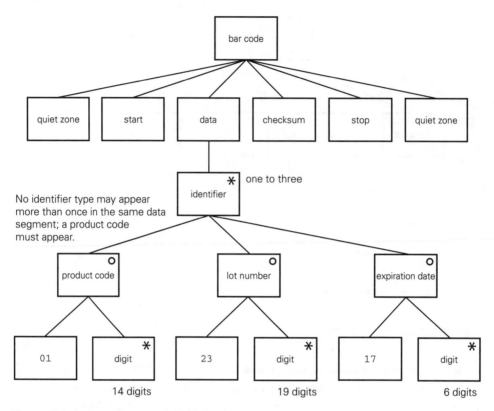

Figure 10.2 Jackson diagram of simple bar-code structure, with annotations

Jackson diagrams are easily extended. For example, a popular extension is to write a plus sign in the upper right corner of a box to mean "one or more." However, the great virtue of Jackson diagrams is their simplicity. No structure notation is particularly intuitive; they all require explanation, such as the legend in figure 10.1. The more extensions you add to the notation, the more explanation it requires and the harder it is to understand. Fortunately, there is a very easy way to add information to the diagram without complicating the notation. Just add annotations, as in figure 10.2. Annotations also allow you to describe unusual sequences not describable in terms of sequence, selection, and iteration, such as palindromes.

In most cases, when you describe a sequence, in addition to presenting the sequence schematically, as in a Jackson diagram, you must also include a textual description of each element in the sequence and an example of the sequence. Most people find it difficult to grasp the set of all possible sequences from the abstract description alone. By looking at the example, people can usually infer the pattern. The schematic view of the sequence confirms or perhaps corrects their inference. The example also grounds the schematic view in something concrete. Abstract ideas for which we know of no concrete example are generally poorly understood abstract ideas.

We've provided an example of the mail server's log file at the beginning of section 10.1. Here's the description of each type of line in the log file:

alias   States that one email address, the *alias*, stands for a list of one or more other email addresses. The mail server redirects email addressed to the alias to each of the addresses in the list. The list may contain aliases, though self-reference, whether direct or indirect, is not allowed.

Format:

alias=address[,*address...*]

If the domain name of the alias is omitted, it defaults to the domain name of the mail server. If the domain name of any of the addresses in the list is omitted, it defaults to the alias's domain name.

send   A record of the mail server successfully sending a message.

Format:

send, *time, from-address, to-address*

receive   A record of the mail server's successfully receiving a message.

Format:

receive, *time, from-address, to-address*

The *time* in both the send and receive lines is the number of seconds since midnight (start of day), January 1, 1970.

We could have made Jackson diagrams for each line's structure, but the above notation is simpler and easier to understand, given the non-hierarchical structure of each line. More sequence notations are described in section 10.4.

10.1.1 Boundary clashes

A word processor is a spectacularly difficult kind of program to specify. The main reason for this is that the various groupings of characters that you need to describe do not form a hierarchical structure. The boundaries of the various elements clash.

The first step in dealing with a boundary clash is to recognize that you have one, and not imagine a hierarchy like that shown in figure 10.3. A single paragraph can

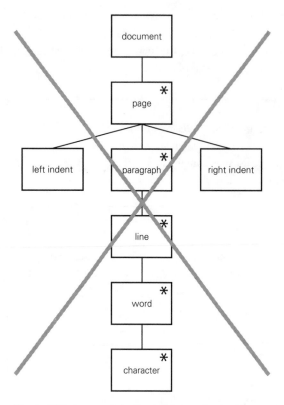

Figure 10.3 Incorrect Jackson diagram for text in a word processor

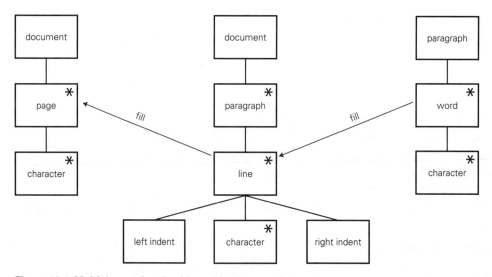

Figure 10.4 Multiple, overlapping hierarchies in a word processor

straddle two (or more) pages; therefore, a paragraph is not a subelement of a page. Similarly, a word can straddle two lines. It's particularly difficult to tell where to put left indent and right indent. The same problem occurs frequently in the output of a report. A page has a header and a footer, and a group of records contains records and a subtotal, but group of records can straddle any number of pages.

The solution is to draw multiple diagrams, one for each hierarchy. The bottommost element in each hierarchy should be the same, as in figure 10.4. Otherwise, you don't have a boundary clash. You simply have hierarchies composed of different elements. You can then define a *mapping* between the hierarchies, requiring further description in text accompanying the diagram. Mappings are discussed further in section 11.5.

10.2 Events

Part of the problem-domain description in any dynamic information problem is a list of all the events within the problem domain that change the answers to queries. Just as the description of a file format lists all possible sequences of the elements of the file, along with a description of each element, a description of events lists all possible sequences of events, along with a description of each event.

Figure 10.5 shows all the events in the lifecycle of a corporate bond from the perspective of a pension fund that keeps a portfolio of bonds (that is, a collection of bonds). The reason for the "from the perspective of" clause is that there are events in the history of a bond that are not shown because they are of no interest to an information system that answers queries about the portfolio. For example, the first event in the history of a corporate bond is that a corporation issues it—that is, makes it available for sale. Many other parties might buy and sell the bond before it reaches the portfolio of interest to the information system. The first event shown in the diagram, however, is purchase: the purchase of the bond by the company that owns the portfolio. This is because the information system is not called upon to answer any queries about the history of the bond before it was purchased.

For each event at the leaves of the tree—that is, the elements of the diagram that aren't broken down into subelements—the development staff needs to know:

- All sets affected by the event: which classes, class members, attributes, and relations are affected by the event

- All parameters of the event: attributes that can vary from one instance of the event to the next

- How the system can find out that the event has happened and what its parameters are: the source or sources of the information

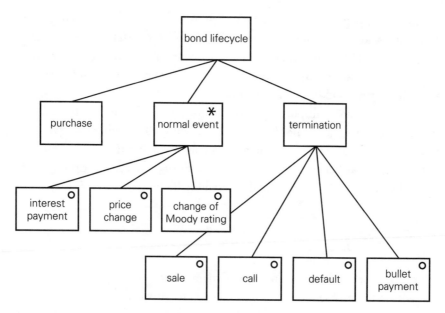

Figure 10.5 Lifecycle of a corporate bond

The first few events in the lifecycle of a corporate bond are shown below. ACS is a fictional accounting system that receives updates from a commercial financial-reporting service and is available to supply data to the portfolio system at night. ACS would be described earlier in the document. Earlier parts of the document would also explain the various entities and attributes involved in the events: bonds, par values, issuers, Moody ratings, and so forth.

The various record types referred to below need not be described in detail in the portfolio system's requirements document, as long as programmers can find them in ACS documentation. However, the requirements document would need to supply a table mapping event parameters to fields in the record types if the mapping is anything less than obvious.

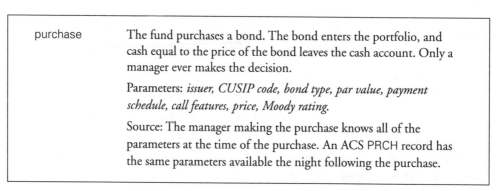

purchase	The fund purchases a bond. The bond enters the portfolio, and cash equal to the price of the bond leaves the cash account. Only a manager ever makes the decision.
	Parameters: *issuer, CUSIP code, bond type, par value, payment schedule, call features, price, Moody rating.*
	Source: The manager making the purchase knows all of the parameters at the time of the purchase. An ACS PRCH record has the same parameters available the night following the purchase.

interest payment	A scheduled payment from the issuer of the bond to the portfolio's cash account.
	Parameters: *payment number.* The amount of the payment is always equal to the amount in the bond's payment schedule corresponding to *payment number.*
	Source: The transmission of a PYMT record from ACS, with ptype = INT, indicates that an interest payment has happened.
price change	A change in the current market price of the bond. Happens continuously, 24 hours a day.
	Parameters: *price.*
	Source: Managers have access to current price data during the day; ACS reports the bond's price at 5:00 p.m. on the last trading day, in a BPRI record.
change of Moody rating	The Moody corporation changes the rating of the bond. A very rare event: roughly 98% of corporate bonds finish their entire life-cycles without a change in Moody rating.
	Parameters: *Moody rating.*
	Source: an ACS MODY record indicates a change. Managers generally know about a change during the day, too, since changes in Moody rating are usually big news.

For purposes of illustration, the sources in this example are deliberately a little bit irregular. In most applications, all the data comes from one source, typically, a data-entry staff. In that case, you can state that once, early in the document, and omit the "Source" paragraph in each event's description. Or, if there are different sources for different data, you might indicate which events are detectable by which information source in a matrix rather than in "Source" paragraphs.

Naming the first event in the history of an object is sometimes difficult. In object-oriented programming, the first event in the history of a piece of data is often called "create." However, that is often a poor name for the first event of the object that the data represents because, often, the object already existed before it entered the problem domain. For example, a book already exists before it becomes the property of a library. If you say that the book is created, then you're talking about stored data, not about books, but in a requirements document, you talk about the problem domain, not the software.

A better name for the book's first event, as seen by the library, is acquire.* A few other good words to keep in mind when naming the first event: discover, purchase, start.

Of course, create is the appropriate word when speaking of something that is really created, like a paragraph in a document or a bubble in a liquid. However, you can often find synonyms for create that apply more specifically to the problem domain: a corporation is incorporated; the first event in a person's life is birth (or conception, depending on what kinds of queries the information system answers).

The first event often has many parameters. Whereas most later events modify a single attribute of a member of a class, the first event usually must supply values for all the attributes at once.

In the bond example, there was an implicit parameter for each event except the first: which bond was affected. This is fine documentation, because it's stated that every event in the diagram pertains to the same bond. However, if a set of events can pertain to more than one object, then each event must include as a parameter which object or objects are affected, and, if necessary, how the source identifies the objects—for example, by employee ID.

10.3 Event responses

The specification for software that describes a dynamic information problem includes, for each event in the problem domain, a corresponding *event response* that updates the model maintained by the software. Event responses also make up the majority of control problems whose solution involves the maintenance of a model, or any other type of problem solved by that technique.

Every event-response description actually lists two events:

- An event at the interface between the software and the problem domain—that is, shared phenomena—that is initiated by a person, software, or hardware in direct contact with the system.

- The resulting change to the model maintained by the system and any other shared events to be caused by the system, such as turning on indicator lights or performing notifications.

A good name for event responses initiated by a person is *operating procedures*. In an operating procedure, the specification dictates how the users should operate the system:

---

* [Cameron 1986] takes a few Jackson diagrams of activity at a library from initial description to program design, discussing some of the theoretical basis for giving such importance to describing complete sequences of events.

when such-and-such event happens in the problem domain, a user is responsible for entering such-and-such data. If there are many classes of user—for example, administrators, managers, and data-entry staff—the procedure should indicate which user is responsible for carrying it out.

Operating procedures indicate not only the data that users enter into the system, but also the specific windows and fields the users enter the data into and any button-presses they need to make in order to reach the right windows and fields. Without this information, testers wouldn't know how to simulate operating the system, and the technical writer wouldn't know what information to include in the user's manual.

If the system rejects data that fails to meet validation rules, the event response should indicate the applicable validation rules and how the system responds to each type of invalid data—with an error message, with a notification to an administrator, update of a log file, and so on. Every error message and every line of text that appears in a log file must be written out, word-for-word, in a specification.

In most cases, the same validation rules apply across many different event responses. To keep the document from becoming unnecessarily repetitious, the validation rules and their accompanying error messages should be collected together into a single table. The statement that the system is to display a certain error message if a validation rule is violated can be placed in the description of the OK buttons on the appropriate screens, rather than repeated over and over again in each event response. Having thus fully documented each error-response, each operating procedure can be made very simple by assuming that all data entered is valid and the user does no backtracking.

There is no need, therefore, to include such statements in event responses as, "If the user clicks Cancel, the procedure is aborted." It's enough that the description of the window says what the OK and Cancel buttons do.

Each operating procedure should be described as a series of action-response pairs: the user performs an action, and the system performs an action in response; the user performs the next action, and so on. The actions are button-clicks, selection of menu items, typing data into a field, and so forth. The responses are the effects on the data model or unusual actions in the user interface, such as a graph appearing. The user's manual should mention such responses as the opening of new windows, but in the specification, the more mundane actions can be left to descriptions of buttons and menu items and left out of event responses. Even for user actions, in most cases it's sufficient merely to state which window must be active for the action to take place; saying "User opens such-and-such window" is unnecessary.

The specification for the system that tracks corporate bonds would read like this:

Portfolio managers are responsible for performing the following procedures in response to bond events:

Event	Procedure
purchase	In *New Bond* window, manager enters issuer, CUSIP code, bond type, par value, payment schedule, call features, price, and Moody rating. System creates a new bond, with the specified attributes.
price change	In *Bond* window, manager selects bond by CUSIP code and enters new price.
change of Moody rating	In *Bond* window, manager selects bond by CUSIP code and enters new Moody rating.

A manager need only enter a price change or change of Moody rating to ensure that system data is up-to-date for reports printed before that night. If a manager omits entering this data, the system will receive it from ACS that night. A manager must enter all purchases, however; the system uses data from ACS only as a check on the manually entered data (see section 4.1).

The agent that performs the responses is "the system." This makes for much clearer reading than passive sentences like "A new bond is created." By what? By whom? Similarly, the agent of each action is stated explicitly in each sentence. In the above examples, the *manager* is the subject of each sentence. More often, the most descriptive word is simply *user.*

Notice that while create was usually a poor name for an event in the problem domain, the event responses speak of creating a bond. Here, create is appropriate, because something new really is being created: a data element inside the system.

Notice also that each description is very terse and written in the present tense. Writing system responses in the future tense mostly creates wordiness and confusion. Also in the interest of terseness, system responses to events that change a single attribute are omitted. It's enough to say that the user enters the data. If the system makes changes to other data—say, to a list of delinquent customers—this must be stated explicitly in the event response.

On most projects, it's helpful to write an interim document that describes the operating procedures without mentioning the windows and fields. The user-interface designer can then design the user interface around this document. The analyst can write the interim document without delving into the details of the user interface. One technique is to create a table of event responses with three columns: the two shown in the example above, plus a column headed "Window." The analyst leaves the third column blank; the user-interface designer fills it in.

10.3.1 Every event

The specification must include an event response for every event in the problem domain. It answers the question, "For each event, what is the system going to do about it?" If the requirements are clearly and simply written, and rigorously describe the set of all possible events, you can check very systematically that the specification addresses every event.

One could say that event responses are use cases. However, the term *use case* is much broader than *event response*. A use case is any single path through system functionality, involving a dialogue between the system and some outside entity that interacts with it—that is, action-response pairs. An event response is much more limited. You define an event response for every event in the problem domain. Thus, event responses are part of a process of rigorously mapping the solution—system behavior—to a well-defined problem. Use cases are much more free form. Also, event responses are very narrowly delimited. Each operating procedure, for example, tells only what a user should do in response to one event distinguished in the requirements document. A use case often tells a longer story, perhaps showing how different users interact with the same piece of data, or tracing one user's activity across several events and several pieces of data.

In addition to covering all the problem-domain events, the specification often needs to define some more events and event responses: those pertaining to administering the system. One of the most elementary is dealing with corrections to data-entry errors. Some poorly designed systems give users only one chance to enter data correctly. If it's wrong, changing it is difficult or impossible.

In addition to correction events, the specification must also describe procedures for installing the software and for backing up and restoring data, as well as any special, administrative users called upon to perform these tasks. Describing administrative procedures is essentially no different from describing other operating procedures. The only difference is that there is no event from the problem domain to map to, so you simply name the procedure: "back up," "restore," "revert," and so on.

10.3.2 Responding to hardware and software events

When interfacing with hardware or software, the specification usually cannot dictate procedures to be followed by that hardware or software; their actions are part of the problem domain, a given. In this case, the event responses are not operating procedures; they're simply events and responses. For the corporate-bond portfolio, each of these events is the receipt of a record from the ACS system during the nightly update. The part of the specification that addresses how the system responds to these records would read like this:

The system responds to records received from ACS as follows:

ACS Record	Response
PRCH	If no bond is in the system with CUSIP code = PRCH.CSIP, append the following message to the ACS log file: (0004) ACS reports purchase of a bond with CUSIP code *csip*, but no such bond was entered during the day. *Rationale:* Managers need all bond purchases to be reflected in reports generated at 5:00 p.m. each night, before the ACS update. Therefore, managers are required to enter purchases manually, making the data received from ACS redundant. The system can still make use of the redundant data, however, by performing the check described here.
PYMT	Mark that the bond with CUSIP code = PYMT.CSIP has received interest payment number PYMT.INUM.
BPRI	For bond with CUSIP code = BPRI.CSIP, change price to BPRI.PRIC.
MODY	For bond with CUSIP code = MODY.CSIP, change Moody rating to MODY.NRAT. See page 30 for table of NRAT codes and corresponding Moody ratings.

Realistically, the system would perform more checking on PRCH records than indicated here. However, checking all the other fields in the PRCH record wouldn't belong in the event response for PRCH because the system should generate an error message only if the PRCH record contains a discrepancy *and* no later records from ACS resolve the discrepancy. Therefore, the rules for generating such an error message belong in a description of how the system responds to the nightly update as a whole, not to any individual record.

For unusual responses, the specification explicitly indicates a rationale. If rationales become too large or there are too many, then collect them into a separate section of the document or in a different document altogether.

Here, since every response is performed entirely by the system, the system need not be mentioned explicitly in each sentence. The imperative mood enables you to describe the responses both clearly and tersely.

You'll notice a certain amount of repetition in the responses. For example, the bond affected by each record is indicated by a field in the record named CSIP. This suggests a way to improve the table. If the table describes responses to many, many records and this pattern continues to hold, then state, immediately before the table, that the bond affected by the record always has a CUSIP code equal to the record's CSIP field. Or make two tables, one for records that follow the pattern and one for all other records.

Rather than complicate the table, the description of the response to a MODY record refers the reader to another table where they can find out how to translate from the codes in the MODY record to the Moody ratings that they stand for.

There is one type of problem where the specification can dictate procedures for other software to follow. That is a software library or operating system—any software that provides services to software to be written in the future. In this case, the event responses form an *application program interface* (API). Such a specification should generally be written by a programmer familiar with APIs, and it should look like an API: a list of function calls, parameters, return values, throw objects, and so on. In fact, there should be little difference between the specification and the programmer's reference manual released with the final product.

10.4 More sequence notations

In the 1960s and 1970s, people invented many different notations for different types of sequences, centering around the basic concepts of sequence, selection, iteration, and hierarchy. This section describes a few more of them. All are well worth considering when writing any requirements document or specification that must describe a set of all possible sequences of one kind.

10.4.1 Backus-Naur Form

Backus-Naur Form (BNF) is mainly used for describing the syntax of computer languages, though there's nothing fundamentally different about describing the set of all possible sequences of characters in a program source file and describing a set of all possible sequences of events. BNF introduces one more concept to the basic quartet of sequence, selection, iteration and hierarchy: recursion. An element in a sequence can be an instance of the very same sequence. The need for sequences that can contain instances of themselves is most commonly needed in programming languages that allow nested block structure, as in this fragment from Pascal:

```
x := 1;
repeat
   y = 1;
   repeat
      a[x, y] := 0;
      y := y + 1
   until y = 10;
   x := x + 1;
until x = 10
```

As the example illustrates, a repeat statement can contain another repeat statement. A tiny excerpt from the full grammar of Pascal shows how BNF describes the above syntax:

<statement> ::= <repeat-statement> | <other-statement>
<repeat-statement> ::= 'repeat' <stmt-sequence> 'until' <boolean-expression>
<stmt-sequence> ::= <statement> | <statement> ';' <stmt-sequence>

A <repeat-statement> can contain a <stmt-sequence>, which can contain a <statement>, which in turn can contain another <repeat-statement>. Thus <repeat-statement> is defined recursively, allowing an infinite number of levels of nesting.

The words in quotation marks are *terminal symbols*: elements that appear in the language exactly as they appear in BNF, without being decomposed hierarchically into other elements. They correspond to the leaf elements of the tree structure shown in a Jackson diagram. Hierarchy is shown simply by referring to an element in one definition and defining it in another.

An element that has a definition is called a *non-terminal* symbol. By convention, all non-terminal symbols are enclosed in angle brackets. Each definition is sometimes called a *production*.

BNF indicates selection by the vertical bar: a <statement> can be either a <repeat-statement> or an <other-statement>. An element can also be optional, shown by enclosing it in square brackets. An if statement, for example, may include an else clause but doesn't have to:

<if-statement> ::= 'if' <boolean-expression>
                           'then' <statement> ['else' <statement>]

Notice that BNF has no symbol for iteration. To indicate iteration in BNF, you must combine selection with recursion, as shown in <stmt-sequence>. Put a single element of the iteration, that is, the shortest possible iteration, as the first option; make the next option the single element followed by the iteration as a whole. Putting another element in between, like the semicolon in the definition of <stmt-sequence>, indicates a separator that must appear between any two consecutive elements of the iteration.

This method of defining an iteration denotes a one-or-more iteration, not a zero-or-more iteration such as is found in Jackson diagrams. A zero-or-more iteration in BNF is an optional one-or-more iteration, that is, a one-or-more iteration enclosed in square brackets and included in the definition of another non-terminal symbol.

BNF is somewhat difficult to use. It describes sequences textually rather than visually, requiring most readers to perform a kind of mental translation in order to understand it. BNF's principal virtues are its great compactness, easy handling of recursion, and facility for describing sequences of text, making it especially suitable for the description of command languages and programming languages which might contain hundreds of different syntactic elements. (Jackson diagrams can also describe recursion, following the same technique: a box lower in the tree has the same name as a box higher in the tree.) Though BNF's assortment of constructs is very sparse, because it's textual, it's very easy to extend.

10.4.2 Syntax diagrams

Another type of sequence notation most commonly used for describing grammars is *syntax diagrams*. Syntax diagrams were brought to wide popularity in the definition of the grammar of Pascal, in [Jensen 1985]. However, syntax diagrams are probably the most readable of all the sequence notations, and they apply far beyond descriptions of syntax. Their arrows make them especially intuitive for describing sequences of events.

Figure 10.6 is the lifecycle of a corporate bond redrawn as a syntax diagram:

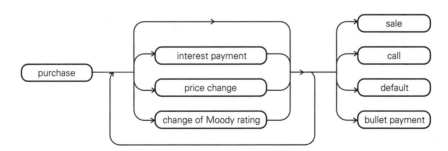

Figure 10.6 Lifecycle of a corporate bond in a syntax diagram

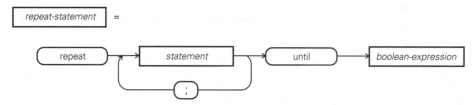

Figure 10.7 Syntax diagram for a repeat statement in Pascal

Sequence is shown by following the arrows from left to right as they take you from from one element to the next. Selection is shown by a line branching out into several lines. Iteration is shown by a line looping back to the left. An option, or a zero-or-more iteration, is shown by an arrow in a selection group that passes through no element, as in the group immediately following purchase.

There is really only one rule for reading syntax diagrams: the set of all possible sequences they describe is the set of all possible paths that you can take by following the arrows. The rules for creating syntax diagrams, however, are very restrictive, ensuring that a reader can examine all possible paths systematically. Elements can be arranged only by sequence, selection, and iteration; lines can't lead just anywhere.

Notice that whereas the Jackson diagram in figure 10.5 included the names normal activity and termination as placeholders, neither of which was a term from the problem domain, the syntax diagram does not include any placeholder terms. Also, the syntax diagram scarcely needs a legend to explain what the symbols mean.

Syntax diagrams show hierarchy in the same manner as BNF: by including a non-terminal symbol in a definition. A non-terminal symbol appears in a box with sharp corners as opposed to rounded corners. Putting the name of the element in italics helps emphasize the distinction. The same device indicates recursion, as shown in the syntax of Pascal's repeat statement in figure 10.7.

Notice that the syntax diagram requires no stmt-sequence to be defined, as in BNF. The semicolon that separates statements is conveniently indicated by drawing it on the leftward-moving line that shows that statement can be iterated.

The primary disadvantage of syntax diagrams is that they take more effort to draw than the other notations. However, this is easily remedied with a modern-day charting program.

In light of the fact that there is nothing in syntax diagrams that is specific to syntax, and because they are perhaps the most intuitive of all the sequence notations, a better name for them might be *sequence diagrams*.

10.4.3 Warnier-Orr diagrams

Warnier-Orr diagrams* add yet another construct to the description techniques of sequence, selection, iteration, hierarchy, and recursion: concurrency. Two elements are said to be *concurrent* if both must be present in a sequence, but they can occur in either order: *A* before *B*, or *B* before *A*.

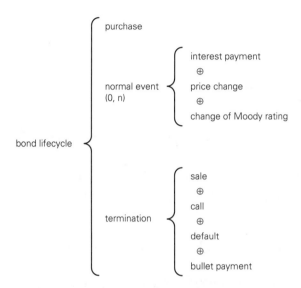

Figure 10.8 Warnier-Orr diagram of the lifecycle of a corporate bond

In the diagram in figure 10.8, the braces indicate hierarchy: that the element on the left is composed of the sub-elements on the right. Sequence is shown by the vertical placement of elements: a sequence starts at the top and continues downward. The ⊕ symbol, meaning exclusive or (either but not both), indicates selection. Iteration is shown by putting the minimum and maximum numbers of iterations in parentheses below the iterated element, as illustrated by normal event. The minimum number of normal events is zero; that the maximum is infinity is shown by writing the name of a variable, n, instead of a number. This variable can then be referred to elsewhere in the documentation where it denotes the actual number of iterations in a specific occurrence.

That two elements are concurrent is shown by a plus sign without an enclosing circle. Aside from the obvious use of describing subprocesses that occur in parallel, concurrency can also describe the simultaneous multiple hierarchies involved in a boundary

---

* Another of the classic 1970s books on converting sequential data structures into program designs was [Warnier 1974], which introduced the basic brace notation that grew into Warnier-Orr diagrams.

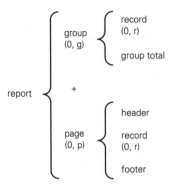

Figure 10.9 Overlapping hierarchies in a Warnier-Orr diagram, expressed as concurrency

clash, as shown in figure 10.9, or any hierarchical but unordered collection, such as the set of parts and subassemblies in an assembly.

Warnier-Orr diagrams tend to fit better on a page than Jackson diagrams, partly because of the lack of boxes, but also due to the vertical rather than horizontal orientation. A page is usually taller than it is wide. A word or phrase, however, is usually wider than it is tall, and in practice, hierarchies tend to have relatively few levels but many items at each level; that is, hierarchies tend to be bushy rather than deep. Consequently it's usually possible to include a lot more information in a Warnier-Orr diagram on one page, whereas the corresponding Jackson diagram might need to be broken up into several pages.

Warnier-Orr diagrams include a great number of extensions beyond the basic sequence-and-hierarchy constructs. Variations on the concurrency operator give Warnier-Orr diagrams a simple way to describe even such things as algebraic expressions. Different idioms specialize Warnier-Orr diagrams for descriptions of processes, descriptions of things, and descriptions of serial data streams. For more information on Warnier-Orr diagrams, see [Orr 1981].

10.4.4 Flow charts

The *flow chart* has been criticized a great deal in the past twenty-five years, but it is quite suitable for describing many simple types of sequences, especially those with a very linear structure with very little branching or iteration. Many business processes are, indeed, this simple.

In a flow chart, as shown in figure 10.10, each rectangle represents an action that has only one possible outcome. An action that involves a decision, or more than one possible outcome, is shown by a diamond with a different, labeled line emerging for each outcome.

The principal danger of flow charts is that when you draw one, you can easily overlook possible sequences. If several actions have several possible outcomes, including going back and repeating previous actions, it's hard to be systematic in covering every possible way that an action can be initiated. Drawing a flow chart is essentially the same as writing a program with goto statements. Beyond a low level of complexity, the program quickly degenerates into spaghetti.

10.4.5 State-transition diagrams

The most common use for state-transition diagrams is to state how something responds to every possible sequence of events, that is, to describe causal rules. However, a state-transition diagram can also simply describe a set of all possible sequences, as in figure 10.11. Each rectangle represents a state that something can be in at a certain time or range of time; each arrow denotes an event that changes its state.

Because state-transition diagrams can make two types of assertions—here is how such-and-such responds to stimuli, and here is a set of all possible sequences—you must indicate which type you mean, as in the introductory sentence in figure 10.11.

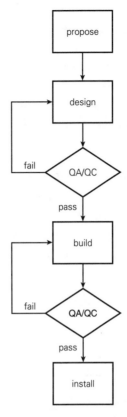

Figure 10.10 Flow chart of a simple design-and-build process; QA/QC stands for "quality assurance/quality control"

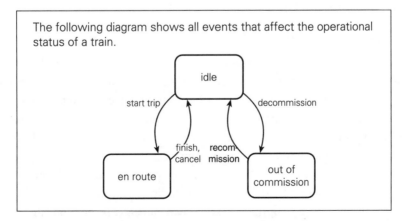

Figure 10.11 A simple state-transition diagram

Notice that the state diagram does not emphasize the events, but what the train is doing when it's not engaged in an event. Notice also that the set of all possible sequences of events shown in figure 10.11 would be awkward to depict in a Jackson diagram or with any of the other techniques that rely exclusively on the sequence/selection/iteration type of breakdown.

The problem is that for any possible sequence that goes *ABC*, there is another that goes *BCA* and another that goes *CBA*, forcing you to draw a separate tree for each one. You can't make *A*, *B*, and *C* alternative subelements of a single interated element because that would imply that *A*, *B*, and *C* could come in any sequence at all.

On the other hand, when the sequence/selection/iteration approach is enlightening, a state-transition diagram often isn't, as in figure 10.12. By emphasizing current state over sequence of events, the diagram wrongly makes it appear that the main fact of interest is whether the bond is in or out of the portfolio.

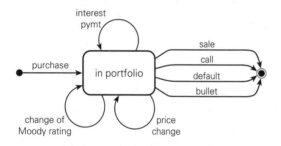

Figure 10.12 Lifecycle of a corporate bond, shown in a state-transition diagram

More information about state-transition diagrams, including guidelines on how to name states, is in section 11.1.

10.4.6 Ad hoc notations

All the preceding notations for describing sequences are quite generic in that they are so well known and so general as to have names. This means that they address only what is common to a great variety of sequences and ignore what is different. However, very often what makes the best documentation is a notation that fits the subject matter very closely, showing the reader exactly what is distinctive about the subject and no more. It doesn't matter if the notation doesn't fit anything else.

You've already seen one *ad hoc* notation in the descriptions of the contents of each line in the mail server's log file. Italicized words indicate text that can vary from line to line, text in brackets indicates optional text, and an ellipsis (three periods in a row) indicates a one-or-more iteration of the preceding text element.

Figure 10.13 *Ad hoc* notation showing sequence of bars in a bar code

Another *ad hoc* sequence notation was the description of the format of a node name. There, a graphic simply divided a six-letter code into three segments and spelled out what characters could go into each segment and what they stood for.

The diagram of bar codes in figure 10.2 becomes much more descriptive when redrawn, as in figure 10.13.

The data consists of a sequence of pairs, with each pair containing an identifier code and identifier contents. The data in each identifier's contents varies according to the identifier code. Code/content pairs can appear in any order, but no two pairs can have the same code.

All this can be indicated by stating it explicitly in text, as in the previous paragraph, and then providing a table:

Identifier	Code	Contents
Container serial number	00	exactly 18 digits
Container type code	01	exactly 14 digits
Batch number	10	up to 20 alphanumerics
Production date (YYMMDD)	11	exactly 6 digits
Expiration date (YYMMDD)	17	exactly 6 digits
Serial number	21	up to 20 alphanumerics
Lot number	23	up to 19 alphanumerics

If there were fifty of these identifier types, the table would be the only reasonable form in which to document them; diagrams would become a mess. Similarly, the width of a quiet zone, the way digits and characters are encoded in black and white stripes, the start and stop codes, and the checksum should all be described in text or tables.

C H A P T E R   1 1

Causation and control

Chapter 10 described events only with respect to the sequence in which they can occur, what they affect, and how the computer can tell when one has happened—enough to define most dynamic information problems. Defining a control problem involves two more kinds of information: what causes the events, and the desired problem-domain behavior. This chapter presents a number of techniques for describing both the causal relations and the desired behavior. These techniques apply both to describing the problem domain and to writing the program specification. In the problem domain, you describe both the rules that objects there obey regardless of how the machine is programmed and the additional rules that the machine is to enforce. In the specification, you describe the causal rules that the machine's input/output devices are to obey.

While this book is concerned only with presenting some patterns that prove useful in a variety of problems (without making a claim of total generality) this limitation applies especially to the discussion of causation. Control problems are among the trickiest and most varied in software, and while we have a few useful patterns, the state of the art is a long way from having a satisfactory library of patterns that map to a set of well defined problems. For causation, we don't yet have anything like the sequence/selection/ iteration/hierarchy technique for imposing a simple order on most sequences. Most research in software engineering to date has focused on how to structure programs and how to describe programs without including all the details, not with how to describe the world outside the software. So, the patterns in this chapter consist mainly of techniques that have been applied to describing programs that solve control problems, adapted to describing the problem itself.

11.1 State transitions

Objects in the world can take on different *states* at different times: the air can take on different temperatures, inventory items can be in different places, proposals can be approved or not approved, a car can move at different speeds or sit stationary, and so on. It is an axiom of states that at any time, an object is in exactly one of its possible states.

Controlling objects in the world entails causing them to take on desired states at desired times. To control them, we must know what causes them to change state. For some types of object, the rules by which they change state are best expressed in the form of mathematical equations. For example, a satellite's location relative to the Earth changes continuously according to a set of differential equations. The density of the air, wind speed and direction, and the positions of the elevators, ailerons, and rudder affect the motion of an airplane according to a set of complex mathematical equations.

Deriving the specifications for software to control such objects is a highly specialized discipline which is a part of *control theory*. Here we will cover only a much more elementary type of causation: discrete events that cause an object to perform an action, possibly switching from one state to another when the action is complete, where the number of states is finite and very small—small enough that you can document each of them one by one. The action performed by the object might vary depending on the object's current state.

A simple example is the light bulb in a room and the switch that turns it on and off. The turn on event moves the light to the on state; the turn off event moves it to the off state. This simple pair of state transitions is shown in figure 11.1(a). Each rectangle represents a state that an object can be in for a duration of time; each arrow represents an event.

Many kinds of objects react differently to the same events, depending on which events have already happened to them. The simplest form of this type of state transition is shown in figure 11.1(b): a light switch that toggles state each time it's pressed.

A more complex example is dialing a telephone. The first digit you dial might be a 7, and the last digit you dial might be a 7, but the two, identical events cause different effects in the telephone system. The first 7 initiates the call, stopping the dial tone; the

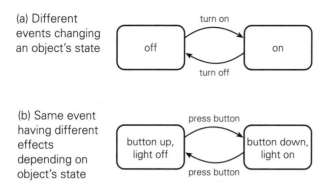

(a) Different events changing an object's state

off — turn on → on
on — turn off → off

(b) Same event having different effects depending on object's state

button up, light off — press button → button down, light on
button down, light on — press button → button up, light off

Figure 11.1 Simple state-transition diagrams

final 7 completes the call, causing the telephone equipment to generate a busy signal, ringing sound, or recorded message, depending on what you dialed.

Figure 11.2 shows the behavior of a telephone line in the United States. There are a number of simplifications: receiving a call (ringing and answering) is omitted, as well as international dialing sequences, operator interruptions, special features like call waiting, and nearly everything else outside the normal procedure of placing a call. The only events are dialing numbers, hanging up and lifting the receiver, doing nothing for too long while the phone is off hook and no call has been placed (timeout), and having the other party hang up.

The diagram shows several fundamental techniques for keeping complexity under control. When the same event has the same effect in many states, you can group the states into a *superstate,* enclosed in a larger rectangle.* The hang up event can happen in eleven different states, and in each case, the result is the same: the telephone line moves to the on hook state. So all eleven states are grouped together into the off hook superstate. Similarly, the timeout event applies to all states in the dialing superstate. Drawing the superstates in thick gray lines helps reduce visual confusion caused by closely spaced parallel lines.

As a complexity-reduction technique, even though there are actually different states for each digit in the area code and each digit in the local number, the diagram collapses them into two states each. There is actually more state information, not shown on the diagram: the telephone number that is accumulated as digits are dialed. The state transition

---

* The simplifying technique of the superstate comes from [Harel 1987]. [Harel 1987] also contains some important extensions to state-transition diagrams not covered here, such as techniques for diagramming concurrent states. Harel's extended form of the state-transition diagram, which he calls a Statechart, is also incorporated into UML; see [Rational 1997].

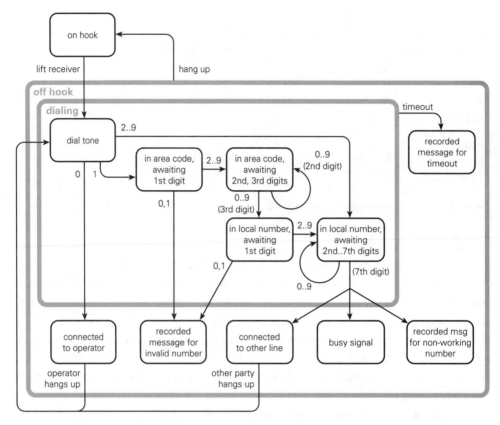

Figure 11.2 State-transition diagram for a telephone line in the United States (simplified)

when the last digit is dialed depends on the state of the other telephone line: busy, available, or not working due to disconnection, change of phone number, and so forth. The rule for which state becomes current after the last digit is dialed is not shown on the diagram because it would cause clutter. The diagram is difficult enough to follow as it is.

You can omit whatever you like from the graphic because you always have the option of explaining it all in text anyway. The more complex or tricky the diagram is, the more you should consider adding an all-text description of the state transitions. Graphics tend to leave important facts unstated, such as whether an event not shown is impossible or is supposed to be ignored, and often there isn't room to describe activity that occurs while a state is current, on entry to a state, on exit from a state, or special conditions that affect which state becomes current in response to a specific event.

UML provides some typographical conventions for putting all this text on the diagram itself—italics means one thing, text after a slash means another, and so on—though many people find them confusing when all are used at once in the same diagram. Always keep in mind that your goal is to fully document an object and its states in the easiest way possible for a reader to understand, not to force every description into a standard graphical notation. Text is the ever-reliable standby.

To fully document an object and its states, you need to include the following information in one form or another:

- A list of all the states

- For each state, what, if anything, the object does during this state, or any externally detectable difference about this state. For example, one state of a garage-door opener is opening, during which the motor pulls the door open. In the light bulb's on state, the light is shining.

- For each state, which events are possible, and for each possible event, how the object responds while in that state: any action that the object performs, and the object's state after the event

- Any additional state information of the sort that does not lend itself well to state-transition diagrams, such as the telephone number accumulated while dialing

- Which state is the start state, if any

- Which state (or states) is the end state(s), if any

The following is a partial text version of figure 11.2.

Five state variables apply to each telephone line, in addition to the states shown in the diagram:

area code	A string of up to three digits: the area code being dialed, if the call is long distance.
local number	A string of up to seven digits: the telephone number within the area code.
timer	A 60-second countdown timer. The timer is either off or counting down (running).
transmit	Where the telephone system sends audio signals originating from the telephone line. Off if not transmitting.
receive	The source of audio signals sent to the telephone line. Off if the telephone system is not sending any audio signals.

Events:

lift receiver	Loop is closed. Possible only in on hook state. *(The loop is the electrical circuit that goes through your telephone, connecting it to the telephone company's equipment.)*
hang up	Loop is opened. Possible only in states other than on hook.
timeout	The timer reaches zero by counting down.
0, 1, 2, 3, 4, 5, 6, 7, 8, 9	A touch-tone or pulse digit is dialed.
other party hangs up	Possible only during a call: the other party hangs up. The other party is either the operator or another telephone line.

States and responses:

State	Event	Action	Next State
on hook (transmit off, receive off, timer off)	0..9	—	on hook
	lift receiver	—	dial tone
	timeout	(Not supposed to happen.) Turn timer off.	on hook
dial tone (transmit off, receive dial tone, on entry, set timer to 60 seconds)	0	—	connected to operator
	1	—	in area code, awaiting first digit
	2..9	local number = *digit*	in local number, awaiting 2nd..7th digits
	hang up	—	on hook
	timeout	—	recorded message for timeout

State	Event	Action	Next State
in area code, awaiting 1st digit (transmit off, receive off, timer runs)	0, 1	—	recorded message for invalid number
	2..9	area code = *digit*	in area code, awaiting 2nd, 3rd digits
	hang up	—	on hook
	timeout	—	recorded message for timeout
in area code, awaiting 2nd, 3rd digits (transmit off, receive off, timer runs)	0..9	append *digit* to area code	if area code now has three digits: in local number, awaiting 1st digit; otherwise: in area code, awaiting 2nd, 3rd digits
	hang up	—	on hook
	timeout	—	recorded message for timeout
(Remaining states omitted for brevity.)			
connected to other party (transmit to line specified by local number, in local area code if no area code dialed, otherwise in area code; receive from same line; timer off)	0..9	—	connected to other party
	hang up	—	on hook
	timeout	(Not supposed to happen.) Turn timer off.	connected to other party

Notice that the table addresses what happens if there's a timeout in each state. Looking only at figure 11.2, it would have been easy to overlook this case, because it's never supposed to happen in some states, but it's not physically impossible for it to happen (the way a hang up event is impossible if the phone is on hook). This is probably insignificant, but you can't know that until you've checked every case. By writing a table, you systematically address every possible case.

While the text doesn't show the big picture the way the diagram does, it does make it easy to understand one state at a time. It's easy to tell what the events are and whether all the events have been covered. It's easy to tell what the actions are. Everything is spelled out, one point at a time. It's easy to read it systematically, from beginning to end, because it has a beginning and an end and a linear sequence leading from one to the other. These are the strengths of a table and the weak points of a graphic. The handling of spurious timeouts always leads back to the state that received the spurious timeout. This is awkward to show in a graphic. All the states that are off hook but not dialing would have to have an extra transition arrow leading back to themselves. But the table has a cell for everything.

Because many states respond the same way to hang up and timeout, you can define these responses in a separate table and refer to it as needed in the main table. This makes it easier to modify the document in future revisions without introducing inconsistencies. However, this also increases the danger of misinterpretation, since each state is not described completely in one place. If there are only a few repetitions, it's best to keep them, in order to retain the simple table structure.

Another way to systematically address every event in every state is to draw a matrix with one row for each event and one column for each state (or the other way around). This works fine under the following conditions: there are no actions other than changing states, there aren't so many columns that you can't fit the matrix on the page, there are no tricky state transitions involving conditions, or if you find another, readable way to organize the information, perhaps by making a separate table of actions and including references to it in the matrix.

The example above is meant to be very general; it's filled with just the sorts of troublesome irregularities that prevent many real life problems from fitting into a matrix. Naturally, apply simpler means to simpler problems, as long as you include all the necessary information.

Note that while the table makes the state-transition diagram in figure 11.2 redundant, the table does not make the diagram useless. In the text, the relationships between the states are difficult to grasp. Typically, a reader will read a little bit about one state, refer to the diagram to check what states can transition to that state, continue a little further in the text, go back to the diagram, and so on. Without the diagram, a reader would either have to visualize everything in their head—very difficult for something like the telephone diagram—or try to comprehend all the state transitions purely abstractly, with no visualization, a feat of which relatively few people are capable.

All this has an important implication for the diagram: you must not slap it out carelessly or let a CASE tool arrange it automatically. Since its sole purpose is to help a reader visualize, you must give careful thought to how you lay out all the elements. The layout should be harmonious. The eye should be able to follow the flow of the diagram easily. The diagram stresses what is conceptually important—something a CASE tool knows nothing about. The dial tone state, for example, is the "home base" of dialing. Therefore, instead of burying it in the middle, figure 11.2 puts it in the upper left, surrounded by much more white space than most of the other states. The recorded message for timeout state is an odd, unusual case, so it doesn't line up with any of the other states.

These are the kinds of considerations to keep in mind when drawing a state-transition diagram. Faithfully representing the transitions is not enough. If you draw a snarl, you might as well draw nothing at all, because the text already provides a complete description (even though it gives the reader no help with visualizing). If you draw a snarl diagram without the text, then you might as well not bother writing a document.

11.1.1 Naming states and events

Be sure to name states in such a way that it is obvious that they are states and not events, and events so that it is obvious that they are events and not states. It's surprisingly easy to do it the other way around. For example, it might be tempting to call the hang up event on hook, since the event consists of making the telephone line "on hook." But that's exactly why you should not call the event on hook: that's the state that persists when the event is done. Another common temptation is to name a state for the event that normally follows it; for example, dial 1st digit instead of dial tone.

The name of an event should be either a verb or a noun (or a phrase that functions as a verb or noun) that clearly suggests an event that happens at a certain time and is over. Another option for hang up, then, is go on hook. In the telephone example, the names for digits are nouns; in context—that is, inside a description of dialing a telephone number—these clearly denote events.

The name of a state should be an adjective or a noun (or a phrase that functions as an adjective or noun) that clearly suggests a state that can persist through time. You should be able to use it in a sentence that says, "An object of this type is either *A* or *B*," where *A* and *B* are state names. A light bulb, for example, is on or off.*

An important type of adjective for naming states is the *participle*: a verb that has been converted into an adjective. English has two kinds of participles: present participles

---

* The words *on* and *off* are also prepositions in English, but in the sentence "A light bulb is either on or off," they function as adjectives. Most words in English can function in more than one part of speech, making it difficult to invent terminology that is both clear and very concise.

and past participles. The present participle is the verb with *-ing* added: blinking, running, printing.* The past participle is usually identical to the past tense: connected, depleted, magnetized. Some irregular verbs have a past participle that is different from their past tense such as broken, shown, and done. If you're not sure which is the past tense and which is the past participle, the past participle is the one that fits into this sentence: "The object is *past-participle.*"

The following are a number of words that are often useful when naming states and events:

States	Events
start	*start*
in header segment	*create*
target *acquired*	*acquire* target
got password	*get* password (or just *password*)
detected intrusion	*detect* intrusion (or just *intrusion*)
received confirmation (or *confirmed*)	*receive* confirmation (or just *confirmation*)
awaiting confirmation	status *changes*
done	*abort*

The word *start* appears in both columns, because it's often useful for both states and events, though not when describing the same object, of course. As a state, *start* is a good name for the state that an object is in before it has undergone any events. As an event, *start* is a good name for the event that begins the process described by the state-transition diagram.

11.1.2 Four interpretations

State-transition diagrams (and tables) suffer from a fundamental ambiguity. They can be intended—and interpreted—in any of the following four ways:

- The events that come out of any state are *the only events possible* when the object is in that state. If an event is not shown, then it is impossible.

- The events that come out of any state are *how the object responds* to events when in that state. If an event is not shown, then it has no effect or is impossible.

---

* The *-ing* ending also indicates another form of the verb, the *gerund*, but this distinction is more subtle than need concern us when naming states.

- The events that come out of any state are *the only events allowable* when the object is in that state. If an event is not shown, then the system must prevent it from happening.

- The events that come out of any state are the *desired response of the object* to events when in that state. If an event is not shown, then it is either impossible or the desired response is to ignore the event.

The first two possible interpretations are as problem-domain description: the first is a description of a set of all possible sequences of events (discussed on page 203); the second is a description of causal rules. The third and fourth interpretations are as prescriptive statements—design decisions to be implemented, whether requirements or specifications.

If you were writing a requirements document for software to control an automated telephone dialer for a business, then the state-transition diagram for a telephone line in figure 11.2 would be purely descriptive. It would tell how the telephone line responds to events, for the purpose of enabling the programmers to design software to control the telephone line. The requirements would say that the dialer places calls to telephone numbers and at times according to rules stated elsewhere in the document. The programmers rely on the truth of the statements in the text form of the table, such as what the transmit and receive lines are connected to in different states, in order to create a design that fulfills the requirements.

On the other hand, if you were writing a requirements document for software to control the equipment at the telephone company that connects calls, then you would intend figure 11.2 prescriptively. In this case, the statements in the text form of the table about what the transmit and receive lines are connected to in different states would be the requirements. The programmers wouldn't rely on those statements being true. Their job would be to make them true. The document would need other, purely descriptive statements that tell what events connect the transmit and receive channels to the various telephone lines, recorded messages, and so on. The programmers would rely on those statements when designing the part of the specification concerned with changing the states of those channels.

To resolve the ambiguity, you must explicitly indicate which interpretation is correct. You can easily accomplish this with a sentence introducing the diagram or table:

> The following diagram shows all events that affect the oxygen sensor:
>
> The oxygen sensor responds to events as shown below:
>
> **R-3.1 For each state of the oxygen sensor, the system allows only the events shown below to occur:**
>
> **R-3.1 The oxygen sensor responds to events as shown below:**

In the third and fourth examples, the fact that the statements are requirements is indicated by giving it a requirement number and setting it in the font reserved for requirements. To make the distinction even clearer, you can add a modal verb, like *must* or *shall*, though if you do so, you should word all requirement statements that way consistently, and modal verbs make some statements rather wordy.* Including it in a section titled "Requirements" also helps, especially if that section contains no domain-description statements.† Finally, by wording the descriptions of the actions as commands, such as "append *digit* to local number," you reinforce that you are making prescriptive statements; by wording them as indicative sentences, such as "*digit* appends to local number," you reinforce that you are making descriptive statements.

In requirements documents for software that controls equipment or other software, often you actually need to write very little description of the causal rules followed by the controlled objects, because this documentation already exists. You can simply refer the reader to the appropriate documentation. (Be sure that it's readily available.) For software that controls new equipment, however, often there is no documentation available which is suitable for use by software developers. A new manufacturing robot is unlikely to have a state table documented already; your task of writing the software requirements is just one stage of the whole job of designing the robot.

The third interpretation most often applies to software that is supposed to guide something through a certain process when it might otherwise go around the process or stop at one point in the process, such as approving a proposal. The following are some states that a typical type of proposal moves through: awaiting approval by department chair, awaiting approval by dean, awaiting approval by provost, awaiting approval by board of trustees, approved. Such a set of state transitions is equivalent to saying: a proposal is not to be marked as approved unless approved by the chair, the dean, the provost, and the board of trustess; the dean is to be notified when the chair approves; the provost is to be notified when the dean approves; and so on.

A state-transition diagram in a specification is not subject to ambiguity between descriptive and prescriptive interpretations because a specification describes only the designed—that is, desired—behavior of the system at the interface between the system and the problem domain. Therefore, only the prescriptive interpretations make sense; you don't need to explicitly disavow the descriptive ones. Furthermore, the specification describes little other than how the system responds to events, so usually only the fourth interpretation is reasonable. The introductory sentence still doesn't hurt, though.

---

* See *Requirement statements* in chapter 15.

† This is a matter of document organization, the subject of chapter 14.

11.2 Actions

Software that solves a control problem causes *actions* that bring about desired results. The desired results are usually functions of other actions, which the software doesn't cause, like button-presses on a photocopier's control panel or changes to a camera's focus to sharpen an image. The software usually can't bring about the desired results directly. For example, the microprocessor in a photocopier can't produce copies directly. The microprocessor can only affect the voltage of wires directly connected to it. State-changes in these wires, in turn, cause a chain of further actions that result in the creation of a photocopy.

Thus, in a control problem, there can be three types of action to document:

- *Spontaneous actions:* those initiated in the problem domain, such as the button-presses at the photocopier's control panel.

- *Immediate actions:* those that the software can initiate directly, such as changing the voltage of wires. An immediate action is shared phenomena; it's simultaneously an action in the software and an action in the problem domain.

- *Mediate actions:* those that are caused by other actions, such as the actual production of the photocopy. A mediate action can be caused by a spontaneous action, an immediate action, or another mediate action.

Most control problems boil down to this: "How can the software make the right mediate actions happen in response to the right spontaneous actions?"

These types of actions are not mutually exclusive. An action that can occur spontaneously might also be indirectly causable by the computer. In this case, it would have two modes of causation: spontaneous and mediate.

The word *spontaneous* might seem inappropriate, since a button-press doesn't really occur spontaneously. A person presses a button, so it might seem to be a mediate event caused by a person, and this action, in turn, might be caused by someone else needing to prepare some hand-outs for a meeting. However, the above classification of actions is strictly in relation to the software. Spontaneous actions are those that, from the perspective of the software, happen "out of the blue," not as a consequence of any other action in the problem domain. A person pressing a button is just something that happens—in this case, something that charges the software with the duty of making something else happen.

The same action does not always cause the same result. The roller that feeds paper into a printer might succeed in getting a sheet of paper and might fail. In a high-precision printer, the roller might bring the sheet into the printer at the wrong orientation.

So the result of roller turns would be the entire set of possible orientations, plus the possibility of not getting a sheet of paper at all.

The words *action* and *event* mean roughly the same thing, though *event* suggests a very short action, perhaps even one that can be located at a single point in time, or the beginning or end of an action. We'll use the word *action* as the more general term, limiting *event* to the narrower sense, especially to mean a short action that affects the state of an object, as described in section 11.1.

The information needed to document each action is as follows:

- The type of causation: spontaneous, immediate, or mediate. Instead of using these somewhat esoteric words, you can simply group actions of each type together, preceded by a statement like, "The microprocessor can cause the following actions directly."

- All of the types of objects involved in the action: the objects that do the action, such as the buttons on the control panel, and any objects that are affected by the action, such as the sheet of paper turned by the feed roller. The objects that do the action might also be affected by it. Direct actions are done by the computer; grouping them with the other direct actions indicates their "doer." The list of objects involved in the action is sometimes called its *signature*.

- Any parameters that the action has: attributes of the action that can vary from instance to instance, such as specifically which objects are affected

- In the case of indirect actions, the condition or event that triggers the action: "happens when."

- If the action continues as long as a certain condition is true, like a servomotor that turns as long as a certain wire is at 9 volts, then say this explicitly: "happens while."

- The duration of the action, unless the action is short enough that its duration can be disregarded

- All the possible results of the action: for each object affected, what effects can there be? The results of an action can themselves be events that trigger other actions or cause state transitions in objects. For example, "successfully connect telephone lines" might be one result of the action of placing a call; "get busy signal" is another. Also helpful is to include the relative frequencies of each result, for example, success 95% of the time, failure 5%.

- If more than one result is possible, how, or whether, the software can detect which actually occurred

Here are two examples of complete documentation of an action. First, from a photocopier:

feed original

Objects:	Feed roller A, original
Happens when:	Output line 0xA0, bit 1 goes high for 0.4 sec.
Duration:	0.4 sec (happens while output line 0xA0, bit 1 is high)
Possible results:	(1) Original is on glass platen, face down. (97% probability if there was an original in the feed slot.)
	(2) Original is not on glass platen. (3% probability if original was in feed slot, 100% if it wasn't.)
	If and only if result (1) has occurred, microswitch B is activated.

Second, from a warehouse:

pick item

Participants:	Stock picker, items, storage locations.
Parameters:	List of one or more items and storage locations where they reside.
Happens when:	Printed order, showing list of items and storage locations, is at printer A, and a stock picker detaches the order.
Duration:	From the time the stock picker detaches the order, less than 5 min. in most cases; if more than 10 min., there is a problem (see below).
Possible results:	(1) The stock picker finds the items and brings them to the packing station.
	(2) The stock picker searches for the items, but fails to find one or more.
	(3) The stock picker never gets the order and/or never searches for the items.
	After 10 min., it is safe to assume that either (2) or (3) has happened.

The fact that an action can have more than one result has an important implication for requirements. What is the desired response for each result? For example, if the feed roller fails to bring a sheet of paper into the photocopier, what should it do? Display a light? Try again? How many times before giving up? In the warehouse, a stock picker goes to the warehouse to get an item and it's not there, even though the database says that it's in stock. What should the software do? Notify someone? Cancel the order? Change the order?

This means that there are two kinds of requirements in a typical control problem: those involving a relation between a trigger event and a desired result, such as "when the start button is pressed, make a copy," and those pertaining to everything that can possibly go wrong in the process that brings about that result—or rather, every alternative sequence of actions within that process.

The above discussion is as general as possible. In the vast majority of control problems, however, you can write documentation that is much easier to understand than a long list of actions. It's quite unnecessary to present the programmers with a jigsaw puzzle of actions to assemble into a sequence that produces the desired behavior because, in nearly all cases, the person who designed the machinery or procedures already understands the sequence in which they're supposed to happen.

Photocopying, for example, consists of a series of events planned out by the engineer who designed the photocopier. You can explicitly describe the intended series of events and then, for each action in the series, ask the engineer what all the possible results are and what is the desired response for each. The same principle applies when asking about and documenting procedures in a business.

Techniques for simplifying the description of the causal properties of the problem domain, based on a designer's intended sequence of events, are given in the next two sections.

11.3 Dependency

A photocopier works as follows. Inside the photocopier there is a surface coated with a substance that is a strong resistor in the dark but a good conductor where exposed to light. In most modern photocopiers, this surface is usually on the outside of a rotating drum or belt, called the *photoreceptor drum* or *photoreceptor belt*. A *corona wire* sprays ions onto the photoreceptor surface, charging it at every point. An image of the paper to be copied is then projected onto the photoreceptor. Wherever light shines, the charge leaks away. Thus, after exposure, the photoreceptor bears an image that is a copy of the image on the paper. The photoreceptor image, however, is made of electric charges rather than ink.

Next, *toner*—tiny, dark particles—is brought into contact with the photoreceptor. The toner has a static charge, applied at the factory where the toner is made, that is opposite to the charge of the photoreceptor image, making the toner stick to the photoreceptor at the regions corresponding to the dark regions of the original.

While the toner is being applied to the photoreceptor, another corona wire charges a blank sheet of paper with a charge of the same sign as that on the photoreceptor but of greater intensity. When the paper is brought into contact with the photoreceptor, the toner moves to the paper. Finally, the toner is fused to the paper by moving through a pair of heated rollers, and the paper is sent to the output tray. Any remaining charge on the photoreceptor is then erased and any remaining toner is mechanically scraped off, readying the photoreceptor for the next copy.

The entire process is shown in figure 11.3.

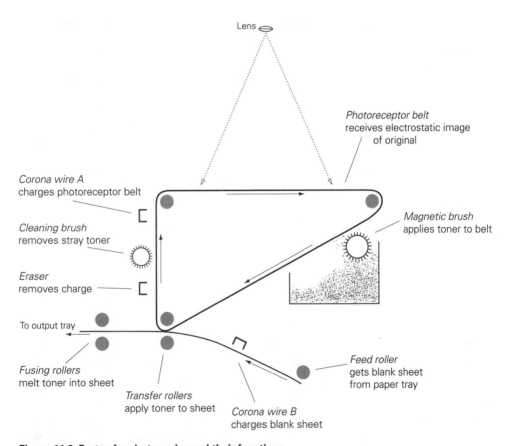

Figure 11.3 Parts of a photocopier and their functions

The requirements for the photocopier's controller are simple:

R-1 When the start button is pressed, if there is an original in the feed slot, the photocopier makes N copies of it, and places them in the output tray.

N is the number currently registering in the count display.

If the start button is pressed while photocopying is in progress, it has no effect.

R-2 The number N in the count display updates in response to button-presses according to the following state table.

At power-on, $N \leftarrow 1$, and current state is start.

State	Button	Response	Next State
start	0	—	start
	1..9	$N \leftarrow$ button	in number
	clear	—	start
	start	—	start
	interrupt	—	start
in number	0..9	If $N \geq 100$, beep. Otherwise: $N \leftarrow N \times 10 +$ button.	in number
	clear	$N \leftarrow 1$	start
	start	—	start
	interrupt	—	start

For simplicity, we'll ignore double-sided copies, sorting and collating, indicating that the fusing rollers are not warmed up yet, and so on. Descriptions of the buttons and how to control the display are simple and are omitted in this example.

How, then, should you describe the process by which the copies are made? Should you explain the principles of electrostatics and the properties of the amorphous selenium on the photoreceptor surface? Should you describe each of the events—the erasing of the charge, the cleaning of the surface, the charging of the surface, the exposure to the image, and so on—in a random order and leave it to the programmers to figure out how to make the copy come out?

Of course, there are much better ways. Since the designer of the photocopier—the system engineer—already knows the sequence in which each action is to occur, you can put this into the requirements. A *dependency diagram,* such as figure 11.4, shows what conditions must obtain before an action is supposed to happen and what conditions can result when the action is complete. Note that the dependency diagram says when actions must occur in order for a certain final result to occur. The preconditions shown in the diagram are not trigger conditions; they do not cause the action to occur. Rather, it is the responsibility of the software to cause the action when the preconditions become true.

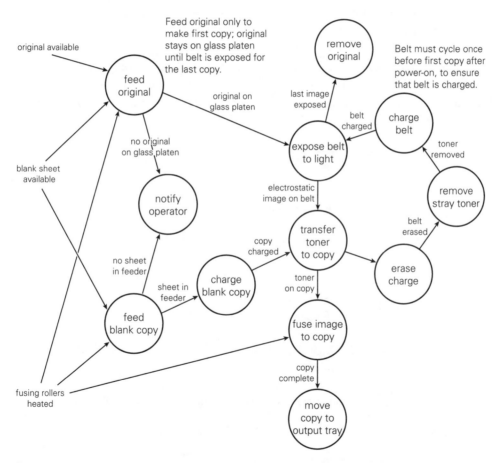

Figure 11.4 Dependency diagram showing results and preconditions of each action in the process of producing a single photocopy

Each circle represents an action; each arrow represents a condition. All the arrows emerging from an action are all the possible results of that action. The results are not necessarily mutually exclusive. All of the conditions resulting from an action could be true at once. An arrow with no label means only "action complete." The arrows leading into an action are the preconditions for that action. When all those conditions become true, the action is ready to begin.

For each condition, you must also document how the software can detect whether the condition is true or false. For software that controls machinery, you can usually accomplish this with a simple table relating bits in input/output ports to conditions. In business applications, some conditions might be accessible only by manual data entry, while for others there are machines to detect them, such as bar code readers that indicate when a part has reached a certain place on an assembly line.

Figure 11.4 makes life much easier for the programmers than simply describing the effects of all twelve actions and telling them to implement requirement R-1. You can also supplement it with text by adding a "perform when" or "ready when" line to each action's description, as in the example below. Another way is to collect all the "perform when" lines together into a section of the document that describes only the process. This is helpful when the same actions are parts of several different processes. The diagram helps readers see how all the actions fit together; the text version is better for systematic reading and double checking.

feed original	
Objects:	Feed roller A, original
Happens when:	Output line 0xA0, bit 1 goes high for 0.4 sec.
Duration:	0.4 sec (happens while output line 0xA0, bit 1 is high)
Possible results:	(1) Original is on glass platen, face down. (97% probability if there was an original in the feed slot.)
	(2) Original is not on glass platen. (3% probability if original was in feed slot, 100% if it wasn't.)
	If and only if result (1) has occurred, microswitch B is activated.
While copying, perform when:	Original available AND blank sheet available AND fusing rollers heated.

Note that the entire process in figure 11.4 is itself an action, and could be represented by a single circle in another, higher-level dependency diagram. The pressing of the start button is omitted from figure 11.4 because the process occurs once per copy, but one press of the start button can produce up to 999 copies. The notation does not easily describe an initial condition for a circular series of actions, such as the initial charging of the photoreceptor belt. The annotation at the upper right simply explains the initial condition in words, along with how to produce it.

Figure 11.4 introduces a new requirement, to address two ways that the process can fail:

R-3 While making a copy, the following events happen in response to failures:

	Action	Failure	Response
R-3.1	feed original	no original on glass platen	Beep, and abort copying process.
R-3.2	feed blank copy	no sheet in feeder	1. Beep, and turn on paper empty light. 2. When start button is pressed, turn off paper empty light, and resume copying process with M copies remaining; $M = N$ - number of copies produced so far.

All the other actions are merely part of the process for fulfilling requirement R-1. You could describe them as requirements, but they're really just the means available to make copies. The people who design the specification are interested in proving that copies get made when the user presses the start button, not that corona wire A charges the photoreceptor belt. The diagram shows the reader how to combine all the actions to make a copy; the real requirement, however, is just to make a copy. If you do make requirement statements out of figure 11.4, be sure to indicate that they are secondary to the main requirement of R-1. The reader should understand that R-1 is the end while the clockwork of actions is the means.

The response of beeping is itself another action, to be defined elsewhere according to the electronics in the photocopier. The software might have to toggle a speaker at a certain frequency for a certain duration or simply pulse a component that makes the entire beeping sound without further intervention.

Further requirements are needed to state the desired response to pressing the start button when the preconditions for copying are false: original available, blank sheet available, and fusing rollers heated. They're omitted here for reasons of space.

It's possible to make figure 11.4 simpler by exploiting this principle:

> The only information about the problem domain of relevance to a control problem is that which pertains to alternative actions that could occur at any point in time.

Most of the actions have only one possible result—or at least, for purposes of the diagram, they are assumed to have only one possible result. Therefore, for purposes of inventing the specification, it doesn't matter what the resulting condition is. All that matters is that the action completed. Figure 11.5 omits the unconditional results, leaving only completion arrows. The belt charged condition remains because it has to be true before the first copying cycle can begin.

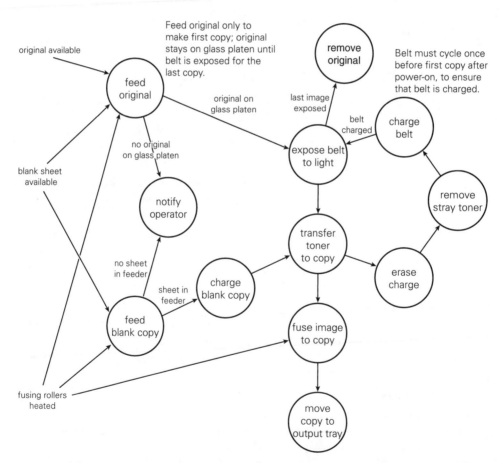

Figure 11.5 Simplified dependency diagram, omitting conditions assumed to occur unconditionally upon completion of an action

Including the conditions can still be valuable in order to show readers in graphical form what the result of each action is. There is a trade off, however. By omitting unconditional results, figure 11.5 directs your eye straight to the conditions that require special treatment in the specification; you can tell at a glance which conditions you need to detect and which conditions are just there for background knowledge. A diagram like 11.4 can provide the necessary background knowledge to understand the dependency diagram, so usually there is no need to repeat it.

The number of actions with unconditional results in figure 11.5 suggests a way to simplify the diagram even more, shown in figure 11.6. In fact, all of the actions from transfer toner to copy to charge belt are, from the standpoint of the software, just one action: rotating the belt. When the blank copy reaches point B, rotating the

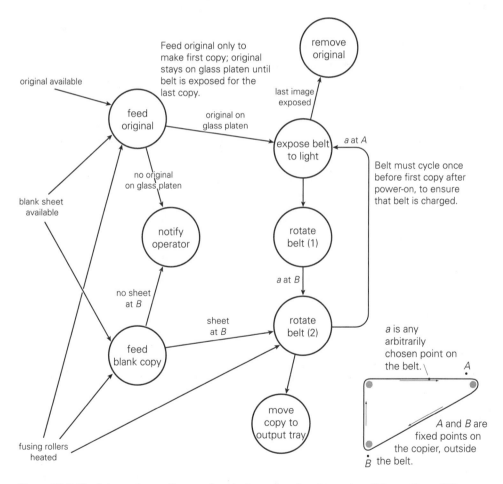

Figure 11.6 Final dependency diagram for photocopier, showing only actions and conditions where the software faces an alternative

belt also rotates the copy through the fusing rollers, so there's no need for a separate step to fuse the toner to the paper. When a portion of the belt passes by a corona wire, that portion of the belt is charged by the ions spraying from the corona wire, and so on.

The two rotate-belt actions are to stop when point *a* on the belt reaches specified fixed points *A* and *B*. How to determine when point *a* has reached points *A* and *B* is a matter for the text. There could be switches at points *A* and *B*, or perhaps the only way for the software to tell is by timing.

These three dependency diagrams, each simpler than the previous, illustrate a very frequent phenomenon in system analysis: the more you think about the problem, the simpler it becomes. Sometimes the opposite is claimed, and indeed sometimes the opposite is true, but one of the most important jobs performed by a system analyst is to boil all the complexity down, discovering the simple, underlying principles and removing irrelevant details. A simple diagram, accompanied by some simple text that includes all the information in an easily understood form, is usually the result of much greater intellectual effort than a sprawling, complex diagram in which secondary or irrelevant details obscure the main facts. A reader should not have to study a diagram for two weeks and then draw his own, simpler diagram; that's the analyst's job.

There are other ways to make dependency diagrams. [Martin 1985] includes (among other variations) notations for indicating that if any of a set of conditions is true, an action should proceed. The approach taken here, however, is that it's easier and clearer to simply write the word "or" in the diagram, and to express in words any information that's difficult to draw in a graphic. Also, note that diagrams 11.4 through 11.6 describe the problem domain, not the software.

The types of concurrent processes described by dependency diagrams are the subject matter of an entire branch of mathematics, known as *Petri nets*. A dependency diagram is really just a somewhat less formal and somewhat more readable version of a standard Petri net diagram.

11.3.1 Interruptions

Complicating most control problems, especially those involving the control of machinery, is the possibility of *interruptions*: spontaneous actions that can occur at any time and that necessitate stopping a process, possibly aborting it, or recovering in some way once the interruption has finished.

For each possible interruption, the requirements document needs to include the following information:

- The nature of the interruption. In the photocopier, examples would be paper jams and door openings.

- Any effects of the interruption. Opening the door of the photocopier, for example, causes all charge to be removed from the photoreceptor belt, destroying any electrostatic image that it might bear.

- Any parameters that can vary from one instance of the interruption to the next

- How the interruption can be detected. For example, detector switches in the photocopier that connect to I/O ports on the microprocessor

- Which actions the interruption can interrupt

- How to respond to the interruption; especially, how or whether to resume the interrupted process

The last item is usually another requirement; it's equivalent to the requirement for how to respond to a failed action. In the photocopier, responding to a jam involves beeping, turning on a light corresponding to the jam, and waiting for the operator to fix the jam. Resuming the interrupted process, however, can be more complicated. Perhaps the current step can be restarted, perhaps it's necessary to back up one or more steps, and so on.

11.4 Flow

Many actions involve two kinds of object: one object that does the action and is not changed by it, and another that is somehow transformed by the action. For example, a person or a section on a shop floor might perform one step of a manufacturing process: parts enter the process, and are transformed into assemblies—or the transformation might be as simple as moving the part from one place to another. Or, in a chemical processing plant, material enters a machine in one state and exits in another, perhaps as a different compound.

We think of the people or machines as active, and the objects that they operate on as passive. The people or machines are the *agents* of the software, performing operations on the passive objects in response to requests initiated by the software, readying the objects for the next phase of the process.*

This kind of process lends itself well to a variation on a dependency diagram, where the circles represent agents (or actions) and the arrows represent objects either

---

* The noun corresponding to *passive* is *patient*, but in contemporary usage, the only patients that we call by that name are the ones found in doctors' offices, so we'll just call them *passive objects* or simply *objects*.

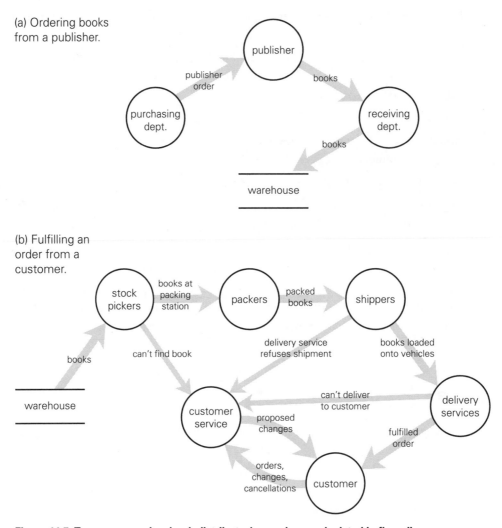

(a) Ordering books from a publisher.

publisher

purchasing dept. → publisher order

publisher → books → receiving dept.

receiving dept. → books → warehouse

(b) Fulfilling an order from a customer.

stock pickers → books at packing station → packers → packed books → shippers

warehouse → books → stock pickers

stock pickers → can't find book → customer service

packers → delivery service refuses shipment → customer service

shippers → books loaded onto vehicles → delivery services

delivery services → can't deliver to customer → customer service

customer service → proposed changes → customer

delivery services → fulfilled order → customer

customer service → orders, changes, cancellations → customer

Figure 11.7 Two processes in a book distributor's warehouse, depicted in flow diagrams

transformed, ready for a transformation, or both. Figure 11.7 shows two examples, from a book distributor's warehouse.

These diagrams are very similar to the much-criticized data-flow diagrams. There are two important differences. The first difference is that what is flowing is not data, but physical objects—in this case, books. For this reason, we'll call this simply a *flow diagram*, not a data-flow diagram.* There is some information flowing, such as the stock

---

* Gane-Sarson charts are a kind of data-flow diagram that also allows "physical flows." See [Martin 1985], p. 103.

pickers' notification that they can't find a book, but the data does not necessarily flow to or from the software. The diagram simply traces objects through a set of transformations by agents.

The second difference is the way we use a flow diagram. A flow diagram describes something that already exists or, at least, that is already designed. It is not a high-level sketch of the program to be designed. Rather, it provides information about the problem domain that is relevant to the design of the program. The accompanying text provides all the remaining detail: how the stock pickers can be told to go to the warehouse to pick books, rules for determining which orders to satisfy and which to reject, and so on. So we aren't trying to design by functional decomposition; we're merely describing a flow in a simple way.

Even though many agents or actions in a flow diagram produce only one result, the diagram shows the result in words in each case. The reason for this difference from a dependency diagram is that the purpose of a flow diagram is to show a reader the continuity from process to process. A reader should be able to easily trace each object as it moves from agent to agent.

Naturally, there is no reason that you can't combine a dependency diagram with a flow diagram. Figure 11.7(b) does that to some extent, with the thinner arrows denoting problems encountered by the stock pickers, shippers, and delivery services.

11.5 Rules

The following is from page 7 of the instructions for the 1997 edition of Form 1040, the form for declaring income, expenses, and taxes owed to the United States government:

IF your filing status is ...	AND at the end of 1997 you were* ...	THEN file a return if your gross income** was at least ...
Single	under 65	$6,800
	65 or older	7,800
Married filing jointly***	under 65 (both spouses)	$12,200
	65 or older (one spouse)	13,000
	65 or older (both spouses)	13,800

Married filing separately	any age	$2,650
Head of household (see page 10)	under 65	$8,700
	65 or older	9,700
Qualifying widow(er) with dependent child (see page 10)	under 65	$9,550
	65 or older	10,350

*If you turned 65 on January 1, 1998, you are considered to be age 65 at the end of 1997.

**Gross income means all income that you received in the form of money, goods, property, and services that is not exempt from tax, including any gain on the sale of your home (even if you may exclude or postpone part or all of the gain). Do not include social security benefits unless you are married filing a separate return and you lived with your spouse at any time in 1997.

***If you did not live with your spouse at the end of 1997 (or on the date your spouse died) and your gross income was at least $2,650, you must file a return regardless of your age.

Here we have a first-rate description of a moderately complex rule.* The description techniques applied here work well on a great many rules. They are:

- Make a table (a matrix).
- Keep complicated exceptions and definitions out of the table and in notes that accompany the table.

---

* The instructions prepared by the United States Internal Revenue Service are some of the finest technical writing in existence. They're hard to appreciate because you read them only to do a task you would much rather not do, but that makes them all the more worthy of appreciation. The instructions are written for an audience that does not want to read them. Much of the audience does not read well or is uncomfortable with arithmetic, and the information to be communicated is tremendously complicated—special cases and exceptions abound. We learn far more from imitating great examples than from abstract explanations—even those in this book—but in the computer field, due to the fact that nearly all work is proprietary, we seldom have opportunity to inspect great examples. But you can learn from other sources, too. In the Form 1040 instructions, notice how complex the information is, how simple the presentation is, and the techniques of wording, layout, and organization that bring about that simplicity. There are clever flow charts, effective use of shading to make numerical charts easier to read, lines of text that don't contain too many characters (see *Page layout* in chapter 15), references to other pages and other documents in place of saying too many things at once, and so on.

A terrible way present this same rule would be to split it into many complete sentences, like this:

R-22 If your filing status was single and at the end of 1997 you were under age 65 and your gross income was at least $6,800, then you must file a return.

R-23 If your filing status was single and at the end of 1997 you were age 65 or older and your gross income was at least $7,800, then you must file a return.

R-24 If your filing status is married filing jointly and you did not live with your spouse at the end of 1997 or on the date your spouse died and your gross income was at least $2,650, then you must file a return.

R-25 If your filing status is married filing jointly and you lived with your spouse at the end of 1997 or on the date your spouse died and at the end of 1997 both spouses were under age 65 and your gross income was at least $12,000, then you must file a reurn.

R-26 If your filing status is married filing jointly and you lived with your spouse at the end of 1997 or on the date your spouse died and at the end of 1997 only one spouse was age 65 or older and your gross income was at least $13,000, then you must file a return.

And so on.

Notice that in the one-statement-at-a-time version, you can't easily see relationships between different parts of the rule. For example, you can't easily see that every rule pertains to whether or not you're supposed to file a return! The fact that each filing status has a cut-off point of age 65 for different minimum gross incomes is also buried in the text. Finally, the text has serious problems with ambiguity because English syntax has difficulties expressing any but the simplest *and* and *or* relationships.*

11.5.1 Mappings and completeness

Every rule is a *mapping*: a set of tuples, each containing an element from one set and a corresponding element from another set (or perhaps involving more than two sets). Rules are thus exactly the same as the relations described in chapter 9.

---

* The practice of writing requirements as long series of nearly identical statements derives from the unfortunate theory that a requirement should be "atomic"—incapable of division into smaller propositions. A much better philosophy is that each proposition should be clear to the reader and that groups of propositions should be numbered according to whatever is most convenient for referring to them in other documents. See *Requirement statements* in chapter 15.

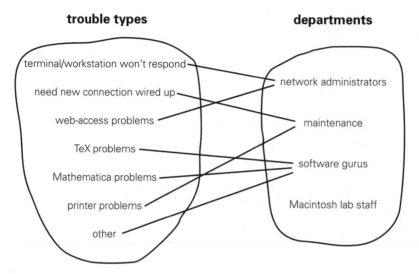

trouble types

departments

terminal/workstation won't respond

need new connection wired up

web-access problems

TeX problems

Mathematica problems

printer problems

other

network administrators

maintenance

software gurus

Macintosh lab staff

Figure 11.8 Domain and range in trouble-ticket rule

However, chapter 9 explained how to describe a set of tuples that could *potentially* be included in a relation—the cardinality of the relation and the kinds of sets that it relates. When describing a rule, you indicate the *actual* tuples in the relation. You don't merely say, "Every combination of filing status, age, and gross income has a corresponding yes or no for whether to file a return." You actually say which combinations of filing status, age, and gross income correspond to having to file a return.

A simple rule is shown in figure 11.8, relating classifications of trouble tickets in a university computer system to the departments that fix them. A piece of software might be responsible for routing trouble tickets to the correct department.

The set on the left, trouble type, is the set of all possible inputs to the rule. The job of the rule is to produce the output that corresponds to a given input. The set of inputs is called the *domain* of the relation; a variable that stands for an element of the domain is called an *independent variable*. The set of all possible outputs is called the *range*; a variable that stands for a corresponding element of the range is called a *dependent variable*.*

A rule is complete and consistent if it maps each element in the domain to exactly one corresponding element in the range. Elements in the range need not map back to the domain in the same way. In figure 11.8, none of the trouble types maps to Macintosh lab staff, and the rest of the departments map back to more than one trouble type.

---

* Unfortunately, the word *domain* also means any set distinguished for the purpose of making propositions about its elements, as in chapter 4, and the word *range* also means a set of elements having a lower bound and an upper bound. Hopefully this multiplicity of senses won't cause too much confusion.

If, for some reason, a single trouble type could map to more than one department, then the range would be "sets of departments" rather than just "departments."

While you can sometimes depict the tuples that make up a rule by drawing lines from one set to another, as in figure 11.8, usually a matrix is your best bet:

trouble type	department
terminal/workstation won't respond	network administrators
need new connection wired up	maintenance
web-access problems	network administrators
TeX problems	software gurus
Mathematica problems	software gurus
printer problems	maintenance
other	software gurus

11.5.2 Discontinuities

In the case of the rule for filing tax returns, the range is very small: {must file tax return, need not file tax return}. But the range is enormous: it's the set of all combinations of all filing statuses, ages, and gross incomes. The complete rule looks like this:

((Single, age 0, gross income \$0), no need to file return)
((Single, age 0, gross income \$1), no need to file return)
((Single, age 0, gross income \$2), no need to file return)
((Single, age 0, gross income \$3), no need to file return)
. . .

The excerpt from the Form 1040 instructions illustrates an important technique in rules with very large domains: exploit *discontinuities* in the rule—borders in the domain between subsets that follow different, simple patterns. Where many elements of the domain follow a simple pattern, you can cover them all in a single row or column of a matrix, as at the beginning of section 11.5. A separate row or column covers the next group, and so on. Thus, you reduce a complex rule to a conjunction of simple ones.

Usually, it's obvious when you can exploit discontinuities, but if you're having difficulty describing a rule, it's wise to see if you can find a relatively small number of discontinuities.

11.5.3 The bird's-eye view

Sometimes it's tempting to describe a rule by writing it in program code or in "structured English" pseudocode. For example, when describing the rule for how lines from the record groups in a report fit onto pages, in between the header and footer, you might write the rule as a procedure, like this:

```
N = 0
print header
while there is at least one more record-line
        print next record-line
        N = N + 1
        if N > page-lines - (header-lines + footer lines)
            print footer
            eject page
        end if
end while
```

Much better is to take a bird's-eye view of the record lines, and talk about entire groups of them at once, like this:

N = page-lines - (header-lines + footer-lines).

Distribute record-lines to pages as follows. Each consecutive page contains either the next N record-lines, or however many record-lines are left to print, whichever is less. For each page, print the following in sequence:

The header.
The record-lines for this page, in ascending order.
The footer.
Page break.

If you take a moment to look at the pseudocode above, you'll notice that it's full of bugs. Despite the best efforts of language designers, general-purpose programming languages are terrible ways to describe almost anything but computer programs. Programming languages, after all, are devices for configuring hardware, not for communicating mathematical relations or business rules or anything else. There is a reason why mathematicians don't talk to each other in Fortran and accountants don't talk to each other in COBOL. Leave programming to the programmers.*

---

* If you're not a programmer, you're probably not accustomed to spotting this kind of bug. Even programmers make these bugs frequently. The bugs are: the header prints only on the first page; the total number of lines printed on each page is one more than page-lines; and the program does not print a footer on the last page or eject the last page unless the last record-line in the report also comes at the very end of a page. It's amazing how many mistakes can find their way into a short segment of pseudocode!

C H A P T E R   1 2

Special topics

12.1 Elicitation

Elicitation, the process of interviewing people to learn about the problem domain and discover requirements, goes beyond the scope of this book, as it includes many elements that are unrelated to documentation, such as:

- Navigating through an organization to find the people who really understand the problem. Because of their thorough knowledge, these people are usually the busiest in the organization and don't have time to talk.

- Asking people questions that, to them, seem stupid or ignorant without losing your credibility

- Resolving contradictions between statements made by different people

- Noticing that different people are using the same term to denote different concepts

- Sensing when people don't understand what you're talking or asking about, and adjusting your presentation to suit them

- Sifting through reams of (usually) out-of-date and badly written documentation to find a few nuggets of fact. How can you tell which are the most likely to be worth staring at for three hours?
- Hearing what people really have to say when you came to ask about something else. The problem domain is often very difficult to ask about because you know little or nothing about it in advance. How can you ask about the requirements of the capacity-planning committee if you've never even heard of the capacity-planning committee?
- Keeping the project from going beyond its scope. Once customers find out that you can give them something, they immediately want more. Should that be included in the current project or contracted for separately?
- The art of asking pertinent questions

However, understanding what content is needed in a requirements document is the most fundamental part of elicitation. If you don't know what kind of information you're searching for, you're going to have a very difficult time asking people for it.

There are two classic mistakes in elicitation that are easily avoided once you understand that requirements pertain to the problem domain, not the software:

1. "The customer don't know what he wants."

If the customer is not an expert in software, it follows that he can't be very specific about how the software should behave, how the database should be organized, or whether the software should have a client-server or three-tier organization, nor can you depend on him to specify backup procedures. The customer understands the problem domain, not the software. It was to bring about some condition in the problem domain that the customer contracted with you to write the software. Ask about that, and miraculously the customer does know what he wants after all.

When analysts pooh-pooh the problem domain in favor of their own domain of expertise, the result is almost always angry customers. Today, you can go to almost any large organization that has paid tens of millions of dollars for custom software to help it manage its procedures and find rancor throughout the staff, still directed at the contractor years after the project failed. Employees will tell you, "They never came around to ask us how we do our work. They never learned our terminology. It was as if they weren't even interested in how people here would use the software. We tried to tell them that the admissions department uses a different approval procedure, but they just wouldn't listen!"

2. Asking the customer to design the software.

The opposite error of ignoring the customer is dutifully taking down and implementing everything the customer says—about the software. "Do you want this to be a Boolean field or a real? Single or double precision floating-point? Where do you want the fields arranged on this screen? Radio buttons or drop-downs?"

This leads to confused customers and poor software. If the customer has some suggestions for things like screen layouts, certainly listen; indeed, solicit such suggestions and always test out prototype screens on real users. But first-rate software development comes from people who know software well and who learn the problem domain well enough to apply their skills.

Documentation is, itself, a tool of elicitation. If the customer can understand the documentation and sees that it's relevant to their business (rather than a lot of jargon that they can't understand), they can provide a lot of valuable information by reviewing the requirements.

If the customer says nothing at the first review of the requirements, except perhaps to nit-pick about wording in a couple places, that is a strong sign that the customer did not understand the document. When people have read and understood a document, they usually have many comments and new ideas, all pertaining to the content, not to spelling or whether the same statement was worded identically each time it was made.

12.2 Object-orientation

Often a junior technical writer is put onto a new project and hears from the programmers that the program is being written in an object-oriented language. Many then ask, "How do you write the user's manual for an object-oriented program?"

The answer, of course, is that it is written exactly the same way as for a computer program written in COBOL-68 or hand-coded machine language. In other words, there is no difference at all. The reason is that object-orientation is a way of structuring program code, whereas a user's manual describes the user interface and, in some cases, the problem domain. Program structure and user interface are two different subject matters—two different domains.

As object-orientation pertains exclusively to program structure, and neither requirements nor specifications describe program structure, it follows that there can be no such thing as object-oriented requirements. "Object-oriented requirements" is a phrase like "roasted effervescence"; the two concepts just don't go together.

Nevertheless, a lot of people in the software industry today are excited about applying object-orientation to requirements. It's worth understanding why because it often leads to a more serious mistake than an incongruous phrase.

12.2.1 Two types of program structure

Back in the days when structured programming—programming partly based on functional decomposition—was the state of the art in program design, some people had the idea of extending it outward to analysis. Thus was born structured analysis.

Programs at that time tended to have what we now call a function-oriented structure. Program code was distributed among a number of subroutines called functions. Each function operated on data in some way, receiving data from a function that invoked it, and generating output data in return. Data that needed to persist from one function invocation to the next was stored in "data stores." Each data store held one type of data. A single data store might hold all the customer data, another all the invoice data, and so on. Any function could access any data store.*

This structure was well suited to data-flow diagrams, as illustrated in figure 12.1.

Structured analysis called upon the analyst to describe system behavior in terms of functions analogous to the functions of programming languages. Just as each program function accepted input data and generated output data, sometimes depositing data in

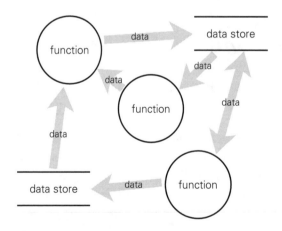

Figure 12.1 Typical data-flow diagram from structured analysis

---

* There's more to structured programming than the function-oriented program structure, but this is all that's relevant to our discussion of applying programming methods to requirements. In fact, the majority of structured programming lives on in object-oriented programming.

or retrieving it from a data store, system functions did the same. A programmer's job was to decompose the system functions into program code. As described in section 3.7, the analyst dictated the high-level structure of the program; the programmers then refined each function into executable code. The functions specified by the analyst would become the design units tested by the testers at the first stage of testing.

Requirements, as described in this book, were still a long way off. Analysis was seen as essentially no different from program design, just not concerned with the details. Hence, it seemed reasonable to extend the principles of program structure to the specification of the program. This, of course, we now see as a mistake. Most fundamental of all is to describe the problem domain and state what the customer desires there in terms of the problem domain. A program specification is properly the description of an interface still written in terms of the problem domain, not the program domain.

In an object-oriented program, data types are bound together with subroutines, called functions or methods. Only the functions associated with a given data type can access or modify data of that type. Other functions can only access the data indirectly by calling those functions. For example, a customer data type might have functions that create a new customer, delete a customer from the database, change a customer's address, retrieve a customer's balance, and so on. The data type in the abstract, along with its functions, is called a *class*. An instance of such a data type, such as data about an individual customer, is called an *object*—hence, object-oriented programming.

The purpose of organizing the program to allow data to be accessed only through restricted channels is to ensure the integrity of the data, as shown in figure 12.2. The get_name and set_name subroutines are the only functions that can access the name data element. Only the get_amount subroutine can access the amount data in an invoice object. For update_balance to access the amount of an invoice, it must call upon get_amount.

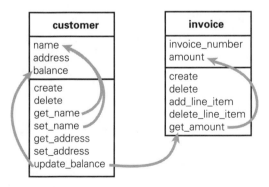

Figure 12.2 Narrow channeling of data flow in an object-oriented design

By limiting access to data through a very narrow channel, when data definitions change—the most common result of a change in the problem domain—an object-oriented program doesn't need to change in as many places as an equivalent function-oriented program. In a function-oriented program, if twenty different functions read or write the customer data store, and the format of the customer data store changes, then twenty different functions need to be modified. Each modification has a small but significant chance of introducing a bug; twenty changes almost guarantee a bug. In an object-oriented program, the only functions that need to be changed are the relatively few and simple ones that provide the interface to the data in the customer class.

12.2.2 The mistake

Now we can understand the temptation to create object-oriented analysis, extending program structure to requirements just as structured analysis did. The job of the object-oriented analyst is to define a set of classes along with their accompanying attributes and operations. The job of programmers is then to convert the class operations into subroutines, adding whatever internal support the programmers find necessary.

You will recognize this as precisely the same mistake at the foundation of structured analysis. Requirements describe the problem domain. Describing program structure is no way to describe the world outside the computer. Attempting to describe the problem domain in programming terms is a force-fit; the problem domain must be distorted to fit the description techniques, instead of the other way around.

The distortion is well illustrated by an example commonly used to introduce people to object-oriented analysis and design. Consider an oven and a cookie. Which gets the bake operation?

Many people reply that the oven should have the bake operation. After all, ovens bake cookies; cookies do not bake ovens.

In a good object-oriented design, however, the bake operation properly belongs in the cookie class. Seeing things this way is the "paradigm shift" that's required in order to do object-oriented analysis.

The reason the bake operation belongs in the cookie class is because there are likely to be many different kinds of food, each with its own set of instructions for how to bake

Figure 12.3 Which gets the 'bake' operation?

it. A roast cooks at a different temperature and for a different time than a cookie or a pie or a soufflé. Some foods need to cook at one temperature for a certain time, and then cook some more at a different temperature. The possibility for special cases in the baking process is endless.

If the oven class contained the bake operation, it would consist of a very large switch statement, where each case contained the instructions for one type of food. Thus the bake operation would have to "know" about every kind of food. It would be a monstrously large subroutine, and people would have to modify it every time a new kind of food was added to the requirements.

If the bake operation is a part of each food class, however, each bake subroutine can be very small. Each bake subroutine only knows how to call the oven subroutines, such as set_temperature. You can add a new food class by simply adding it; you don't need to modify any existing code. Thus the program organization is much more resilient. The most likely changes to requirements will lead to very small changes to the program structure, each with a virtually negligible chance of introducing a bug elsewhere in the program. Therefore the requirements document should state that cookies do the baking, and ovens merely have their temperatures set.

Now wait just a minute. What is the state of affairs *in the problem domain?* In the problem domain, there is simply the action of baking, involving both an oven and a cookie. The action occurs as long as there's a cookie in the oven and the oven is on. Different types of food have different oven temperatures and durations of baking.

That is all. We do not need a "paradigm shift" to understand the rules for how ovens bake cookies. So how did the description become so warped when object-orientation got hold of it? Notice that all of the reasons for associating the bake operation with cookie had to do with program maintainability and program simplicity. But what relevance does program maintainability have to baking? In the pure problem-domain description, there was no need to associate baking with just the oven or just the cookie. The need to attach an operation to just one class is part of object-oriented design. An object-oriented program consists of a number of classes with associated subroutines. A subroutine can be associated with one class, no more.* In the real world, by contrast, there are no such limitations, and we have no reason to conform to such limitations when describing the real world.

---

* One might object that friends in C++ enable bake to operate on both classes without being bound to either, and that so-called generalized object models do not require operations to be bound to a single class. Indeed, whenever we discover a misfit between program elements and the problem-domain elements they are supposed to map to, we can define new kinds of program elements. Thus, progress in software methods marches ever onward. However, this is all beside the point. Allocating the bake operation to cookie *is* good design. The lesson is that we should describe the problem domain in its own terms, not translate it into program terms. That's the programmers' job.

Douglas Bennett gives the name *behavior allocation* to the act of choosing which subroutines to associate with which classes, and which subroutines call which other subroutines. "The behavior-allocation decision has the biggest impact on the system."* Behavior allocation will become a central concern of the programmers when they design the program, but it is of no concern to a requirements document or a specification (except, as usual, in that requirements and specifications provide the information needed by the programmers to make the design).

So the next time an object-orientation enthusiast tells you that their classes and operations are an abstraction—that is, a description—of the problem domain, you will know better. If the description includes predicates involving message-passing or one subroutine (or "function" or "operation" or "method") calling another, then you will know that it's really a description of a program.

The opposite, and more common, mistake from distorting the description of the problem domain to suit a particular method of structuring programs is to have the analyst design the classes and methods. Whereas in structured analysis, the analyst specifies the top-level subroutines for programmers to implement, an object-oriented analyst specifies the top-level classes and methods for programmers to implement (methods just being subroutines that interface to the data in classes).

This is an even worse disaster than merely writing down a distorted picture of the problem domain. Behavior allocation is not only one of the most momentous decisions in program design, it is one of the most difficult to do well. Object-oriented design is just as prone to spaghetti as function-oriented design. The difference is that in the hands of a skilled practitioner, an object-oriented design can be much cleaner and open to likely modifications than the best function-oriented design. If the system analyst does not have experience with object-oriented programming, then it is very unlikely that their choice of behavior allocation will turn out well once the programmers flesh it out in code. Here we see the fallacy of top-down design all over again (see section 1.1).

Notice also that object-oriented analysis implicitly casts all software problems into the workpiece frame. This is not necessarily a disaster. You can certainly create a functioning information system by treating it as a set of workpieces that users can create, view, update, and delete. But during analysis, it's better to keep one's focus on the problem domain: to describe the real world of things and sequences of events, rather than to start by inventing the operating procedures and computer activity that respond to those events—the "use cases" that are popular with object-oriented methods (see section 12.3).

---

* [Bennett 1997], p. 132.

12.2.3 A different kind of design pattern

The explicit recognition of design patterns began in the object-oriented programming community.* As this book advocates an approach to requirements based on known design patterns, it may seem that object-oriented programming might still have something to offer requirements. Alas, it is not so.

The types of patterns of concern to requirements are patterns of entire software systems and the problems they solve. These patterns, such as the information system and the controller, are based on a wide variety of techniques in computer programming: well-known algorithms, data structures, the principles of relational databases, I/O buffers, standard user-interface elements, lookup tables, parsing methods, and so on. Most of these techniques apply to more than one problem frame, but the existence of these techniques guarantees that, in most cases, a problem that fits any of the frames can be solved. We've learned to recognize the patterns at the level of the software system as a whole mainly because people have combined the underlying techniques—the program-level design patterns—so many times. Ideas such as hash tables and state-table-driven parsers enabled us to write software that solved problems that we did not know how to solve before. Writing a compiler was once a research project. Now that the tools and techniques are well understood, students write them in undergraduate courses.

Object-oriented design is a different kind of innovation. It pertains to how to organize the program code that implements the other kinds of ideas. It is not itself a new algorithm or data structure, and it does not solve a customer's problem.† Rather, it solves a problem of the programmer's: how to manage the complexity of a large program and allow its data types to change without requiring massive changes throughout the program. Anyone who has written a program of 1000 lines or longer knows what an important problem this is.

However, object-orientation provides no new capabilities to the world outside the computer. No new requirements-level problem frames can be defined for object-oriented techniques.

An example of a type of software innovation that does entail a new problem frame is encryption algorithms. Encryption could conceivably be forced into the control problem's frame, in that encryption enforces rules about who can and can't access data. However, different encryption methods involve different kinds of parameters than those that pertain to control in general. The major questions to answer before choosing and implementing a known encryption technique are what kinds of keys there are and

---

* [Gamma 1995] is the watershed work.

† Except, perhaps, to reduce bugs and lower maintenance costs.

how each party is to access the keys. The particular algorithm itself might be specified in the requirements.

Encryption techniques, like the methods of sorting and searching, enable us to solve new kinds of problems in software. All object-orientation can add is very clean ways of delimiting encryption subroutines from the rest of a program.

12.3 Use cases and feature-interaction

There is a style of programming known as "hacking around."* When you hack around, you write a little bit of code to address one case that the program needs to handle. When another case comes along, you tack on a little more code. When you discover a problem, you tweak a little bit of code here and a little bit there until the problem goes away.

The resulting program is a "hack"—a patchwork of little snippets of code and little fixes, usually containing more bugs than anyone could find and correct in several lifetimes. The reason for the bugs is that each little fix addresses only one case without considering its impact on other parts of the program. Nearly all programs, no matter how well-structured, have complex interactions between all their parts. Changing one part of a program often necessitates changing other parts, too. The more hacks, the more complex the interactions, and the more damage can be done by the next hack.

A *use case* is a description of one case of a program being used—a single path through system functionality, showing each action initiated by a user, piece of hardware, or other software (collectively called *actors*) and the program's response.† The program can also initiate a use case, such as when performing a scheduled event. A use case is, thus, a little dialogue between one or more actors and the program. A use case might have a few alternative behaviors to handle unusual conditions, but a use case should flow linearly from beginning to end; otherwise, it's not one case but several.

Here's a typical use case:

Check out book
Librarian scans in library card of borrower. If the card won't scan, do *Replace card* and try again. Librarian scans in bar code from book. If the bar code won't scan, the librarian types in the book number. The system marks the due date of the book two weeks later than the current date, and the small printer prints out a slip showing the due date. The librarian gives the slip to the borrower.

---

* Not to be confused with the practice hacking into computer systems—that is, gaining unauthorized access.

† Use cases were first presented in [Jacobson 1992], pp. 159–166.

The great virtue of use cases is that they are very easy to understand. The great danger is that, by themselves, they are unsystematic. You probably noticed a common theme in chapters 4 through 11: always have a systematic method for covering all possible cases. Only by getting a bird's-eye view of all possible sequences of events can you see all possible cases and understand how changes made to one case affect others.

Use cases take the opposite approach. Writing software requirements by simply writing use cases as they come to mind is the equivalent, in requirements, of programming by hacking around. There are two main problems. First, because use cases describe interaction between the system and the outside world, use cases are specification, not requirements. They are descriptions of interfaces in terms of information flow, leaving out such matters as screens. This means that you're plunging into interface design before you've understood the problem domain.

Second, a sprawl of use cases is a terrible problem frame for all but the simplest problems. How do you know when you're done writing use cases? How can you tell if the use cases conflict? How can you tell if the use cases leave any gaps? Check out book, display book availability, make new card, replace card, add new book, delete book. Are those all the use cases? No, there's also: send mail for late fees. The mail is sent electronically if the borrower has an email address, and by regular mail if not. Are those two use cases or one? Are we done? No, there's also a use case to change a book's information if it's wrong. But that's all going to be on the same screen as the use cases for adding and deleting, so do we really need a separate use case for it? Now, suppose that the customer wants the system to support something new, such as, borrowers from outside the university who have to pay $40 a year for borrowing privileges and have a different amount of time that they can borrow books. Do you make new use cases for this new kind of borrower or do you modify the old use cases? Which use cases have to change?

A good problem frame constrains the problem, enabling you to be systematic. The types of frames shown in chapter 4 apply only to specific types of problems: for control problems, you document the causal rules that govern the problem domain and the additional causal rules to be imposed on it; for information problems, you document all possible behavior in the problem domain and all information about the problem domain to be supplied, and leave out causation; and so forth. Recognizing one of those problems, you have the beginnings of a systematic approach (though only the beginnings, of course).

Use cases can't constrain a problem, because they can fit any problem. The "use-case frame" looks like figure 12.4. The requirement is: the system responds in specified ways when the actors act in specified ways, or the other way around; in other words, the system interacts with actors. What *wouldn't* fit this problem frame? Because the use-case

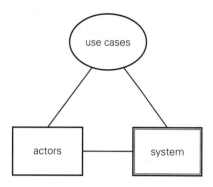

Figure 12.4 Problem frame for use cases

frame applies equally well to all software problems, it includes no information specific to any software problem. It gives you no pertinent questions to ask in researching it, and it provides no help in finding the seams in the problem for purposes of dividing it into smaller pieces. The only question it leads you to ask is the most generic one: "What would you like to do with the system and how would you like it to behave?"

If your requirements document is a set of sixty somewhat-connected use cases, you need to reframe the problem. No one will ever be able to understand how they all interrelate. Even software for a small college library can easily grow to over a hundred use cases.

On the other hand, use cases can be applied in a disciplined manner—not as requirements, but as parts of a specification that solve a problem that has been well defined in the requirements. If the requirements document describes the lifecycle of a book, showing each stage that the book goes through, from being acquired, through borrowing and returning, and finally being lost, sold, or given away, you can write a use case for each of these events. This type of use case is described in section 10.3 as event responses and operating procedures.

When you write an operating procedure, you begin with a very specific question derived from the problem: "How do I get the system to know that a borrower is attempting to borrow a book?" or "How do I get the system to know that a book has been returned?" The problem itself is not framed in terms of use cases, but in terms of controlling books and tracking events that change the state of books.

If the library's administration or lending procedures change, you now have a systematic way to see which operating procedures the change affects. You have diagrams showing all possible sequences of events. The diagrams show you which event descriptions to change. Because the event descriptions map to operating procedures, you know which operating procedures to change. The process is seldom this mechanical, but having a well defined problem that maps to a suite of simple operating procedures makes it much easier to update software in response to changing requirements.

Another place for use cases is as helpful redundancy: just to describe common scenarios, but with no attempt to exhaustively specify the software. A sequence of action-response pairs is a good way to describe a scenario.

12.3.1 Feature interaction

Whenever you write requirements or specifications, you need to be on guard against a problem that plagues nearly all such descriptions: feature interaction. Feature interaction is unanticipated overlap between two different descriptions, such that they conflict or leave a gap. They're best illustrated by two use cases:

Call forwarding on busy

Caller *A* places call to caller *B*. Caller *B*'s line is busy, and caller *B* has call forwarding on busy active. The system reroutes the call to caller *B*'s forwarding number. Go to *Connect call.*

What could be a simpler and more logical description than this? It covers just one case, covers it very clearly, and even covers it from the user's point of view.

Now let's move on to call waiting:

Call waiting

Caller *A* places call to caller *B*. Caller *B*'s line is busy, and caller *B* has call waiting active. The system sends a ringing sound to caller *A* and makes a clicking sound on caller *B*'s line. If caller *B* hangs up for between one and two seconds and then goes on hook again, the system terminates caller *B*'s original call and connects caller *A* to caller *B*.

Again, this is a perfect use case. It covers exactly one complete flow of events from start to finish, including the alternative paths, and it's easily comprehensible.

There's just one problem. What if caller *B* has both call forwarding on busy and call waiting active at the same time? Looking at one use case at a time, you would think that all system behavior during calls had been covered perfectly. But in fact, the two features *interact*. If the requirements leave out how the system is supposed to behave in this case, the decision may be made randomly—by whatever falls out when the programmers implement the two identified cases.

It's unlikely that anyone would seriously consider writing the requirements for a full-scale telephone switch as a set of use cases, but this example illustrates why use cases are dangerous. Here, the problem has been grossly misframed. The problem is to describe the behavior of certain telephone equipment: which telephone lines are supposed to connect to which other telephone lines in response to which events. The telephone equipment is not even mentioned in these use cases, due to a misguided focus on "the user." By systematically describing events that affect specific categories of telephone equipment, the interaction would be obvious.*

These two use cases also contain an ambiguity, common when use cases are applied to complex software: which actions in the use case necessarily happen, and which could happen another way, in another use case? If you make "Call to busy line" one use case, and "Call to open line" another, then you must indicate which events in each use case distinguish the use case from all others, which events the designers can safely assume will happen, and which events the designers are required to make happen. You might also consider describing the activity in terms of state changes, or any way you can think of that enables you to see all possible alternatives at once.

12.4 Reviews

Before signing off on a requirements or specification document and sending the team off to implement it, you should have the document reviewed by everyone concerned:

- The customer
- The project manager
- The user-interface designer
- The programmers
- At least one tester
- At least one technical writer

These people can help improve both the form of the document and the design decisions† expressed in it. Each reviewer can see problems that you couldn't have anticipated, because your concerns and areas of expertise are so different.

The classic work on the subject of document reviews (as well as code reviews) is [Yourdon 1989b]. It's filled with useful procedures and techniques (as well as psychological insights into many of the participants) explaining why they sometimes get derailed from the task of improving the document. None of that will be repeated here, except this one principle: during the review, the participants bring up problems that they

---

* See [Zave 1993] for an excellent introduction to feature-interaction, including many wonderfully thorny examples from the world of telephony.

† Remember, requirements are design. See section 2.3.

would like to see addressed, and that is all. There should be no attempt made to reach a consensus about how to best solve the problem. Afterward, you talk to each reviewer about how you've decided to solve the problem, or perhaps you solicit suggestions for solving it. If you try to combine both problem-identification and solution in the same meeting, you probably won't get through the document in an entire afternoon, unless it's only two pages long.

12.4.1 Document ratings

One type of feedback that you should not solicit is numerical ratings of the document on various scales, such as completeness, clarity, precision, and so on. There are several problems with these ratings. First, few people will give you a zero for clarity even if they didn't understand the document. Few people want to hurt their co-workers' feelings, and fewer still are willing to risk looking stupid by admitting that they didn't understand something that everyone else might have understood. Most people are intimidated by badly written documents; they assume that the problem is with them and not the document.

Second, these scales pertain to global attributes of the document and are, therefore, of little use in spotting and solving problems. They're similar to the testing done by the early airplane inventors (described in the footnote about the Wright brothers in chapter 1), testing attributes of the whole instead of testing targeted to specific parts of the document's content. During the review, you should be trying to determine if people have understood specific ideas that you wanted to get across. You can't find that out by asking them to numerically rate their understanding of it. You find that out by striking up a conversation with them about it. "What did you think of the rules for detecting invalid nucleotide sequences?" is a better question than "On a scale of one to ten, how feasible are the requirements?" The former question might elicit such useful answers as, "Oh, sorry, I didn't read that part," "I thought that was a great strategy," or "Since any possible sequence can occur within an intron, how can any nucleotide sequence be invalid?"

Finally, the scales themselves are often vague and/or impossible for reviewers to have informed opinions about. How can the programmer tell whether the document "addresses customer need" so accurately that he can distinguish a quality level of eight out of a possible ten from a quality level of nine? Does "completeness" refer to how completely the problem domain is described, or whether there is enough information to enable a programmer or user-interface designer to start designing interfaces?

Numerical answers to such questions are inherently arbitrary. It's no wonder that most are in the range of five to ten, clustering around 7.5, regardless of the scale or the quality of the document.

(On scales of one to five, most people pick four regardless of the level of quality. Picking three would merely be "average" and therefore negative, because everyone wants to be above average. Picking five, however, would suggest perfection, so four is the perfect compromise.)

Document ratings grow out of the unfortunate theory that if we are assigning numbers to things, we are gathering data precisely and scientifically. Better to heed the words of John von Neumann: "There's no sense in being exact about something if you don't even know what you're talking about." Just find out if the readers know what you're talking about and whether they agree with it. You accomplish that by asking meaningful, specific questions and keeping your ears open for answers and topics that you didn't expect.

12.5 Requirements jargon

The requirements jargon used in this book is far from standard. The software field lacks any well standardized terminology for the requirements-and-specifications phases of development. However, if you have to work with requirements documents that are written according to the theory that requirements are a high-level sketch of the program, then you'll need to know some of the other terms in use.

The chart below lists some terminology in common use. Note that many terms are often used to indicate the very distinction that another term was created for. The more correct definition is given first when there are more than one.

user requirements	What the user requires of the software or the system as a whole; what the user wants. User requirements are either written by the user or taken down by a system analyst in consultation with the user.
system requirements	1. What is required of the system as a whole: both hardware and software together; desired system behavior
	2. What is required of the software; desired software behavior
	System requirements are developed by engineers, as a refinement of user requirements, by translating them into engineering terms.

software requirements	1. What is required of the software; desired software behavior
	2. User requirements for software
	Software requirements are developed by engineers, as a refinement of user requirements by translating them into engineering terms.
functional requirement	1. An action to be performed by the software, including its input, the processing to be performed, perhaps including interaction with a user or other hardware or software, and the resulting output. Similar to a use case except that functional requirements often feed into one another, the output of one being the input of another. Functional requirements appear in user requirements, system requirements, and software requirements; they're a category of requirement within each level of requirement.
	2. Any system requirement or software requirement, as distinct from a user requirement
non-functional requirement (NFR)	An attribute of a functional requirement, such as how easily the function can be modified or how easily users are able to use the function
performance requirement	One type of non-functional requirement: how long it takes the system to perform the function
constraint	A design constraint, as defined in section 8.1, as well as the hardware platform and operating system
reliability, safety, maintenance, etc. requirements	Various non-functional requirements brought over from other engineering fields, such as mean time to failure; described under global characteristics in section 8.1.

If you don't see much difference between user requirements and software requirements, you're not alone. Many requirements documents, attempting to conform to the user/ system/software breakdown, double their size by including functional requirements (software requirements) that are identical to the user requirements, with just the wording changed, as in the following example:

> UR-3 User shall be able to store grocery inventory data.
>
> UR-4 User shall be able to retrieve grocery inventory data.

Later, in the Functional Requirements section:

> FR-3 System shall store grocery inventory data.
>
> FR-4 System shall retrieve grocery inventory data.

A traceability matrix might show that FR-3 implements UR-3 and that FR-4 implements UR-4, just in case that isn't clear. This is one strange result of the "start high-level and become more detailed" view of requirements and software development.

The above jargon might seem confusing. It is. The hardware that software is supposed to run on is a constraint? A non-functional requirement pertains to a function? Most people would think that's a requirement that doesn't work. User requirements are what is required by a user, but system requirements are what is required of the system? Who is the user in the requirements for a programmer's library to aid user-interface designers—the programmers who use it, the user-interface designers who use it, or the end users who use the user-interfaces? It's no wonder that customers are little more than baffled as they skim through documents couched in such jargon.

Even people who've been using the old jargon for a long time seldom have a clear idea what it means. If the above terminology is in use at your company, an interesting experiment is to ask different people what a functional requirement is. Seldom do two people give the same answer.

By making the principal divisions in software documents pertain to subject matter rather than to level of detail, you avoid the theoretical problems that gave rise to the old jargon, and you can have much clearer, precise, and useful definitions of the content that you put in each section.

12.6 Cutting corners

You say that you don't have the time or resources to do it right? Well, here are some tips how to do it wrong. Be warned, however, that for every corner that you cut for short-term gain, there is a long-term loss. It is a fact of life, though, that sometimes this is a wise trade-off. Sometimes, if you don't take care of the short-term now, there will be no long term in which to enjoy long-term benefits. Many software companies routinely cut the corners described below, yet they are still in business and have satisfied customers, so cutting a corner does not mean the end of the world. (However, their development costs could probably be lower and their quality could probably be higher.)

To put it another way, there is a risk to writing documentation: it delays the writing of code. If imperfection is not a concern, the risk of being late may well outweigh the risk of having bugs. It is the job of management to weigh these risks anew on every software project.

Cut these corners	*Face these risks*
In the requirements document, omit the description of the problem domain. That is, write requirement statements only. This results in a vastly shorter document—perhaps one or two pages of terse requirement statements with no commentary.	When the system analyst leaves or works on a different project, it is likely that no one else will understand the customer's business. Maintenance of the program will be difficult, and people will fall into the pattern of "I don't know why it's in there, but we'd better not change it because there might be a reason for it." Leaving out the problem-domain description also pre-empts creative solutions. By understanding the customer's world, reviewers or interface designers can often come up with solutions that the analyst would never have thought of, or they may suggest new and useful requirements. Given only the requirements—the analyst's final solution—with none of the background, people can only implement it unquestioningly. One more risk is that the requirement statements themselves will be easy to misinterpret, when not understood in relation to the world that gave rise to them.
Omit the requirements document altogether. That is, write only the specification: a description of the software behavior at the interface to the outside world.	Without any definite requirements, the programmers and user-interface designers are free to design whatever they find most fun. They're likely to include features that the customer has little use for, and omit or downplay features that the customer thought critical.

Omit the user-interface document. Just prototype, or even omit prototyping, and let a programmer design the user interface while coding it.	Expect a mediocre user interface that frustrates end users with its obliviousness to the problem domain and its insistence that users think in terms of the program domain. Human nature being what it is, programmers are tempted to skip user-interface ideas that are tedious or time-consuming to implement. A dedicated user-interface designer typically pays more attention to the small details that make a user interface easy to use in ways that people seldom notice, and the "Anything is possible to the man who doesn't have to do it himself" syndrome frees the designer to include unusual or imaginative features that many programmers would rather not think about.
Omit the specification documents as well as the requirements. That is, skip writing any of the documentation described in this book. Thus, the programmers specify the software only implicitly and concurrently with program design, with a vague idea of the requirements communicated only through oral tradition (see section 13.1).	In addition to all of the above risks, expect the software to be released with numerous bugs because, lacking a specification, the testers cannot create a test plan. If you regularly cut this corner, you probably don't have any testers, anyway.

Expect to have conversations like this with your customer: "Oh, is that why you wanted that feature? Oh, yeah, I guess the way we did it isn't very useful, after all."

Realistically, when you go this far in omitting documentation, often you do not achieve even short-term benefits. The bugs, confusions, and unnecessary rewrites often result in more man hours spent to deliver the first release, not fewer.

Note that writing documentation that no one can understand or that no one reads is equivalent to not writing it at all, except that it costs more. |

12.7 A few good books

The following are a few good books, well worthy of a location on or near any analyst's desk. This is not an exhaustive list, just a few books that the author has found especially stimulating and/or useful in daily practice:

Software Requirements and Specifications: A Lexicon of Practice, Principles, and Prejudices, by Michael A. Jackson, ACM Press, 1995
An intellectual journey. This is the book in which Jackson presents such ideas as problem frames, shared phenomena, and connection domains. A wide variety of topics in software engineering are covered, and some topics beyond it, in a set of 75 short articles meant to be read in no particular sequence. Each time you wander through it, you see connections between areas that you thought had nothing in common; you see fundamental principles that you had never dreamed of. You return from the journey a wiser software engineer.

Analysis Patterns: Reusable Object Models, by Martin Fowler, Addison-Wesley, 1997
We learn best from examples, and here is a book of example "conceptual models" of a variety of problem domains, mostly in the business world—inventory, accounting, corporation finance, and others. These "models" are primarily the types of domain descriptions covered in chapter 9. When you start mapping out a new domain, you can often find similar problems in one of the domains that Fowler covers, saving you from reinventing a number of difficult wheels.

Envisioning Information, by Edward R. Tufte, Graphics Press, 1990
Not a book on software, but a classic work on informational graphics. It contains example graphics, from the most brilliant to the most opaque, showing information about an enormous variety of subjects. Tufte transforms bad graphics into lucid ones, showing you how to revise, and illustrating the principles he uses. Ultimately, the book trains you to look at problem domains more perceptively, as you become aware of the types of relations that a good graphic can make clear.

Two more books on graphics by Tufte, *The Visual Display of Quantitative Information* and *Visual Explanations,* emphasize types of graphics that are less frequently applicable to software engineering, but are also well worth reading.

PART 3

Style

C H A P T E R   1 3

Documentation

13.1 Why document?

On any project involving two or more people, there arises an *oral tradition*. Peter tells Larry how he's planning to structure a certain interface. Larry mentions this to Margot in a conversation about a data structure that he's working on. Charles hears about a new requirement and mentions it to Margot, but it never gets around to Peter.

None of this information gets written down, but it exists in the way that Homeric tales existed in ancient times. Each bard learns the story from another bard. Human memory being what it is, each person distorts a little bit, and human inventiveness being what it is, each person embellishes a bit. There is still a story circulating and evolving out there among the bards, but no two bards have the same version.

A software project will always have an oral tradition, and we should make no attempt to stop it. It's how people work together. However, in a software project of any size, an oral tradition is not enough. Here, "any size" means roughly four or more people, including the people who test, design the user interface, and write the manual. If the tester wasn't in the room when the programmer convinced the user-interface designer to make a change, the tester should not have to waste hours writing a test plan for a feature that's no longer a part of the software.

The cure, of course, is writing things down. Here are the principal benefits of documentation—two obvious ones, and three less well known:

1. Extends what the mind can grasp and remember

In any project large enough to need requirements, the amount of information is more than any one person can retain, even after an eight-hour meeting that covers every detail. The written word can be referred to later, and it doesn't fade the way human memory does.

2. Gives the same story to each member of the team

A written document is exactly the same each time it's read. So the user-interface designer, programmers, testers, and documenter can all read the same material, which they surely wouldn't be able to do if they were all given the information in individual conversations.

3. Introduces new team members to the project

People on projects come and go. A new tester, for example, has a hard time catching up with the oral tradition. A well-written document can bring them up to date in only a few days.

4. Protects intellectual equity

Very often, only one or two people at a software company understand the problem domain or the design of the software. They're the only people who can intelligently judge proposed changes, notice holes in reasoning about the application, or even think of new ideas for software to write. If these people's precious knowledge is put into written form, the company is no longer so dependent on them. Their intellectual equity won't walk out the door if they get a better job offer.

5. Helps the writer to better understand the problem	Describing requirements or a specification in written form inevitably forces one to adopt a higher standard of rigor than spoken conversation calls for. Anyone who's ever documented requirements has had the experience of discovering holes or even conceptual incoherence in their understanding of the problem. This is the observation that leads people to conclude that "the document isn't important, only the documenting is." As we've seen above, the document is important for other reasons, as well.

Of all the things to document, requirements are the most important for the long term and specifications for the short term. The specification tells the programmers and testers exactly what to do and what to test for. But they won't have the background knowledge to make trade-offs intelligently or to propose new ideas for future development. The requirements are usually people's only source of information about the problem domain. If they're left to the oral tradition, the team must contact the system analyst or resort to guessing. In practice, by the time development begins, the system analyst has usually flown to another part of the country to do the scope of work for another project, so guessing is the only option.

Understanding what the benefits of documentation are, we can target our methods of documentation at providing those benefits. Many companies take documentation of requirements very seriously, but they don't realize many of its benefits because, in their practice, oral tradition is the only way that real information is communicated, only the system analyst understands the problem domain, and so on.

If we want the programmers to refer to the document to supplement what they remember from meetings, then we must make the reference information easy to find. Scattering it throughout the document will defeat benefit #1, even though the document would still be complete and correct.

If we want the members of the team to have the information in the document, then we must write the document in such a way that they will read it. Many requirements documents go unread because people can't understand them and they seem irrelevant to their jobs.

We can see now that while cranking out text is easy, achieving the benefits of documentation will take some thought.

13.2 Broad principles

The following are a number of very broad principles of technical writing. The list is far from exhaustive, of course, but these are helpful to bear in mind when writing and especially when learning about writing. They guide many of the techniques discussed throughout this book.

1. Writing is a craft

Reading a book on woodworking will not make you an expert carpenter, or even a mediocre carpenter. The problem is not with the book; it's that woodworking is an enormously complex craft. Making a cabinet involves thousands of tiny decisions about precise placement of each tool, the sequence in which to perform operations, fine muscle control when cutting the curves, and so forth. These decisions are mostly unconscious for an expert carpenter because years of practice have made them second-nature, enabling the carpenter to draw upon them as needed while his or her mind focuses on just a few, key aspects of the work.

Technical writing is the same way. There is no rote procedure or ten simple steps for creating an excellent technical document. Rather, the difference between a document that is readable and gets read and a document that no one can understand and no one is willing to read is thousands of tiny decisions—each word choice, each choice of sentence structure, each choice of where to place objects on graphics. No one of these decisions makes much difference. Making thousands of them well or thousands of them poorly makes an enormous difference.

As with woodworking, reading a book about technical writing won't make you very good at it. Acquiring the skill takes practice, and no matter how good you get, you can always get much better with another year of practice. Learning technical writing is a lifelong activity. Every document has something new to teach you: a helpful phrase, a trick for breaking up sentences, a bad habit to unlearn.

The same is true of other people's documents. In fact, other people's documents are even more helpful. Many analysts have read only their own documents and never benefit from seeing how other people solve the same problems. A good document has techniques to imitate. If someone else's document is hard to understand, you can figure out what made it hard to understand and avoid making that mistake yourself or think of a better way to express it. However, if your own document is hard to understand, often you don't notice that because you already know what it's supposed to say. Other people's bad documents are the easiest to learn from. The best technical writing flows so easily that you can't tell that there were any problems to be solved while writing it.

If writing documents is a large part of your job, as it is for most system analysts and program designers, it pays to be literate. People will judge you not on the basis of your thinking, but on the basis of your writing.

2. Write for human beings

There is an awful truth about software requirements: most requirements documents go unread. Booch writes of an 8,000-page requirements document that "no one could understand."* Even the more ordinary 50- to 100-page requirements documents go unread. The usual reason is that they are written to conform to abstract standards of correctness rather than to communicate project-specific information to real human beings—more like writing a program than writing in English.

Such abstract standards usually derive from "methodologies" or from overly specific documentation standards. These methodologies usually propose expressing a very limited set of information about the software in a very limited set of ways of expressing it— one notation for all diagrams, one sentence structure for all requirements, one table of contents for all documents.

Conforming to the standards becomes an end in itself. If anyone is able to decipher the document, that is merely a benign side-effect. Not surprisingly, when most people look over such a document, they figure it was made only to satisfy some arbitrary rules and not to communicate anything to them, so they put it aside after a few minutes of skimming and find some other way to get their information. Many programmers are now convinced that writing requirements documents is a waste of time and that, however flawed it may be to jump straight into program design after some informal talks with the customer, at least that strategy avoids the time and expense of writing an enormous document that serves no purpose.

Writing for human beings means constantly asking yourself questions such as the following:

- Is there a way to express this that would be easier to understand?

- Am I overloading the reader with too much information at once? Should I provide some sort of roadmap, or break it up into smaller sections or smaller sentences?

- Which details are more important to my readers and which are less important? How can I make clear which details are which?

- Is this statement too abstract for my readers to understand without illustration? Are these details too narrow and disconnected for my readers to understand without explaining the underlying principle common to all of them?

---

* [Booch 1996], p. 17.

- What reasonable misinterpretations could my readers make when reading this passage?

- Will my readers see any benefit in reading this section? How does it relate to any specific reader's job? Does anyone have a reason to care about this? Will people see this as a waste of their time?

- What is the feel of the writing—formal but friendly, stuffy and pompous, scatter-brained and rambling, simple and direct, flows like sludge?

- Is the document boring? Would anyone want to read it? Will anyone read it?

It may seem strange to be concerned about whether or not a document is boring or not. Shouldn't your readers read it whether they like it or not? That's what they're paid to do, isn't it? That attitude, unfortunately, is likely to make people only briefly peruse your documents. If you describe a problem that your readers have made a career of solving, then your readers will find it interesting.

People generally want to do a good job, and they enjoy doing it. Testers want to devise test cases, user-interface designers want to think up ways to present information, programmers want to write code to implement specifications. A requirements document or specification that is pure content all the way through is anything but boring to these readers. A document that hides the content behind requirements jargon and a gauntlet of bureaucratic sections, or omits most or all of the content (not so unusual), would be boring to anyone.

If you really want to learn to write for human beings, try working in their capacity for a little while, with someone else's requirements document. Trying working in the testing department for a week. Try programming. If you want to understand the frustrations that people go through when reading requirements documents, there's no better way to learn than first-hand. "Why is this information missing?" "Why is this information buried so deep in this document, when it's the only information that actually counts, anyway?" "It took me a week to figure out what these thirty pages meant, but it's actually so simple! Why does it have to be such a struggle to decipher these documents?" When you've suffered trying to read a bad requirements document up against a dead-line, then you'll have some ideas about how to write one.

None of the above questions have to do with the correctness of the information in the document. A good technical document is much more than correct: it is geared to human readers.

3. Alternatives, not rules

Many books on writing state rules like "never end a sentence with a preposition" and "never write in the passive voice." Some even go as far as to prescribe precise rules for the number of sentences in a paragraph: some say "no more than ten" while some even say "every paragraph should be three sentences long."

These rules are nonsense.* The skill of writing is not that of following rules, but of exploring alternatives and choosing the one that best fits the content. Sometimes the passive voice emphasizes exactly what you want to emphasize and deemphasizes exactly what you want to deemphasize; converting to the active voice would obscure your point.† You should be able to consider both the active and the passive voice, rather than treating one as a sin even in thought. In the vast majority of cases, you'll probably want to choose the active voice, but that doesn't mean that there is something wrong with choosing the passive voice in the remainder of cases. The point here is that you should *choose,* consciously, rather than thoughtlessly write in one or the other.

Just as in part II, this book tries to give you sets of alternatives to consider, without prejudging which alternative best fits the problem you're currently solving, or even claiming to have identified all possible alternatives. In many cases, when you're stuck with a difficult sentence, all you need is for someone to come along and point out an alternative that you hadn't considered.

This book also supplies principles for choosing among alternatives. These are principles, not rules. A principle is a fundamental insight or idea from which good decisions or other principles follow. The same principle can apply in very different ways to different problems. To apply a principle to a new problem, you need to see the unique way in which that principle applies to that one problem.

For example, "Write for human beings" can lead you, in one instance, to reject one sequence of presenting material in a document because the early sections of the document don't seem to have any purpose until a very late section explains them. People need to know why information is in a document in order to retain it and understand it. So, when you reject that sequence and begin to search for another, you are applying the principle by imagining yourself in the position of a reader, thinking of what will go on in people's minds while reading the document—going beyond making the document technically correct, and adjusting it for real people. On the other hand, you might

---

* Winston Churchill is reported to have said, upon being corrected for violating the rule about ending a sentence with a preposition, "That is the sort of arrant pedantry up with which I will not put." The superstition about ending a sentence with a preposition was started by 18th-century grammarians who believed that Latin had the one, true grammar, which all other languages should emulate. In Latin, prepositions work differently than in English and, indeed, there's no place for them at the end of a sentence. No ancient Roman would need to be told this, of course, any more than you need to be told that "Clapping margarining the" is not a valid sentence. The mythical rule against split infinitives started the same way.

† [Pinker 1994], p. 228, gives an excellent illustration of the passive voice, showing how the corresponding sentence in the active voice would "feel like a *non sequitur.*"

notice, while looking over a first draft of a document, that it seems somehow boring and monotonous. You discover that you used the same sentence structure in ten consecutive sentences, so you vary the sentence structures to keep from losing the reader's interest. Again, you're drawing upon your empathy with human readers to make the document more than correct—same broad principle, but a very different application.

Thus principles of writing are similar to legal principles. The principle of freedom of speech is not applied mechanically, the way one would apply a rule like "no paragraph shall have more than three sentences." Judges try to understand the basis of the principle—the way the principle brings about justice—and apply it only in situations where the basis of the principle can be found. They must simultaneously consider other legal principles and weigh all the consequences of each possible decision. So, limited censorship is allowed in wartime, there is no right to receive subsidies for publication, and so forth.

Principles of technical writing seek to bring about clarity, the same way legal principles attempt to bring about justice. You can't apply them mechanically, but they are nevertheless an indispensible aid in choosing among the many different ways to write a sentence or organize a document.

4. People like lists

When people create a specification or a test plan or a program, they want to have systematic way to check that their creation meets every requirement. Nothing fulfills this need better than a list. Readers can check each item on a list one by one; when they are finished with one item, they can forget it. As much as possible, try to make evaluation criteria—requirements and preferences—stand out from the rest of the text, and submit to systematic, one-step-at-a-time reading. Naturally, some information just can't be presented this way, but when you have information that can, this is the first option to consider.

5. Form follows content

Rather that expressing the content in a form chosen in advance of writing the document, choosing the way in which to say something should derive from the content. The opposite approach is particularly dangerous when, say, the prefabricated table of contents does not include slots for all of the content needed in the document. Furthermore, sometimes a table is better than a diagram; sometimes a diagram is better than a table. Making policy decisions about these things achieves the fairly negligible goal of uniformity at the expense of clear presentation in each instance.

This principle is taken up in more detail in chapter 14.

6. A place for every detail, and every detail in its place

This is the fundamental principle of organization. A document's organization is a set of slots for holding details: big slots for holding big details that are made up of small details, the sequence of slots chosen carefully so that each detail is prepared by all the previous details, and so on. Without a consciously designed document organization, you can easily omit details for lack of a place to put them or repeat the same details in many places for the same reason.

Document organization is the subject of chapter 14.

7. Reinforcement, not repetition

Sometimes it is said that a requirements document should contain no redundancy, but this is not quite true. Repetition is seldom a good idea because it adds length to the document unnecessarily and confuses readers about which statement is definitive, if the repetitions are not all identical. Repetition is also decoy text (see section 13.3), dissuading the reader from taking the text seriously. The reader is encouraged to skip and skim rather than read carefully because it seems that new content appears only occasionally in the document rather than in every sentence.

But repetition is not the only form of redundancy. *Reinforcement* is giving confirmation to a reader's understanding of the material, through logical harmony between different elements of the document, and through repetition of the same content but in different forms. For example, a reader's understanding of an abstract statement is reinforced by giving an example or two. Strictly speaking, the examples add no new content, but they confirm or correct the reader's understanding of a statement that is prone to misinterpretation. If readers understands why a certain feature is useful to the end users, this reinforces their understanding of the feature or perhaps clarifies the feature. If the feature does not have any apparent use, a reader may doubt that have understood it correctly.

An overview is 100% redundancy, but a necessity in all but the smallest documents. When a reader reads the details left out of the overview, his understanding of the details is confirmed by the fact that they make sense in light of the overview, and his understanding of the overview is confirmed by the details.

Graphics often express the same information that's found in the text, but in different form. Graphics can express subtle or complex relationships in an easily perceivable form. While reading the text, readers can refer repeatedly to the graphic, each time verifying that they have understood the text correctly.

Even skillful choice of section headings is reinforcement. If it seems that a variety of requirements all work in service of one goal, say, performance monitoring, then the reader's understanding of the role of those requirements is confirmed by including them all in a section titled "Performance Monitoring."

Reinforcement is one of the technical writer's basic tools for making complex material understandable. It's also an instance of the principle of writing for human beings. Reinforcement has no place in machine language; if the machine language is correct, the computer performs correctly. But any form of human communication needs a great deal of redundancy in order for the listener to be sure that they understand.

The rest of this chapter describes a number of common violations of these broad principles.

13.3 Decoy text

The nineteenth-century French novelist Victor Hugo peppered his novels with essays describing the periods of history in which his stories were set. They're fascinating essays, but many people find them a distraction from the plot. People who want to skip them encounter a problem, illustrated by the essay on the Battle of Waterloo in *Les Misérables*.

After fifty pages and eighteen chapters of description and analysis of Waterloo, there's a discussion of what happens at night after a battle. "The day after a battle dawns on naked corpses."* At night, a little army of thieves robs all the valuables, including clothes, from the dead soldiers still lying on the battlefield. Hugo describes one of these thieves stealing a silver cross of the Legion of Honor from an almost-dead nobleman. The thief's name is Thènardier, and both he and his loot turn out to be important elements of the story. A reader who skipped these digressions would miss the important plot points buried within them.

You might think that there's no harm in adding some extra text to a document. After all, the reader can just skip it if it doesn't apply to them.

But there is harm. All text that isn't part of requirements—purpose of document, purpose of task, summary of task, inclusions, exclusions, acceptance criteria—obscures the genuinely relevant information. It's *decoy text*.

As in *Les Misérables*, a reader can't easily know in advance whether a section or paragraph is decoy text or not. By including decoy text, you're encouraging the development staff to skip and skim rather than to read carefully. You're saying, "much of the text in this document doesn't really matter." In other words, you're saying, "I'm

---

* [Hugo 1862], p. 352.

wasting your time." This is not a good message to send if you want your readers to review a document carefully.

Various types of decoy text are described below. The way to fix all decoy text is simple: delete it.

13.3.1 Metatext

The most common type of decoy text is *metatext*—text that describes the text that follows. Sometimes metatext is necessary, but usually it's decoy text. If the title of the document is "BPM Requirements," you don't need a Purpose of Document section that says "The purpose of this document is to describe the requirements for BPM," perhaps followed by another sentence or two just to make the section a little longer.

For more information, see *Metatext* in chapter 15.

13.3.2 Generalities

All information in a requirements document should be specific to the software to be built. A requirements document or specification is not the place to give people a course on general principles of good data modeling, user-interface design, program design, or even how to evaluate requirements.

Some requirements documents contain small dissertations on what makes a good requirement:

Requirements shall possess the following attributes to be considered acceptable:

Atomic: The requirement shall describe one and only one function.

Complete: The requirement shall describe the system behavior in response to all inputs.

Testable: The requirement shall be observable.

Non-redundant: The requirement shall be unique and contain no overlap with other requirements.

Unambiguous: The requirement shall not be open to interpretation.

Traceable: The requirement shall be able to be tracked forward to change requests, code modules, and test scripts.

And so on.

These lists of required attributes of requirements usually have a number of problems. First, despite their call for precision, they're ambiguous. What is "one and only one function"? Second, they often make no distinction. How could a requirement not be traceable, as defined above? Third, they're often impossible to achieve. Some things, like user-friendliness, just can't be quantified precisely. Response time can, with a frequency-distribution function, but that's unnecessarily precise for most applications. And in many cases, it makes more sense to have some requirements overlap instead of cramming them into a single, huge sentence.

What is a reader to make of such a list? He could object to nearly every requirement in the document for failing to meet these standards. Or he could be sane and ignore the list. Now consider his position: "Clearly this section was never meant to be taken seriously. But how am I to know which of the remaining sections were intended seriously and which were intended to be ignored? I guess I'll just ask someone." This is the decoy principle in action, driving people away from the benefits of documentation and back to the oral tradition.

More dangerous is a requirement that expresses a generality:

> R/UI-8.5.2 Each input screen shall fit entirely within the window and shall use as little scrolling as possible to display and/or retrieve information.

This is not merely decoy text, this is a decoy requirement. A good user-interface designer knows this principle already and will try to apply it to the information that this particular program needs to display. Sometimes you can make everything fit in one window, and sometimes you can't. That depends on the information to be displayed—which is what the document should be talking about.

13.3.3 Piling on

Piling on takes its name from a type of foul in American football. The ball carrier has already been tackled and is at the bottom of a pile of defenders. The play is over and the whistle has been blown, but one more defender throws himself onto the pile, further pinning the already immobile ball carrier, and costing his team a penalty.

Something similar happens in requirements documents. A two-paragraph description of a functional requirement has just made the requirement clear. Instead of another requirement or some new problem-domain information, the next section expresses the same requirement in input-process-output format. The section after that says the same thing again, this time in the form of a use case, complete with its own introductory description that says everything that's been said before.

Piling on can be observed at a large scale or a small scale—even inside the title of a document. At a small scale, it consists of piling words onto a word or phrase that has already made its meaning clear, as in the following examples.

Before piling on	*After*
Requirements	Requirements Specification
Use Case	Business Use Case

13.3.4 Including other documents

There are a number of important documents produced in software development that are neither requirements nor specifications. A common temptation is to throw them into the requirements document.

Scope of work

A document describing each of the tasks to be carried out during development and any associated deliverables; usually written for the purpose of billing and/or scheduling.

Because scope-of-work information is similar to some requirements, it causes confusion when inserted in a requirements document. Notice the incongruity between the following two "requirements":

R2.5 Resolve Discrepancy

Inputs: Discrepancy record.

Process: IF discrepancy valid THEN operator resolves discrepancy and marks discrepancy resolved ELSE operator moves discrepancy to rejection list.

Outputs: Discrepancy log, rejection list.

and:

R2.6 User Manual

Inputs: Requirements document, design document.

Process: Research and documentation.

Outputs: User manual.

The general rule is: describe the requirements and problem domain or, in a specification, describe the software; but don't describe the development process that will produce the software. That's another topic, for another place.

The one exception is that a requirements document should list materials needed by the development staff: documents from the customer describing protocols, customer-supplied data files, and so forth.

Schedules

Schedules change much more frequently than requirements do, and they pertain to all aspects of development, including testing, coding, delivery, and training. Therefore, a schedule is best made a separate document.

Acceptance criteria

Acceptance criteria, like specifications, need to be carefully crafted after requirements are complete.

Approval signatures

A form for approvals is signed once by a few parties, but the requirements document is printed out 30 to 100 times, over years. Make a separate form; have the parties involved sign it, and keep it in a special place—not inside the requirements document.

Traceability matrix

It's not entirely unreasonable to include a traceability matrix in the requirements document and fill it in over the course of the rest of the project. However, for people not accustomed to their use, seeing a traceability matrix with only the left column filled in is baffling. "Oh well, yet another arbitrary section to ignore," they say.

If you have a document management system, or even a directory on a network drive, it's probably best to put the traceability matrix there, near the requirements document. If your company has procedures for sign-offs on changes to documents, there will probably be much more ceremony to change a requirements document than to change a traceability matrix. Also, filling in a column on a traceability matrix does not throw the requirements out of date—an important consideration in an ISO 9000 company. (ISO is the International Organization for Standards.)

Feedback forms

Feedback forms are not entirely unreasonable to include, but they generally are regarded as more fluff, especially if the form is more than one page long. Also, as with approval forms, a requirements document needs to be printed out many more times than a feedback form. See also section 12.4.

No one of the last several extra documents is particularly bothersome to include in a requirements document. However, the attitude of "there's no harm in throwing one extra thing in" soon leads to throwing all of it in, and then people can't discern the purpose of the document.

13.4 More common mistakes

Decoy text is certainly the most common mistake in both requirements and specifications. This section describes a few more.

13.4.1 Jigsaw puzzles

A popular pastime is assembling jigsaw puzzles with large numbers of pieces—sometimes thousands. Here's a piece that's part of a sail. Where's another sail piece that connects to it? It's probably very far away, buried in that large pile with all the other pieces. To solve the puzzle, you must keep in mind that you're looking for a sail piece as you slowly sift through the pile, simultaneously looking for missing pieces in other small groups.

Many requirements documents are jigsaw puzzles in their own way. It says on page 16 that a grant deed has grantor, grantee, consideration, and address, but on page 45 it lists grantor, grantee, title company, consideration, and property transfer tax—whatever those are. So I guess the attributes of a grant deed are the union of those two sets. "No," replies the author of the document, "in the use case on page 62, there's a step where the user types in both address and assessor's parcel number. You really should read the document more carefully."

When searching through the document and finding what appears to be a definitive statement of the attributes of a grant deed on page 16, a reader is simply not going to expect to have to read any more, certainly not some use case on page 62. Always bear in mind that people skim at first to get a general idea of what the document says, and then refer to the document afterward for specific information.

To read a document like this one, you have to keep the whole thing in mind at once. You have to treat it as a sea of details, just like the sea of pieces in the jigsaw puzzle. However, no human brain can do this.

Note, however, that nearly every large document is a jigsaw puzzle to a slight extent. Your objective is to reduce the number of places where a reader can make a reasonable interpretation of text in one place that turns out to be wrong because of some other statement made very far away.

That does not include situations where you write an unfamiliar word or phrase in one place but define it elsewhere. The fact that the word is unfamiliar tells the reader to expect to find a definition elsewhere, such as in an overview or a glossary.

Principles of organization—mostly, the prevention of jigsaw puzzles—are presented in chapter 14. The most basic principle for fixing jigsaw puzzles is to collect a description that is scattered and implied throughout a document and put it all in one place. In the above example, the solution is to have a single section that definitively lists all the attributes of a grant deed. Then the reader doesn't have to puzzle it together by gathering use cases from throughout the document.

Sometimes, though, you can't cover all related information in one section. To help guide your reader, add page references to related material. For example, if there is something on page 62 that you need to know to properly understand what it says on page 16, then on page 16 write, "See page 62 for more information about grant deeds." There's nothing wrong with including a lot of cross-references within a document; the far graver danger is leaving these cross-references implicit.

13.4.2 Means confused with ends

Some requirements documents confuse description of the problem domain with requirements. For example, there might be a connection domain consisting of a program called HOLA, which can answer certain queries about some domain of interest. It would be a mistake to write:

> R-15 The system shall communicate with HOLA.

Of course the system's going to communicate with HOLA: it's a source for information about the real world that another requirement says the system is to produce in response to queries. Describe the relevant part of the real world, the queries, the information that HOLA can supply, and the protocols for communicating with HOLA, and you are done. R-15 is really a redundant requirement, obscuring the problem by confusing it with the solution.

These kinds of requirements also undermine the coherence of the document—the opposite of the reinforcement principle mentioned in section 13.2. Is this a requirements document or a specification or maybe a partial specification or maybe some sort of mixture of the two? Does the document describe the problem domain or the system's behavior? The reader really can't tell your intention, if you mix the two.

13.4.3 Force fit

The following is the way, in some forms of structured analysis, to indicate that the software is supposed to accept some data as valid and reject other data as invalid. You define

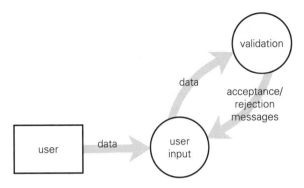

Figure 13.1 Data-flow diagram for data validation

a user input function and a validation function. You say that the user input function receives data from the user and sends the same data to the validation function. You then say that the validation function sends other data back to the user input function; this other data is a stream of messages indicating acceptance or rejection of the data sent by the user input function.

The documentation consists of a data-flow diagram like figure 13.1, and a set of requirement statements like these:

R-4 The user input function shall receive data from the user.

R-4.1 The user input function shall send data to the validation function.

R-4.2 The user input function shall receive acceptance and rejection messages sent by the validation function.

R-4.3 The user input function shall reject data received from the user corresponding to rejection messages received from the validation function.

R-5 The validation function shall validate data.

R-5.1 The validation function shall receive data from the user input function.

R-5.2 The validation function shall send acceptance and rejection messages to the user input function, in response to the data received from the user input function.

R-5.3 The validation function shall send an acceptance message to the user input function for each data element that has a value greater than or equal to zero and that has a value less than or equal to 26.

R-5.4 The validation function shall send a rejection message to the user input function for each data element that has a value less than zero or that has a value greater than 26.

The data-flow diagram shows three data streams, each of which must be documented, precisely describing each element of each data stream, but without saying anything about how the data stream will be implemented.

Now just a minute here. Forgetting structured analysis and everything else you know about requirements, how would you say that the system rejects numbers typed in by the user that are not in the range 0..26? Maybe something like this:

R-4 The user is not allowed to type in a number outside the range 0..26.

The same principle would apply if the validation rules were more complex. You'd put the validation rules in a big table, preceded by this:

R-4 The user is not allowed to type in data that violates the rules in table 1.1.

How, then, did half a page of dizzying text plus a data-flow diagram get produced just to make this tiny statement? The enormous version is the result of force-fitting the content to a very limited form of expression. If your entire vocabulary is functions and data flows, you have no choice but to force-fit everything you say into functions and data flows.

If you find yourself taking that much text to say something so simple, it's time to put aside your first strategy for describing it and search for another way. Try talking to someone who is totally unfamiliar with what you want to describe. Very often, you find yourself explaining it very simply just by speaking out loud to a person who doesn't already know what you have to say. Or if you can get that person to put it in his own words after you explain it to him, you might have a much better strategy for explaining it.

Notice that all of the above requirements are really program design, not requirements or even specification.

13.4.4 Duckspeak requirements

In the preceding set of requirements from structured analysis, you may have noticed a certain gnawing vagueness. Consider the following requirement:

R-461 The airplane reservation data validation function shall validate airplane reservation data.

What does that mean? Why write that sentence? How would you test it? Try saying it out loud. It's remarkably similar to the *duckspeak* described in the novel *1984*. Duckspeak was speech intended to agree with the official standards, but spoken so quickly and in such a monotone that it hardly mattered what the words were. All that counted was the dutiful, predictable tone.* Usually duckspeak requirements come in great numbers, one after the other, something like the requirements on page 281, but more of them. Reading them is hypnotic; they put people to sleep.

Duckspeak requirements are the worst type of force fit: requirements that say nothing at all, included in the document only to conform to standards. Strictly speaking, they're decoy text.

If you find yourself writing meaningless sentences only to conform to a standard, consider reframing the problem. Chapter 5 provides a variety of ways to frame a problem. You should try to find some strategy of presentation or document organization that does not include any slots that demand to be filled by sentences whether meaningful or not.

Framing all problems as a set of of functions—that is, as a set of transformation problems—is often the cause of awkward descriptions. Even a transformation problem can be described straightforwardly, though. Just describe the inputs, the outputs, and the rule relating them.

Another cause of duckspeak is the practice of treating requirements as high-level program design. The analyst is trying to describe subroutines that exist inside the software, but without including any implementation details—a self-contradictory goal. Leave the subroutines to the programmers and describe only the problem domain (or phenomena shared between the software and the problem domain, in a specification), and you'll avoid the dilemma of choosing between statements that are specific but bias implementation and statements that say nothing about implementation because they say nothing at all.

13.4.5 *Unnecessary invention of terminology*

Another ill effect of force-fitting all requirements into functions and data flows is that you have to invent an enormous amount of terminology that no one will ever use. For example, you need to define a "user input function," a "user presentation function," an "airplane reservation data validation function," and so on. These phrases gum up your prose, and yet no one will ever talk about the things they mean. The testers and programmers just talk about screens and validation rules. So do the users, and therefore so do the technical writers who put together the user's manual. The force fit to functions requires that

---

* [Orwell 1949], p. 254.

readers translate between their simple concepts that directly refer to the reality of the software or the problem domain, and the awkward language of functions. You might as well save them the trouble and write only in terms that readers will actually use.

13.4.6 Mixing levels

Another mistake you can see in the preceding examples is that even though they claim to be requirements, they're really high-level program design. Many requirements documents jump back and forth between program design and specification, often saying very little about the problem domain. They dabble a bit in user-interface design, saying what happens when the user clicks the OK button and that the user can click the Cancel button at any time to cancel the changes, almost in the same breath with statements about leasing policies or approval procedures. Suffice to say, this is confusing.

The solution is to be rigorous about what sort of content you include in the document. As described in chapter 1, a requirements document is only about the problem domain. It does not describe the software (except, of course, for realized domains). Don't slip into user-interface design or even describing the software behavior, unless, of course, the customer insists on some design ideas of their own. And don't slip into program design, describing subroutines internal to the software, with inputs, outputs, and processing. It doesn't matter if you describe the program at a high level, leaving out details; that's still describing the program, and leaving out details makes it even more confusing.

If you're writing a specification, then simply describe the shared events and shared states that constitute the interface. The shared states of a user interface are the screen; the shared events are the input from the user and the changes to the screen. In a hardware or software interface, you simply describe the rules for how the system responds to inputs.

If the customer does include some special provisions about the user interface or any other aspect of the software, be sure to indicate that these intrusions into interface design or program design are special requests of the customer—design constraints. If you mix design constraints with normal requirements without some indication that that's what you intend, you harm the coherence of the document.

13.4.7 Prefabricated table of contents

One source of a lot of force fits is a prefabricated table of contents, usually called a *template*. These templates usually have many sections and subsections, and it is company policy that each be filled out in every requirements document. For describing the functionality of the software, the software is to be divided into a set of functions, and each function is to include a set of inputs, some processing, and an output. We've already seen on page 281, how these lead to convoluted descriptions of simple things.

As noted in chapter 8, starting with a prefabricated table of contents is equivalent to forcing the content of one document into the table of contents of another. Document organization is not a task that you can do once and copy over and over again, the way type can be designed and repeated identically millions of times in millions of documents. Inventing a document structure is one of the tasks of writing a document, and it is seldom an easy one. The other tasks are choosing the content, and filling the organization with the written and graphical expression of that content.

Another side-effect of a prefabricated table of contents is that, often, no two people interpret the headings the same way. (A worthwhile experiment is to go around to everyone in your department and ask them to define *functional requirement*. The amount of variety is astounding.) Typical sections are Assumptions and Dependencies. What's the difference? If you look at how different people fill out these sections, you can see that they have radically different ideas about what they should contain. There is often an Inclusions section—apparently that would have to contain the entire document. Next there's an Exclusions section—apparently a list of everything that the software will not do. A long list, probably.

Most analysts simply fill these sections with a little bit of perfunctory gobbledygook and move on. No one is really sure why they're there. In review meetings, however, clashes about what belongs in each section sometimes lead to semantic arguments about what a use case "really is," or exegetical schisms over how to interpret the headings and template instructions.

If you're stuck in this situation and you have some content that desperately needs to go into the document, even though the prefabricated document structure has no room for it, there is usually an out: put it in an appendix. If you have to, put 99% of the information in a set of appendices that are the equivalent of a logically organized document.

None of this should be construed as an argument against template files that contain style definitions, handy macros, and even a tiny amount of starter text. These kinds of files greatly speed the writing of a document because they make consistent formatting either automatic or very close to automatic. These template files are only a speed-up for the word processor, however; they are not a speed-up for document organization and choice of content.

13.4.8 *Inconsistent terminology*

While people are deciding on requirements, they often invent and then change terminology several times as they get new ideas for terminology and as their understanding of the problem improves. A common side effect of this is that the document accumulates both older and newer terminology for the same things. Here it's an *angle,* there it's a *rotation,* and there it's an *orientation.* Before you release the document, be sure to do a global search-and-replace on all the old terminology. If you've been maintaining a glossary during the discussions, this will be very straightforward.

13.4.9 *Writing for the hostile reader*

Your writing must satisfy many different kinds of readers—not just readers with different jobs, but readers with different reading styles. There are detail-oriented readers, who methodically examine each detail one at a time without worrying about why each detail is as it is; big-picture readers, who don't trust their understanding of any detail unless they can deduce it themselves from the underlying principles; and so on. There is another kind of reader that many analysts go out of their way to try to satisfy: the hostile reader.

The hostile reader, upon reading any statement, tries to misinterpret it—and always succeeds. If you write, "Each inventory item has a unique identification code," the hostile reader counters: "*Each* inventory item? In the whole world?" So you change it to "Each inventory item in the XYZ warehouse has a unique identification code." The hostile reader is not yet satisfied: "Tables and chairs and dollies in the warehouse are items. Do they have unique identification codes?" No, that's not what you meant, so you change it to "Each item in the XYZ warehouse that is bought from a supplier or sold to a customer has a unique identification code." Still not good enough. The hostile reader objects: "So if you get an item for free and have not yet sold it to a customer, it has no identification code?" You fix that, and the next objection, and so on, and on each iteration, the sentence becomes ever longer and more difficult to understand.

You can try defining a term once and reusing it many times, so you don't have to write the definition into each sentence to satisfy the hostile reader. That won't work, though. The hostile reader never reads more than one sentence at a time. What the context of a sentence supplies, the hostile reader ignores. So you resort to the strategy of saying everything in the document in every sentence.

Before you get too worried about the hostile reader, see if you can remember the last one you met in person. If there are any genuinely hostile readers, they must be very rare. The author has not met one. There are a few testy readers out there, who don't try as hard as they possibly could to answer the question, "What is the author's intention here?" but they're also rare, and they're especially rare among people who are reading a requirements document in order to learn the next problem upon which to ply their skills. The hostile reader is a bogeyman. You don't need to fear him.

The hostile reader illustrates a fundamental principle of language: speaking assumes a cooperative listener, and listening assumes a cooperative speaker.* The same principle

---

* [Pinker 1994], p. 228.

applies to written language, of course. There is another principle: while you can't make yourself understood to the hostile reader, by trying to do so, you make yourself incomprehensible to all real readers.

This is why many legal documents are so opaque. They're written for a hostile reader assumed eager to find a loophole by exploiting the ambiguities inherent in natural languages. Even legal documents don't succeed in ruling out all possible unreasonable interpretations. They do succeed, however, in being incomprehensible. Sometimes the meaning is exactly the opposite from what the lawyer intends, the swirling syntax being so byzantine that not even the author can follow it.

Furthermore, when you read legal verbiage, your first thought is to try to find a loophole. When treated with hostility, naturally, you react with hostility. By writing in such a way that you do not draw upon the reader's intelligence to understand you, you turn the reader's intelligence to misinterpreting you—you make them a hostile reader.

13.4.10 Putting the onus on the development staff

When grumblings are overheard from the development staff about lack of good requirements, management sometimes proposes to solve the problem by putting the onus on the staff. "Before we sign off on a project, we will show you the requirements document, and we won't proceed without your approval. If there's anything you don't understand, point it out and the analyst will clarify it or get it corrected. You will have every opportunity to make sure the document is just right. And then, once you do sign off, you will be accountable. There will be no more pointing fingers or complaints that the document wasn't correct."

This solution is also proposed when management learns that no one on the development staff is reading requirements. "We'll make them read the requirements documents by announcing that they'll be accountable if there's something wrong with them."

The United States Congress has failed to balance the federal budget for many years now. Some have proposed an indirect type of solution: change the process by which Congress makes budgets by requiring them to balance the budget, as one of the rules that they have to follow. Yet there is a law on the books, passed in the 1970s, already requiring a balanced budget. A constitutional amendment would face the same problem: who's going to make Congress balance the budget, and what decisions will this party make regarding how much funding to give to each department and program? These process solutions don't work because the only way to balance the budget is to *balance the budget.*

Similarly, the only way to make requirements documents readable is to make them readable. When programmers read a poorly written requirements document, they see a maze of information that appears to be of no relevance to them. Why are there user requirements that are almost identical to functional requirements, except that the wording is slightly different? What's this ferociously complex data-flow diagram for? Why does each function have inputs and outputs that aren't inputs and outputs? They appear to be destinations for data, since some of them are called data stores, but the data itself is missing.

Faced with a document in which so little is understandable to you, you're likely to infer that it was never intended for you to read. Perhaps managers understand and have a use for all that strange prose. Maybe the legal department insists on having an Exclusions section that lists what's not to be included in the software, and maybe there's a reason why that list isn't infinite. All through the document, the same things are said three or four times, often on the same page. No one could have made a document so intricate if there weren't good reasons for it.

So you give your approval, meaning "the few little bits that seemed to have something to do with my job seemed okay." You figure that you'll get most of the information that you need by word of mouth. After all, that's how it's always been done.

On the other hand, if only three or four things seemed wrong or unclear, then you'd know exactly what to object to. Changing the approval process won't get the document to that level of clarity. Only improving the document will.

The above should not be taken to mean that well-honed and well-defined business processes are unimportant. Indeed, the development staff should review requirements documents and sign off on them only when they contain all the information they need to do their jobs. However, process improvements, at least those concerning interaction between people, should always be understood as a way of enhancing the division of labor, not as a substitute for the labor itself.

13.5 Poor uses of documentation

13.5.1 Documentation for the sake of documentation

Documentation is sometimes put to uses unrelated to or contrary to getting the software completed and functioning correctly. One is conformity to documentation standards. For example, a poorly designed ISO 9000 quality process or the standards for a government contract might specify that a requirements document describe the software, perhaps by casting it into the concepts of structured analysis, and fit all the information into a one-size-fits-all table of contents.

The theory behind this is that in order to have consistent quality, we need a set of quality criteria that can be defined independently of any particular project. A person should be able to judge the quality of the requirements document without knowing anything about the problem domain, and without any experience as a programmer. Is there a Gane-Sarson chart? Yes. Is there a section titled Dependencies? No—return to system analyst for revision. Suffice to say, this is focus on non-essentials.

A project where this kind of documentation is written tends to be a project that is not focused on delivering a high-quality, correctly functioning product. Instead of the requirements document being a vehicle to enable the development team to do its jobs, writing the requirements document and many other documents is an end in itself. The hundreds or thousands of pages of documentation prove that we did everything correctly, in accordance with official standards, so if there's something wrong with the product, it's not our fault. Many of these kinds of projects never reach completion and, perhaps, were never intended to.

This book won't help you write that kind of document. If you're forced to work with such standards, one strategy is to write two documents: one to conform to the standards, and one for real human beings to read. Indeed, many project managers provide this service to their teams when a requirements document is incomprehensible. The manager talks to the system analyst, learns what the requirements really are, and then makes a list that fits on a page or two of all the requirements that the team really has to address.

13.5.2 Doubletalk

Another highly questionable use of documentation is impressing the customer, not with the accuracy of your analysis, but with how much more you know than the customer. The theory is that the customer sees all the arcane terminology, sections with no intelligible purpose, and indecipherable graphics, and thinks, "It's a good thing we didn't attempt this ourselves! There's no way we could have produced anything like this. These people sure must know what they're doing."

That might work sometimes. Of course, it also breaks the link between the requirements document and the customer. So, the written description of the problem domain never gets verified by the domain experts. Also, the programmers can't understand such a document, so they miss out on the content that's buried within it, whether it's right or wrong.

If the customer has ever dealt with requirements documents before, you're sure to impress them much more with a simple, short, clear one. Impress the customer with the clarity of your document and the completeness of your analysis. "Wow, you really understood our situation here. No one has ever done that before."

If you absolutely must write a mystifying document to impress a customer, be sure to write a second document that is useful to the development team.

13.5.3 CYA documents

One more unfortunate attitude toward the writing of requirements and specifications is to treat them as *CYA documents*. (You will have to use your imagination to tell what this acronym stands for.) Such a document does not provide anyone with information necessary to do a job. Instead, its purpose is to have something to point to if disputes arise late in the development process.

The procedure is as follows. First, write a hopelessly convoluted set of specifications, filled with references to documents that are difficult to find, impenetrable requirements jargon, lots of repetition so that it's difficult to tell which of a set of statements is the definitive one, and statements whose import can't be properly grasped without first reading a seemingly insignificant subordinate clause in a sentence that comes 61 pages later.

Next, the customer sees the document. The customer doesn't read the document, of course, because that's not humanly possible. The customer is perhaps awed by how much more arcane is the discipline of software description than they ever imagined. The customer figures, or perhaps just hopes, that everything that was talked about in the preceding discussions must be included in such a long, complex document. After skimming the text a while, perhaps finding a sentence or two to reword, the customer signs off.

Now the development team takes over. Naturally, 90% of the information about the software will be communicated orally because no one on the team can understand the document, except for a few tables that the system analyst tells them to look at. But let's suppose that the software is written exactly as specified.

At last the software is delivered. The customer tries out the software and notices that there's a backup feature but can't figure out how to restore. It turns out that the software can't restore; it can only back up. The programmers said there was an unusual technical snag with restoring, so the system analyst decided to make it a possible future enhancement.

"How can you deliver a piece of software that lets you back up without restoring?" the customer bellows.

"Look under Acceptance Criteria, on page 73. It doesn't list any criteria pertaining to restoring," the analyst replies coolly, like a chessplayer who's just cornered his opponent.

"But what's the point of backing up, then? What if a hard disk crashes?"

"I'm sorry, but you signed off on the specification document, and the contract states that you will make final payment for the software if it meets the acceptance criteria in that document. If you want additional features, we can discuss new development work to add them." Checkmate?

Suffice to say, the customer probably won't be interested in new development. What happens now is that the customer refuses to pay—regardless of what it says under Exclusions in the CYA document. So the sales and marketing folks are brought in. To try to retain the customer, they offer some sort of sweet deal—on support, on training, on the next job—in addition to promising to add the needed features for no charge.

A CYA document does not cover you in case of disputes arising late in development. Not only does it force most information needed by the development staff to be communicated by oral tradition, it tends to backfire and anger the customer.

A better way to handle such disputes is to try to prevent them. Driving safely protects you much better than an airbag.

First of all, the contract must budget for change, simply because we can't spot every requirement at the beginning, and we probably won't get the specification perfect at sign-off time, either. Even today, many customers think that software engineering works like manufacturing. So, you need to tell the customer about these imperfections of requirements gathering and software design at the beginning of the job. Each time you change a requirement or part of a specification that the customer signed off on, you'll need to get agreement from the customer and charge the new costs to the change budget. If the customer knows that the changes are coming, this won't be so painful.

Second, instead of hiding information from the customer with an opaque document, try to make the document as clear, short, and simple as possible—though never at the expense of relevant detail, of course. If the document is made to be read and understood, the customer will probably read and understand it. The customer would then notice early on that, for technical reasons, the restore feature is deferred to a later release. There wouldn't be any big surprise at the end, where the customer is made to feel hoodwinked.

Finally, never forget that the customer is the first participant in the division of cognitive labor that produces software.

C H A P T E R   1 4

Organization

14.1 Content first

The first principle of organization is: a place for every detail, every detail in its place. Organization is the process of inventing places for all the details. Therefore, to organize, you must first have some details in need of organization.

In elementary school, you were probably taught that the first step in writing a document is to make an outline. First you state all your main topics. Then you break each topic down into subtopics, and, if necessary, you break those down into subsubtopics. Each bottom-level topic will correspond to exactly one paragraph. Once you finish the outline, writing the document then becomes very simple and systematic: just write the paragraph corresponding to each bottom-level topic.

Of course it never works so easily in practice, except in simple examples from elementary school. Alert readers will recognize the top-down approach, already criticized in chapter 1: how can you tell if the overall structure of the document is any good until you've written the paragraphs? How do you know that it makes sense to break down the subject matter along the lines of your top-level topics, instead of some other way?

There is a further problem with writing an outline first: it doesn't make sense to choose an organization without first having some content to organize. Therefore, your first step in writing a document should be to make a list of the content that you want to include—an unordered list containing big topics, tiny topics, concepts, propositions, ideas for graphics, and anything else that you want to include in the document. Just add items to the list as you think of them without worrying about the sequence or hierarchy in which they'll appear in the final document or about whether an item corresponds to one paragraph or two or twenty. Don't even worry, at this point, if some items overlap. Part II of this book provides guidance for identifying the content items appropriate to the document that you're writing.

An outline processor is a wonderful device for creating your list of content. You can begin grouping related items together and choosing a sequence as you type them in, but don't become attached to the first way of organizing the document that occurs to you. You want to make use of the outline processor's ability to let you quickly make radical changes to the way the document is organized.*

There are two principal aspects of organization: how information is grouped together into units, and the sequence in which information is presented. Choosing a good grouping and a good sequence is a matter of identifying the *logical structure* of the content, that is, which items logically depend on which. The following two sections provide guidance on making this choice, though the full subject of logical structure is far beyond the scope of this book.

14.2 Grouping

Ideally, information that is more closely related to other information logically should be located closer to it in the document physically, and the principal divisions in the document should correspond to the principal logical divisions in the content.

---

* Very early in writing this book, I made a list in an outline processor of about 600 content items to organize. Organization was very difficult, and I had to abandon many early attempts. The original idea of having one chapter per problem frame, containing all the documentation techniques needed for that type of problem, just didn't work: nearly all of the documentation techniques overlap between two or more problem frames. Presenting requirements techniques in one section and specification techniques in another didn't work, either, again due to the overlap problem. An early attempt at presenting a complete, example requirements document for each frame didn't work: most readers didn't want to trudge through even a ten-page requirements document to see the techniques in action. I had to scrap about 100 pages of writing in response to that piece of feedback. The point of this example is that it's typical. Organization of any document longer than a couple pages is almost always difficult, requiring careful thought and a willingness to delete, reorganize, and rewrite.

These ideals can be difficult to achieve in practice. For example, if many different classes participate in the same sequence of events, you would likely have one section for each class, followed by one section to describe the sequence of events. The class documented in the first section, however, is logically related no less closely to the sequence of events than all the other classes. Thirty pages may well separate the first section from the section describing the events. These are the kinds of trade offs you make when organizing a document. Each event in the sequence is related more closely to the sequence as a whole than to the classes, so you have to bundle the events into one group, even though this means distancing them from the classes.

Fortunately, you've already done most of the work of finding the logical seams in the subject matter when you framed the problem as described in chapters 4 through 6. In a requirements document, each domain naturally fits into one section. Each requirement oval can also make a section, or you might put it at the end of a section about one domain. (See the tips for classes and events below; the same decision applies to them.) The rest of this section focuses primarily on smaller choices about how to combine details into groups.

The following are a few ways in which two or more propositions (statements) can be logically close and, thus, candidates for inclusion in the same group:

Logical relationship	Example
Propositions A and B are about the same subject.	A gene consists of a sequence of codons. A gene codes for a specific protein.
Propositions A and B have the same predicate.	Servomotor 3 can close valve G. A member of the maintenance staff can close valve G.
Propositions A and B have subjects in the same class, or that are different values of the same variable.	I/O port 0x7000, bit 0, turns on servomotor 3. I/O port 0x7000, bits 4–7, select one of 16 speeds for servomotor 3.
Propositions A and B have the same kind of predicate—that is, answer the same question or have parallel structure.	Data mining must happen before data analysis. Data analysis must happen before data transmission.

However, it is virtually impossible to deduce from general principles whether a given set of content items should be grouped together or not. Better to systematically consider alternatives and use your common sense. Usually, just by looking over some alternatives, you can easily see which fits your subject matter best.

Here are three ways to group classes and events:

(1)	(2)	(3)
class *A*	class *A*, including events	class *A*
class *B*	class *B*, including events	class *B*
class *C*	class *C*, including events	class *C*
class *D*	class *D*, including events	events that affect *A*, *B*, and *C*
events		class *D*, including events
		class *E*
		class *F*
		events that affect *E* and *F*

Organization (1) makes sense if the set of events straddles classes *A*, *B*, *C*, and *D*. Organization (2) is more appropriate when each sequence of events affects only one class. Naturally, within each section, you describe the class in one subsection and the events in another subsection; you don't let one complicate the other. Organization (3) is a more general case: a mixture of the previous two. There's no need to consistently follow one grouping strategy throughout the entire document.

You can see that classes and events are just one instance of a common pattern of logical relationship: one set of naturally grouped propositions pertains to one or more other sets of naturally grouped propositions. The vast majority of grouping decisions, whether at the level of paragraphs, tables, or sections, boil down to choosing from among the above three types of organization.

A type of grouping mistake to avoid is illustrated by an application that has a set of queries as well as the capability for a manager to decide which employees can run which queries. The temptation is to say, along with the description of each query, that a manager can decide which employees can run it:

query *A*, manager can set up authorization
query *B*, manager can set up authorization
query *C*, manager can set up authorization
query *D*, manager can set up authorization

This violates the most fundamental principle of organization—"a place for every detail, and every detail in its place"—replacing it with something closer to "every detail in every place." You need to choose *one* place to say that a manager can set up authorization for any query. Once you've recognized this, you can see that you have an instance of the type of logical relationship shown in organization (1), above.

14.2.1 One thing at a time

The fact that it is so very tempting to complicate the descriptions of the queries with the description of the authorization capabilities raises another principle of organization, well stated by G. Polya, the mathematics professor who brought the study of heuristic to the twentieth century:

> The first rule of style is to have something to say. The second rule of style is to control yourself when, by chance, you have two things to say; say first one, then the other, not both at the same time.*

Trying to say two things at once almost guarantees incomprehensibility. The reason that it's so often tempting is that much of the information in a technical document is usually tightly interrelated in many different ways. You fear that if you talk about query *A* without talking about the authorization capabilities, the reader will think that any user can run query *A* unconditionally. You're trying to avoid the jigsaw puzzle problem described in section 13.4.

However, the repetitious organization clearly won't do. That organization will create even worse problems if there are more capabilities that affect all the queries. This is one of those awful trade offs that you face nearly every time you write a technical document: there is some risk that a reader will read the section on queries without reading the section on authorization. That risk, however, is outweighed by the greater risks (of confusing the reader or persuading them to stop reading altogether) that are brought on by repetition and saying too many things at once. In reality, the risk of confusing the reader is very minor if the document is clear, concise, and includes nothing but useful content all the way through.

If you're looking for a principle of logical relationships that guides this decision, here it is:

> The propositions that define something are more closely related to each other than are propositions related to it in any other way, such as telling how it is used.

* [Polya 1957], p. 172.

For example, what defines a query is its content and any other information that is inherent in the query, such as its input or output formats. They say what the query *is*. That information belongs all in one place, uninterrupted by anything else. The ability to decide who can run a query is, something that presupposes a query to talk about and, therefore, does not belong within the same group.

However, a fine compromise is to create a larger group, containing two parts: one part describing the queries, and the other describing the authorization capabilities. Usually, you don't even need to explicitly designate these as members of the same group; you can simply place the section on authorization immediately following the section on the queries. Then the reader will learn about authorization immediately after learning about queries and will hardly be able to help noticing that they're related. The basic grouping principle pertains to keeping related statements close together in the document, not necessarily keeping them in the same section.

Another helpful standby, whenever you want to be sure that a reader understands that information elsewhere in the document affects what a certain section says, is the *cross-reference*. Just write "See section 2.4" or "See page 17 for information on which users can run each query."

14.2.2 Seven plus or minus two

In the 1956 article "The Magical Number Seven Plus or Minus Two," almost certainly the most widely read article ever published in cognitive psychology, George A. Miller wrote about some interesting "limits on our capacity for processing information."

Many have understood this article as scientific proof that a graphic should have no more than 7 ± 2 circles or rectangles in it because then the mind won't be able to understand it; more circles or rectangles would exceed our capacity for processing information. Some have gone further and taken the article as scientific proof that the human mind cannot understand a section in a document that contains more than nine subsections. $7 + 2 = 9$, therefore nine subsections is the limit; if the section contains ten subsections, then the readers can't help but become confused. A procedure cannot have more than nine steps, or people won't be able to carry it out reliably, and so on: whenever any group contains more than nine elements, it's beyond human comprehension.

If you think something must be wrong with this idea, you're right. In fact, the article made no such statements. More importantly, those statements are not true, as a few observations will demonstrate. The Old Testament is not any less comprehensible for having Ten Commandments rather than Nine. A road map shows you thousands of symbols at once, and yet people navigate with road maps every day. A typical dictionary contains 50,000 subsections all grouped together—one for each word—and yet people have no trouble using it. You can carry out a written procedure with a hundred steps by just doing one step at a time and then reading the next step. The English alphabet is 26 letters long, and yet children learn it. You have probably understood sentences containing more than nine words, and whistled melodies of more than nine notes.

When a subtle idea becomes popular, it often becomes distorted; a simplistic substitute takes the original idea's name in popular culture. Miller's article is actually about two main subjects. In the first section, the majority of the article, he observed that in many experiments involving quick, perceptual measurements of stimuli that varied along a single axis—such as the pitch of a tone, the loudness of a tone, the salinity of water, the length of an arc—most people could accurately distinguish only about seven different levels, give or take quite a lot depending on the type of stimulus. Miller called this range of levels the *span of absolute judgement.*

Given that the span of absolute judgement is only about seven levels, this raises an important question: how, then, are we able distinguish such complex phenomena as faces? We all recognize far more than seven faces, and with amazing accuracy. Miller doesn't provide a definitive answer, but he discusses some tricks, such as, judging stimuli that vary on several dimensions at once to achieve a much greater number of distinctions.

The article then turns to the *span of immediate memory:* how much information we can keep in our short-term memories at once, measured by giving someone some information that they have never heard before and asking them to recite it back. Most people, upon hearing a random sequence of binary digits, can recite it back correctly only if the sequence is no longer than about nine digits. This would seem to indicate that the span of immediate memory is about nine bits of information.

Now here is the truly noteworthy part of the article, at least for writing documentation. There is a trick by which you can accurately recite back a string of *forty* binary digits. When you hear five digits, think of the corresponding decimal number from zero to thirty-one: for example, when you hear 10010, think "18" and forget the 10010. Do the same with each group of five digits. This breaks the string down into eight decimal numbers, which you can keep in your head all at once (just barely), and use to reconstruct the original binary number. It takes some practice, but anyone can do it.

In the terminology of information theory, this trick is called *recoding.* By recoding the binary digits, you've increased the amount of information you can keep in your head at once from nine bits to forty bits—a huge increase, considering that every increase of one bit doubles the number of distinctions that you can make. The span of immediate memory is therefore properly measured in chunks, not bits, and through recoding, each chunk can be worth many, many bits. The number of chunks you can hold in your immediate memory varies somewhat according to the type of chunk. For simple things like digits, it's as high as nine, but more often it's around seven or even five for arbitrary lists of words.

Recoding is far more commonplace and of far more importance than as a parlor trick for reciting binary digits. Just as our brains have means for extending the span of absolute judgement to astounding levels in order to recognize thousands of faces, we also have means for extending the span of immediate memory, enabling us to consider problems of spectacular complexity—like software requirements and computer programs. Recoding is foremost among them, and it's everywhere; you do it all the time. It's how you're able to read a 400-page book and not get lost. When one topic is done, you put it and all its details away in your mind, and think about the next topic. If the two are connected in some way, you can mentally reopen the first topic, as needed, to understand the consequences of the connection and then forget about it again.

So, if you have 700 elements that belong in a table, make a table with 700 elements. Just make the table so that the reader can read it one row at a time and so that there is an obvious commonality to all the rows. Commonality allows the reader to chunk the table, thinking of it as only one thing, such as, "the table that lists all the field mappings." If you have a procedure with eighteen steps, the same principle applies: make your description such that the reader can read one step at a time, knowing his place in the whole procedure without having to keep all 18 steps in mind at once.

So here is the real lesson to learn from Miller's famous article:

> *The Recoding Principle:* Make it *easy* for your readers to recode, or chunk, the information, so that they seldom or never have to consider more than four or five things at once (not nine!).

In fact, you can set up nearly all documentation so that a reader never needs to think about more than one or two things at once. There are almost always a few complicated parts that require juggling three or four or five at once, but, through skillful grouping—saying one thing at a time—you can keep those to a minimum.

14.3 Sequence

The ideal sequence in which to present information is such that no statement ever appears before any statements that are logically required to understand it.

Like the ideals for grouping information into sections, this ideal is much harder to put into practice than it sounds. Especially in software, it seems that all the parts are so tightly intertwined that no one part can be described in isolation. The key to solving this problem—to the extent that it can be solved—is to put that which is more *logically fundamental* first. Every new piece of material builds on all the previous pieces, ultimately creating the desired logical structure in the reader's mind.

For purposes of understanding material, the rule for deciding which of two concepts or propositions is more fundamental is simple:

> If a concept or proposition *B* refers to another concept or proposition *A*, then *A* is more fundamental and should come first.

The principal way that one concept refers to another is by including it in its definition. For example, you can't understand what a two-pair connection is until you understand what a pair is and what a connection is.

A proposition refers to another proposition by extending it, varying it, talking about it, or including it. For example, you can't understand "If a timeout occurs, resynchronize the channel" until you know that it is possible for timeouts to occur and that it is possible to resynchronize the channel.

A proposition refers to a concept by including it. You can't understand what "Inside plant is equipment located in a central office" means until you understand what "inside plant" and "central offices" are.

Here are a few heuristics for determining which of two pieces of information is logically more fundamental:

- Facts not within one's power to choose are more fundamental than facts that one can choose. So descriptive statements should generally come before requirements, as requirements are really just descriptions of conditions that the customer chooses to make true. To put it another way, the problem is more fundamental than the solution.

- *Things* are more fundamental than their attributes, relations between them and other things, and the actions they can do or have done to them. For example, you need to understand what nations are (things) before you can understand foreign policy (action). This is the principle that guided the placement of classes before sequences of events in all the examples in section 14.2. Similarly, in a class description, the definition of the class precedes the description of its attributes.

  - A corollary: Relations are less fundamental than what they are relations between. This includes relations between actions, such as causal relations.

  - A corollary: Actions are less fundamental than what gets changed during the action.

  - A corollary: Attributes are less fundamental than what they are attributes of. This includes attributes of relations and actions, or even of other attributes.

- The normal case is more fundamental than the exceptional cases. Exceptional cases are variations or extensions of normal cases.

- What a thing *is* is more fundamental than any roles that it plays in different situations or how it is used.

- A description of agents should usually precede a description of the passive objects that they act on. For example, usually a detailed description of users should precede detailed descriptions of the things they act on. Both, however, tend to be very intertwined: the agents are defined by what they do to the passive objects, and the passive objects' capabilities are exercisable only by certain agents. The reason for putting the agents first has less to do with logical structure and more to do with the fact that there are usually few agents and many passive objects. Describing the agents first leads to fewer forward references.

You'll notice that these suggestions can easily conflict. What if a class *A* contains attributes that refer to class *B*, and class *B* contains attributes that refer to class *A*? That's very common because that's the situation each time you have a relation between two classes. In this case, you simply have to choose one or the other, knowing that the reader might be temporarily perplexed the first time reading through the document.

The above tips can help you minimize incomprehensibility due to one piece of information's logically depending on a later piece of information, but they can't guarantee you a way to eliminate it. As with difficulties in grouping, you can always refer to a later section or page number to help the reader find the information that hasn't been covered yet.

However, there is a simple technique for giving the reader enough information in advance of any section to understand it on first reading, even if it refers to information in later sections: an overview. An overview should try to follow the principles of logical sequence inside itself. This is easier than in the main text because an overview leaves out nearly all detail. However, the overview provides enough information so that readers have some introduction to all the main concepts, enabling them to understand sentences that refer to those concepts, even if they haven't read about them in detail.

14.4 Emphasis

Emphasis is a way of distinguishing the two percent of the content that is most important from the remaining ninety-eight percent. It is not a way of indicating that certain information is important. Of course, every statement is so important that your reader should know about it; otherwise you wouldn't have put it in the document.

Importance is mainly the proposition's location in the logical structure of the document. The most important statements are those that bear directly on many other statements. Thus, an important statement is one that a reader needs to bear in mind in order to properly understand other statements.

For example, in the requirements for a photocopier, a reader needs to understand that the purpose of the whole thing is to make copies. Understanding this, a reader can look at all the details with a critically focused eye: "If this happens and then that happens, how is that supposed to produce a copy? What if such-and-such happens first? How would you recover from that?" Burying so important a statement deep in the document would leave the reader with a heap of seemingly arbitrary details, and no good questions to ask about each one. In a photocopier, this wouldn't be a problem, but what if the reader did not know the purpose of the equipment in advance of reading about it?

Emphasis is the way to prevent that from happening—to give statements a visual importance that matches their logical importance. Here are a few techniques of emphasis, ordered by roughly decreasing strength:

- A graphic emphasizes its content.
- Whatever appears first is automatically emphasized.
- Whatever you refer to many times is emphasized—not page and section references, but references in which you talk about one thing in many places, in the context of many other things, each time adding more information.
- Surrounding content with white space emphasizes it. Look at page 300. Which sentence do you see first?
- Bullets emphasize.
- Repetition in another form emphasizes; for example, giving an example or drawing a graphic.
- Taking more space emphasizes. A long section seems to be more important than a short section.
- Any kind of contrast emphasizes the contrasting element. If one row in a table is shaded and the rest are not shaded, the shaded row is emphasized. If one row is unshaded and the rest are shaded, the unshaded row is emphasized.
- Italics are the last resort, and much weaker than any of the above techniques. Italics for emphasis indicate that you want to want a word or phrase to be read in a louder or more strained tone of voice than the surrounding text—seldom needed in technical documents.

It may seem surprising to hear that taking more space could be a good thing to do in a document, as a way of giving a piece of information its proper degree of emphasis.

However, "express everything in the fewest words possible" is a crude rule and, if taken literally, would lead to incomprehensibly terse (but literally correct) documents. It is better to understand that you have alternatives, and those alternatives include a wide range of different lengths.

If you want to make a section longer, you can: add examples, or add more examples or more-detailed examples; add a graphic; add an explanation of the rationale for the information in that section; add usage scenarios; say the same information in more than one way.

Be aware that all the techniques of emphasis can work in reverse, too. Whatever you put first will be emphasized, whether you want it emphasized or not. If you start the document with a lot of bureaucratic sections, the principle of "whatever appears first is automatically emphasized" causes the genuinely important text to be deemphasized. This is essentially why decoy text is the bane of good documentation.

Strangely, talking about importance explicitly usually backfires. Writing the words "IMPORTANT!" or "NOTE:" before important statements often makes people skip over them.

Furthermore, such extreme forms of emphasis, or emphasis applied to much more than the two percent that genuinely touches nearly every other statement in the document, undermines your credibility. Italicizing every *not* makes you sound like a person who continually raises his voice or repeats himself—that is, a person who does not expect anyone to listen to him. Usually when people expect to be ignored, it's because they have reason to: they know that what they have to say is not relevant to other people's concerns. You probably don't want to communicate to your readers that what you have to say is irrelevant to their jobs. Say everything once, with no more and no less emphasis than each statement deserves.

C H A P T E R   1 5

Small details

A good document organization and wise choice of content are only as effective as the small details that fill out that organization and present that content. This chapter is a collection of short articles covering a wide range of small details of technical writing that often come up when writing software requirements and specifications. Some of the articles are about individual words. These are marked by headings in quotation marks. Others cover the basics of broader topics, such as, how to make useful TABLES and how to write a DEFINITION.

acronyms

Whenever possible, try to avoid inventing new acronyms. They're opaque to the uninitiated, and, of course, you're writing for the uninitiated. They take a person a lot longer to learn than a word or a two-word phrase. However, if an acronym is already part of the vocabulary of the problem domain, then you must explain it in the requirements document.

The meaning of an acronym is seldom made clear by indicating what its letters stand for. If you know that OSS stands for "operations support system," do you know what an OSS is? For more information, see DEFINITIONS and GLOSSARIES.

"affect/effect"

Words easily confused. *Affect* is most often a verb, and *effect* most often a noun:

> *Affecting* something is causing an *effect* within it.

Adding to the confusion are a noun usage of *affect*, having a completely unrelated meaning, and a verb usage of *effect*, meaning "make" or "bring about." Fortunately, these additional senses are seldom needed in technical documents.

"always"

It is sometimes claimed that a requirement should never assert that something is to always or never happen. For example, a requirement should not say that the system should always reject an order from a customer on credit hold. This is because a requirement is supposed to be finite, and an "always" or "never" statement pertains to a potentially infinite amount of time. The reason for wanting requirements to be finite is because requirements are supposed to be testable, and it's impossible to test an infinity of cases.

This is a mistake. Test cases are necessarily finite. You test a system, say, for three weeks. The purpose of testing is not to determine that the system worked for three weeks. The purpose of testing is to either gather evidence that supports an inference that the system will meet requirements indefinitely far into the future, or to uncover evidence that it won't. Testing is always imperfect. Even finite requirements that have a mere quadrillion possible cases (many fewer than in most real-world system) are impossible to test one by one. Testers carefully choose their test cases to expose evidence that has as much logical leverage as possible, to learn as much as possible about how the system will perform during the potentially infinite span of time when it is not being tested.

Furthermore, the people who design specifications and write programs are not trying to produce a system that works only during testing. The problem they are trying to solve is, "How can we make such-and-such always happen?" The requirements document should state that problem and not confuse it with the separate problem of how to verify that the software meets the requirements.

To put it another way, the customer will be somewhat nonplussed if you write that the cutting blade will not fall while a person is in the cutting area—but only during the first three weeks of operation.

assumptions

The word *assumption*, like its frequent companion DEPENDENCY, is vague. There are a wide variety of things in software development that are equally well named by the word *assumption*, so you can never safely—ahem—assume that the reader will understand the one that you intended, without providing some clarification.

Faced with a template containing a section named Assumptions, it can be tempting to include anything you can think of, only for the sake of having something to include in that section:

1.8 Assumptions

This document assumes that DEX will be developed according to XYZ Corporation Software Development Standards, doc. no. 045-71001.

And what if the staff does not develop the software according to *XYZ Corporation Software Development Standards?* What useful information does this sentence communicate to the reader? Since it communicates nothing, it should be deleted.

Assumptions worth stating are those where you can identify something in the document that would have to be changed if the assumption were changed. Identifying an assumption is useful only if you explicitly indicate what would have to be changed.

For example:

This user interface is designed on the assumption that it will be implemented in Visual Basic. If we switch to a different tool, we would probably need to change the appearance and functionality of a number of the controls.

It's neither necessary nor possible to state exactly which controls would have to be changed, without redesigning the user interface for every other available tool. But even though this paragraph doesn't go into detail, it communicates useful information to the reader. If a programmer is considering switching to a different tool, they will be on the alert for user-interface decisions that exploit capabilities of Visual Basic that are not available in the new tool. If a user-interface designer is considering a different tool, they will also be on the alert for compromises made in response to the limitations of Visual Basic that don't need to be made with the new tool.

Notice that this definition of *assumption* includes all problem-domain information. If the objects in the problem domain have different attributes than those you describe, or if events can come in different sequences than those you describe, then, of course, you would change the document. The majority of a good requirements document is problem-domain description, but there's no need to call it "assumptions." Reserve this word only for specific assumptions about the development process on which you have premised some of the decisions expressed in the requirements document or specification.

"click on"

A small improvement, to decrease wordiness, is to consistently write that a user "clicks" an object rather than "clicks on" an object.

"compose/comprise"

Two surprisingly tricky words that occur often in requirements. The standard usages are:

> The whole *comprises* the parts.
>
> The parts *compose* the whole.
>
> The whole *is composed of* the parts.

Comprise, in other words, means to encompass, or include. *Compose* means to fit together to form something larger, like the way that musical notes together form a musical composition.

Therefore the digits do not comprise the identification code, but they do compose the identification code. The identification code is not comprised of digits (a nonsensical phrase), but it is composed of digits, and, to say the same thing, it also comprises the digits.

With such a subtlety of English usage, it may be most prudent to abandon tradition and simply treat these words as synonyms. Fewer and fewer people know or care about the difference, anyway.

A better solution is to not word a sentence in such a way that a reader's ignorance of the distinction could lead them to misunderstand. One way to do that is by always providing redundant clues indicating which word you intend as the whole and which you intend as the parts. This is very easy because, as in "digits" and "identification code", the whole is normally singular and the parts are normally plural.

Another way to avoid the confusion is by using different words altogether, like *consists of*:

> The identification code consists of 9 hexadecimal digits.

The simple word *is* is often even better:

> The identification code is a series of 9 hexadecimal digits.

Includes and *contains* are poor substitutes, since they suggest that more might be included than what you list. "The identification code includes 9 hexadecimal digits." And what else does it include?

conventions

The following text demonstrates both some recommended typographical conventions and a good way to describe them:

> This document observes the following typographical conventions.
>
> *Requirements* are testable effects or conditions to be created by GEO: services to be provided to users, rules to be enforced, etc. Requirements are written in **bold sans serif type** and given an identification number preceded by an R. For example:
>
> **R-5   A user can enter a separate orientation for each of a structure's attachments, independently of the structure's orientation.**
>
> *Data* to be stored by GEO is written in sans serif type, to distinguish it from real-world objects and attributes that it represents. For example: a structure is an outdoor object, such as a telephone pole or building, to which cables can connect; but a structure is a collection of data stored in the GEO database about a structure. A structure type is one of the pieces of data in that collection.
>
> *Named data values* are written in *italic sans serif type*. For example, the possible values of structure type are: *pole*, *pedestal*, *building*, *manhole*.
>
> *String literals*—alphanumeric data to go into the system exactly as shown, such as filenames—are written in sans serif type.
>
> *Program code* is written in the Courier font.
>
> *Names of windows and controls* are written in *italic sans serif type*.
>
> *Preferences* are evaluation criteria for choosing between two or more designs that meet the requirements. There's no way to test a preference; a preference only provides guidance in making the most useful possible design. Preferences are written in **bold sans**

serif type and given an identification number preceded by a **P**. For example:

P-1   *Preference:* **GEO's user interface should give priority to ease of use in working with copper networks over hybrid fiber-coax networks.**

Invariants are conditions that are not to be changed by any event, or by a specified set of events, though they might be changed temporarily during the event. Invariants are a redundant check on the correctness of the requirements. If any requirements describe an operation or possible sequence of operations that could result in an invariant being violated, the requirements are incorrect. Invariants are written in **bold sans serif type** and given an identification number preceded by a **V**. For example:

V-1   *Invariant:* **No structure's orientation ever points into a sector narrower than 5 degrees.**

Notice that all of the examples to illustrate the conventions are taken from later in the document, and the name of the software—GEO—is mentioned explicitly, instead of a generic term like "the system."

Naturally, omit any paragraphs for conventions that don't apply to the document that you're writing. You may well omit the entire discussion of the conventions, if you're sure that your readers don't need to have them explained. Good typographical conventions are intuitive enough that they really need no explanation, though the above text also provides a place to explain the concepts of requirement, preference, and invariant, which might be unfamiliar to many readers. Even if you include the section explaining the typographical conventions, you should still strive to write the remainder of the text so that someone could understand it without having read the discussion of the conventions. Most readers skip that section anyway.

There is a little bit more to the conventions that a reader does not need to know, but that you need to know when writing the document:

- The identification numbers of requirements, preferences, and invariants are out in the left margin, away from the main body text (see PAGE LAYOUT).

- A requirement, preference, or invariant is always in a paragraph by itself, separated from preceding and following text.

- In a definition, the name of the concept being defined is italicized, except in the GLOSSARY (see DEFINITIONS). Another good convention for defined terms is to put them in **bold serif type**. This makes the terms very easy to spot when scanning over a page, but it can also clutter the page if there are a lot of them or the page also contains requirements or other bold text.

- When describing a variable that must be replaced by a definite number or sequence of characters in any concrete instance, the variable's name is in *italic serif type,* even if the surrounding text is in the sans serif font. For example:

> Landbase filenames have the format lb*xxxyyy*.dwg, where *xxx* and *yyy* are the *x* and *y* co-ordinates of the upper left corner of the map, respectively.

The convention of writing requirements, preferences, and invariants in **bold sans serif type**, putting them on separate lines from the rest of the text, and putting the identification numbers in the left margin, makes it easy for a reader to scan through the document looking for "just the meat." This way, you can add commentary to each requirement without the extra text camouflaging the requirement statement.

The reason for the convention of putting variables in *italic serif type* even when inside sans serif text is that *italic sans serif text* does not stand out very well. For example, in lb*xxxyyy*.dwg, the coordinates do not stand out nearly as well as when they're written in the serif font.

"correct"

Similar remarks as for INVALID.

cross-references

If you find yourself needing to repeat something explained at length elsewhere in the document, keep in mind that, instead of repeating it, you can refer to it by page number or section number. Cross-references are an indispensible weapon against the temptation to say everything in one sentence, bore the reader through repetition, or create a jigsaw puzzle.*

When you make a cross-reference, be sure to include the page number or section number explicitly, via a special instruction to the word processor, rather than write "the following section" or "above." Later, you might insert another section, necessitating that you change the cross reference to "two sections below" or "two sections before this one." If you let the word processor fill in the page number or section number automatically, you won't have this problem.

There's nothing wrong with referring forward in the document. The ideas in a requirements document or specification are usually so interconnected that there's no way to avoid forward references.

---

* See section 13.4.

"data"

Some grammarians and editors insist that you treat the word *data* as a plural noun because it's a borrowing from Latin, where it's the plural of *datum*. For example, they'd insist that you reword "This data represents the pH of the aquarium" to "These data represent the pH of the aquarium."

However, usage in computers has established a singular meaning of *data*, which has proven too convenient to abandon because of etymology. Most people today don't even know the connection with *datum*, and when trying to follow the rule "*data* is plural," have often fouled up otherwise readable sentences for lack of a singular. If you're editing someone else's document, don't push this obsolete rule.

To indicate plurality, write "types of data" or "sets of data."

definitions

A *definition* is a statement that identifies what a concept refers to, by identifying the concept's location in the conceptual framework of which it is a part. A proper definition achieves this by indicating the broader concept, called the *genus* (plural: *genera*), of which the concept being defined is a special case, and one or more distinguishing characteristics, called *differentiae* (singular: *differentia*), that distinguish the concept from others of its genus.

Some typical definitions:

name of concept being defined   genus   differentia distinguishes concept from others of its genus: in this case, materials that do conduct electricity

An insulator is a material that does not conduct electricity.

name of concept being defined   genus

Distortion is degradation in the quality of a signal, not due to decrease in the strength of the signal as a whole, but to variations in the relative intensities of the signal at different frequencies.

differentia distinguishes concept from others of its genus: in this case, other forms of degradation in signal quality

A common temptation when writing a definition is to omit the genus. This results in an unclear definition because, often, a reader can't infer the genus and consequently can't tell what kind of thing you're talking about. Definitions that are phrased "is when" or "is where" almost always omit the genus, and are almost always unclear.

A *compiler* translates source code into machine language.	A *compiler* is a program that translates source code into machine language.
What performs this translation? A computer? A person? If you're writing for someone who doesn't know what a compiler is, you can't expect him to know that it's a kind of program.	
An *overplot* is when two things overlap.	An *overplot* is an overlap between two or more graphic entities drawn at the same place on a page.
An overplot is not a point in time, but this definition seems to say that it is.	
HC: Identifies the house count at a telephone pole.	HC: The number of houses that connect to a single telephone pole: "house count."
This definition makes a reader ask what thing does the identifying. *In fact, nothing does; see the definition at right.*	

Notice that a definition is much more than a synonym for a word. A definition indicates a way of mentally dividing reality for purposes of talking and thinking about it. Italicizing the word or phrase for the concept being defined is a helpful cue to the reader to interpret the sentence as a description of a named mental distinction, rather than an assertion about the things included within that distinction.

A circular definition is one that includes the concept to be defined in the genus or differentia. Of course this is illegitimate, because the definition is meant to communicate a concept to someone who doesn't already know it. A definition draws upon the reader's knowledge of all the concepts in the genus and differentia to help the reader form a new distinction.

This does not imply, however, that the words that describe the genus or differentia can't be among the words that name the concept to be defined. For example, the following is a perfectly good definition:

> A *patron request* is a request made by a patron for a bibliographic item, without specifying the lending institution from which the bibliographic item is to be retrieved.

The fact that the name of the concept being defined is *patron request* does not mean that there's anything wrong with referring to patrons and requests in the definition. A patron request is a certain kind of request, and what (partly) distinguishes it from other types of requests is the fact that a patron makes it. Many made-up terms contain their genus and differentia within them; that's what makes them self-explanatory terms.

Here are some helpful genera for tricky definitions: *the act of, a method of, the responsibility to, a commitment to, a set of, a type of* x *that, information about, facts about, the amount of, the number of, a measure of, the ratio between.* A few examples:

> *Final post* is the act of permanently recording all additions, deletions, and changes made to physical plant, once all work on a work print has been completed.
>
> A *booking* is the commitment of a seat on a specific flight and day to a specific passenger.
>
> *dBmV* is a measure of the voltage level of a signal, equal to $20 \log_{10}$ mV, where mV is the number of millivolts measured across a resistance of 75 ohms.

Some concepts are actually tuples—that is, groups of two or more kinds of things mentally grouped together. Since you probably don't want to have to define the concept *tuple,* you can give the genus as *combination,* as in "a *problem* is a combination of data, an unknown, and a condition relating the unknown to the data."[*]

When defining an attribute, often it helps to write "said of" to indicate the type of thing that the attribute applies to. In this case, you don't need to explicitly state the genus as "attribute of entity-type *x.*" The same technique is sometimes helpful when defining relations and actions, too. For example:

> aerial: Suspended from poles or similar overhead structures; said of cable, strand, anything that can be hung from poles.
>
> attenuate: To decrease in strength; said of a signal passing through a transmission medium.

The above is a typical format for a definition in a GLOSSARY: the term to be defined at the left, and just the defining information at right, instead of a complete sentence. If you were to include the *aerial* definition inside a narrative paragraph, you could word it this way:

> Cable or strand is said to be *aerial* if it is suspended from poles or other overhead structures.

---

[*] This is G. Polya's "problem to find," which he wrote much about in [Polya 1957].

Some concepts are too fundamental to be defined: they don't have a genus, or there are no concepts to relate them to others of the same genus. Examples are: *entity, attribute, relation, action, event, state, quantity, quality, point in time, type.* Some concepts, like *record, field, responsibility, commitment, program,* and *data,* do have definitions, but they require more theoretical discussion than you probably want to include in a requirements document. You seldom need to communicate the meaning of such a term, but if you do, don't try to give it a proper definition. You may have to rely on synonyms; better yet, give an example that guides the reader to see how the concept is abstracted. For example, "Entities are objects that possess attributes, engage in actions, or participate in relations, as a person has height and weight, can travel from one place to another, and can be the parent, sibling, or child of another person."

Other concepts are difficult to define because we form the distinction perceptually. Who, other than a biologist, can define *tomato?* We distinguish tomatoes from other foods by appearance, not by an easily verbalizable relation with other concepts. Fortunately, there is almost no need to define such concepts. It's enough to say "a type of vegetable" (or "a type of fruit" if any biologists are around); that is, provide the genus but skip the differentia. If you must indicate to a reader enough information to help him recognize a plant or other visually distinguished type of object, then provide a picture.

To define a particular kind of *state* or *status,* list the complete set of mutually exclusive states. For example, "A proposal's *approval status* is its current stage in the process for granting or denying it: *awaiting department approval, awaiting chair approval, awaiting board approval,* or *denied.*" The word *current* is helpful when defining states.

Some concepts are distinguished only by their level in a hierarchy. For example, a typical copper-wire telephone network has three levels of cables: *feeder cables, distribution cables,* and *drop cables.* Obviously, a good genus to define these concepts is *cable* or *cable in a copper-wire telephone network,* but differentiae like *top-level, mid-level,* and *bottom-level* would not communicate much. There are two solutions here: define each cable by the things that it connects to, and draw a picture.

Wirecenter: the geographical area served by a single central office.

Central office: a building where local call switching takes place.

Main distribution frame: a large connector at a central office, which connects the switching equipment to feeder cables.

Feeder cable: a large cable that connects to the main distribution frame at a central office and feeds into distribution cables.

Distribution cable: a cable that connects between a feeder cable and one or more terminals.

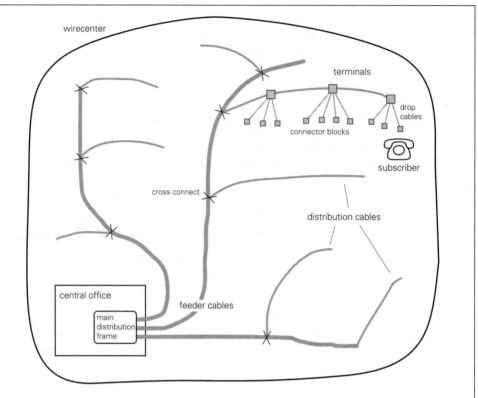

A wirecenter in a copper network, showing cable route from central office to subscriber. Terminals, drop cables, and connector blocks are shown on only one distribution cable.

Drop cable: a small, usually two-pair cable that connects between a terminal and the connector box at a subscriber's building.

(Remaining definitions omitted.)

As this last example illustrates, concepts often come in groups where each concept is distinguished by its relation to the others. A diagram that simultaneously depicts all of them is an indispensible way to help a reader grasp each distinction, much better than words alone can. If you bombard the reader with a series of terms and definitions—wirecenter, central office, call switching, main distribution frame, feeder cable, distribution cable, drop cable, terminal, dead end, and cross connect—he can't possibly retain it all. The diagram presents the same number of concepts without being overwhelming. A reader can refer to it many times while reading the text, each time able to see how each concept relates to all the others, not just to the one or two listed in each definition.

dependencies

The word *dependency* is vague. There are many ways in which one thing can depend on another. So, as when writing about ASSUMPTIONS, you must be explicit:

Vague	*Explicit*
XYZ depends on the following software:	The following software must be complete before programmers at ABC Corp. can begin developing XYZ:
XYZ depends on the following software:	The following software must be installed on any computer on which XYZ is to run:

Don't say that the customer cannot depend on the software to generate correct results if the users don't carry out the operating procedures as described in the specification or user's manual. If you're going to say that, you might as well say that the customer can't depend on the software if the users make random patches to the executable file. See "Writing for the hostile reader" in section 13.4.

document titles

The title of a document should be clear and terse, instantly informing potential readers of its content and purpose. Shown below are some ways to improve common document titles:

Wordy, unclear, or confusing	*Direct*
XYZ SRS	XYZ Requirements
XYZ Software Requirements Specification	
XYZ Requirements Specification	
XYZ Requirements Specifications	
XYZ Detailed Functional Requirements Specifications Document (DFRSD)	

Wordy, unclear, or confusing	Direct
XYZ High-Level Requirements	XYZ Preliminary Sketch *or* Preliminary Sketch of XYZ Requirements *The reason for this change in wording is to avoid suggesting a higher degree of rigor or commitment than a "high-level requirements" document actually delivers. Calling it "preliminary" is also an invitation for wide-ranging comments and suggestions.*
XYZ Functional Specification XYZ Functional Requirements	XYZ Specification *or* XYZ Program Specification
XYZ Logical Data Entities and Attributes	XYZ Data Dictionary
XYZ User Interface Requirements	XYZ User Interface *or* XYZ User-Interface Design
XYZ External Interface Requirements	XYZ/ABC Interface *or* XYZ/ABC Interface Design *or* Interface Between XYZ and ABC *An important improvement here is that ABC is mentioned explicitly in the title.*
XYZ Guidebook to Terminology and Nomenclature	XYZ Glossary

See also TITLE PAGE.

"entry"

Can denote either the act of entering, or an item in a list. In the latter sense, *entry* is usually awkward and confusing. Try substituting *item* or *element*. For example, a pull-down menu contains "items," not "entries."

fancy cover

A requirements or specification document is scaffolding. Especially before customer sign off, it's incomplete, not fully thought through, and continuing to change as the result of reader feedback. The appearance of the document should reflect this.

If the purely cosmetic details of the document are too refined, such as a fancy, glossy cover, or an artistic typeface, the document sends a different message to its reader. It leads the reader to understand that it contains the final, perfected result of the best expertise your company has to offer. Consequently, any flaw, such as missing details about the customer's business processes, a section that's hard to understand, or grammatical or spelling errors tends to be seen as a reflection on your level of competence. You probably don't want a customer to take that attitude toward your document. The customer should see flaws not as reasons to reconsider the deal, but as opportunities to help improve the software, and as a normal, expected part of the design process.

These documents should certainly be as professional and readable as you can make them, but it's unwise to polish their appearance. Stapling the document or putting it in an old, three-ring binder is good enough.

first sentence

The first sentence of a requirements document should tell the reader what *thing* the requirements pertain to—the piece of software to be developed. The structure of this first sentence should follow the same principles as a DEFINITION. For example, the very beginning of a document titled *GEO Requirements* might read:

1.1 Overview

GEO is a program to allow users to add *x, y* coordinates to objects stored in the DBG database.

This sentence tells the reader what the document is about: GEO. The rest of the paragraph might describe the DBG database, *x, y* coordinates, and the sorts of objects stored in the DBG database. It's almost always worthwhile to supplement this opening description with a very simple block diagram—perhaps a diagram derived from the frame diagram you made while thinking through the requirements, or the frame diagram itself. Now the reader knows what you're talking about, and you can start making statements about GEO: its problem domain, its requirements, the platform it's supposed to run on, and so on.

The thing that the requirements are about is the single most important, most fundamental piece of information to include in a requirements document. That's why it should come first. Yet this information is often entirely omitted from requirements documents, in favor of a useless "purpose and scope" section, like this one:

1.1 Purpose and Scope

The purpose of this document is to describe the requirements for GEO.

Notice the difference between this sentence and the one recommended above. The "purpose" sentence communicates nothing that wasn't already clear from the title of the document. If the reader did not already know what GEO is, this sentence doesn't help.

The recommended sentence gives the reader new information: it answers the question, "What is GEO?" Without an answer to that question, the reader will have a very hard time understanding the rest of the document. A little later on the page, once you've introduced all the main concepts, you can spell out details such as which version of the software the document applies to. (This information should also be on the TITLE PAGE.)

Since you're defining a particular thing rather than a concept, finding the genus can be tricky; you have a lot of options. Fortunately, almost all of them are good. Here are some helpful genera to choose from: *program, software, piece of software, software package, library, API, database, system.*

More example first sentences:

Labcon is a C++ library for controlling laboratory instruments manufactured by Exsys, Inc.

Erasmus is a full-text database of medieval literature.

VERBIS is a software package to track all aspects of a human-resources department: fringe benefits, vacation time, job postings, job descriptions, employee skills, company organization, and employee training.

The *Mensis 2000* is a court-reporting machine: a machine to enable court reporters to transcribe courtroom conversation and print it out word-for-word later. This document describes the requirements for the software inside the Mensis 2000.

Italicizing the name of the product further indicates that the sentence is the definitive, fundamental statement of what the product is.

The last example ends with a sentence similar to the "purpose" sentence, with the difference that the preceding sentence renders it meaningful, by describing the machine that the software is a part of. This strategy of "describe the machine first, then say that this document describes the software for the machine" is suitable for most embedded applications, where the software has no name of its own.

glossary

In a glossary, place each term in the left margin (see PAGE LAYOUT), as it would appear in the middle of a sentence. That is, write the term in lower case unless it's always capitalized. If you capitalize all the terms, the reader won't know whether to capitalize them in the middle of a sentence. Put the terms in bold sans serif type, to make them easy for a reader to scan through when searching for a specific term.

Write the DEFINITIONS in a column to the right of the terms. You don't need to put any METATEXT between the glossary heading and the first term.

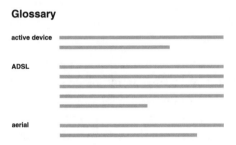

Often, a single term has more than one sense (more than one distinct concept that the term can mean). In this case, number the senses and define them in separate paragraphs, like this:

---

tap   1. A place where a cable's SHEATH has been opened for the purpose of connecting to one or more of the PAIRS inside.

2. In a BROADBAND network, a type of SPLITTER that connects DROP CABLES to a DISTRIBUTION CABLE. A tap typically has 2, 4, or 8 ports for supplying signal to 2, 4, or 8 SUBSCRIBERS. Some common symbols for taps:

           (23)   [23]   ⟨23⟩

    2-port tap   4-port tap   8-port tap

The number on the inside indicates the tap value, or approximate amount of signal strength, in dBmV, lost by the tap between the input and each tap port. This is not the INSERTION LOSS of the tap; the greater the tap value, the lower the insertion loss.

The above example shows two other techniques helpful in writing a glossary. First, a glossary is a good place for adding a little bit of supplementary information in addition to the pure definition. Don't try to say everything you know about the concept, but it helps to hint at why the concept is important, add extra introductory information such as typical sizes or typical values, and clarify any likely misunderstandings. A glossary is also a good place to explain graphical symbols for the concepts being defined.

Second, if you use a term in a definition that is defined elsewhere in the glossary, write the term in small capitals the first time it appears in the definition.

When defining an ACRONYM, it is seldom enough to say what each letter stands for. You must also define the concept that the acronym as a whole denotes:

OSS	Operations Support System: As defined by the FCC, a computer system and/or database used at a telephone company for pre-ordering, ordering, provisioning, maintenance and repair, or billing.

Often, during a project you change terminology several times, or you find it necessary to revise your definitions of problem-domain terminology. Be sure to make all the terminology in the document consistent before you release it. It helps a lot if you update the glossary every day as you talk with the customer and write the document.

On a large project with many different requirements documents, you might want to make one big glossary for all the documents. This saves a lot of cutting, pasting, and inconsistency. This cumulative glossary can be quite a useful repository of knowledge for future projects. Another strategy is to collect all the new terms from each project and add them to a company-wide glossary. People can cut and paste from the company glossary on new projects. The company glossary can even help introduce new employees to their jobs.

"i.e." and "e.g."

Two Latin abbreviations, often confused. Their meanings:

i.e.   that is

e.g.   for example

If you can't keep them straight, your readers probably can't, either. Just write "that is" or "for example" and you can't go wrong.

"invalid"

A statement disallowing "invalid data" can be appropriate in an overview or preliminary sketch, but not in a requirement, unless "invalid data" is precisely defined. It should not be up to the programmers to invent their own criteria of what sort of data is valid or invalid. Their job is to implement the actions described in the requirements or specification: if the input data is in such-and-such format, store it; if it's in such-and-such format, display such-and-such error message; if it's in yet another format, display yet another error message. When describing the desired output of the program at this level of detail, there is no need for the concepts *valid* and *invalid,* except to help a reader understand why it's useful for the computer to take this or that action.

metatext

Metatext is text that describes text in the document rather than the document's subject matter. For example, "The following paragraph describes..." or "This chapter describes..." Some metatext is unavoidable, such as a description of typographical CONVENTIONS, or a documentation guide to describe a set of documents or the contents of a large document. However, most metatext is nothing but clutter. It distracts from the ordinary text and therefore from the content; deleting metatext almost always improves a document.

A common place to put metatext is right after a section heading. The concern is that if you don't explain what's going to come in the section, a reader won't be able to understand it. For example:

---

3. Email
This section describes email.

4. Format of Email Messages
This section describes the format of email messages.

4.1 Address Part
This subsection describes the address part of an email message.

The address part consists of four name/domain pairs . . .

Much better than merely repeating a section heading in a sentence (a practice that is somewhat condescending to the reader) is to start by presenting some content that itself introduces the rest of the section. The most likely candidate for introductory content is a DEFINITION. Another good way to introduce content is to sketch it out, similar to an overview.

With introductory content in place of metatext, the above example could read like this:

> **3. Email**
>
> Email is electronic mail: documents sent electronically from one user at one computer to one or more other users, possibly at different computers.
>
> **4. Format of Email Messages**
>
> A single email message consists of an address part, a body part, and zero or more attachments.
>
> **4.1 Address Part**
>
> The address part consists of four name/domain pairs . . .

If you find yourself writing metatext, try deleting it and seeing if the text is hard to follow. If it's easier to follow, as it usually is when interruptions are removed, then leave the metatext out. If it's harder to follow, then either put the metatext back—sometimes it is indeed necessary—or consider adding content that you may have skipped, like definitions, or rearranging the content so that each piece of information helps introduce the next, as described in section 14.3.

Good metatext is usually very short. Here's a very quick way to distinguish some examples from other text:

> An address has the format *login@domain*, where login is the user's login name and *domain* is the name of the computer that exchanges mail for that user.
> *Examples:* george.gibbons@paydirt.com, v3873092@bryant.edu.

This same quick technique also makes a nice introduction to digressions about rationale or special implications that you want the reader to understand. The word *Rationale* or *Implication* followed by a colon is the bare minimum of metatext you need and, therefore, the right amount.

Your motto as a technical writer should be "content right now," not "content next paragraph."

"model"

One of the most overworked words in the computer field. Save this word to mean an object that has been made to bear a useful analogy to something else, so that the model can be observed to learn something about what it is a model of. Model-building is a fundamental technique in software: the data stored in a computer is a model of the part of the world that the data represents. Often, users read the data to learn about some part of the world, hoping that the analogy between the data and the real world holds for the information they're trying to learn. Models themselves are neither true nor false, though the inferences that we base on them are.

Don't write *model* to mean *concept, abstraction, conceptual framework, specification, process, description, diagram,* or anything other than the plain sense of the word *model.*

It's too confusing, especially to customers unfamiliar with the strange linguistic habits of the software community.

Here are a few simple substitutions to illustrate how to fix phrases that contain these non-model senses of the word model:

Confusing	*Clearer*
waterfall model	waterfall process
requirements model	requirements
use case model	use cases

page layout

The following is a recommended page layout for a requirements document or specification.

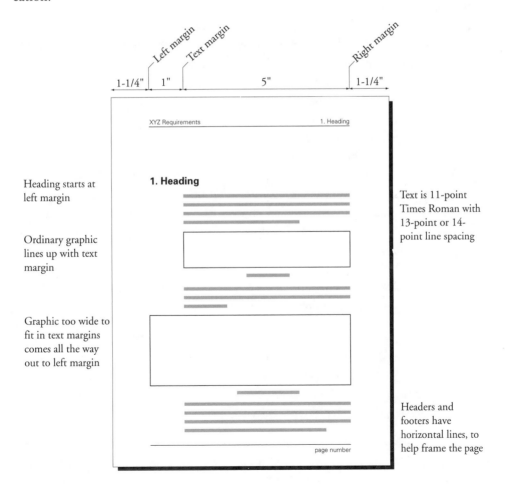

You can adjust this layout slightly—for example, you might move the outer margins around if you're making a double-sided document—but there are a few important aspects of it that you should retain.

The goal of a good page layout is to place everything harmoniously on the page so that it's easy to read, the reader's attention is directed to what they need to find, and the reader is never distracted by the page layout itself. This is a very easy goal to achieve, but some word processors' defaults create a cluttered layout that's difficult to read. Especially in a document that presents complex material that a reader must consider very carefully, you do not want the physical appearance of the page to make the material seem harder to understand than it really is.

Typical defaults in a word processor set the font to 10-point Times Roman with a line spacing of 11 points, and a text margin that is only 1/2" in from the left margin. The result is quite difficult to read, not just because the type is small, but because there are too many characters per line. Optimal readability is at about 40–70 characters per line; the defaults make lines with around 100 characters per line. By increasing the font size and making the left indent on normal text a whole inch, the number of characters per line is reduced to about 80. That's still above optimum, so you need another trick to improve readability: increase the line spacing.* With a line spacing of 14 points, even 11-point Times Roman at 80 characters per line looks quite spacious and readable.

This might seem complicated, but fortunately you only need to set it up in your word processor once; then you can forget about it.

The other important consideration in the recommended page layout is to frame the page. An 8-1/2"×11" page is so large that it loses its visual unity if text and graphics don't line up with the margins. Adding horizontal lines to the header and footer also helps the reader perceive the page as a cohesive whole. The left edge of screen shots should line up with the left margin or text margin, instead of being centered. Only very small graphics should be centered.

Paragraphs should be in block style: with one line of space between them, and not indented. This helps requirement, preference, and invariant statements fit harmoniously onto the page, in their highly emphasized format.

"paradigm"

A word to avoid in most circumstances, due to its vagueness.

Philosopher Thomas Kuhn started the contemporary usage of the word paradigm in the book *The Structure of Scientific Revolutions,* where it was part of his theory that normal science is puzzle-solving with a well defined puzzle type—which he called a

---

* [Schriver 1997], pp. 260–263, presents some of the research on line spacing, line length, and readability.

paradigm (remarkably similar to a problem frame).* Scientific revolutions, in his theory, are periods when scientists abandon one puzzle type for another.

Since then, the term has entered popular usage and changed somewhat. With Kuhn's original idea now faded and forgotten, *paradigm* serves mostly as a conveniently vague word to resort to when you don't want to go to the effort of clearly identifying what you want to say and then saying it—or, worse, where you want to impress someone with fancy language. Here are a few examples of how to improve sentences that contain the word *paradigm*:

Vague	*Clearer*
The DEX and VERBIS systems operate on different paradigms.	There is no one-to-one mapping between the data elements stored in DEX and VERBIS.
VERBIS represents a new paradigm in printed-circuit assembly.	*Better to say nothing at all, or else write:* The following features in VERBIS have never before been implemented in software for automation of printed-circuit assembly: *followed by a list of specifically what differentiates VERBIS from its competitors—though a survey of the market and the competition does not normally belong in a requirements document.*
The alarm-response process conforms to a three-step paradigm.	When an alarm appears on the main monitor screen, the security staff carries out the following three steps: *or* When the system receives an alarm signal, it checks the following three conditions to ensure that it's not a false alarm:

---

* The older meaning of *paradigm* was an example that illustrated a pattern in its most ordinary or archetypal form. An example is *amo, amas, amat, amamus, amatis, amant,* illustrating the pattern of inflections of one of the major types of verbs in Latin, by showing how just one verb, *amare,* meaning "love," is inflected. Memorize the paradigm and you can inflect another verb that follows the same pattern: *secare,* meaning "cut," goes *seco, secas, secat, secamus, secatis, secant.* This sense of the word *paradigm* is very useful, and not unduly vague. Unfortunately, most people are not familiar with it, and that's a reason to avoid it in most circumstances—in addition to its having been supplanted by the vague variations on Kuhn's sense of the word.

Vague	Clearer
Accommodating the data warehouse will require a shift to a new paradigm.	The types of read requests initiated by the data warehouse software differ from the read requests that our software fulfills, in the following ways:
	or
	We will need to redesign our record-locking scheme from scratch in order to accommodate the data warehouse.

Here are some words that can replace *paradigm,* depending on your meaning: *system, method, framework, scheme, description, technique, structure, set, set of predicates.* Don't just replace *paradigm* with *model,* unless, of course, you're really talking about a MODEL.

"represents"

Representation is the relation between computer data and the real world. When we devise a convention for setting computer data to one of a set of states to indicate that something in the real world is in one of a corresponding set of states, we are making the data *represent* the real world.

Thus representation is one of the basic concepts of computers. Other sorts of representation implement the same principle: a sales representative informs potential customers of the offerings of the company that he represents. Both the human representative and the computer data "re-present" something that exists somewhere else and can't present itself directly.

Unfortunately, all too often people write the big word *represents* as a synonym for the little word *is.* For example:

> Compliance with the new tax laws represents the most important goal of the new accounting system.

No, compliance with the new tax laws does not represent anything. It's not stored information or an indirect way of communicating. Sentences like that are usually the result of trying to make things more complicated than they really are. Better to just write:

> Compliance with the new tax laws is the most important goal of the new accounting system.

Write the word *represents* only when you really mean it.

requirement statements

There are three main ways to word a requirement statement: in the present tense, with a modal verb like *must* or *shall,* and in the imperative mood (as a command).

In the present tense:

R-1   A user can view landbase files in AutoCAD format.

R-2   A user can run any of the following queries on demand:

R-3   When the passcode is entered at the gate, the gate toggles between locked and unlocked.

R-4   WATCHCOM notifies the user when the gas pressure on any pressurized cable falls below its allowable minimum.

With a modal verb:

R-1   A user must be able to view landbase files in AutoCAD format.

R-2   A user shall be able to run any of the following queries on demand:

or

R-2   VSYS shall answer any of the following queries on demand:

R-3   When the passcode is entered at the gate, the gate must toggle between locked and unlocked.

R-4   WATCHCOM shall notify the user when the gas pressure on any pressurized cable falls below its allowable minimum.

In the imperative mood:

R-1   View landbase files in AutoCAD format.

R-2   Answer any of the following queries on demand:

R-3   When the passcode is entered at the gate, toggle the gate between locked and unlocked.

R-4   Notify the user when the gas pressure on any pressurized cable falls below its allowable minimum.

It's hard to go wrong with the present-tense format. It easily accommodates mentioning both the user and the system, if necessary, and it is especially well suited to describing required problem-domain activity without mentioning the system, as in R-2 above.

Writing requirements with a modal verb almost always creates longer, more obscure sentences, and is therefore not recommended. For example, where the present tense allows you to say "a user can," the modal-verb format requires "a user shall be able to." Unfortunately, some organizations, including the United States government, require use of the word *shall* in requirements as part of the terms of the contract. In this case, you have no choice; but if you have a choice, you should pick one of the other two formats. Also, if you write requirements with a modal verb, be sure to make it consistently *must* or consistently *shall* throughout the document. The modal verb *should* is best reserved for preferences, not requirements, as it does not connote the kind of finality that you want in a requirement statement.

The imperative mood creates the simplest requirement statements. However, as in R-1 and R-2 above, sometimes it omits too much. If the user is supposed to activate some capability of the software, such as a query, it's best to mention the user explicitly, as the present tense allows. The imperative mood works best for requirements involving notifying a user: there the sentence can mention the user as the object of the verb. You can mix requirement statements in the present tense and indicative mood in the same document, reserving the indicative mood for notification and the present tense for all other types of requirements.*

It's usually best to avoid the future tense in requirement statements. The future tense is best reserved for describing development activity to occur after the document is complete, like "Future versions will add support for more landbase formats, as needed."

Often, a requirement contains a lot of small details: various different activities that are supposed to occur depending on several different conditions. Rather than write an enormously complex sentence, or a series of many nearly identical sentences, make the requirement refer to a TABLE describing the rule. The table from the tax instructions in section 11.5, along with the accompanying "many sentences" version, gives a good illustration of how much more readable the table is. You can word the requirement statement that precedes the table like this:

R-5   **Send delinquency notices to customers as described in the following table:**

---

* Technically, mood and tense are two independent variables of a verb. The first group of requirement statements shown above is in the indicative mood and the present tense, and the third group is in the imperative mood and the present tense. For most purposes, though, it's enough to call them "present tense" requirements and "imperative mood" or "command" requirements.

or

R-5   **Send delinquency notices to customers as described in table 1.1.**

Rules are abstract. Because requirements almost always describe rules, requirements are also abstract, and, consequently, they can be difficult to understand without some commentary. Typical helpful commentary is definitions, examples, and explanations of rationale. By putting requirements into bold sans serif type, as noted under CONVENTIONS, you can easily weave short comments into the requirements without creating confusion.

Here's an example. The figure 10 referred to below is a graphic illustrating each concept, omitted here for brevity. Page numbers that the example refers to are indicated by XX.

R-6   **A user can view the following landbase features:**

R-6.1   –   **Right-of-ways, including text.**

A *right-of-way* (ROW) is any street, road, alley, etc. Most right-of-ways have names; hence the "text" clause of this requirement. Figure 10 shows four right-of-ways, including text: N. Roanne St., W. Greenleaf Av., W. Greenacre Av., and N. Geneva St.

R-6.2   –   **Centerlines.**

A *centerline* is a line in a landbase drawn down the middle of a right-of-way. Some landbases do not have centerlines. More information about centerlines is on page XX.

R-6.3   –   **Property boundaries and addresses.**

Property boundaries are lines that show where one street address ends and another begins. The rectangular shapes surrounding the right-of-ways in figure 10 are property boundaries.

<table>
<tr><td>R-6.4</td><td>–</td><td>**Span footages.**</td></tr>
</table>

Some landbases, though not all, include graphical representations of spans. These are lines from structure to structure, showing the footage of the span. Figure 10 shows many span footages; the two pointed to are 95' and 124'. A landbase might measure span in meters, not feet. Being able to see the footage in meters is often helpful for a user to find out where a structure should go on a landbase, especially during network design (see page XX).

Notice that the principles of grouping and sequence discussed in chapter 14 are at work in this example. All the information grouped under R-6 has a simple and obvious common denominator: landbase features that a viewer can view. All of this information is collected together in one place, not scattered throughout the document. However, the description is not allowed to stray from its purpose. The reader is referred elsewhere for more details about centerlines and network design; these are covered in depth in other sections. The principles of sequence are at work in the decision to describe centerlines after right-of-ways: the DEFINITION of *centerline* refers to right-of-ways in its differentia and, therefore, requires the reader to first understand what a right-of-way is.

In addition to showing how to intersperse commentary with requirements, this example also demonstrates a simplifying technique that is almost indispensible in any requirements document: writing many endings to a single sentence. If you need to write several requirements about the same thing, write the common part as the beginning of a sentence, and write the different parts as "sentence-completions."

The following is mind-numbing:

R-7	**A calling application shall be able to read bibliographic data from the AV database by direct function call.**
R-8	**A calling application shall be able to read bibliographic data from the AV database through a secure firewall connecting to the Internet.**
R-9	**A calling application shall be able to read bibliographic data from the AV database through a direct TCP/IP connection.**
R-10	**A calling application shall be able to write bibliographic data to the AV database by direct function call.**
R-11	**A calling application shall be able to write bibliographic data to the AV database through a secure firewall connecting to the Internet.**

And so on.

The following says the same thing, but is much simpler and easier to understand:

> **R-7**   **A calling application can create, read, update, and delete bibliographic data in the AV database:**
>
> R-7.1   –   **By direct function call.**
>
> R-7.2   –   **Through a firewall connecting to the Internet.**
>
> R-7.3   –   **Through a direct TCP/IP connection.**

The en dashes help to visually relate the sentence-completions to the sentence-beginning at the top. They're especially valuable if you intersperse commentary with the requirements, as in the example of R-6, above.

Usually you can combine create, read, update, and delete into a single requirement statement. People think of them as four aspects of a single capability: full access to a database. While, technically, they are four separate capabilities and will require at least four separate test cases, writing them as four separate statements usually makes the information seem four times as complex as it really is.

tables

Almost any group of very similar statements is best communicated with a table. If you find yourself writing a very long series of sentences that have the same structure, a table is likely to be both clearer and easier to make.

Confusing

The Address group contains street addresses and is stored on layer 20. The Drops group contains drop cables and is stored on layers 11, 12, 50, 65, 66, 102, 104, and 119. The Land group contains all landbase features and is stored on layers 1 through 50. The Quartz group contains Quartz output and is stored on layers 123 through 244 and 251 through 255. The PoleNo group contains attribute text of utility poles and is stored on layer 70.

Clearer

Group	**Layers**	**Description**
Address	20	Street addresses
Drops	11, 12, 50, 65, 66, 102, 104, 119	Drop cables
Land	1–50	All landbase features
Quartz	123–244, 251–255	Quartz output
PoleNo	70	Attribute text of utility poles

Confusing	*Clearer*		

A bug must be assigned to both a programmer and a tester unless its status is Code or NFBC, in which case it need not be assigned to either, except that a bug in Fixed status must be assigned to a programmer but doesn't have to be assigned to a tester.

status ↓	Must be assigned to:	
	programmer	tester
Code	○	○
Release	●	●
Test	●	●
NFBC	○	○
Fixed	●	○

Notice how few horizontal and vertical lines a table needs. Many tables need no lines at all. The fewer lines you can draw on a table while still grouping all information that needs to be grouped, the less clutter you add and the more you emphasize the contents of the table.

title page

You can reduce the apparent complexity of the document by putting information on the title page that would otherwise go into separate numbered sections, each introduced by METATEXT.

If the table of contents can fit on the title page, then it belongs on the title page. There it provides a quick overview of the document, inviting people inside if the headings appear relevant to their work.

Information to include on the title page:

- The title of the document
- The version number of the software
- The date of the last revision of the document
- The name of your company and, optionally, your company logo
- Who prepared the document
- The name of the party for whom the software is being developed
- If your company has codes for billing time spent on the software, the code for this particular project

- If necessary, the words "proprietary and confidential," or whatever your lawyer advises

- The table of contents, if the whole thing fits without making a mess of the page

An eye accustomed to reading English normally scans a page from upper left to lower right. Since the company logo is merely a nicety rather than information specific to the project, put it in the upper right or lower left, out of the eye's customary path. Whatever you do, don't center it.

Under "Prepared by," note that these aren't movie credits, so you need only mention the people who actually wrote the document. There should only be one or a few such people. You don't need to mention every manager, programmer, tester, or customer representative who reviewed the document, nor the company that catered the meetings.

Mention names of people, not merely a company. A phrase like "Prepared by: Splenetix Corporation" hides the people involved, suggesting that no one wants to take responsibility for the contents or to be contacted if there is a problem. Including your name says, "*I* did this, and I stand by it."

"type"

Everything seems to have a "type" or "type code" of some sort. That's what makes the word *type* so vague. But there's an easy solution: coin a phrase (there's no need for an ACRONYM) that explicitly states the type of the type. Inside a gravel class, you might have a type attribute to indicate whether it's lawn gravel, parking-lot gravel, and so forth. Name this attribute gravel type, even though it's in the gravel class. That way, elsewhere in the same application, you won't be confused by the type codes in the truck, scale, mine, and pulverizer classes. Those attributes, of course, you should name truck type, scale type, mine type, and pulverizer type.

Naturally, before being satisfied with such a generic strategy, first try to find substitute words at a lower level of abstraction. pulverizer type might be better named pulverizer method or pulverizer size—or you might need both attributes.

underlining

Don't underline. Underlining is a substitute for italics, invented for typewriters and handwriting. When applied to a proportional font such as Times Roman or Arial, it adds clutter more than emphasis.

The exception is monospace fonts like Courier, which have no italics or bold face. (Most software can create an italic or bold version of them, but only by mechanically slanting or darkening the letters, resulting in an ugly and unreadable distortion.) Underlining is meant for monospace fonts, and only for monospace fonts.

"use"

Every time you write the word *use,* think a second time. Usually you can replace it with a more specific verb, though not always. *Use* is an extraordinarily vague word: it means any sort of process involving an object to yield a result. If the reader does not already know this process, they won't understand. The writer, however, is often baffled by this lack of comprehension because when the writer sees the word *use* in the same context, he unconsciously fills in the details of the process. When you write it, you might be thinking, "the system reads the barometric pressure from the sensor and plugs it into the forecast formula," but a reader won't understand that if all they see is, "the system uses the sensor to make forecasts."

Some alternatives: a user *runs* a program; the system *reads* or *stores* data; a variable or state *indicates* some condition (instead of "the system uses this variable to check some condition"); a program or function *calls* a function or service. Spell out the meaning as concretely as possible.

The phrase *is used to* is especially confusing. Very often, you're trying to say what something *is,* but *is used to* describes what people do with the thing rather than the thing itself. If you say that a function in an API "is used to" calculate some value, you're writing vaguely about why a programmer might write code to call that function, but you haven't said what the function *does.* If the function is used to calculate some value, does that mean that it returns that value or that it performs some intermediate calculation that "is used to" calculate the final result in combination with other processing? Just say what value the function returns or what effects it has. It is often useful to explain why a function in an API is useful to a calling program; but do so in a separate sentence or paragraph, after you've explained what the function does.

Vague or wordy	*Clearer*
The Permissions window is used to set up the authorization database.	In the Permissions window, the system administrator sets up the authorization database.
Test 16A is used to test the report generator.	Test 16A tests the report generator.
The Monitor window is used to choose which track to disable.	In the Monitor window, a user disables a track by selecting it and clicking the disable button.

Notice how much clearer sentences become when you mention the user explicitly.

"valid"

See INVALID.

voice

A verb is said to be in the *active voice* if its subject is the agent of the action denoted by the verb, or in the *passive voice* if its subject is the object of the action. For example, the verb in "VSYS prints month-end reports" is active; the verb in "Month-end reports are printed by VSYS" is passive.

The active voice emphasizes the agent of the action; the passive voice emphasizes the object. Emphasizing the object entails de-emphasizing the agent. This is especially so when a sentence with a passive verb omits the agent entirely, as in "Month-end reports are printed."

While both forms of emphasis have their uses, the passive voice is often a terrible temptation. You should use it only consciously and deliberately to achieve an unusual form of emphasis, not as your habitual way of framing a sentence. The temptation comes from the fact that when you're writing, especially about something in computers, what's on your mind is how some object is affected by an action, not the agent of the action, and often it's hard to identify any distinct agent. However, for a reader to understand the action you're talking about, often you must make the agent explicit.

The following are a few examples of how to convert passive sentences to active:

Vague passive	*Explicit active*
When the Scheduled Reports window is closed, the month-end report is printed.	When the user closes the Scheduled Reports window, VSYS prints the month-end report.
Obsolete bar codes prevent products from being identified.	The system cannot identify a product if it has an obsolete bar code.
	or
	An auditor cannot identify a product if it has an obsolete bar code.
MDU data is exported only once to VSYS.	Once a caller has exported MDU data to VSYS, it can never export it again.
	or
	VSYS requests MDU data from a caller only once per session.

Sometimes a sentence has every verb in the active voice but still has the vagueness or woodenness usually associated with the passive:

Active in form, passive in spirit	*Explicit and direct*
Failure to include an authorization record will result in rejection of the file by VSYS.	If the caller does not include an authorization record in the file, VSYS rejects the entire file.

If your word processor has a grammar checker, it probably tries to tell you what proportion of verbs in a document are passive, or perhaps flags every passive verb with the recommendation that you change it to active. However, many verbs that have the appearance of being passive actually refer to states and not to actions. For example, most grammar checkers would flag *is loaded* as passive in the sentence "If a tape is loaded, the tape drive begins reading it." However, *loaded* in this context is actually an adjective referring to the state of the tape: loaded or not loaded. States don't have agents, so there is no way to reword the sentence to make the verb active, at least not without talking about something else; the *if* part of the sentence is not about an action.

PART 4

Examples

C H A P T E R   1 6

Bug Log requirements

The example documents in chapters 16 and 17 are taken from a successful real-world project at Information + Graphics Systems, Inc., in Boulder, Colorado. In review meetings, readers had much to say about the content—their understanding of the problem domain and new ideas for results to be achieved by the software and/or improvements to the user interface. Readers did not nitpick about conformance to documentation standards or minutiae of wording. The documents also generated comments like "I've been to a lot of requirements review meetings, but this is the first time I've ever read the document all the way through."

The project is very small, but by no means is it a toy project. The problems solved in this project are typical of many larger information systems, just on a much smaller scale.

Despite the success, each document has been edited for purposes of this book. The documents have been shortened somewhat to save space, proprietary information and names of customers have been deleted or changed, and a few things have been added in order to better illustrate the principles taught in this book. The documents have not, however, been edited for perfection. These are real documents of realistic quality, made in all the rush and chaos of a real project.

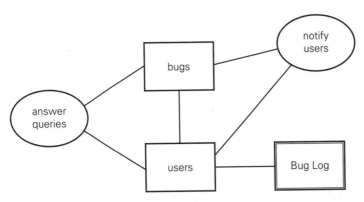

Figure 16.1 Main problem frame for the Bug Log

The first document is the requirements for a program called the Bug Log: a program for tracking bugs as people discover and fix them during software development. The two main problems solved by the Bug Log are shown in the frame diagram in figure 16.1. The answer queries requirement refers to queries about bugs that users need to be able run on demand. The other requirement oval, notify users, refers to the the need to inform users when they are responsible for performing a task related to a bug: a programmer needs to know when he's been assigned to a bug, so he can fix it; a tester needs to know when the fix is complete, so he can test it; and so on.

Notice that the Bug Log is not connected to the bugs. Only the users have direct interaction with bugs, so the frame diagram indicates that the Bug Log depends entirely on the users to get information about the bugs. Even though the users are a party that requests information about bugs, the users are also a connection domain for supplying that information to the Bug Log.

Different users have direct access to the same bugs, introducing a connection problem: different users can discover the same bug, but they can enter it into the system differently. We don't want different programmers being notified that they need to fix the same bug. It's enough for the requirements document to describe the connection problem; it will be the job of the specification to solve it—imperfectly, just as all connection problems are solved imperfectly.

In addition to the two information problems, the Bug Log also solves a small workpiece problem, shown in figure 16.2. Managers need to assign bugs to other users or have the Bug Log assign them automatically. These assignments are not acts that occur outside the Bug Log; the Bug Log must realize the assignments inside itself, as is usually the case when a domain involves human commitment or responsibility. For purposes of the first frame diagram, the act of assigning bugs to people is considered part of the

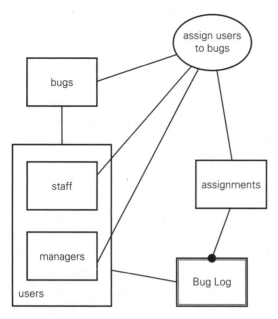

Figure 16.2 Small workpiece problem solved by the Bug Log

activity in the bugs domain; notifications and the results of queries depend on which bugs have been assigned to which people.

The frame diagrams immediately suggest a way to organize the document:

1 Overview and expectations

2 Users

3 Bugs, including software-development activity that pertains to bugs

4 Assignments

5 On-demand queries

6 Automated notifications

7 General information, such as scale and platform

The overview and the section on general information don't come from the problem frames, of course; they're parts of nearly every requirements document. Each of the remaining sections corresponds to either a domain rectangle or a requirement oval.

Thus, the frame diagrams make grouping the major parts of the subject matter easy. The choice of sequence derives from the principles presented in section 14.3. Users are described before bugs because users are the agents and the bugs are the passive objects. Assignments come after bugs because assignments pertain to bugs.

Queries and automated notifications come after bugs and assignments because they reflect information about bugs, whereas bugs can be described without mentioning the queries and notifications.

Naturally, the final table of contents is not exactly the same as that shown above. The actual document groups miscellaneous software-development activity into a separate section before a complete section on bugs. The section on bugs includes assignments, which turn out to require very little documentation. Queries and notifications are similar enough that they go into a single section. Within each section, descriptions of events follow the descriptions of the things involved in the events.

There are a couple of other small realized domains in the Bug Log: the Bug Log assigns ID numbers to bugs and allows managers to assign each bug a priority, and there are rules about how a bug's status is allowed to change, requiring that the Bug Log not merely track status but exert some control over it. These are too small to affect document organization. The document simply includes them under the description of bugs.

Just like many other business applications, the Bug Log can also be framed as solving a control problem instead of two information problems (plus the workpiece problem of creating assignments). In that case, the requirement would be, "Get bugs fixed, tested, and so on." Indeed that is the reason that Bug Log is being written: to aid in getting bugs fixed, tested, and so on.

However, so much is involved in that activity, including decisions that the Bug Log can't make, that it's more straightforward to think of the Bug Log mainly as informing people about the status of bugs and their responsibilities for working on them. Very importantly, there aren't any rules of desired behavior that we would want the Bug Log to enforce. The customer simply wants managers and the development staff to know about bugs as they're discovered and worked on; there are no hard and fully general rules about bug fixing that would be suitable for encoding into software. Best to leave those decisions to human beings; hence, the principal requirements say to give human beings information, not to cause bugs to be fixed.

The shaded areas in the following document are the author's asides to readers of this book.

Bug Log Requirements

Last updated: October 14, 1996
Document ID: I-CORE/BUG-209-01
Prepared by: Ben Kovitz

1. Overview

The Bug Log is a program, to be developed and used internally at IGS, for tracking bugs found in the course of software development. The Bug Log replaces a program already in use at IGS, called BT.

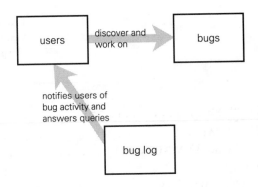

Figure 1 The Bug Log

Software development at IGS, for both new software and upgrades to existing software, normally consists of a requirements-gathering stage, followed by design, coding, testing, and documentation. The Bug Log is strictly for tracking small, delimited changes made during the testing stage and after software is released to clients, not for tracking changes to requirements or tasks performed during the initial coding stage. Most, but not all, of these changes are to correct defects—bugs—in the software; some, however, are suggestions for minor improvements or code changes due to very late changes to requirements.

As shown in figure 1, the Bug Log's main jobs are to notify users of activity pertaining to bugs and to answer queries, either on-screen or printed, about the status of bugs. The notifications tell users when they are responsible for performing some task related to a bug: fixing the bug, verifiying that the fix was successful, etc. Managers assign bugs to the other users.

1.1 Expectations

The current bug-tracking program, BT, was written somewhat hastily in Microsoft Access and has a number of deficiencies. The principal reason for writing the Bug Log is to fix the following complaints from users:

- There is no defined process for how to fill in the fields that describe each bug, or whose responsibility it is to fill them in. For example, a bug is assigned to a programmer, but who makes this assignment? The person who enters the bug? The manager of the project? If the person who enters the bug is supposed to assign it to a programmer, how do they know which programmer to assign it to? Should a programmer query for "bugs assigned to me" or "bugs that pertain to the project I'm working on"?

- There is no automated mechanism for notifying people that bugs they need to fix have been entered. Users must actively query for bugs. Some users stay logged into BT and query frequently; others rarely log into BT and consequently often are unaware of new bugs for several days.

- It's not clear when a bug fix is ready for testing because, even though a programmer has marked a bug "fixed" after making the change, the change isn't available for testing until the next internal release of the software, which can be as long as a day or two later.

- It's difficult and error-prone to create queries and reports. To create a query, one must manually define joins between tables. Often, bugs are left out of reports because one must override Access's default join type— an item of Access minutiae known to few users of BT.

- To run a report, a user must sift through a menu listing all the reports created by all other users of BT, most of which are irrelevant to any one user's tasks.

- There's no way to search for a specific bug by ID.

- There's no user interface for administrative functions, such as, creating new users, entering new pick-list values (such as product names), and archiving old bugs. These tasks can only be performed by people with intimate knowledge of Access and the BT tables, or the database can easily be corrupted.

- The current BT is astonishingly slow. The slowness is increased by the need to fill in a large number of fields for each bug instead of having BT pre-populate them with default values. During a typical session, a user enters several bugs in which nearly all the fields are identical, so there's a lot of room for speeding up data entry with intelligent defaults.

- In the user interface, it's not obvious how to create a new bug: you click a button that has a triangle and an asterisk on it.

- Because users don't log in to BT, Access doesn't know who they are, and they must manually fill in the "created by" field of each bug.

- A few IGS employees are not at the Boulder office, but still need access to BT. The slowness of the program prevents them from running it via modem even though they can log in to the Boulder network via RAS.

2. Software Development

Software development at IGS, insofar as it is of concern to the Bug Log, involves the classes of objects shown in figure 2.

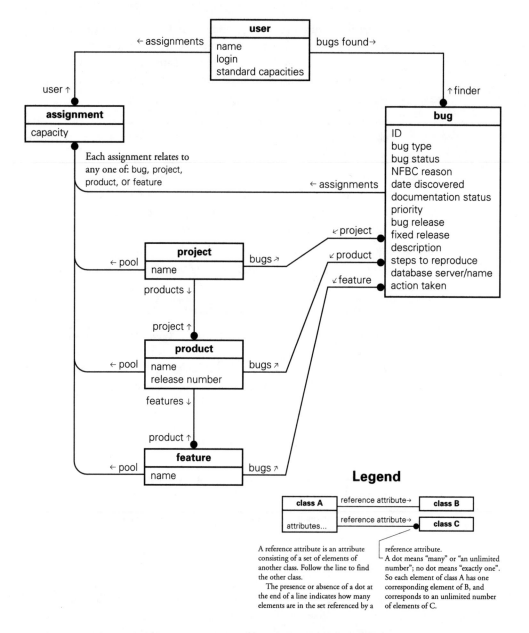

Figure 2 Classes and relations of concern to the Bug Log

Class	Description	See Section
user	Any person at IGS who finds bugs or needs information about bugs.	2.1
bug	A defect in IGS software in need of change, or a small improvement to be implemented.	2.3
project	A billing category at IGS: a project to which work performed is billed.	2.2.1
product	A single piece of software or a software package, developed as part of one project.	2.2.2
feature	Part of a product.	2.2.3
assignment	Data to be stored in the Bug Log indicating who is responsible for working on a specific bug, project, product, or feature, and in what capacity.	2.3.1

2.1 Users

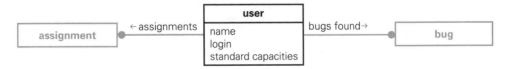

Figure 3 User and related classes

The *users* of the Bug Log are everyone at IGS who finds bugs in software under development or needs information about those bugs. All users have access to IGS's local-area network, including users who work at sites other than the Boulder office. Users outside the Boulder office access the local-area network via RAS, usually on laptop computers with 28,800-bps modems.

Attribute	Description
name	The user's full name.
login	The ID with which the user logs in to IGS's local-area network.
standard capacities	A list of the capacities in which the user most frequently works on bugs. See below for a description of capacities.
assignments	Specific bugs, projects, products, and features that the user is assigned to, and in what capacity. See section 2.3.1.

Notice that none of the descriptions starts with the words "this is".

A user can work on bugs in zero or more of the following *capacities:*

Since there are so few capacities, simply listing them all defines the term capacity *very clearly, while simultaneously defining each distinct capacity.*

A *programmer* fixes bugs.

A *tester* verifies that bugs have been fixed correctly.

A *documenter* updates user's manuals to reflect bug fixes.

A *manager* decides which bugs to fix, what priority to give each bug, and who should work on which bugs and in which capacities.

Most users work in only a single capacity on all the bugs that they work on. Occasionally, however, there are exceptions. A programmer might be called in as a tester on a programming tool, or if a tester is out of the office one day, a documenter might fill in for him. The standard capacities are the user's normal capacities, not the exceptional roles.

The capacity of finding bugs does not have a name; any user can find a bug.

Currently no two users have the same name, but some might in the future. No two users can ever have the same login.

Current numbers of users who work in each capacity:

Capacity	Number of Users
programmer	35
tester	6
documenter	3
manager	11

This table presents valuable information about scale, enabling programmers to choose suitable implementation tools.

2.1.1 User Activity

The following events affect users:

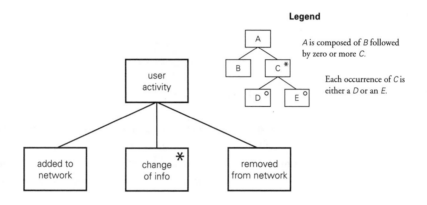

Figure 4 User activity

Event	Description
added to network	The IGS system administrator creates a login for the user on the local-area network at the Boulder office.
	Parameters: *name, login.* Optional parameter: *standard capacities.*
change of info	Any data pertaining to a user can change at any time.
	Parameters: One or more of *name, login, standard capacities.*
removed from network	The IGS system administrator removes the user's login from the local-area network.
	Parameters: *user.*

The sources of information from which the Bug Log can learn when the above events occur are the system administrator and the user's manager.

Events that affect the user's assignments are described in section 2.3.1.

2.2 Projects, Products, and Features

2.2.1 Projects

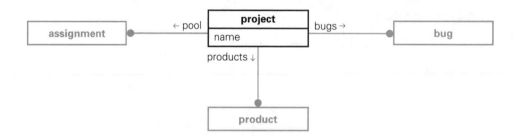

Figure 5 Project and related classes

A *project* is a billing category to which the accounting department at IGS bills work performed. Some projects are internal, some are external. The accounting department bills customers for time spent on external projects; time spent on internal projects is part of our operating expenses.

Attribute	Description
name	The name of the project: no more than six characters. Most external projects have names that are abbreviations for a specific IGS customer. For example, SPLNX is the project name for work billed to Splenetix Corporation. Most internal work has the project name CORE. No two projects have the same name.
products	The set of all products that are included in this project.
pool	The set of people assigned to this project.
bugs	The set of all bugs that have been found in all products within this project, whether fixed or not.

2.2.2 Products

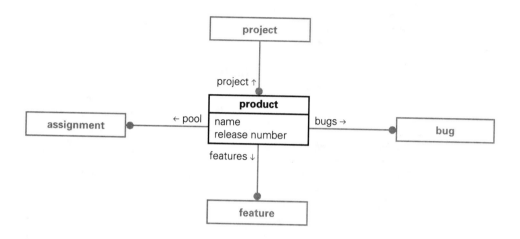

Figure 6 Product and related classes

A *product* is a single piece of software or software package developed at IGS.

Attribute	Description
project	The project to which work on this product is billed. Every product is part of one and only one project.
features	The set of all features, if any, into which this product has been subdivided for purposes of tracking bugs.
pool	The set of people assigned to this product.
bugs	The set of all bugs that have been found in this product, whether fixed or not.
name	The name of the product. Up to 30 characters. No two products within the same project have the same name, but two different projects can have products that are named the same but include very different source code.
release number	The current release number of the product.

A release number consists of four numbers, each separated from the next by a period:

The first number is the *major release number,* incremented only on releases that introduce major new functionality.

4.00.00.001

The second number is the *minor release number,* incremented on any new version, except that when the major release number changes, the minor release number is set back to zero.

The third number is the *patch number,* incremented only for special releases that contain only small fixes.

The fourth number is the *build number,* incremented each time the program is compiled and linked. Build numbers are for internal use only and are not included in release numbers in documentation for clients.

Each number inside a release number can be up to three digits long. Sometimes release numbers are written without leading zeroes, but there is also a standard format, as follows:

major release number	No leading zeroes.
minor release number	At least two digits: add leading zeroes if necessary.
patch number	At least two digits: add leading zeroes if necessary.
build number	At least three digits: add leading zeroes if necessary.

Some users are accustomed to writing the first and second periods in a release number as underscores. This practice is a carryover from when we put entire release numbers into MS-DOS filenames, which could include only one period, preceded by up to eight characters and followed by up to three characters.

2.2.3 Features

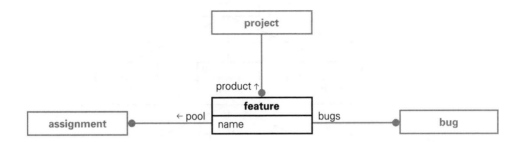

Figure 7 Feature and related classes

A *feature* is part of a product, typically a part for which a single programmer is responsible (see figure 7).

Attribute	Description
product	The product of which the feature is a part. Every feature is part of one and only one product.
pool	The set of people who are assigned to the feature.
bugs	The set of all bugs that have been found in this feature, whether fixed or not.
name	The name of the feature. Up to 30 characters. No two features within the same product have the same name, but two different products can have features that are named the same.

2.2.4 Project Activity

Software development work within a single project consists of the events shown below in figure 8. At any time, any number of projects can be in progress simultaneously.

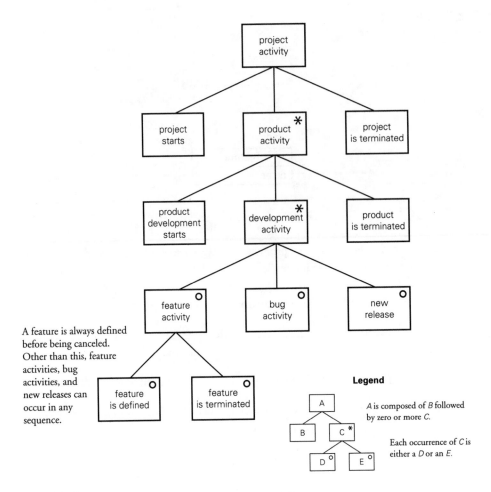

A feature is always defined before being canceled. Other than this, feature activities, bug activities, and new releases can occur in any sequence.

Legend

A is composed of B followed by zero or more C.

Each occurrence of C is either a D or an E.

Figure 8 Project activity

The source of information for all events listed below, with the exceptions of bug activity and new release, is IGS management.

Event	Description
project starts	IGS management defines a new project.
	Parameters: *name* of project.
project is terminated	IGS management decides to bill no further work to a project.
	Parameters: The terminated *project*.

Event	Description
product development starts	IGS management decides to start development on a new product. Parameters: The *name* of the new product, and the *project* of which it is a part. A product's initial release number is 0.00.00.000.
product is terminated	IGS management decides to stop work on a product. Parameters: The terminated *product*.
feature is defined	IGS management defines a new feature within a product, for purposes of assigning responsibilities. Parameters: The *name* of the new feature, and the *product* of which it is a part.
feature is terminated	IGS management decides to stop work on a specific feature. Parameters: The terminated *feature*.
bug activity	A wide variety of events, described in section 2.3.
new release	The programmers compile and link a new release of a product, and configuration management makes it available to the rest of the staff and/or the customer. Every new release changes the release number of the product. On average, there are roughly twenty new releases that change only the build number (that is, internal releases) for each release that changes any of the other parts of the release number (external releases). Parameters: The *product* that had the new release, and its new *release number*. Source: Configuration management.

2.3 Bugs

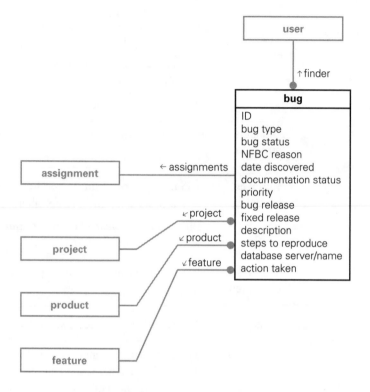

Figure 9 Bug and related classes

A *bug* is a defect in a piece of IGS software, a small improvement to be made to that software, or a group of small, related improvements and/or defects. This usage of the word *bug* is somewhat broader than industry standard, in that it includes more than defects, but it's become part of usage at IGS as a result of the BT program's user interface, which referred to both defects and improvements as bugs.

Making the change called for by a bug is called *fixing* the bug, whether the bug is a defect or an improvement.

Attribute	Description
ID	A number uniquely identifying the bug, assigned by the Bug Log.

Attribute	Description
bug type	Which of the following categories describes the bug:

	bug	A defect that needs to be corrected: a failure to meet requirements.
	suggestion	A suggestion for improvement, not specified in requirements. We often implement small suggestions to improve the quality of the software even if the customer doesn't specifically ask for them and we receive no additional payment for them.
	enhancement	A change request going beyond the original written requirements for the software, requiring contractual agreement with the customer before being assigned to a programmer to implement.

Attribute	Description
finder	The user who found the bug. Often two users find the same bug. Approximately 1 in 7 bugs entered into BT were superfluous duplicates. For simplicity, we'll say that every bug has a single finder but that two bug records stored in the Bug Log can be duplicates.
date found	The date that someone first found the bug. (No queries pertain to the dates when more people found the bug, if any.)

Attribute	Description
bug status	The current stage in the process of fixing the bug. There are six statuses:

assign	The bug is awaiting assignment by a manager to a programmer and tester.
code	The bug is assigned to a programmer and awaiting change to the source code.
build	The programmer has changed the source code to fix the bug; the version of the software containing the fix is now awaiting release.
test	The version of the software containing the fix has been released; the bug is awaiting testing by a tester.
NFBC	"Not Fixed But Closed": IGS has decided not to fix the bug. See NFBC reason, below.
fixed	The bug has been fixed and the fix has been verified by a tester.

An early version of the requirements document named the bug statuses awaiting assignment, awaiting coding, and so on, as recommended in section 11.1.1. These had the advantage of being self-explanatory but were wordy. During user-interface testing, the staff decided to change the names of the statuses to the shorter names shown here, due to the frequency with which people would use them in spoken conversation, even though they are properly the names of actions, not statuses.

The first four bug statuses, *assign*, *code*, *build*, and *test*, are collectively referred to as *open*. The final two, *NFBC* and *fixed*, are collectively referred to as *closed*.

Attribute	Description
NFBC reason	The reason why the bug was marked *NFBC*. One of the following:

	not reproducible	IGS staff was unable to reproduce the bug.
	deferred	IGS is not going to fix the bug now, and will make a decision about whether to fix the bug later.
	software constraint	IGS has decided not to fix the bug due to limitations in our development tools; for example, the bug is due to a limitation in Powerbuilder.
	canceled	IGS has decided not to fix the bug, or the bug is not a genuine problem with the software.

A bug has an NFBC reason only if its bug status is *NFBC*.

Attribute	Description
documentation status	The current stage in the process of updating end-user documentation to reflect the bug fix. There are three documentation statuses:

	none required	Fixing the bug entails no change to the documentation.
	awaiting documentation	A change is required and pending.
	done	A documenter has completed the change.

Attribute	Description
project, product, feature	The project, product, and feature that the bug pertains to. All bugs pertain to a single project and product; some bugs pertain to a specific feature and some do not.

Attribute	Description
assignments	The programmer, tester, and documenter that the bug is assigned to. A bug can be assigned to a maximum of one person in each of these three capacities.
	At different times, depending on bug status, there must be a person assigned to the bug in a specific capacity. Details are in section 2.3.5.
priority	A measure of how important it is to fix the bug. Programers decide which bugs to work on first, according to their priority; it is the responsibility of managers to assign priorities. There are four priority levels:

critical	Bug renders the software unusable in a catastrophic way, such as crashing it.
high	Bug should be fixed before the next external release, if possible. It definitely needs to be fixed before the final release.
medium	Bug needs to be fixed before final release, but isn't so important that it must be fixed in the next external release.
low	Bug would be nice to fix, but is not necessary to fix in final release.

	A bug has a priority level only when a manager assigns it. Before then, the bug has no priority at all.
bug release	The release number of the software in which the bug was found. Release numbers are described in section 2.2.2.
fixed release	The release number of the software that incorporates the bug fix. A bug has no fixed release until it's fixed. Release numbers are described in section 2.2.2.

Attribute	Description
description	Free-form text describing the bug. Bug Log must allow at least 1K of text.
steps to reproduce	Free-form text telling a programmer how to reproduce the bug. Bug Log must allow at least 1K of text.
database server/name	If applicable, the name of the database to connect to in order to reproduce the bug, along with the name of the database's server.
action taken	Free-form text describing the actions that the bug's programmer and/or documenter have taken so far to fix the bug; written by the programmer and/or documenter. Bug Log must allow at least 1K of text.

2.3.1 Assignments

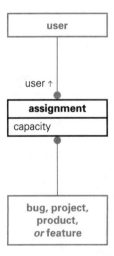

Figure 10 Assignment and related classes

An *assignment* is data stored in the Bug Log indicating that a particular user is responsible for working on a bug, product, or feature in a specific capacity.

Attribute	Description
user	The person assigned.
capacity	The capacity in which user is assigned: manager, programmer, tester, or documenter (described on page 350).
bug, project, product, or feature	The bug, project, product, or feature to which user is assigned.

2.3.2 Events that Affect Bug Status

Figure 11 and the accompanying table show all events that affect a bug's bug status (as described on page 360).

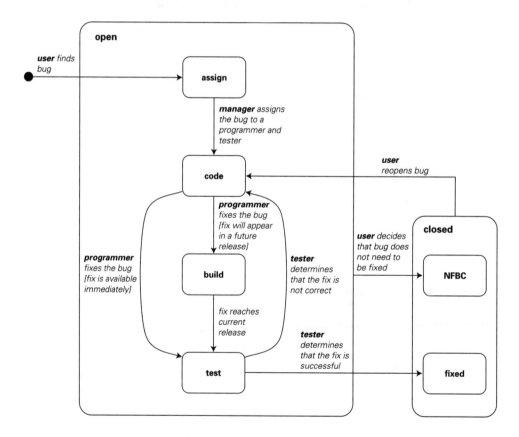

Figure 11 Events that affect bug status

Event	Description
user finds bug	A user finds the bug. Bug status begins at assign.
	Parameters: *bug type, project, product, feature* (if applicable), *description, steps to reproduce, finder* (the user who found the bug), *database server/name* (if applicable), *bug release.* Optionally, the user can assign the bug a *priority.*
R-1	**The Bug Log assigns the bug a unique ID.**
	This same event also sets a bug's documentation status; see section 2.3.4.
manager assigns bug to programmer and tester	The manager responsible for the product that the bug pertains to assigns the bug to both a programmer and a tester. If the bug does not have a priority, the manager gives it one. Bug status changes from assign to code.
	Parameters: *bug, programmer* and *tester* assigned, *priority* (if applicable).
programmer fixes the bug	The programmer modifies source code and/or database tables in an attempt to fix the bug.

Finding out when bug fixes appear in new releases is the hidden, tricky connection problem in the Bug Log, and it is the trickiest thing to design for. Without careful focus on the problem domain, including asking questions like "what source of information can the Bug Log rely on to find out when bug fixes get released?" it would be easy to overlook this problem. The BT software, which the Bug Log replaces, was designed by starting with the database tables and user interface and had no recognition of a distinct build state—the time between the programmer's fixing the bug and its being released and ready for testing.

Sometimes, the fix is available immediately to a tester for testing. In this case, bug status changes directly to test. The most likely reason for the fix being immediately available is that the only change was to a database table.

Otherwise, the fix must go through configuration management to be included in a new release. In this case, bug status changes to build. Sometimes the programmer knows the release number in which the fix will appear; other times, the fix must wait until other programming is completed, and the programmer does not know when the fix will be released. The most common case is that the fix comes out in the next release, and the programmer knows this immediately upon completing the fix.

Parameters: *bug, new bug status, fixed release* (if known), *action taken.*

Event	Description
fix reaches current release	The bug fix reaches the current release, through configuration management, and is available for testing. Bug status changes to test. Configuration management does not know which bug fixes are included in each release. Only the programmers know. Parameters: *bug, fixed release* (equal to current release).
tester determines that fix is successful	The tester tests the program and determines that the bug has been fixed. Bug status changes to fixed. Parameters: *bug.*
tester determines that fix is not correct	The tester tests the program and determines that the bug has not been fixed. Bug status returns to code. Parameters: *bug.*
user decides that bug does not need to be fixed	A user decides that the bug does not need to be fixed, for one of the reasons described under NFBC reason on page 361. Bug status changes to NFBC. Parameters: *bug, NFBC reason.*
user reopens bug	A user decides that a closed bug needs to be fixed. Bug status changes to code or assign, at the user's discretion. If bug status was NFBC, the bug loses its NFBC reason. Parameters: *bug, new bug status.*

2.3.3 Who Can Change Bug Status

The Bug Log is responsible for ensuring that only authorized employees change the data representing bug status. That is, we want the Bug Log to enforce certain rules about who can change bug status, not merely track changes to bug status. These rules are described below.

R-2   **The Bug Log allows data representing bug status to change from one value to another only by users assigned to the bug as shown in the table below:**

From ↓	To					
	assign	code	release	test	NFBC	fixed
(non-existent)	any user	—	—	—	—	—
assign	—	—	—	—	any user	—
code	—	—	programmer	programmer	any user	—
build	—	programmer, tester	—	programmer	any user	—
test	—	programmer, tester	programmer, tester	—	any user	tester
NFBC	any user	any user	—	—	—	tester
fixed	any user	any user	—	—	any user	—

There is one exception to the table:

R-2.1   **Any IGS manager can change data representing bug status from any value to any other value, subject to the validity conditions described in section 2.3.5.**

This is how bug status moves from assign to code.

> *This comment on requirement 2.1, while small, is critical. Whenever tabular data or a set of statements together imply a conclusion of importance to the reader, you must state that conclusion explicitly or expect the reader not to grasp it.*

2.3.4 Events that Affect Documentation Status

Figure 12 and the accompanying text show all events that affect a bug's documentation status (as described on page 361).

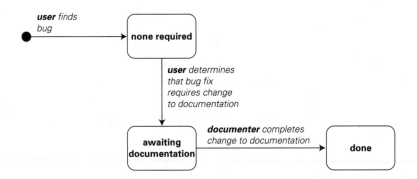

Figure 12 Events that affect a bug's documentation status

Event	Description
user finds bug	A user finds the bug. Documentation status begins at none required.
	Parameters: none that affect documentation status.
	The same event also affects bug status; see section 2.3.2.
user determines that bug fix requires change to documentation	A user determines that user's manuals or online help need to be updated to reflect the bug fix. Usually the tester makes this determination.
	Parameters: *bug*.
documenter completes change to documentation	The documenter makes the needed change to the user's manuals or online help.
	Parameters: *bug*.

Documentation status is not as important to track or control as bug status. Consequently there are no requirements limiting who can change the data in the Bug Log that represents documentation status.

2.3.5 Validity Conditions

R-3 **Data representing bugs always meets the conditions shown in the table below, to ensure internal consistency:**

status ↓	Bug must be assigned to:			Bug must have:			
	programmer	tester	documenter	bug type	priority	fixed release	NFBC reason
Assign	○	○	○	●	○	○	○
Code	●	●	○	●	●	○	○
Build	●	●	○	●	●	○	○
Test	●	●	○	●	●	●	○
NFBC	○	○	○	●	●	○	●
Fixed	○	○	○	●	○	●	○

● = required   ○ = not required

These validity conditions could have been deferred to the user-interface design. However, because so many of the Bug Log's requirements pertain to the data stored by the Bug Log—that is, to realized domains—it's best to cover these validity conditions in the requirements document. Notice how much more complex this information would appear had it been written as one individual ("atomic") requirement statement for each black dot in the table.

3. Queries and Notifications

3.1 Queries

R-4   **A user can query at any time to see a list of bugs and information about them, specifying filter criteria, sort order, and output format, as described below.**

R-4.2   **Filter criteria: determine which bugs appear in the output of the query. Filter criteria are any combination of values of the following attributes:**

R-4.3

project
product
feature
bug status
programmer
tester
documenter
manager
bug release
fixed release
date created
NFBC reason
documentation status
bug type
priority
finder

> *Requirements R-4.2 and R-4.4 were written somewhat hastily: does a "combination" of attributes mean just a Boolean and of attribute values, or does it allow any combination of Boolean and, or, not, and parentheses? The description of sort orders left out the ability to specify multiple attributes so that one attribute can break a tie when two bugs have the same value for another attribute. Fortunately—and really, not surprisingly—these ambiguities did not lead to any problems in user-interface design.*

R-4.4   **Sort order: bugs can be sorted according to any of the attributes listed under R-4.2.**

R-4.5   **Output format: A user can view the output of a query either on screen or in a printed report.**

R-5   **A user can examine the history of the following actions taken in regard to a bug:**

The bug is found.

The bug's bug status changes.

The bug's documentation status changes.

The bug's description, steps to reproduce, action taken, or NFBC reason changes without a simultaneous change in bug status.

The bug's programmer, tester, or documenter changes, either from one user to another, or from being unassigned to being assigned to a definite user (or vice versa).

A history query displays the following data:

R-5.6   –   **Which of the above actions occurred.**

R-5.7   –   **For changes of bug status, documentation status, programmer tester, and documenter, the new value of the changed attribute.**

R-5.8   –   **The user who performed the action.**

R-5.9   –   **The date and time (hours and minutes) of the action.**

R-5.10   **Just as with bug queries, a user can view the history of a bug on screen or in a printed report.**

3.2 Notifications

R-6   **The Bug Log notifies a user when any of the following events occurs:**

R-6.11   –   **A bug becomes "current" for the user, as defined below.**

R-6.12   –   **A bug ceases to be current for the user.**

R-6.13   –   **Any of a bug's attributes, other than bug status, changes while the bug is current for the user, and after the user has read the notification that the bug has become current.**

> *Rationale:* This ensures that, for example, a programmer working on a bug is notified if the tester modifies the bug's description or steps to reproduce.

R-6.14   ***Exception:* The Bug Log never notifies a user of the user's own action.**

So, for example, a programmer is not notified when when a bug ceases to be current for that programmer, if the reason it ceased to be current is that the programmer fixed the bug and changed its bug status to build.

What exactly constitutes a "notification" will be determined during user-interface design: whether it's an email message, a special query that a user must actively perform, a special message box stored in the Bug Log, or something else.

P-1   *Preference:* **Users do not want their email boxes cluttered by large numbers of automatically generated messages.**

Usage patterns in BT suggest that email might be the best notification method for a few users but not for most. Programmers and testers normally stay logged into the Bug Log all day long. Documenters and managers had much less need to access the Bug Log, consequently did not log in often, and consequently did not find out about bugs for which they had responsibility for long periods of time—usually, only when someone notified them by telephone.

A bug is *current* for a user if the user now has a responsibility to perform some action in regard to the bug. The conditions under which a bug is current for each type of user are shown in the following table:

Type of User	Bug is Current If
programmer	Programmer is assigned to bug and:
	Bug status is code.
tester	Tester is assigned to bug and:
	Bug status is test.
documenter	Documenter is assigned to bug and:
	Documentation status is awaiting documentation.
manager	Manager is assigned to bug's product, and any of the following conditions hold:
	Bug status is assign.
	Or:
	Documentation status is awaiting documentation and the bug has no documenter assigned.

Certainly a more elegant way to handle the need to notify a manager that a bug needs a documenter assigned would be to define an equivalent assign *state for documentation status. The Bug Log is now in use, and no one complains about this, so it must not have been a very important imperfection.*

4. Runtime Environment

R-7   **The Bug Log client program runs on the following platforms:**

R-7.15   –   **Windows 3.1 and 3.11.**

R-7.16   –   **Windows NT 4.0 and later.**

R-7.17   –   **Windows 95.**

R-8   **The Bug Log server is accessible through the Boulder local-area network.**

R-9   **Users log into the Bug Log with their own passwords.**

R-10   **The Bug Log is accessible to IGS employees outside the Boulder office via modem connection through RAS.**

R-10 is implicitly a performance requirement, in that it implies that the connection between the Bug Log client and server uses little enough bandwidth that it's feasible to run it over a modem.

It might seem strange to refer to the client and server parts of the Bug Log in the requirements. However, this is a particularly clear example of the way that requirements, to answer all the needed questions relevant to implementation, must premise some implementation decisions. This little section also gathers together some "global characteristics" required of the Bug Log: a little bit about security, and a performance requirement, expressed with no more precision than necessary.

5. Likely Changes

Future versions of the Bug Log are likely to have requirements for:

- Trouble tickets called in by customers, including installation and configuration problems as well as bugs.

- Data entered directly into the Bug Log by customers.

- Queries to display counts of bugs in various categories, broken down by priority and the age of the bug.

- Tracking more of the software development process, including initial definition of requirements, interface design, and all change requests.

- Ordinal priority levels instead of the critical/high/medium/low classification described in this document. Ordinal priority levels would allow a manager to say, for any bug, that it is of higher or lower priority than any other given bug, in effect telling programmers the desired sequence in which to fix bugs.

6. Glossary

bandwidth   A measure of the capacity of a communication channel, such as a telephone line or a cable connecting computers in a network. The greater the bandwidth, the more data the communication channel can carry in a given amount of time.

bug   In this document, refers to either a defect in a piece of software or a small addition to functionality.

client   A program or computer that requests services or another, central program or computer that it's connected to via a network. Compare SERVER.

configuration management   The department at IGS responsible for archiving and tracking changes to program source code, informing staff of new internal and external releases, and creating deliverables, such as tapes and disks, for clients.

current   In this document, a bug is said to be *current* for a user if the user now has a responsibility to perform some action in regard to that bug. Details are provided on page 372.

fix   In this document, to make the change specified by a bug, whether it's a correction of a defect or an implementation of new functionality.

Powerbuilder   A commercial program for building CLIENT programs with graphical user interfaces that connect to database SERVERS through a network. In common use at IGS.

RAS   Remote Access Services. A facility standard in Windows 3.11 and Windows NT for linking a user into a local-area network via modem.

release   A complete, installable, runnable version of a piece of software. Between one release and the next, features are normally added and/or bugs fixed. An external release is a release delivered to the end user of the software, usually but not necessarily a client outside IGS. Most external releases are preceded by many internal releases: releases created for use by the testing and documentation staff.

server   A program or computer that accepts requests from other programs or computers connected to it via a network, processing data for them and/or sending them data they've requested. Compare CLIENT. Typically, a client program provides a human-friendly user interface to a server, and the only other way to control the server is by typing Unix command lines.

CHAPTER 17

Bug Log user interface

This chapter presents the program specification for the Bug Log—the first stage of the solution to the problem defined in the requirements. The Bug Log interfaces only to people, so the only interface document is the user-interface design.

The complete user-interface design document was about 80 pages long. This chapter only includes a few excerpts to show you the general technique of how to document a graphical user interface: a list of operating procedures, and a bunch of screen shots and tables of buttons and fields with terse descriptions of how they behave.

The user-interface design document was almost three times the length of the requirements document. This illustrates the most common pattern in normal software development: the requirements document is fairly short; the interface documents are two or three times as long, especially if they're user interfaces; and the program is longer and more complex still.

This might come as a surprise because the real world is far more complex than a user-interface design or program. However, the increasing complexity of each stage is readily explained by two facts. First, while reality as a whole is far more complex than any program or user-interface that we invent, we always frame the software problem so that it includes only a relatively simple and narrowly delimited part of reality—the tiny bit that is relevant to the design of the program.

Second, each stage embodies not only all of the information from the preceding stage but also a large set of elements from the domain being designed. The user interface embodies everything in the requirements and all the complexity of menu bars, access keys, and numerous types of on-screen controls. The program embodies everything in the requirements and user interface and all the complexity of accessing a database, calling upon services from the operating system, memory allocation, passing and returning parameters between subroutines, and so on.

Bug Log
User Interface Design

Last updated: January 19, 1997
Document ID: I-CORE/BUG-210-01
Designer: Ben Kovitz

1. How the Requirements Are Implemented

> *The following short, descriptive paragraphs are much more useful than a standard traceability matrix, which lists only section numbers and leaves it to the reader to figure out how all the pieces of the puzzle fit together. They also provide a quick introduction to the design.*

The Bug Log user-interface design implements its requirements as described below.

R-1 Bug Log assigns each bug a unique ID when the bug is found.

Happens when user clicks *New Bug*. See section 2.3.

R-2 Restrictions on who can change bug status.

Bug Log checks the rules for who can change bug status in the *Status/Action* tab of the main window. Error messages are in section 5.

R-3 Validity conditions.

Bug Log checks validity conditions whenever a user attempts to leave a bug. Error messages are in section 2.2.

R-4 Queries.

The user is always viewing a query. Different tabs in the *Main* window show a list of bugs or different attributes of a bug. User prints a query via File|Print.

A user can change the current query in the *Query Builder* window, as well as save queries for later reuse.

Users type in the data that appears in queries as they find and work on bugs. See operating procedures in section 3.

The Bug Log user interface introduces one new type of user not mentioned in the requirements: the Bug Log administrator. As described in section 3, the Bug Log administrator is responsible for entering new release numbers and for setting up data describing users.

R-5 History data.

The *History* tab of the *Main* window shows the history of the current bug. See section 4.5.

R-6 Notifications.

A user has the option, settable in the *Users* window (see section 4.13), to receive notifications via email. There is also a special bug attribute that users can query on, *Awaiting Action By*, that includes bugs that are current for a specified user; see section 4.8. Most users will run this query to find out which bugs they need to work on. So, except for the email option, users receive notifications only by actively polling.

R-7 Compatibility with all Windows platforms.

The user interface is drawn entirely in standard Windows controls available in Visual Basic.

R-8 Server accessible through Boulder local-area network.

Not applicable to user-interface design.

R-9 Passwords.

The user had to supply a password to log in to Windows, and the Bug Log knows the user's Windows login ID, so there's no need to specially log in to the Bug Log.

R-10 Accessible via modem.

Not applicable to user-interface design.

2. General Information

The Bug Log user-interface design assumes that it will be implemented in Visual Basic. Switching to another development tool, such as Powerbuilder, would probably necessitate changes to a number of the screens and controls due to different capabilities in the two tools.

The Bug Log contains the following windows:

Window	Description	Section
Main	User views, edits, and creates bug records.	4.1
Query Builder	User defines and edits queries.	4.6
Saved Queries	User views and loads saved queries.	4.11
Save Current Query	User saves currently active query.	4.12
Users	User, usually the Bug Log administrator, views lists of users and their capacities.	4.13
Create User	Administrator adds a new user.	4.14
Projects	Manager or administrator views list of projects, products, and features.	4.15
Assign	Manager assigns people to projects.	4.16
New Project	Manager adds a new project.	4.17
Change Current Release	Administrator enters release number of new release of a product.	4.18
Print	User prints a report.	4.19

2.1 Current Bug and Current Query

At all times, there is a *current bug* and a *current query*.

The current bug is available for editing in the *Description* and *Status/Action* tabs of the *Main* window. The user can edit no other bug than the current bug. Changing the current bug from one to another is called *moving* from one bug to another.

The current query consists of filter criteria, a sort order, and, optionally, a user-specified set of columns. All bugs that match the filter criteria of the current query are shown in the *Bug List* tab of *Main*. The current query affects which bug the user moves to when moving to the next or previous bug.

2.2 Leaving a Bug

Leaving a bug is any of the following actions:

–   Moving to another bug.

–   Clicking the *New Bug* button in any of the *Main* window tabs.

–   Attempting to close the *Main* window or exit the program.

If, when a user tries to leave a bug, any of the messages in the table below applies to the bug, the attempt to leave the bug fails, the message is displayed, and the focus is left on the indicated control on the *Main* window. If more than one message applies, only the first is displayed.

> *Notice that every error message is spelled out explicitly here, down to the smallest details of punctuation and capitalization. We can't get away with a table of validity conditions like that in the requirements document. Notice also the little trick of describing the condition that the program tests for in the error message itself. This ensures that the error messages are detailed enough: if they're detailed enough for the programmer, they should be detailed enough for the user. (If you want to omit detail from an error message, describe the part that only the programmer sees in commentary next to the message.) There are no useless, generic error messages like "Data was invalid; please re-enter."*

Message	Control with Focus after Message Is Displayed
Bug has "NFBC" status, but no NFBC reason. You need to either fill in the NFBC Reason field or change the bug to a different status.	*NFBC Reason*

Message	Control with Focus after Message Is Displayed
Bug has no project. You need to fill in the bug's Project field.	*Project*
Bug has no product. You need to fill in the bug's Product field.	*Product*
Bug has "Code" status, but has no programmer assigned. You need to either fill in the Programmer field or change the bug's status back to "Assign".	*Programmer*
Bug has "Code" status, but has no tester assigned. You need to either fill in the Tester field or change the bug's status back to "Assign".	*Tester*
Bug has "Build" status, but has no programmer assigned. You need to either fill in the Programmer field or change the bug's status back to "Assign".	*Programmer*
Bug has "Build" status, but has no tester assigned. You need to either fill in the Tester field or change the bug's status back to "Assign".	*Tester*
Bug has no bug release number. You need to enter the release number of the product in the Bug Release field.	*Bug Release*
Bug release numbers must have the format nnn.nnn.nnn.nnn. You need to re-enter the release number of the product in the Bug Release field.	*Bug Release*
Bug release numbers must have the format nnn.nnn.nnn.nnn. You need to re-enter the release number of the product in the Fixed Release field. (No error if *Fixed Release* is *Next Release* or *Future Release*.)	*Fixed Release*
Bug has no type. You need to enter "Bug", "Enhancement", or "Suggestion" in the Type field.	*Type*

Message	Control with Focus after Message Is Displayed
Bug has "Build" status, but fixed release is neither "Next Release", "Future Release", nor a specific number. You need to indicate in the Fixed Release field which release will contain the fix.	*Fixed Release*
Bug has "Test" status, but fixed release is not a specific number. You need to indicate in the Fixed Release field which release of the software contains the fix.	*Fixed Release*
Bug has "Fixed" status, but fixed release is not a specific number. You need to indicate in the Fixed Release field which release of the software contains the fix.	*Fixed Release*

2.3 Defaults When Creating a New Bug

When the user creates a new bug, the Bug Log pre-populates its fields as described in the table below. In the table, the phrase "the current bug" means the current bug at the time the user created the new bug (that is, when the user clicked the *New Bug* button on the *Main* window), not the newly created bug.

ID	A unique number, greater than the ID of any other bug.
Project	The *Project* of the current bug.
Product	The *Product* of the current bug.
Feature	The *Feature* of the current bug.
Bug Release	The *Bug Release* number of the current bug.
Type	Blank.

Found By	Blank, if the currently logged-in user is not defined in the *Users* screen (see page [omitted]). Otherwise, the user's name.
Bug Description	Blank.
Steps to Reproduce	Blank.
Database Server	The *Database Server* of the current bug.
Database Name	The *Database Name* of the current bug.
Programmer	Blank.
Tester	Blank.
Documenter	Blank.
Priority	Blank.
Fixed Release	Blank.
NFBC Reason	Blank.
Status	*Assign.*
Documentation Status	*None Required.*
Action Taken	Blank.

2.4 Online Help

At all times, pressing F1 opens the online help to the page for the current screen, and, if appropriate, the current tab.

3. Operating Procedures

Name	Event(s) Addressed	Procedure
find a bug	(Various.)	There are three ways for a user to find a bug: 1. If the user knows the bug's ID, user clicks the *ID* button in the *Description*, *Status/Action*, or *History* tab, and enters the new ID. The bug with the specified ID becomes the current bug. 2. The user can define a query by any combination of bug attributes in the *Filter Criteria* tab of the *Query Builder* window, and scroll through the bugs listed in the *Bug List* tab. 3. The user can run a special query to search for text in the *Description*, *Steps to Reproduce*, and *Action Taken* fields, by defining a query using the *Special Filters* tab of the *Query Builder* window.
notification that bug is not current for a user	All the events that affect whether a bug is current for a user: user finds bug, manager assigns bug to programmer and tester, programmer fixes bug, fix reaches current release, tester determines that fix is successful/ not correct, user reopens bug	There are two ways for a user to be notified when these events occur: 1. If the user has the email preference flag set to *Yes* in the *Users* window, the Bug Log sends the user email announcing that the user is now responsible to perform some action. See section 5. 2. The user can run a query on *Awaiting Action By*, in the *Special Filters* tab of the *Query Builder* window. The first method is recommended for documenters and managers who only occasionally need information from the Bug Log. The second method is recommended for users who log in to the Bug Log every day, such as programmers and testers.

Name	Event(s) Addressed	Procedure
other notifications	Changes to bug attributes and a bug's ceasing to be current, as described in requirements R-6.2 to R-6.4.	Bug Log sends affected user email for these events, regardless of setting of email preference flag. See section 5.
create new bug	user finds bug	User should run a query on the bug's project, product, and feature and look through the most recent bugs to see if another user has found the same bug. If the bug has not already been entered into the Bug Log, user clicks *New Bug...* in *Main* window, fills in *Type*, *Project*, *Product*, *Feature* (if applicable), *Description*, *Steps to Reproduce*, *Bug Release*, and *Database Server/Name* (if applicable). If the Bug Log recognizes the user's login ID, the Bug Log fills in *Found By*; otherwise, the user must fill it in manually.
assign bug	manager assigns bug to programmer and tester (also documenter)	Manager finds the bug and fills in *Programmer*, *Tester*, and *Priority* fields in *Status/Action* tab.

Name	Event(s) Addressed	Procedure
done fixing bug	programmer fixes the bug	Programmer finds the bug, then:

1. If the fix is immediately available for testing, programmer sets the bug's status to *Test* in the *Status/Action* tab and enters current release into *Fixed Release*.

2. If programmer knows that the fix will be available for testing in the next release, programmer sets the bug's status to *Build* and enters *Next Release* in *Fixed Release*.

3. If the fix won't be available in the next release, but the programmer knows the release number in which it will be available, programmer sets the bug's status to *Build* and enters the release number into *Fixed Release*.

4. If the programmer does not know when the fix will be available for testing, programmer sets the bug's status to *Build* and enters *Future Release* in *Fixed Release*.

In this last case, the programmer is responsible for checking each new release to see if the fix is included. Automatic email notification reminds the programmer to do this; see section 5. |
| update release number | new release, fix reaches current release | Whenever a new version of a product is released, the Bug Log administrator enters its release number in the *Change Release Number* window.

The Bug Log automatically changes the bug's status if its *Fixed Release* was *Next Release*, and sends notifications as described in section 5. |

Here we see the solution to the connection problem involving how to inform the Bug Log that a bug fix has become available for testing. The chosen solution is to impose some responsibilities on the programmers, described at right.

The remaining operating procedures (there are many: every event described in the requirements is addressed) are omitted for brevity. Documenting these procedures is especially critical for the people who will write the user's manual and online help. Most of these procedures involve tasks that users are responsible for performing. Without this documentation, people would have to guess what their responsibilities are.

4. Screens

Unless otherwise indicated:

— All backgrounds and buttons are light gray.

— The background color of all edit controls is white.

— All lines are black.

— All buttons are raised 3D.

— All fields are sunken 3D.

— Controls in a window's title bar—control menu, minimize button, maximize button, and close button—are not documented here and have standard Windows 95 functionality.

— The focus starts on the first control in the tabbing order when a new window is opened or a new tab is brought to the top.

— Any controls that are not shown (for example, controls visible only to an administrator) are automatically left out of the tabbing order.

— When a control is said to receive the focus, if the control is on a tab, that tab is brought to the top, if it wasn't already.

— When a control or menu item is said to be grayed, it is also disabled.

— Window captions, menu text, and dialog-box text have the Windows default attributes.

— All other text has the following attributes:

Color: black

Font: MS Sans Serif

Size: 8 points

Style: regular (not bold or italic)

Access keys are shown by an underline, both in graphics and descriptions. Example: Bug.

4.1 Window: Main

Overview: The *Main* window is the first window displayed when the user starts the Bug Log. *Main* displays lists of bugs and all information about individual bugs.

Bug Log icon

Menu Bar

Tabs

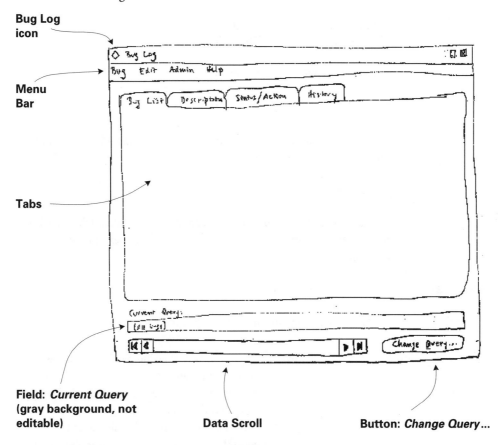

Field: *Current Query* (gray background, not editable)

Data Scroll

Button: *Change Query...*

The ideal way to get screen shots into the design document is to design them in a prototyping tool and capture them. However, the above method—drawing them with pencil and paper and scanning them in—is also very effective. It's much easier than, say, fiddling with a word processor's table or graphics capabilities. However you draw them, you must include screen shots in a user-interface design document, and they must show every feature of every screen. You can tweak for aesthetics after the screens are working.

Window attributes:

Resizable?	No.
System buttons:	Close, Minimize.
Enter-key action:	No effect, except when cursor is in a mult-line edit; then, inserts a new line.
Esc-key action:	No effect.
Modal/modeless:	Modeless.

The *Bug List* tab is on top when the user first opens the *Main* window. Each tab is described in a separate section.

Tabbing order:

Depends on which tab is on top; see sections on individual tabs for tabbing orders. *Change Query...*, *New Bug*, and *Print...* appear inside each tab's tabbing order.

Menu Bar

The *Main* window's menu bar contains the following items:

Bug			
	New <u>W</u>indow	Ctrl-W	Opens a new *Main* window. Both windows operate simultaneously. The new window has the same tab on top as the original window, and it has the same values in all controls in all tabs. This overrides all default values for controls specified elsewhere in this document.
	———		Separator.
	<u>N</u>ew Bug	Ctrl+N	Same as pressing the *New Bug* button in the *Bug List*, *Description*, and *Status/Action* tabs (see page [omitted]). Grayed when *New Bug* is grayed.
	<u>P</u>rint...	Ctrl-P	Same as pressing the *Print* button.
	———		Separator.

	Close		Closes the *Main* window. If only one such window is open, the Bug Log exits.
Edit	Undo		See below (page [omitted]).
	Undo Last Edit	Ctrl+Z	See below (page [omitted]).
	Cut	Ctrl+X	Cuts currently selected text to clipboard. Grayed when no text is selected. "Currently selected text" is: Selected text in a text box, when that box has the focus. The selected item in a drop-down or list box, when it has the focus.
	Copy	Ctrl+C	Copies currently selected text to clipboard. Grayed when no text is selected. Same comment as for Cut.
	Paste	Ctrl+V	Pastes clipboard text to current cursor position. Grayed when cursor is not in a place where text can be inserted and when clipboard does not contain text.
Admin	Users...		Opens the Users window.
	Projects...		Opens the Projects window.
Help	Help Topics		Opens the online help at the contents page.
	About the Bug Log		Opens the About the Bug Log window.

Information about the Edit|Undo *commands (about four pages) is omitted for brevity.*

Field: *Current Query*

Shows:

The text form of the current query;

Or, if the current query is a saved query with a name different than its text form, shows:

The saved name of the current query, in italics.

See section 4.6 to find out how a query is translated into text form.

Not editable; gray background.

Examples:

SPLNX Connectivity   A typical query, in text form.

Master bug report   A saved query.

Data Scroll

Moves from one bug to another. Buttons function as follows:

Button	Action When Clicked
⏮	Moves to the first bug in the current query.
◀	Moves to the previous bug in the current query.
▶	Moves to the next bug in the current query.
⏭	Moves to the last bug in the current query.

If the action specified above is impossible to carry out—for example, if the user clicks the "move to previous" button, and the current bug is the first in the query—then the button has no effect. (No beep!)

In the space between the buttons, the following message is displayed:

Bug *nnn* of *mmm*

where *nnn* is the ordinal number of the current bug in the current query (the first bug is 1, the second bug is 2, etc.), and *mmm* is the total number of bugs in the current query.

If the current query is empty, the following message is displayed instead:

(No bugs in current query)

Buttons

Button	Action When Clicked
New Bug (common to all tabs)	Brings the *Description* tab to the top, if it wasn't already. Creates a new bug, pre-populating fields as described in section 2.3.
Print... (common to all tabs)	*Opens the Print window (section 4.19).*
Change Query...	Opens the *Query Builder* window (section 4.6).

Section 4.2, "Tab: Bug List", is omitted for brevity.

4.3 Tab: *Description*

Overview: The *Description* tab (part of the *Main* window) contains all fields that the user needs to fill in when entering a bug: everything that describes the bug, but nothing about what action was taken to fix the bug or the status of the bug.

Field: *ID* (gray background; not editable)

Button: *ID*

Buttons: *New Bug* and *Print...*

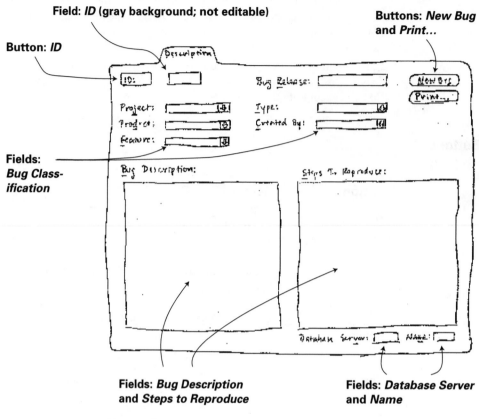

Fields:
Bug Class-
ification

Fields: *Bug Description* and *Steps to Reproduce*

Fields: *Database Server* and *Name*

Tabbing order:

    Project
    Product
    Feature
    Bug Release
    Type
    Created By
    Bug Description
    Steps To Reproduce
    Database Server
    Name
    New Bug
    Print...
    Change Query...
    ID (button)

There is no default button (button activated when user presses Enter).

Field: ID

Shows the ID of the current bug. Gray background; not editable except when the *ID* button is down (see below).

Double-clicking the *ID* field has the same effect as clicking the **ID** button.

Has the same location on all tabs that contain it (*Description*, *Status/Action*, and *History*).

Button: ID

Has the same location on all tabs that contain it (*Description*, *Status/Action*, and *History*).

Behaves as follows:

State	User Action	Response	
Up	Clicks button.	If the current bug does not meet the validation criteria in section 2.2, the appropriate error message from that section is displayed, and the *ID* button returns to the *Up* state.	
		Otherwise: the *ID* field's background turns white, and all other fields in the window go gray and uneditable. The focus moves to the *ID* field, and all text in that field is selected. The *ID* button stays Down.	
Down	Presses Enter or clicks *ID* button.	*Value of ID field*	*Response*
		Blank	*ID* button returns to *Up* state, and *ID* field returns to the value it had before the user clicked *ID*.
		ID of any bug in the database, whether or not in the current query	Identified bug becomes current bug, and *ID* button returns to Up state.

	A non-numeric value	Message box: A bug ID can contain only numbers.
	A number that is not the ID of any bug	Message box: There is no bug with ID *nnn*.
Clicks any other button, presses Esc, or brings the Bug List, History, or Bug Counts tab to the top.	*ID* button returns to Up state, and *ID* field returns to the value it had before the user clicked *ID*.	

Whenever the *ID* button returns to the Up state, all fields return to their normal state (*ID* gray, others white).

Fields: Bug Classification

Field	Items in Drop-Down List	Special Actions
Project	All projects in database.	
Product	All products defined for the selected project. Empty list if *Project* is blank.	If the user changes the *Project* field to a project for which only one product is defined, *Product* immediately changes to that product. If there is more than one product for that project, *Product* goes blank. Blank if *Project* is blank.
Feature	All features defined for the selected product. Empty list if *Product* is blank.	If the user changes the *Product* field to a product for which only one feature is defined, *Feature* immediately changes to that feature. If there is more than one feature for that product, *Feature* goes blank. Blank if *Product* is blank.
Bug Release	(No list.)	When user selects a new project/ product/feature combination (or project/product combination, for products not subdivided into features), automatically changes to the current release, unless any user had already manually entered a release number (in the current session or any other).
Type	All valid bug types (*Bug, Enhancement, Suggestion*)	
Found By	All users in the database.	

Fields: Bug Description and Steps To Reproduce

Multi-line edit boxes, with automatic word wrap according to current width of the field.

Special keystrokes:

Enter or Ctrl-Enter	Inserts a paragraph break.
Ctrl-Tab	Inserts a tab.
Ctrl-I	Toggles between italic and normal text attributes for current selection, or, if no text is selected, for next text entered.

Fields: Database Server and Name

Single-line edits, containing the server and name of the database to use to reproduce the bug. No special behavior.

The remainder of the Bug Log user-interface design is omitted for brevity. Mostly it contains more screens and descriptions of fields and buttons, just like the ones on the Description tab.

G L O S S A R Y

analyst Short for SYSTEM ANALYST.

assertion A program statement that specifies a condition that is never supposed to be violated during execution of the program; the only
way the condition can be violated is if there is a bug in the program. If the condition is false when the assertion is executed, the
assertion halts the program and displays an error message indicating which assertion failed, helping a programmer to find the cause.
Assertions generate executable code only in a debug or test version,
not in the final version shipped to the customer.

For example, if one of a subroutine's parameters is supposed to be
in the range 1..10, the first statement of that subroutine might be
an assertion that the parameter does in fact fall within that range.
If another subroutine passes a value of 0 in that parameter, the
assertion would fail, and a programmer could inspect a core dump
to find out which subroutine passed the invalid value. Well-written
requirements can suggest many useful assertions to include in programs, helping catch bugs very early in development.

cardinality In a RELATION, the minimum and maximum number of elements of CLASS *A* corresponding to a single element of class *B* (or to a single ORDERED SET of classes *B, C,* and so on).

CASE tool Software to aid in many aspects of software development: Computer-Aided Software Engineering.

class 1. Loosely defined: a set containing like or comparable elements. For example, the class of all employees at Splenetix, Inc., or the class of all dishes on a restaurant's menu. Most classes include a set of attributes that apply to most or all of the members of the class: name, employee number, position, and hourly wage; or name and price.

2. More rigorously defined: a set of TUPLES in which each tuple has the same number of elements, the ith element of each tuple is from a set S_i, and S_i can be anything at all—the set of all numbers, the set of all possible 20-character strings, and so forth. The tuples correspond to the employees or restaurant dishes in the previous definition. The tuple elements are the attributes, and the sets from which the tuple elements are taken are the sets of all possible values of an attribute.

class diagram A diagram depicting one or more CLASSES and their RELATIONS to each other. When describing the structure of an object-oriented program, a class diagram can include subroutines associated with each class, though not when describing a PROBLEM DOMAIN.

class description A description of a CLASS, including a definition of the type of object that it contains, all of its attributes and all of its RELATIONS to other classes.

connection domain A DOMAIN that shares phenomena with two other domains, enabling one domain to have an indirect connection with the other.

connection problem   A problem to be solved by software, in which the software is to simulate SHARED PHENOMENA between two or more DOMAINS that are connected only by a CONNECTION DOMAIN. Connection problems usually arise in conjunction with other problems. For example, in many INFORMATION PROBLEMS, the software has no direct access to the relevant part of the world. Therefore, some form of indirect access must be created, such as a manual data-entry system.

control problem   A problem to be solved by software, in which the software is to cause a certain DOMAIN to behave in a specified way.

data structure   A way of allocating memory in a computer to data, along with algorithms for manipulating the data and retrieving it.

For example, a simple data structure is the *linked list.* A linked list consists of any number of blocks of memory, each of which contains both data and the address of the next block in the list. Elements can be inserted into, removed from, or shuffled throughout the linked list by manipulating just the addresses. This is much faster than storing all the data contiguously in memory, which would require copying large amounts of memory from one place to another.

data flow   Data sent between a FUNCTION (subroutine) and either an ultimate source or destination of data, such as, an end user or remote system, another function, or a DATA STORE.

data store   A repository for data when it is not being accessed by a program, such as a file on a hard disk.

decoy text   Text in a document that does not contain information of the sort that the document purports to be about. For example, text that explains how to evaluate requirements for completeness and consistency, placed in a document whose title says that it's about the requirements for a specific project. A user looking for information pertinent to the specific project must guess, upon encountering each section, "Is this one a decoy or does it contain relevant information?"

deliverable A tangible artifact to be produced at any stage of software development, such as a requirements document, a user's manual, or the software itself.

differentia One of the elements of a definition: the aspect of a concept that distinguishes it from others of its GENUS. For example, the differentia of *compiler* is "converts programs written in a high-level language into machine language." That's the difference between compilers and other programs. Also called the *distinguishing characteristic*.

directed attribute An attribute of CLASS *B* that has different values for different elements of class *A*. For example, the same product can have a different price for each vendor that sells it.

direction problem A CONTROL PROBLEM in which the computer can only direct people to perform actions that fulfill the REQUIREMENTS, as opposed to causing these actions directly.

domain Any collection of things, actual or potential, physical or conceptual, as described with a specific set of concepts; a set of predicates and potential individuals that they apply to. People distinguish domains for purposes of understanding and describing problems.

domain expert An expert in the PROBLEM DOMAIN.

dynamic information problem An information problem in which change is an important feature of the relevant part of the real world, such as keeping track of inventory in a warehouse or monitoring weather conditions in cities all over the world.

embedded system A piece of machinery containing a small computer, such as a typical modern microwave oven.

entity-relation diagram An older form of CLASS DIAGRAM. Entity-relation diagrams, unlike class diagrams, were strictly for describing the PROBLEM DOMAIN, not for describing program structure.

ERD	ENTITY-RELATION DIAGRAM.
exploratory engineering	Engineering characterized by exploration of new kinds of designs. Compare ORDERLY ENGINEERING.
event response	An action, described in a program's SPECIFICATION, for the computer to take when a certain event happens in the PROBLEM DOMAIN, such as updating a database. Some event responses include an operating procedure for users to carry out when the event happens.
formal methods	Rigorous methods of describing a program or its problem domain, derived from mathematical notations.
function	1. A mapping between two sets D and R such that for each element of D, there is one element of R to which it maps. A single element of R may map to many elements of D. Also called a one-to-many relation. The set D is called the domain of the function, and R is called the range.
	2. In many programming languages, a subroutine that accepts parameters from callers and returns a value. Often, "function" is used as a synonym for "subroutine."
	3. In some requirements documents, a capability of the software to receive inputs and generate outputs; see FUNCTIONAL REQUIREMENT.
functional requirement	A requirement stated in terms of inputs and outputs to the software or between elements of the software. Each such mapping between inputs and outputs is called a *function*. The input of a function might be the output of another function, and its output might be data sent to a DATA STORE.
genus	One of the elements of a definition: the kind of thing that the concept being defined is distinguished within, as opposed to distinguished from. Every instance of the concept is also an instance of the genus. For example, the genus of *compiler* is *program* because a

compiler is a program, and compilers are distinguished from other types of programs. Compare DIFFERENTIA.

hash table	A type of data structure that enables rapid searching for stored data elements. Whereas most search techniques take more time if there are more elements to search through, hashing usually takes the same, very short amount of time regardless of the number of data elements. The disadvantage is that the maximum number of elements must be known in advance and space allocated for all of it. Thus, hashing is most appropriate for applications such as looking up words in a spelling checker, where the size of the dictionary is known in advance and does not increase much at runtime.

Notice that this is not a true definition. It tells what hash tables are useful for, as well as some of their properties, but it doesn't tell what a hash table *is*. In fact, a hash table is a data structure that collects elements into small groups, each element being mapped to a group by a "hash function." A programmer must invent a hash function for each application, carefully designing it to distribute elements evenly among the groups. This information, however, is of little relevance for a book on requirements, so it's left out of the definition. This is an example of how a good definition is one that fits the reader and the reader's purpose in reading—not necessarily one that explains what is truly most fundamental about the concept being defined.

individual	Any uniquely distinguishable element of the world about which it is possible to assert or deny a given PREDICATE.
information problem	A problem to be solved by software, in which the software is to supply information about some part of the real world.
integer	A whole number: a number with no fractions or digits after the decimal point. Typically, integers are the kinds of numbers appropriate for counting things: the number of books you own is an integer, the number of people in your family is an integer. Negative whole numbers and zero are also integers. Compare REAL NUMBER.

I/O port	Short for input/output port. A piece of computer hardware that sends and/or receives signals from other hardware. When the computer changes the state of the I/O port, the state of something in the outside world changes, too—or, conversely, when the state of something in the outside world changes, the state of the I/O port changes, enabling the computer to respond to it. For example, by changing the state of an I/O port, your computer sets the graphics mode currently displayed on the monitor. Macintosh computers poll the monitor through I/O ports to determine what graphics modes the monitor supports. An I/O port typically has a numerical *address*, like 0xF00, distinguishing it from all other I/O ports in the same computer.
ISO 9000	An international standard for businesses, especially manufacturers, requiring the existence of quality procedures and that all company procedures be documented.
jigsaw puzzle	A document in which closely related information is scattered throughout, requiring the reader to piece it together as if assembling a jigsaw puzzle.
legacy system	Software already in place at a customer site. Sometimes new software replaces a legacy system, and, sometimes new software needs to communicate with one or more legacy systems that stay in place. In the latter case, legacy systems are often the most complex part of the problem domain.
monospace font	A font in which each character has the same width, such as `Courier`.
multi-frame problem	A complex software problem that contains different, overlapping parts.
OMT	Object-Modeling Technique. A set of techniques for describing the structure of an object-oriented program, now subsumed and superseded by UML.

pattern decomposition	The technique of breaking down a known type of successful design into the known design elements of which it is composed.
predicate	Something that can be asserted or denied of one or more INDIVIDUALS, forming a true or false proposition. For example, *open* and *closed* are predicates that can be asserted or denied of a given electrical switch; *delinquent* is a predicate that can be asserted or denied of a given customer.
preference	A criterion for making design trade-offs, or choosing between different designs that meet REQUIREMENTS. For example, a preference might state that the user interface should give priority to efficiency in the hands of experienced users over ease of learning.
problem domain	The part of the world where the problem solved by a piece of software resides, and in terms of which that problem is defined.
proportional font	A font in which different characters have different widths, such as Times Roman, Helvetica, and Arial.
object-oriented programming	A method of programming in which one structures the program as a set of data structures combined with sets of subroutines that operate on them, as opposed to a collection of subroutines that all have access to all the data.
open-ended problem	A situation in which we believe that some improvement is possible, but we have no definite criteria for measuring improvement. Discovering good criteria is, itself, part of the problem. Compare WELL-DEFINED PROBLEM.
oral tradition	The body of knowledge communicated informally among the development staff during a project and never written down. Often, the oral tradition contains more information and is more up-to-date than the documentation.
ordered set	A set whose elements have a specific order; you couldn't rearrange them and have the same ordered set. To illustrate, the set of all cities in Canada has no particular order. You might write the names

of the cities in alphabetical order, but the cities themselves do not have any order. By contrast, if you travel from one city to another, you can define a set (Saskatoon, Medicine Hat) indicating the start point and destination of your journey. The first element is the start point; the second element is the destination. This is an ordered set. Exchanging Medicine Hat with Saskatoon would describe a different journey. (There are definitions having a more mathematical character. See [VNR 1975], p. 324 or any book on set theory.)

orderly engineering Engineering characterized by application and slight variation of time-tested designs. Compare EXPLORATORY ENGINEERING.

realized domain A domain that does not exist tangibly outside the software and is, therefore, realized within the software in order to be controlled. For example, debts that one party owes another have no tangible existence. To control them, we must create a proxy for them within the software, which both parties agree will constitute a debt. Other types of realized domains are the documents created on word processors and the imaginary worlds realized in video games.

real number A number of the sort that applies to continuously variable quantities—a number that can have any number of digits after the decimal point. The distance from the Earth to the Sun is a real number; your weight is a real number. Compare INTEGER.

reference attribute An attribute of a CLASS consisting of a subset of elements of another class (or perhaps the same class). For example, one of the attributes of an invoice line item class is the corresponding element from an inventory item class; one of the attributes of an invoice class is one or more invoice line items.

relation A set of TUPLES that maps elements from one CLASS to elements of one or more other classes. For example, a customer-invoice relation might map customers to their invoices by containing tuples like (George Gibbons, #20647), (Charles Mangano, #20648), and so on. Each tuple maps one element from the customer class to one element from the invoice class.

requirement	A condition to be achieved in the PROBLEM DOMAIN by virtue of an engineered artifact, such as a piece of software.
sans serif font	A font without serifs on the letters, such as Helvetica or Arial.
serif font	A font with serifs, such as Times Roman or Courier.
shared phenomena	Events or states shared by two or more DOMAINS. For example, the event of selling a product in a vendor domain is also the event of buying a product in a customer domain. Typing something into a computer is also, in the computer domain, receiving data. It is only through shared phenomena that one domain causes effects in another or that information flows.
SME	Subject-matter expert.
specification	A description of the SHARED PHENOMENA between a piece of software and its problem domain: the events in the problem domain that are also events in the software, and the events in the software that are also events in the problem domain, as well as the states they share, such as the states of the screens in the user interface. Put more simply, a software specification is a description of how the software interacts with everything in direct contact with it.
static information problem	An information problem in which the relevant part of the real world changes seldom or not at all, such as the way that drugs interact or the text of Dante's *Inferno*.
system	A piece of software together with the procedures for using it.
system analyst	A person in the software development process whose task is to research and document the PROBLEM DOMAIN and the REQUIREMENTS.
traceability matrix	A matrix, sometimes used in engineering, having one row for each REQUIREMENT and one column for each DELIVERABLE. Each cell in the matrix contains a number identifying a location in the deliverable: a requirement number, section number, source-file name,

and so forth. The matrix, thus, correlates each item in the requirements document with each place in the other deliverables that
address it. For example, you can see at a glance that requirement
R-5 is addressed in section 3.2 of the test plan.

transformation A problem to be solved by software, in which the software is to
problem map elements of an input set to elements of an output set, such as
converting data files in one format to another, data into graphics,
or converting between the CMYK and RGB methods of specifying
colors.

TSR Terminate-and-stay-resident utility. A type of program that runs
under MS-DOS, which stays in memory and continues executing
even while the user runs other programs. TSRs perform functions
like displaying address books in response to a hot key, communicating with special hardware, and extending or modifying the
operating system.

tuple An ORDERED SET; especially, an element of a set in which each element is a tuple having the same number of elements. CLASSES and
RELATIONS are both sets of tuples.

UI USER INTERFACE.

UML Unified Modeling Language: a set of graphical notations designed
by Rational Software Corporation for describing the structure of
object-oriented programs.

use case A dialogue between a designed system and people or objects that
interact with it.

user interface SHARED PHENOMENA between a computer and the users who
interact with it: screens, keyboard commands, rules for responding
to mouse clicks, and so forth.

well-defined problem A set of criteria according to which proposed solutions either definitely solve a problem or definitely fail to solve it, along with any ancillary information, such as which materials are available to solve the problem. Compare OPEN-ENDED PROBLEM.

workpiece problem A problem to be solved by software, in which the software is to enable people to create and edit objects that exist within the software, such as documents and graphics.

BIBLIOGRAPHY

[Alexander 1977] Christopher Alexander, Sara Ishikawa, Murray Silverstein, Max Jacobson, Ingrid Fiksdahl-King, and Shlomo Angel. *A Pattern Language: Towns, Buildings, Construction.* New York: Oxford University Press, 1977.

[Bennett 1997] Douglas Bennett. *Designing Hard Software: The Essential Tasks.* Greennwich, Conn.: Manning Publications, 1997.

[Bradshaw 1992] Gary Bradshaw. "The Airplane and the Logic of Invention." *Minnesota Studies in the Philosophy of Science* 15 (1992): 239–250. Ed. Ronald N. Giere. Minneapolis, Minn.: University of Minnesota Press, 1992.

[Booch 1996] Grady Booch. *Object Solutions: Managing the Object-Oriented Project.* Reading, Mass.: Addison-Wesley, 1996.

[Cameron 1986] J.R. Cameron. "An Overview of JSD." *IEEE Transactions on Software Engineering* SE-12, no. 2 (February 1986): 222–240. The Institute of Electrical and Electronics Engineers, Inc. Reprinted in [Cameron 1989], 216–234.

[Cameron 1989] J.R. Cameron. *JSP & JSD: The Jackson Approach to Software Development.* The Institute of Electrical and Electronics Engineers, Inc., 1989.

[Cayley 1809] Sir George Cayley. "On Aerial Navigation." *Nicholson's Journal of Natural Philosophy, Chemistry and the Arts* (November 1809).

[Date 1977] C.J. Date. *An Introduction to Database Systems,* 2nd ed. Reading, Mass.: Addison-Wesley, 1977.

[Davis 1993] Alan M. Davis. *Software Requirements: Objects, Functions, and States.* Englewood Cliffs, N.J.: Prentice/Hall International, 1993.

[Gamma 1995] Erich Gamma, Richard Helm, Ralph Johnson, and John Vlissides. *Design Patterns: Elements of Reusable Object-Oriented Software.* Reading, Mass.: Addison-Wesley, 1995.

[Gause 1982] Donald C. Gause and Gerald M. Weinberg. *Are Your Lights On?* Winthrop Publishers, 1982. Reprinted by New York: Dorset House Publishing, 1990.

[Harel 1987] David Harel. "Statecharts: A Visual Formalism for Complex Systems." *Science of Computer Programming* 8 (1987): 231–274. Amsterdam: North Holland Publishing Co.

[Hoare 1985] C.A.R. Hoare. *Communicating Sequential Processes.* Englewood Cliffs, N.J.: Prentice/Hall International, 1985.

[Hugo 1862] Victor Hugo. *Les Misérables.* Trans. Charles E. Wilbour, Lee Fahnestock, and Norman MacAfee. New York: New American Library, 1987.

[Jackson 1975] Michael A. Jackson. *Principles of Program Design.* London and New York: Academic Press, 1975.

[Jackson 1983] Michael A. Jackson. *System Development.* Englewood Cliffs, N.J.: Prentice/Hall International, 1983.

[Jackson 1995] Michael A. Jackson. *Software Requirements & Specifications: A Lexicon of Practice, Principles and Prejudices.* New York: ACM Press. Association for Computing Machinery, Inc., 1995.

[Jacobson 1992] Ivar Jacobson, Magnus Christerson, Patrik Jonsson, and Gunnar Övergaard. *Object-Oriented Software Engineering: A Use Case Driven Approach.* Reading, Mass.: Addison-Wesley, 1992.

[Jensen 1985] Kathleen Jensen, Niklaus Wirth, Andrew B. Mickel, and James F. Miner. *Pascal User Manual and Report.* New York: Springer-Verlag, 1985.

[Joseph 1916] H.W.B. Joseph. *Introduction to Logic,* 2nd ed. Oxford University Press, 1916. Oxford: Clarendon Press, 1906, 1967.

[Knuth 1973] Donald E. Knuth. *The Art of Computer Programming: Sorting and Searching.* Vol. 3. Reading, Mass.: Addison-Wesley, 1973.

[Kuhn 1970] Thomas S. Kuhn. *The Structure of Scientific Revolutions,* 2nd ed. Chicago: The University of Chicago Press, 1970.

[Martin 1985] James Martin and Carma McClure. *Diagramming Techniques for Analysts and Programmers.* Englewood Cliffs, N.J.: Prentice/Hall, 1985.

[Mazza 1994] C. Mazza, J. Fairclough, B. Melton, D. de Pablo, A. Scheffer, and R. Stevens. *Software Engineering Standards.* New York: Prentice/Hall, 1994.

[Metzger 1981] Philip W. Metzger. *Managing a Programming Project,* 2nd ed. Englewood Cliffs, N.J.: Prentice/Hall, 1981.

[Miller 1956] George A. Miller. "The Magical Number Seven Plus or Minus Two: Some Limitations on Our Capacity for Processing Information." *Psychological Review* 63, (1956): 81–97. Reprinted in *The Psychology of Communication: Seven Essays,* New York: Basic Books, 1967; and *Psychological Review* 101, no. 2 (1994): 343–352.

[Montalbano 1974] Michael Montalbano. *Decision Tables.* Worthington, Ohio: Science Research Associates, Inc., 1974.

[Orr 1981] Ken Orr. *Structured Requirements Definition.* Topeka, Kan.: Ken Orr and Associates, 1981.

[Orwell 1949] George Orwell. *1984.* New York: Harcourt Brace Jovanovich, 1949. Paperback edition reprinted by New York: New American Library.

[Parnas 1986] David Lorge Parnas and Paul C. Clements. "A Rational Design Process: How and Why to Fake It." *IEEE Transactions on Software Engineering* SE-12, no. 2 (February 1986): 251–257. The Institute of Electrical and Electronics Engineers, Inc.

[Pinker 1994] Steven Pinker. *The Language Instinct: How the Mind Creates Language.* New York: William Morrow and Company, 1994. Reprinted by New York: Harper Collins, 1995.

[Polya 1957] G. Polya. *How to Solve It,* 2nd ed. Garden City, N.Y.: Doubleday, 1957.

[Pressman 1996] Roger S. Pressman. *Software Engineering: A Practitioner's Approach,* 4th ed. New York: McGraw-Hill, 1996.

[Rational 1997] *UML Notation Guide, version 1.1.* Rational Software Corporation, 1 September 1997.

[Sawyer 1955] W.W. Sawyer. *Prelude to Mathematics.* Baltimore, Md.: Penguin Books, 1955, 1961.

[Schriver 1997] Karen A. Schriver. *Dynamics in Document Design.* New York: John Wiley and Sons, 1997.

[Sommerville 1989] Ian Sommerville. *Software Engineering,* 3rd ed. Reading, Mass.: Addison-Wesley, 1989.

[Tufte 1983] Edward R. Tufte. *The Visual Display of Quantitative Information.* Cheshire, Conn.: Graphics Press, 1983.

[Tufte 1990] Edward R. Tufte. *Envisioning Information.* Cheshire, Conn.: Graphics Press, 1990.

[Tufte 1997] Edward R. Tufte. *Visual Explanations.* Cheshire, Conn.: Graphics Press, 1997.

[VNR 1975] W. Gellert, S. Gottwald, M. Hellwich, H. Kästner, H.Küstner, eds. *The VNR Concise Encyclopedia of Mathematics*, 2nd ed. New York: Van Nostrand Reinhold, Routledge, 1975.

[Warnier 1974] Jean-Dominique Warnier. *Logical Construction of Programs*, 3rd ed. Trans. B.M. Flanagan. New York: Van Nostrand Reinhold, 1974.

[Yourdon 1989a] Ed Yourdon. *Modern Structured Analysis.* New York: Yourdon Press, 1989.

[Yourdon 1989b] Ed Yourdon. *Structured Walkthroughs*, 4th edition. New York: Yourdon Press, 1989.

[Zave 1993] Pamela Zave. "Feature Interactions and Formal Specifications in Telecommunications." *Computer* 26, no. 8 (August 1993): 20–30. The Institute of Electrical and Electronics Engineers, Inc.

[Zave 1997] Pamela Zave and Michael Jackson. "Four Dark Corners of Requirements Engineering." *ACM Transactions on Software Engineering and Methodology* 6, no. 1 (Jan. 1997): 1–30. Association for Computing Machinery, Inc.

[Zave 1998] Pamela Zave. "'Calls Considered Harmful' and Other Observations: A Tutorial in Telephony." *Services and Visualization: Towards User-Friendly Design.* New York: Springer-Verlag, 1998.

index